T0329528

THE

PUBLICATIONS

OF THE

SURTEES SOCIETY

VOL. 228

THE

PUBLICATIONS

OF THE

SURTEES SOCIETY

ESTABLISHED IN THE YEAR

M.DCCC.XXXIV

VOL. CCXXVIII

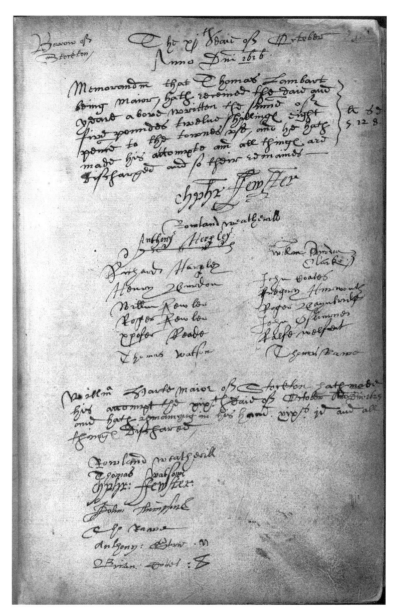

Figure 1   Book of Orders and Accounts: Example 1 (p. 1 of MS)
The first full accounting entries after the tabbed index, recording
handovers of mayoral accounts in 1616 and 1625.

BOOK OF ORDERS AND ACCOUNTS FOR THE BOROUGH OF STOCKTON-ON-TEES

EDITED BY

JOHN LITTLE

THE SURTEES SOCIETY

THE BOYDELL PRESS

First published 2024

A Surtees Society Publication
published by The Boydell Press
an imprint of Boydell & Brewer Ltd
PO Box 9, Woodbridge, Suffolk IP12 3DF, UK
and of Boydell & Brewer Inc.
668 Mt Hope Avenue, Rochester, NY 14620–2731, USA
website: www.boydellandbrewer.com

ISBN 978-0-85444-085-6

ISSN 0307-5362

A catalogue record for this book is available
from the British Library

Details of other Surtees Society volumes are available
from Boydell & Brewer Ltd

The publisher has no responsibility for the continued existence or
accuracy of URLs for external or third-party internet websites referred
to in this book, and does not guarantee that any content on such
websites is, or will remain, accurate or appropriate

FSC
www.fsc.org
MIX
Paper | Supporting
responsible forestry
FSC® C013056

Printed and bound in Great Britain by
TJ Books Limited, Padstow, Cornwall

CONTENTS

ILLUSTRATIONS

The editor and publisher are grateful to all the institutions and persons listed for permission to reproduce the materials in which they hold copyright. Every effort has been made to trace the copyright holders; apologies are offered for any omission, and the publisher will be pleased to add any necessary acknowledgement in subsequent editions.

ACKNOWLEDGEMENTS

I first came across a mention of the 'Book of Orders and Accounts' in Tom Sowler's *A History of the Town and Borough of Stockton-on-Tees*. When Sowler was writing his history of the town, the volume was held in the Town Clerk's department at Middlesbrough Town Hall. Why it was there and not in Stockton is not clear, as it had been presented, when re-discovered, to the mayor of Stockton. It seems to have had various homes during the re-organisations of local authorities in recent times.

Thanks are due to Stuart Pacitto formerly of Teesside Archives for alerting me to its location, at Preston Hall Museum, where it is on loan from Teesside Archives and on public display. Ruth Hobbins, manager of Teesside Archives, arranged the high-quality digital photography of the whole volume, without which this transcription would have been immensely more difficult, and general permission to use the source. Christine Hutchinson, collections officer of Preston Hall Museum, arranged physical access to, and inspection of, the book. Geoff Braddy, chair of Cleveland and Teesside Local History Society, and other committee members, generally encouraged and supported the digitisation of the volume and the use of information from articles in *Cleveland History*. John Banham, secretary, and Mark Egan, editor, of Durham County Local History Society, allowed me in the Introduction to use some portions of text from an article in that society's journal.[1] Thanks to Sheila Ripper, who prepared the maps, to Alan Heesom, who first agreed to and encouraged this work, and to Angus Winchester, who brought to bear his huge experience of early modern sources, scholarship and editing, applied with considerable energy.

John Little
Cambridge, UK

---

1   John Little, 'The other James Cooke: trade on the Tees in the seventeenth century', *Journal of Durham County Local History Society*, No. 82 (March 2018), pp. 5–25.

ABBREVIATIONS

Bayley, 'Genealogical Additions'	Bayley, W. D., '"Genealogical Additions" to the History of Stockton upon Tees', in J. G. Nichols (ed.), *The Topographer and Genealogist*, Vol. II (1853), pp. 73–123 and 550–9
BCTLHS	*Bulletin of Cleveland and Teesside Local History Society* (renamed *Cleveland History* from Vol. 61 (Autumn 1991) onwards)
Brewster, *History*	Brewster, John, *The Parochial History and Antiquities of Stockton-upon-Tees* (Stockton, 1796; revised edn 1829; reprinted 1971)
Cal.Cl.	*Calendar of Close Rolls*
Cal.S.P.Dom.	*Calendar of State Papers Domestic*
CTLHS	Cleveland & Teesside Local History Society
DCLHS	Durham County Local History Society
DCRO	Durham County Record Office
DULASC	Durham University Library Archives and Special Collections
Fordyce, *History & Antiquities*	Fordyce, William, *The History and Antiquities of the County Palatine of Durham*, 2 vols (Newcastle, 1857)
Green, *Hearth Tax*	Green, Adrian G., 'Introduction', *County Durham Hearth Tax Assessment, Lady Day 1666* (London, 2006)
Heavisides, *Annals*	Heavisides, Henry, *The Annals of Stockton-on-Tees* (Stockton-on-Tees, 1865)
Mackenzie & Ross	Mackenzie, Eneas and Ross, Marvin, *An Historical, Topographical and Descriptive View of the County Palatine of Durham*, 2 vols (Newcastle, 1834)

NEID	North-East Inheritance Database, Durham University Library, http://familyrecords.dur.ac.uk/nei/data/neisearch.php
ODNB	*Oxford Dictionary of National Biography*
OOP	Stockton St. Thomas Parish Records, Overseers of the Poor Accounts, 1718–1732 (SRL, Microfilm No. 54; originals in DCRO)
P&W	Parsons, William and White, William, *History, Directory and Gazetteer of the Counties of Durham and Northumberland*, 2 vols (Leeds, 1827)
Richmond, *Local Records*	Richmond, Thomas, *The Local Records of Stockton and the Neighbourhood or A Register of Memorable Events* (London, 1868)
Sowler, *History*	Sowler, Tom, *A History of the Town and Borough of Stockton-on-Tees* (Teesside Museums and Art Galleries, 1972)
SRL	Stockton-on-Tees Reference Library
SS	Surtees Society
Surtees, *History*	Surtees, Robert, *The History and Antiquities of the County Palatinate of Durham* (London, 1823; reprinted East Ardsley, 1972)
TA	Teesside Archives, Dorman Museum, Linthorpe Road, Middlesbrough
TNA	The National Archives, Kew
TWAS	Tyne and Wear Archive Service, Discovery Museum, Blandford Square, Newcastle
VCH Durham III	William Page (ed.), *The Victoria History of the County of Durham, Volume III* (London, 1928)

INTRODUCTION
THE 'BOOK OF ORDERS AND ACCOUNTS'

The 'Book of Orders and Accounts belonging to the Borough of Stockton', so titled on the front cover, is held by Preston Hall Museum, Stockton-on-Tees, where it is usually on display but not routinely available to researchers. In May 1923, the weathered-looking volume was discovered in the library of the YMCA in Stockton-on-Tees. A Mr. Lang there contacted Councillor Alexander Livingstone, proprietor of a ladies' and gentlemen's outfitters in the town, to alert him to the find. He in turn wrote to Mr. Downey, the town clerk, explaining that the mayor had seen it, and 'attached much importance to it'. Preparation for a formal handover of the book to the council was immediately scheduled as an item on the General Purposes Committee. At the next council meeting Mr. Copeland, honorary secretary of the YMCA and a 'foreign correspondence secretary at one of the large works', made a brief presentation and handed over the 'Old Minute Book'.[1]

The manuscript 'minute book' was in fact the 'Book of Orders and Accounts' for the town, covering the period 1616 to 1835. It could have easily been lost or discarded. Thomas Richmond wrote in 1868 that:

> It will be right to remark here that some deficiencies in this work would have been obviated could a reference have been made to the old order book of the Corporation, which is now unfortunately lost, having been intrusted some years ago to a gentleman, then employed in an inquiry regarding the anchorage and plankage dues, but not returned.[2]

Who that person was and where the volume was between 1868 and 1923 is unknown. More recently, due to the vicissitudes of local

---

1   For this correspondence, see below, Appendix 1.
2   Richmond, *Local Records*, Preface.

government reorganisation, it seems to have spent time at Stockton Town Hall, Middlesbrough Town Hall and Cleveland County Archives before being loaned by Teesside Archives to Preston Hall Museum in Stockton.

John Wilford Wardell, a former historian of Stockton and Yarm, gave up on studying the town's history in 1963, writing that he was abandoning his history as 'the sources were too scanty and the old town was disappearing'.[3] But some of these scanty sources were under-exploited. This is certainly true of the 'Book of Orders and Accounts'. The book appears not to have been used by local historians before the 1960s. In 1972, Tom Sowler quoted selective extracts from it amounting to less than five per cent of the content.[4] He also used some of the content in his *Town House, Stockton-on-Tees*,[5] in which he sets out the financing of the Town House, using also information from the Durham Bishopric Notitia Books. Otherwise it has not been referenced by local historians other than by the editor of this volume in one paper and in unpublished presentations.[6]

The volume has an alphabetical index at the front with tabbed pages. These pages are not numbered. The pages containing the main entries are numbered as far as p. 480, by whom we do not know, but there has been removal of pages and renumbering/overwriting of numbers. The entries in the 'Book of Orders and Accounts' commence in 1616,[7] but one entry has a backdated reference to 1612.[8] It is possible that Thomas Lambert, mayor in 1616, was responsible for starting the book. The first entry was in 1616, but on the same page is an entry from 1625. The next entry dates from 1623, and is a restatement of the ancient customs and rights to levy duties, such as a portion of any corn shipped into the port, signed by over thirty

3   John Wilford Wardell, *A Short History of Stockton-on-Tees* (Stockton-on-Tees, 1963), foreword.

4   Tom Sowler, *History of the Town and Borough of Stockton-on-Tees* (Teesside Museums and Art Galleries Department, 1972).

5   Tom Sowler, *Town House, Stockton-on-Tees* (Stockton-on-Tees Museum Services, revised edn, 1986).

6   John Little, 'People and prosperity in seventeenth-century Stockton-on-Tees', unpublished lecture for 'Prosperity and Discord: The North East in the Seventeenth Century', Teesside University/CTLHS Joint Day School, 11 March 2017.

7   Sowler (*History*, pp. 465–79) gives the covering dates as 1626–1835. The date of the first full entry could perhaps be read as '1626', but reads more convincingly as '1616' (see Figure 1). Thomas Lambert was mayor in 1616.

8   p. 41, below.

burgesses. Then follow short entries from 1629 and 1633, followed by a retrospective summary of payments for anchorage and plankage dues to the bishop. Thereafter the usage of the book is a consistent annual record of handover of money from one mayor to the next. Mayoral oaths appear from 1664, and orders issued by the corporation start to appear from about 1680. There are references to a mayor's file which no longer exists,[9] but in the earliest pages there is some more detailed accounting for expenditure and income items.

The earlier part of the volume covers the period of development of the town from a poor, thatched hamlet, in the shadow of the bishop's fortified manor house, to a smart Georgian town with a paved high street, a new parish church and a new Dutch-style Town House. The later part of the volume covers the increasingly prosperous eighteenth-century port and market town,[10] through to the dawn of the railway age, which together with local iron ore discoveries in the region would precipitate the sudden growth of neighbouring Middlesbrough, and the transition to an industrial Teesside sub-region.

Many of the entries are routine and repetitive, for example when the mayor's oath of loyalty at the court leet was recorded, or his accounts were handed over to his successor (they were all men). But this allows us to trace the continuity and turnover in burgesses, mayors and influential families and merchants. All of the entries are countersigned by several burgesses, and some entries are signed by twenty or more, sometimes in their own hand, sometimes by making a mark.

Other entries relate to the anchorage, plankage and metage, under a lease from the bishop of Durham; rules for the appointment of burgesses and mayors; duties on coal, malt, salt and timber; erection of market stalls; development of free quays; fishing rights and town management orders relating to the town clock, brickmaking, dealing with sewage, and improvements to the highway. In the late seventeenth and eighteenth centuries, there is an increase in the number and length of orders relating to town improvements. There is an increasing trend towards the wealthier burgesses funding such improvements or lending the borough money for that purpose, and

9   e.g. below, p. 41.
10 See Tony Barrow, *The Port of Stockton-on-Tees 1702–1802*, Papers in North Eastern History, No. 14 (2005) for an important account of the commercial life of the town in the eighteenth century.

*Figure 2   Book of Orders and Accounts: Example 2 (p. 156 of MS)
Analysis of debts to burgesses who had borne expenditure on behalf of
the borough, discharged by granting them rights to parcels of waste
ground granted to the borough by the bishop of Durham, 1701.*

being reimbursed. A large number of decisions are recorded from the court leet when held at Stockton.

Official records relating to the borough and its finances are recorded here, but not the minutiae of everyday complaints, misdemeanours and administration. There is an extended period at the beginning of the book when the courts are not mentioned. Presumably they were either taking place away from Stockton or being recorded elsewhere. In the late eighteenth and early nineteenth centuries, dedicated committees (for example for repairs and auditing) and municipal borrowing and debt make an appearance. Appointments of teachers at the grammar school are agreed.[11] In the early nineteenth century, orders relevant to the Clarence and Stockton and Darlington railways appear, usually relating to the acquisition or disposal of land and property.

As with any historical source, we must be aware of its limitations. There are key aspects of Stockton's history at the time which are not even mentioned, such as the survey of the castle in 1647[12] and its subsequent sale and demolition, the Civil Wars, Scots invasions, the plague and the Dutch Wars. While the state papers of the second half of the seventeenth century are full of maritime incidents off the east coast, troop and supply movements and reports to central government by local officials, and the Exchequer Port Books show increasingly voluminous trade on the Tees in that period, the book's entries stick fairly narrowly to the official business of the town's mayor and burgesses and give few hints of wider events, though there is circumstantial evidence that some of the town's merchants thrived in this period and the economy grew.[13]

The construction of a new parish church in 1712–13 does not feature here,[14] and it is clear that this volume does not give a total picture of the local economy, unsurprisingly given that the bishop of Durham largely controlled most of it in the first half of the period. But the financing of the new Town House, butchers' Shambles, market cross and new quays do appear. We know from the Exchequer Port Books, wills and probate inventories, and other sources, that many of the men signing this book as burgesses were merchants, a number

11   The first mention of the grammar school was in 1785, erected by subscription on land leased to the corporation by the bishop. The schoolmasters in this period are listed in Brewster, *History*, p. 250.

12   See Sowler, *History*, pp. 81–2 and 445–7.

13   See Little, 'The other James Cooke'.

14   See Tom Sowler, *The Parish Church of Stockton-on-Tees* (Stockton-on-Tees, 1990).

of whom were wealthy enough to finance or partly finance the improvement of the borough through paving, provision of clocks and water pumps, construction of municipal buildings, including the sergeant's house, and development of port facilities.

It is perhaps the number of signatories, mainly of burgesses, mayors and aldermen, that is the key feature of this volume. They allow a view of the town's governing oligarchy over two centuries. Names are always valuable in the linking of data across multiple sources, albeit the task of distinguishing father from son and grandson with the same name is frequently challenging and sometimes impossible. Not many women are mentioned, and none as signatories. As is often the case, available records document the middling and wealthy sorts rather than the poor, and this is generally the case here, the signatories being burgage holders, merchants and mayors.

The strengths of this source are its long life over two centuries, and its transactional nature (seemingly lacking any propaganda, political spin, or pitches at posterity) and the large number of individuals named, with dates. We can cross-reference burgesses and merchants who signed the entries here with merchants mentioned in the Exchequer Port Books, Sound Toll Registers[15] and Hearth Tax returns. We can also link them to the parish registers, wills and probate inventories, Protestation returns and Hearth Tax returns. While successful merchants appear, there were few truly wealthy people in the town and its hinterland, the most notable being the occupant of Blakeston Hall, Sir Thomas Davison, who in 1666 had 17 hearths, compared to the 6 or 7 in the dwellings of Stockton's and Norton's leading merchants and yeomen, and the large number of dwellings having 1 to 3 hearths.[16]

Appendix 5 shows personal marks of signatories, giving some indication of literacy among these burgesses, but it is not a large enough sample to draw quantitative conclusions. That issue is discussed briefly in that appendix.

The volume is leather-bound, with three straps made from re-used vellum strengthening the spine. Part of one is missing. One of the straps contains 4 lines of text in English in a late-medieval hand, which are neither clear nor substantial enough to be reconstructed.

---

15   See below, p. 19, for explanation of Sound Toll Registers.

16   For an analysis, see John Little, 'Merchants, mariners and yeomen: What does the Hearth Tax tell us about early modern Stockton?', *Cleveland History*, No. 105 (2014).

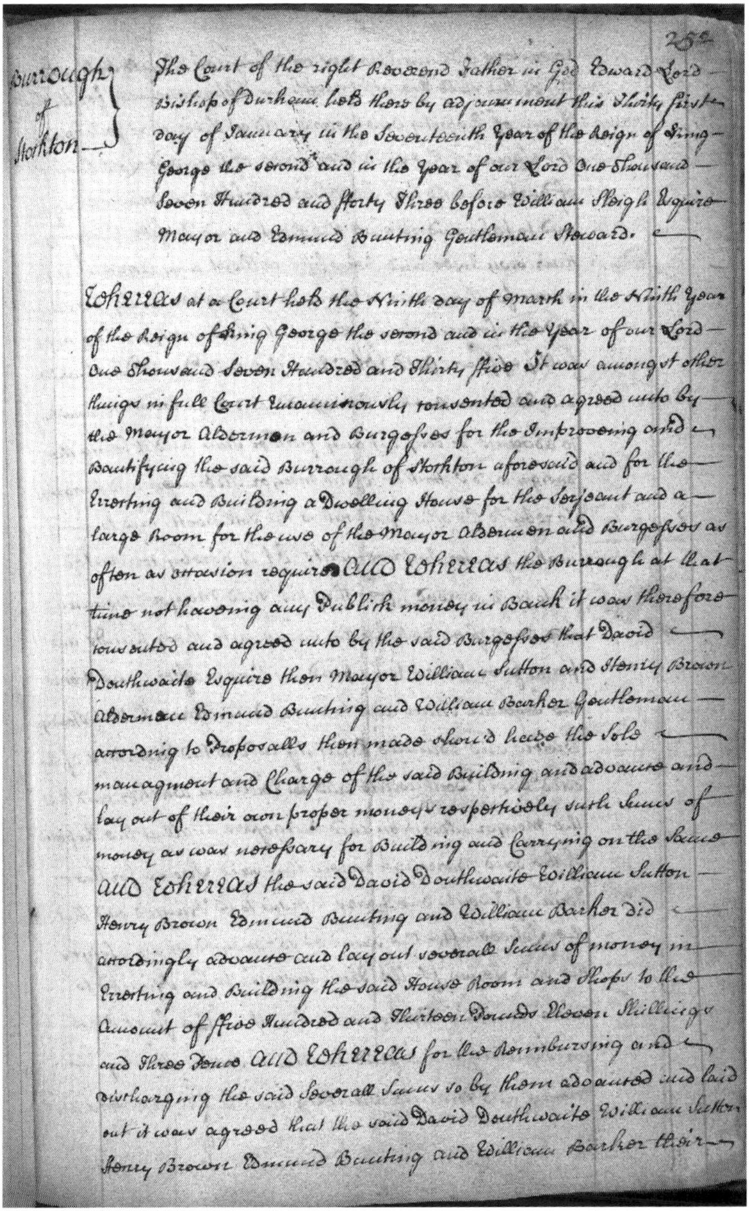

252

Burrough of Stockton

The Court of the right Reverend Father in God Edward Lord Bishop of Durham held there by adjournment this Thirty first day of January in the Seventeenth Year of the Reign of King George the second and in the Year of our Lord One Thousand Seven Hundred and forty Three before William Sleigh Esquire Mayor and Edmund Bunting Gentleman Steward.

Whereas at a Court held the Ninth day of March in the Ninth Year of the Reign of King George the second and in the Year of our Lord One Thousand Seven Hundred and Thirty five It was amongst other things in full Court unanimously consented and agreed unto by the Mayor Aldermen and Burgesses for the Improveing and Beautifying the said Burrough of Stockton aforesaid and for the Erecting and Building a Dwelling House for the Serjeant and a large Room for the use of the Mayor Aldermen and Burgesses as often as occasion requires And Whereas the Burrough at that time not having any Publick money in Bank it was therefore consented and agreed unto by the said Burgesses that David Douthwaite Esquire then Mayor William Sutton and Henry Brown Aldermen Edmund Bunting and William Barker Gentlemen according to Proposalls then made should have the sole management and Charge of the said Building and advance and lay out of their own proper moneys respectively such sums of money as was necessary for Building and Carrying on the same And Whereas the said David Douthwaite William Sutton Henry Brown Edmund Bunting and William Barker did accordingly advance and lay out severall Sums of money in Erecting and Building the said House Room and Shops to the Amount of Five Hundred and Thirteen Pounds Eleven Shillings and Three Pence And Whereas for the Reimbursing and discharging the said Severall Sums so by them advanced and laid out it was agreed that the said David Douthwaite William Sutton Henry Brown Edmund Bunting and William Barker their

Figure 3 Book of Orders and Accounts: Example 3 (p. 252 of MS) First page of a lengthy entry from 1743 concerning the financing of the recently built (1735) Town House by key burgesses.

The Borough or Corporation

A charter for the incorporation of the borough of Stockton has never been found, though it was probably created by one of the bishops of Durham at around the same time as Hartlepool and Newcastle were created by King John.[17] Many royal powers were effectively delegated to the prince bishops of Durham. The borough had a common structure involving a mayor and burgesses, the latter electing the former. Its powers, including imposition of duties on trade, markets, shipping (anchorage and plankage), and operation of local courts, were granted by the bishops, who were effectively lords of the manor of Stockton. Hence the 'Book of Orders and Accounts' includes material pertaining to the court leet and court baron proceedings, commercial relationships with the bishopric, and details of the burgesses' dues to the bishop. In this case the court leet was a branch of the bishop's judiciary rather than the monarch's.

Brewster[18] quoted a manuscript from the time of Charles II said to reside 'in the Townhouse closet', stating that the court was very ancient. Before 1770 the court had been neglected and, on the advice of an eminent sergeant at law, was revived. Brewster set out the format of court notices, proclamations, oaths, warrants, summons, and plaints for court leet and court baron.[19] The court baron was originally largely concerned with internal and routine manorial issues and would meet every few weeks, whereas the court leet or 'head court' (*curia capitalis*), which also had a policing and peace-keeping role on behalf of the crown, met twice a year. Court leet proceedings are documented in the book from 1680 to 1824. From 1770 the courts leet and baron were both held at the Town House, though the business and juries were kept distinct. The court leet also appointed the mayor on the first Tuesday after New Michaelmas Day, 29 September. In or just before 1823, Robert Surtees wrote that 'The steward of the bishops' court leet (in which court the mayor is elected) usually acts as the law officer of the corporation; the situation is now held by Leonard Raisbeck Esq'.[20]

In Stockton, the steward of the court, though acting for the bishop, was usually a gentleman or merchant of the town, and was later often known as the recorder. The town's sergeant was constable of

---

17   This is discussed in Brewster, *History*, p. 125, and Sowler, *History*, p. 18.

18   Brewster, *History*, p. 130.

19   *Ibid.*, pp. 133–49.

20   Surtees, *History*, p. 175.

the borough and bailiff of the bishop's courts. Before 1680, the entries are mainly brief summaries of the handover of borough money from one mayor to another, countersigned by some of the burgesses and aldermen, and records of which burgesses had paid for their rights of anchorage and plankage from the bishop.[21] After 1824, the entries are described as meetings of the mayor, burgesses and aldermen without mention of courts.

The word 'corporation' is used from 1650 onwards, but there is no indication of a fixed body of men or sub-set of the burgesses. The signatories vary in nature and number throughout. All burgesses had a right to elect the mayor. Certain burgesses were more heavily involved in financing developments such as paving the streets, building the Town House and rebuilding the butchers' Shambles. These individuals are often known to be leading merchants. For court leet and court baron entries, the signatories are presumably those in attendance at court sessions. In the later years, lawyers and bankers become prominent. Leading families show a persistent presence in the affairs of the town. These groups have been referred to as 'oligarchies' as they exercised considerable control and influence, albeit not being representative in any democratic sense.

The definition of the parish changed during the period covered by this volume. Stockton was part of Norton parish until it became a parish in its own right in 1713, having consecrated its own church in 1712,[22] though a chapel of ease, possibly named after Thomas Becket, had served Stockton from about 1235. The bishop's borough was therefore a small part of the parish in terms of geographical area. In the seventeenth century, although part of Norton parish, Stockton's Protestation returns, Hearth Tax returns and other records were reported separately. The two communities had different demographics, and these diverged substantially in the later seventeenth century.[23] Norton had a longer ecclesiastical history, and as a settlement in early medieval and pre-Norman times probably

---

21 Brewster (*History*, pp. 123–56) describes the operation of the borough and courts in the late eighteenth and early nineteenth centuries, when he was writing. He gives examples of the notices used to summon to court, and various oaths sworn at court by affeerers (assessors), witnesses, juries, sergeants, leather-searchers and ale tasters.

22 *An Act for making the chapelry of Stockton in the County of Durham a distinct parish*, 1713 (Private Act, 12 Anne, St.1, c.8) and *An Act for making more effectual an Act concerning Stockton Parish*, 1714 (Private Act, 1 Geo 1, St.2, c.42).

23 See Little, 'Merchants, mariners and yeomen'.

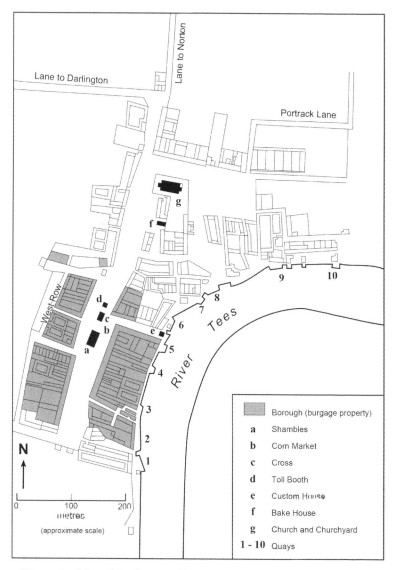

Figure 4   Map of Stockton-on-Tees in 1724. After 'A Copy of a Map of Stockton (Tho. Pattison del[t] 1724)', bound into Richmond, Local Records.

Key   1: James Cooke's Quay &c.; 2: John Cooke's Quay; 3: Ald. Raisbeck's Quay; 4: Readman's Quay; 5: Jackson's Quay; 6: Atkinson's Quay; 7: White's Quay; 8: Douthwaite's Quay; 9: Smith's Quay; 10: Hall's Quay.

had more interaction with settlements to the north of Stockton, such as Carlton and Bishopton. Stockton, because of its riverside location and the borough planted by the bishop, arguably developed partly because Norton did not, the latter being a relatively stable community of yeomen centred around St. Mary's church.[24] Figure 4 shows Stockton town centre as it was in 1724.

Care is needed in referring to the port of Stockton, as Peter Barton pointed out.[25] Not only was Stockton a sub-port of Newcastle for a long period, the 'port of Stockton' extended at times as far as Seaham in the north and Saltburn to the south. At times it incorporated Hartlepool. The river's meandering course and shifting shoals meant that it could take two days or more to sail up to Stockton and four up to Yarm. Larger vessels might be filled from smaller lighters downstream of Stockton, therefore much of the activity, especially before the river was twice straightened in 1810 and 1828, was not in the town centre.[26] Figure 5 shows the course of the river in 1760 and clearly illustrates why Portrack was so important in the handling of vessels, which would often unload onto smaller vessels (lighters) at that point.

A Brief History of the Town

One historian of Stockton wrote, 'It is Stockton's misfortune to be compared unfavourably with her neighbours. For most of recorded history, the town has stood in the shadow of larger and richer communities nearby.'[27] He was referring to Norton, Yarm and Middlesbrough, and suggests that Stockton only dominated the Tees from 1730 for about a century, though it has probably been an urban settlement for eight hundred years.

---

24 See Robin Daniels, *An Archaeological and Historical Survey of the Township of Norton in Cleveland* (unpublished BA Dissertation, University of Leicester, 1979), which suggests that Norton was the head of a shire-like organisation to the north of the current town before Stockton developed significantly.

25 Peter Barton, 'The port of Stockton-on-Tees and its creeks: a problem in port history', *Maritime History*, 1 (2) (September 1971), pp. 55–75.

26 *A Plan for Altering the Course of the River Tees between Stockton and Portrack.* Printed by R. Christopher, Stockton (1791) (copy in SRL). See also Sowler, *History*, pp. 227–76 (which includes a map of the various river schemes) and sources there cited.

27 Barry Harrison, 'The importance of Stockton's history', in Sowler, *History*, pp. xxi–xxv.

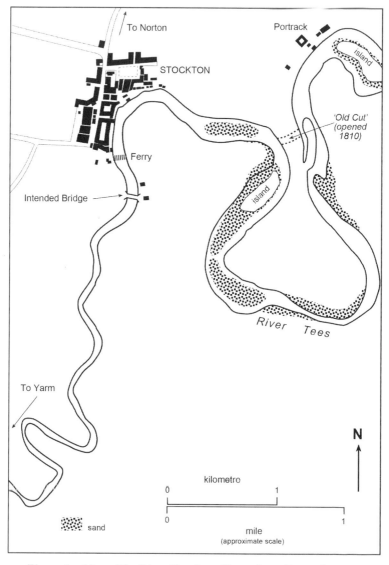

Figure 5   Map of the River Tees from Thornaby to Portrack, 1760.
After map by John Bell, for which see D. W. Pattenden, The History
of the River Tees in Maps, *3rd edn (Middlesbrough, 2001).*

In medieval times, the trade out of the mouth of the River Tees, and the customs activities, were centred around Hartlepool, a strong, defensible harbour, and Yarm, much further upstream, but the base for well-connected yeomen and merchants trading in butter and other agricultural produce. As early as the reign of Edward I, Hartlepool was mentioned, along with Hull, Newcastle, Scarborough, Whitby and Ravenscar, in letters to the sheriffs of counties and bailiffs of ports, ordering the mustering of ships, commandeering of supplies for the war in Scotland, or the prevention of monks being transported out of England without the king's permission.[28] There is no mention of Stockton or Yarm in these communications and others like them. At that time customs duties were spread across these ports but were payable at Yarm rather than Stockton. Numerous further records mentioning Hartlepool and Yarm, but not Stockton, occur across state papers from the thirteenth to fifteenth centuries. For example, in 1333 John Nesbitt was appointed 'controller of the custom of 2s. on every tun of wine, the custom of 3d. in the pound, and other small customs and prests in the ports of Hartlepool and Yarm'. Stockton is not mentioned.[29]

Yarm and Hartlepool were outside the control of the bishops of Durham, Hartlepool being owned by the Brus family and then the Cliffords, with ongoing disputes about its place in the bishopric, and Yarm being outside the bishopric altogether, in Yorkshire. The bishops had all the rights to anchorage and plankage[30] along the north bank of the Tees. They maintained a fortified manor house at Stockton and a wooden ferry boat there. The bishop's house was surrounded by fertile demesne lands, and a market was held from 1310. While Bishop Pudsey probably planted the town of Stockton between 1183 and 1197,[31] with a view to revenues from burgage rents, he did not seem inclined to allow too much enterprise, or the community in Stockton at that time had not the capacity to deal with it.

So, in the Middle Ages the importance of Stockton was the bishop's manor house, his ferry and demesne lands, and the economy was

---

28 *Cal.Cl. Edward I, 1296–1302*, pp. 77, 100–2, 215–16.

29 *Cal.Cl. Edward III 1333–1337*, p. 40.

30 Anchorage was money charged for the right to anchor; plankage was a toll for the use of a gangplank at a wharf. The bishop of Durham had the right to impose these charges on the River Tees, but he would sell on that right to the burgesses of Stockton.

31 Sowler argues for Bishop Pudsey planting the borough in this period, rather than King John, who created many other boroughs in the region from 1199 onwards: Sowler, *History*, pp. 17–20.

largely agricultural. There is little evidence of organised trade and quays.[32] In the fifteenth and sixteenth centuries the economy of Stockton reached a very low state, with almost nothing raised in anchorage and plankage dues.[33] For much of the sixteenth century the economic growth of north-east England was dominated by coal, especially the shipping of coals to London, but agricultural produce dominated the trade of the Tees. The number of ships to and from Stockton at the beginning of the seventeenth century was tiny even in comparison with Hartlepool. In 1601–2 only one ship inwards from overseas was recorded, and that from Largo (Fife), and none leaving for overseas.[34] Six ships delivered inwards and five outwards along the coast, so presumably one left empty or carrying ballast. These ships were mainly based at Burlington (Bridlington), Blakeney and Wells in Norfolk, and Whitby.[35]

**

The seventeenth century in England saw profound changes in the economy, government, culture and science. In local administration, as it related to urban settlements, there was a general movement from the Elizabethan system of justices of the peace, the remnants of parish administration by the church (and in County Durham's case by the bishopric) and the Crown, to a more locally driven system of decision making by town oligarchies, linked into Parliament, which by 1714 was supreme.[36] These oligarchies no doubt had a different flavour in each town, but economic resurgence after the Restoration would often provide greater opportunity for them to commercialise their agricultural holdings, develop new trades and industries, and develop a middle-class 'shopocracy'. The extent

32   See Linda Drury, 'The bishop of Durham's horse ferry, Stockton, c.1469', Cleveland History, No. 75 (Summer 1999), p. 13; 'Estate records of medieval Stockton', ibid., No. 83 (Winter 2002), p. 12; 'Estate records and medieval Stockton: the coroner of Stockton Ward', ibid., No. 86 (Spring 2004), p. 1; and 'Records of the bailiff of Stockton manor or castle', ibid., No. 91 (Winter 2006), p. 21.

33   Barry J. D. Harrison, 'The borough of Stockton in the late Middle Ages', BCTLHS, No. 49 (Autumn 1985), pp. 1–8.

34   TNA, E190/186/1.

35   TNA, E190/186/2.

36   See Christopher Hill, The Century of Revolution 1603–1714 (2nd edn, London, 1980) and Continuity and Change in the Seventeenth Century (revised edn, London, 1991); Keith Wrightson, English Society 1580–1680 (London, 1982).

to which any given town might thrive perhaps depended on the national economy's resurgence but required individuals to take economic and administrative action on the ground. Some towns thrived because individuals and groups exercised initiative, determination and commercial skills. Such influential groups, often of very old and long-standing families, existed in Stockton in the first half of the seventeenth century. Their activities were in some instances undisturbed or occasionally even reinforced by the Civil Wars. There is evidence that some of the town's merchants were becoming successful before the Restoration,[37] but it is easier to find evidence of wealth from 1650 onwards, in Hearth Tax returns, primage accounts at Trinity House Newcastle, and better survival rates for wills and probate inventories. So the 'Book of Orders and Accounts', which records the people involved, the activities of the mayor, burgesses and aldermen, their commercial rules and town orders and accounts, throughout the seventeenth century is helpful in assessing the civic strength (or otherwise) and the identities and dynamics of the people involved, before and after the Restoration.

In 1602, a renewal of the old market charter was made by Bishop Matthew, and a list of the burgesses at that time, and their position in the High Street, included many names who feature repeatedly in the early part of the 'Book of Orders and Accounts': Bainbridge, Bunting, Burdon, Fewler, Fleatham, Harperley, Hart, Heron, Lambert, Osburne, Swainston, Watson, Weatherell and Wilson. The name Fewler appeared on more plots than any other.[38] Some surnames in 1602 do not feature in the book at all: Tunstal, Halliman,[39] Saire and Symne. These families might have moved on or simply never participated in the signing of orders and accounts, becoming mayors or aldermen, or getting involved in the town's finances.[40]

In 1609, a royal proclamation encouraged a growth in commercial activity in the area. The importation of alum was banned nationally, on account of the discovery of alum in Yorkshire.[41] This local alum trade was not through the town of Stockton, but through subsidiary

---

37   Little, 'Merchants, mariners and yeomen'.
38   Richmond, *Local Records*, pp. 29–30.
39   Richard Halliman was a churchwarden at Norton in 1635: Richmond, *Local Records*, p. 33.
40   Brewster, *History*, pp. 99–100. Richmond presumably took the list from Brewster, but the editor has not found the source of the 'plan of the borough holders in the time of Queen Elizabeth' to which Brewster refers.
41   *Cal.S.P.Dom. James I, 1603–1610*, p. 521.

ports or creeks such as Coatham, Cargo Fleet and Dabholme,[42] though these would have been under Stockton for customs purposes. In the early seventeenth century, coal was already being shipped from Weardale to Dabholme and Cargo Fleet for use in alum shale processing.[43]

In 1620, the mayor and burgesses of Stockton brought a case seeking the right to control the anchorage and plankage on the north bank of the Tees themselves, but the bishop defeated them.[44] Nevertheless, the burgesses paid their 9s. per burgage in return for a share of the trade and the right to impose charges on visiting ships, raise taxes (e.g. 'causey money' for the upkeep of roads) and take a share of any corn being traded.[45] So there was a desire to make money, and to develop as merchants, before the Restoration. A small number of families was involved in the town's orders and accounts, and we can trace the changes in governance and the strengthening of the oligarchy through the seventeenth century as it gradually shook off the bishop's control.

When the Bishops' Wars broke out, several cheesemongers of London petitioned to have two thousand firkins of butter, then at Stockton and Whitby, shipped to Berwick and Newcastle for the Northern Expedition. This shows that Stockton was an active port in 1638–9, with contacts with London merchants.[46] In August 1640, Bishop Morton of Durham was 'at my castle at Stockton', where he had held up shipment of six hundred pounds of butter, which was licensed to be sent to London, but which he thought that the king's man, Conway, might need for the northern campaign. He also mentioned that he had used his own troops to protect some of the king's possessions in convoy.[47] In that year, the Treaty of Ripon agreed that the River Tees would be the 'bounds of both armies,

---

42   Cargo Fleet was variously called Caldecotes, Cauldgate Fleet, Cleveland Port and other variants. See D. W. Pattenden, 'Cargo Fleet or Cleveland Port', *BCTLHS*, No. 48 (Spring 1985), p. 1.

43   For a recent account of the north-east coast alum industry, see Peter Appleton, *A Forgotten Industry: the alum shale industry of north-east Yorkshire* (Skelton, 2018). There is some unpublished analysis of alum and coal shipments in the late Peter Barton's files in Teesside Archives, Acc7360, U/BSH.

44   Richmond, *Local Records*, p. 31.

45   For 'causey money', see below, pp. 30, 45–6, 48, 66; for corn dues, see below, pp. 16, 30, 40–1, 45–8, 76.

46   *Cal.S.P.Dom. Charles I, 1639–40*, p. 563.

47   *Cal.S.P.Dom. Charles I, 1640*, p. 647.

excepting always the town and castle of Stockton and the village of Egglescliffe'.[48]

Occupation of Stockton Castle by Captain James Levingstone, acting as governor, and his troops, was using up the winter fodder of the inhabitants of Thornaby village just over the river.[49] They had complained both to the bishopric and to the Committee of War in York, who had both written to the captain to no avail. His soldiers were taking livestock and goods at will, broke a windmill and drew swords upon peaceable petitioners, who were getting hungry. Whether any immediate action was taken or the situation improved we do not know.[50] We do know that in 1642, an act of parliament instructed that £7 2s. 8d. be distributed to the people of Stockton for the billeting of the king's army.[51] In 1644, the earl of Callendar took Hartlepool and Stockton, 'places of importance for the Parliament'.[52]

During this period, some merchants managed to build up their trade and resources, as several wills and inventories show significant resources: stores of grain, shares in ships and cargoes, debtors and creditors and shop contents. Some in this period benefited from the destruction of Stockton Castle (as the manor house was now described), with James Cooke and Major John Jenkins[53] (a soldier serving Cromwell who settled in the town) apparently constructing houses more solid than the usual cottages, using stone from the castle.

The port was used to ship supplies to combatants, but to a lesser degree than Hartlepool, which had a good defensible harbour and was regarded as militarily more important. Stockton's role was perhaps more about landing of supplies, and Teesmouth's as a safe haven and capacious shelter from the storm. This safe haven role would become very important in the Dutch wars, when hostile ships, especially 'capers', would often loiter in north-eastern waters looking for easy merchant prey. The navy in both Cromwell's time and Charles II's would have to organise convoys, rescue parties and raiding parties. Convoy escorts would often collect convoys which had been sheltering in the Tees Bay.

48 Richmond, *Local Records*, p. 36.
49 *Cal.S.P.Dom. Charles I, 1638–1639*, p. 563.
50 *Cal.S.P.Dom. Charles I, 1641–1643*, pp. 470–1.
51 Richmond, *Local Records*, p. 34.
52 *Ibid.*, p. 35.
53 John Jenkins left 52 shillings per annum to the poor of Stockton, to be paid every sabbath in white bread: Brewster, *History*, pp. 323, 345–6.

There seems to be some evidence that Stockton was an active, experienced and useful port, from the correspondence of both royalist and parliamentary forces. No Exchequer Port Books for Stockton survive for this period but there is evidence of trade in the primage accounts in the Trinity House records for the Tees,[54] though care is needed, as Stockton was a 'creek' of the port of Newcastle and its customs records often subsumed those of Yarm, Coatham and later even Hartlepool.[55]

Some key Stockton figures certainly benefited from the 'compounding' process whereby Parliament sequestered property from those who had been loyal to the king, and rewarded those loyal to Parliament with some of the proceeds. The Burdon family acquired all of the demesne lands near the castle by a warrant of 28 February 1644, for a year.[56] Rowland Burdon was warranted by the parliamentary sequestrators to execute the office of bailiff of Stockton on 23 August 1644. On 16 September of that year, he was issued a certificate stating that he was 'well affected to the Parliament'.

Circumstantial evidence, strongly suggestive of economic growth in this period, can be found in the wills of Stockton merchants, especially that of James Cooke,[57] who first features in the 'Book of Orders and Accounts' in 1634, and also in Exchequer Port Books in the 1630s. By the mid-1660s he seems to have become wealthy by local standards, involved in both agricultural and maritime activities, and owned a ship.[58] It is not credible that the wealth in such wills and inventories was created only after the Restoration, though Stockton's trade did, from Exchequer Port Book evidence, grow rapidly from 1660 onwards. If James Cooke had developed his business before the Restoration then he had done well to maintain it throughout this period, and avoided forfeiture to compounding committees which were used by the Cromwellians to remove assets from the 'disloyal'. The former assets of the bishop at Stockton passed into the hands of

---

54   TWAS, GU.TH series nos. 109, 160, 203, 214.

55   See Barton, 'Port of Stockton-on-Tees'.

56   Richmond, *Local Records*, p. 35. In 1645, they were then let to George Lilburn for a year: *Records of the Committee for Compounding with Delinquent Royalists in Durham and Northumberland 1643–60* (SS Vol. 111), pp. 7, 24, 35. See also Surtees, *History*, p. 173. Similar fines, penalties and pardons had been levied/ granted in 1570 after the Northern Rebellion: see Sowler, *History*, p. 51, quoting a passage from TNA, E137/133/1.

57   NEID, 1667/C18/1–4 (James Cooke).

58   See Little, 'The other James Cooke'.

William Underwood and James Nelthorpe in 1647, as Parliament, after ordering a survey of the town, had ordered destruction of the castle, or fortified manor house, which was carried out in 1652.[59]

The gap in Exchequer Port Book records is partly filled by Trinity House records. Teesmouth was overseen and buoyed by Trinity House from an early date, and a lighthouse was built in this period.[60] From 1634 to 1661 the same person, Thomas Watson, paid the primage dues for Stockton.[61] There is no mention of this role in the 'Book of Orders and Accounts', so there must have been some mechanism separate from the mayoralty. Possibly there was a group of burgesses overseeing it, but their accounts do not survive. Other Trinity House records show payments for overseas vessels in 1643 and 1644,[62] and coastal traffic in 1649 and 1650.[63] Then there is a gap in surviving records until 1658.

The Sound Toll Registers, the accounts of the toll which the king of Denmark levied on the shipping through the strait, or sound, between Sweden and Denmark, show nothing for Stockton ships before 1668, despite being a remarkably thorough and complete set of records.[64] This suggests that whatever trade was taking place through Stockton in the Civil War and Commonwealth period did not include the extensive Baltic trade that developed after the Restoration and contributed to the rebuilding of the town and many of its neighbours. Before 1660, most shipping trade was perhaps coastwise.

At this time, Bishop Cosin issued letters demanding regularisation of the rentals on his properties, including Stockton, and later renewed the charter for Stockton market.[65] By 1666, the Lady Day Hearth Tax returns provide an overview of the town's prosperity. Most residents of Stockton and Norton had only one or two hearths, and quite a number were exempt from the tax, but there were several yeomen, merchants and mariners who were already prosperous, and

59 Sowler, *History*, pp. 81–2 and 440–7.
60 TWAS, GU.TH.213: Covenant to build lighthouse on the Tees, 1641.
61 TWAS, GU.TH.203/1: Tabulation of money paid to Trinity House from Stockton, 1623 to 1661.
62 TWAS, GU.TH.203/2: Stockton outwards 'crossing the seas', 1643–4.
63 TWAS, GU.TH.203/3: Stockton inwards and outwards, 1649–50.
64 Sound Toll Registers Online. Danish National Archives (Rigsarkivet) at http://www.soundtoll.nl/index.php/en/over-het-project/sonttol-registers.
65 Sowler, *History*, pp. 90–2 (English translation of Latin text from Brewster, *History*, pp. 464–5).

this also shows up in their wills and probate inventories. Stockton was picking up the pace of its seaborne trade, merchant activity, and trade with its hinterland while rebuilding the town itself.[66]

The Restoration in 1660 saw economic stability and prosperity start to return to the North-east, despite the eruption of the second conflict with the Dutch in 1665. It may be that Stockton's skills – shipbuilding, rope-making, sailcloth manufacture and food shipment – even benefited from such conflicts. The combination of borough governance through established families, and a growing commercial middle class, would now see the town (and other towns which the port supplied) substantially rebuilt, often with Dutch influence, as with Stockton's Town Hall. The Customs Office was moved from Hartlepool to Stockton in 1680, and the town's quays were extended between 1680 and 1683, both developments which signalled the increasing importance of Stockton as a port. Increasing trade, both regionally and nationally, fuelled prosperity and more luxury goods. A progression from proto-industries such as alum, flax, jet and copperas to a full industrial economy would eventually commence with the shipbuilding industry moving from wooden construction to iron ships. But Stockton would flex its entrepreneurial muscles more as a port and market town than as a heavy industrial centre for some time yet.

In the early eighteenth century, Daniel Defoe commented briefly on the town, describing both Stockton and Yarm as towns of no great note, but commenting on the importance of the lead and butter trade at Stockton. A later edition, after his death, noted its transition from 'poor pitiful village to well built corporate town of great resource and business'.[67] The maritime trade of Stockton not only served its hinterland, with a growing network of turnpike roads feeding the outgoing traffic in butter, lead and grains, but was also central to the rebuilding of the town and many other settlements in its neighbourhood and trade networks, using Dutch pantiles as well as designs, together with Baltic timber. But the town was not without its poor: a workhouse was also built, in 1730.[68]

66   See Little, 'The other James Cooke' for a general discussion of economic growth in this period.
67   Daniel Defoe, *A Tour through the whole island of Great Britain* (London, 1762), p. 210. His original tour was supposedly in 1724–7, but how much of his narrative was based on personal experience is debated. Other authors, including Samuel Richardson, were involved in many editions after Defoe's death in 1731.
68   Richmond, *Local Records*, p. 60.

In his definitive account of the trade of the port, Tony Barrow demonstrated that the grain trade was a major engine of growth for Stockton in the eighteenth century, and the town was a conduit for the consumer revolution, channelling luxury goods and foodstuffs. He describes the activities of some key merchants: David Dowthwaite, John Hutchinson and Henry Hutchinson,[69] who all appear in this volume, and John Headlam and the Backhouse bankers, who do not. Barrow concluded that 'Stockton was already an established centre of commerce and maritime-related industry at the accession of George I, exploiting an extensive hinterland throughout South Durham, Cleveland and the Yorkshire Dales'.[70] In 1771, a new stone bridge over the Tees became its lowest crossing point, and cemented the growing importance of Stockton compared to Yarm.

Publications from Stockton in the later eighteenth century show that there was by then a well-developed print culture, implying the presence of a literate middle class. In the eighteenth century the town became sufficiently prosperous and diversified that it could attract satirical attacks on the airs and graces of its key personalities. Joseph Ritson was well known for his testiness and combativeness, and he applied it to his home town in a notorious pamphlet called *Stockton's Jubilee*, published in 1781, applying Shakespearian quotations to fifty-eight thinly disguised citizens of the town; he particularly disliked customs officers. This is perhaps evidence of the commercial and mercantile flavour of the town in the late eighteenth century. The other thinly disguised characters he lampooned were a more varied cross-section of the community.[71]

The population of Stockton is hard to determine precisely before the national census commenced in 1801 and civil registration of births, deaths and marriages began in 1837. Possible benchmarks are Protestation returns in 1641, Hearth Tax returns in 1666 (the most complete for County Durham) and the 1801 census. Estimates for 1641 based on Protestations are 686 for Norton and 585 for

---

69   John and Henry Hutchinson founded The Tees Bank in 1785. John's son, George William, shared his father's taste for literature and contributed to *The Stockton Bee*, a local magazine. The Hutchinsons' bank was subjected to a robbery in 1824, a box containing £8,000 being stolen from the mail coach in front of the Vane Arms Hotel: Heavisides, *Annals*, pp. 22–3.

70   Tony Barrow, *The Port of Stockton-on-Tees, 1702–1802*, Papers in North Eastern history (North East England History Institute, 2005), p. 3.

71   See John Little, 'Joseph Ritson and the Stockton Jubilee', *Cleveland History*, No. 110 (2016).

Stockton.[72] The Hearth Tax returns for Lady Day 1666 produce estimates of 712 for Norton and 925 for Stockton.[73] These are highly tentative figures but do suggest that Stockton had started to pull ahead of Norton, which was essentially static, while Stockton's trade expanded, possibly attracting more migrants. The 1801 census recorded 4,009 people.

A further complication is migration. There would be large-scale migration to the Teesside iron and steel industries, from Staffordshire, South Wales, Ireland and elsewhere, in the nineteenth century, but there is indirect evidence that ports like Stockton and Sunderland were growing by the seventeenth century, diverging from the national picture of a static, or even declining, population in the second half of the seventeenth century.[74] A closer study of Stockton's population history is needed, but there does seem to have been rapid growth, against wider trends, a trait shared at the time with another growing port, Sunderland. Growth in Stockton, from 1641 to the 1801 census, is probably around 300 per cent on reasonable assumptions, and may well have involved substantial inward migration as the trade of the port increased. Growth in County Durham towns seems to have been greater in medium-sized towns with specialist industries (e.g. Whickham) or growing ports (Sunderland, Stockton). After 1801, growth was more in line with neighbouring medium-sized towns.[75]

If it is the case that Stockton grew rapidly in the second half of the seventeenth century, the engines of growth may have been the re-granting of the market charter by Bishop Cosin in 1666,[76] the growth of seagoing trade and shipbuilding, and the growth of

---

72   Using a multiplier of 3.5. There were 196 males over 18 in Norton and 167 in Stockton: H. M. Wood (ed.), *Durham Protestations*, SS Vol. 135 (Durham, 1922).

73   Based on a multiplier of 3.5 but adding 25 per cent in view of Green's estimate of 25 per cent under-reporting. These are highly tentative, assuming Norton and Stockton have the same multiplier and level of undercounting

74   John Little, Review of *Sunderland Wills and Inventories 1651–1675* in *The Local Historian*, 52 (1) (January 2022), pp. 83–5, draws some brief parallels between Sunderland and Stockton. See also R. I. Hodgson, *Demographic Trends in County Durham 1560–1801* (University of Manchester School of Geography Research Paper No. 5 (March 1978) and Maureen M. Meikle and Christine M. Newman, *Sunderland and its Origins: Monks to Mariners* (Chichester, 2007), pp. 145–6.

75   Hodgson, *Demographic Trends*, p. 17, Table 1. Stockton shows the biggest proportional growth in south Durham, especially up to 1674.

76   Brewster, *History*, pp. 464–5.

industry and the London trade along the Tyne, with feeder and spillover effects on Stockton. Growth and commercialisation may also have benefited from the exercise of local initiative, such as the burgesses fighting the bishops' right to anchorage and plankage dues, enclosure in 1658–62,[77] and people migrating into the town. Corroborating evidence for commercial growth includes extension of the old quays in 1680–3, by 1,000 feet,[78] a new highway along the quays in 1706, a new church by subscription commenced in 1710 and completed in 1712, an act of parliament separating Stockton from Norton parish in 1711, and an order for paving the streets in 1717.[79]

The industrial era significantly impacted Stockton only in the nineteenth century. Until then it was a market town and port, and it traded in grains, butter and imported foodstuffs, luxury goods and building materials, including for shipbuilding. Wooden ships had been built in Stockton since medieval times, but possibly spasmodically using casual labour. Betteney suggests that about 150 wooden ships were built in Stockton and Thornaby between 1740 and 1835.[80] A map of 1828 shows a sailcloth manufactory and rope walk.[81]

Stockton had a role in the lead industry, exporting lead from Teesdale, Weardale, Swaledale and Arkengarthdale, and an alum trade was recorded from an early date. It was the railways, first the Stockton and Darlington Railway, connecting the Tees to Darlington and Shildon and beyond, then the Clarence Railway, connecting it to Hartlepool, that precipitated involvement in coal, iron and engineering, albeit largely as the result of the frantic growth of

---

77 Sowler, *History*, pp. 445–64 reproduces a transcript of the enclosure award from Court of Chancery, in the papers of S. V. Morris (TA, U/SVM 3.13); Brewster, *History*, pp. 461–4 includes a briefer abstract.

78 Sowler, *History*, pp. 300–1; Brewster, *History*, pp. 185–7 quotes the commissioners appointed to address the case for free quays. Their locations are given in relation to quays already held by James Cook, Robert Jackson, Mr. Atkinson and Thomas Crowe and land owned by Matthew Wiggoner. Brewster (*History*, pp. 187–90) also sets out the limits of the port of Stockton, from Blackhall Rocks in the north to Hunt Cliff by Saltburn in the south, and quotes a later commission which extended the limits to Ryhope Nook (nearer to Sunderland) and Hunt Cliff, and extended the customs rights granted by the bishop to Worsell Wath, well inland of Yarm.

79 Brewster thought that this 'very generally improved' the High Street: *History*, pp. 229, 232–3).

80 Alan Betteney, *Shipbuilding in Stockton and Thornaby* (Tees Valley Heritage Group, 2003), pp. 94–6.

81 Map entitled 'Stockton in 1828' bound into Brewster, *History*.

Middlesbrough through first coal shipments then iron ore from the Cleveland Hills. This would bounce back into Stockton as Teesside as a whole became engaged in heavy industry. Stockton's shipbuilding, like that at Sunderland and Newcastle, would move to iron and then steel ships, and in the late nineteenth and early twentieth centuries, the river, particularly the stretch at the seaward end of the town and the North Shore, became a place where about 10 per cent of the world's iron ships were built,[82] and the south bank, called Thornaby or South Stockton, became home to large iron and steel works.[83] Around the town, ironworks and engineering developed. The workforce in this period grew through inward migration, from Ireland (particularly into Middlesbrough), Staffordshire and South Wales, but also from the surrounding region, the Borders and Cumbria. The Welsh influx was significant enough for Eisteddfods to be held on Teesside well into the twentieth century.

At the time of the last entry in this book, in 1835, the industrial age had not fully arrived in Stockton, though the railway had, and its neighbour Middlesbrough was developing and expanding rapidly. Municipal government was slowly taking a more modern form. The 1835 Municipal Reform Act was a major step in that direction, establishing a nationwide system of municipal borough and town councils, elected by ratepayers and subject to audit. Stockton's borough had already started to develop a committee structure, and a further step was taken towards democracy in local government.[84]

That reform, following on from the 1832 Great Reform Act, was partly the outcome of considerable unrest across the country from 1811 onwards. Public notices had been issued by Mayor Henry

---

82   See Betteney, *Shipbuilding* and G. A. North, *Teesside's Economic Heritage* (Cleveland County Council, 1975), pp. 33–7, which includes startling statistics, such as the north-east of England being responsible for 42 per cent of all the world's merchant shipping by 1892 (when the UK produced 82 per cent).

83   The village of Thornaby was about two miles south of the Stockton bridge. It was small but ancient: the church of St Peter's Ad Vincula dated from the twelfth century. The parish stretched up to the bridge (and the ferry before that), but had few buildings north of the village. When the area opposite Stockton centre was developed industrially it became known as South Stockton; it became a new borough called Thornaby in 1892.

84   On 29 June 1832, when the Parliamentary Reform Bill was passed, a procession, fair and a dinner for 1,700 people were held. On 26 December 1835, there was said to be considerable interest in the election of councillors: Richmond, *Local Records*, pp. 163, 171.

Hutchinson in Stockton in 1817, imploring the population to act peaceably and volunteer for peacekeeping duties.[85] The 'Book of Orders and Accounts' makes no comment on those issues, and public meetings and orders to appoint constables and address unrest in the town are not mentioned in this volume. Nor did municipal reform squash the unrest. Shortly after the reforms and after the 'Book of Orders and Accounts' was discontinued, the Chartist movement would cause panic in the town in 1839–40, with special constables being appointed, as the possibility of a general strike exposed tensions between the comfortable middle class ('shopocracy') and those determined to push for universal suffrage.[86]

The book is largely silent on industrial development and technology. There is no mention of gas, though the town was first lit by gas in 1822,[87] nor of shipbuilding, potteries, sugar refining, rope-making, mills or even brickworks, though all existed before 1835.[88] By 1827, there were eight agents (shipping, land and wharfinger), seven insurance offices, thirty-nine inns, nine attorneys, five auctioneers, five printers, binders and stationers, three brewers and boot and shoe makers, plus many more.[89] As municipal reform approached, Stockton possessed the attributes of a fully urban community. Indeed, the length and volume of entries in the orders and accounts in the 1820s illustrate an increased complexity of civic and civil affairs in the town.

It is evident that the decisions for the borough were made by a select few burgesses, initially dominated by old families, then increasingly by merchants and financiers. If the number of signatures in the volume is compared to a plot of the population, however estimated, then we find that in the seventeenth century, although the number of signatories increases, the population increases even more rapidly, and so the 'oligarchy' becomes less representative. In the eighteenth century, both the population and the number of citizens involved in civic affairs increased. In the early nineteenth century, a nascent representative democracy was on the horizon.

---

85 Relevant material in Teesside Archives includes the Pargeter Collection (TA, U/PG), which contains original public order notices.

86 Malcolm Chase, 'Chartism 1838–58: Responses in two Teesside towns', *Northern History*, 24 (1998), pp. 146–71; *idem, Chartism: A New History* (Manchester, 2007), pp. 99–100, 121.

87 Sowler, *History*, p. 359.

88 *Ibid.*, pp. 345–71, gives a selective overview of industry in Stockton.

89 P&W, pp. 315–16.

The cessation of entries in this volume in 1835 was because the 1835 Municipal Corporations Act was implemented, creating more consistent governance for a set of 178 reformed boroughs, including Stockton-on-Tees, governed by town councils, elected by ratepayers and served by unelected town clerks and treasurers, separating political from administrative responsibilities.[90]

90   Appendix 2 reproduces the report on Stockton-on-Tees by the royal commission which informed the act.

EDITORIAL METHOD

The layout of the MS pages presenting financial material has been retained as far as is necessary for clarity and to preserve the meaning.

In the transcript, the pages of the alphabetical, tabbed index (pp. 28–36 below), unnumbered in the MS, have been numbered editorially using Roman numerals. The main text retains the latest versions of the MS Arabic page numbers; pages after MS p. 480 have been numbered editorially in the same sequence, in italics.

Original spelling has been retained. Abbreviations in English and Latin have been silently expanded where the meaning is not in doubt. Capitalisation has been modernised. Punctuation has been added where it aids clarity in long, legalistic passages. The interchangeable use of 'i' and 'j' and 'u' and 'v' have been modernised. Line fillers have been omitted.

Vertical columns of signatures have been transcribed sequentially as comma-separated names, taking the columns from left to right. For clarity, [*col. 1*], [*col. 2*], etc. are used to identify names in each column, the column numbers running from left to right. Personal marks among the signatures (presented as images in Appendix 5) are noted by an asterisk.

The following editorial conventions have been adopted:

*	Signatory's personal mark (see Appendix 5)
\ /	Insertion in same hand
\\…//	Insertion in different hand. Footnotes highlight apparently later additions/editing
[——]	Unknown/uncertain text (Length estimated/given in footnotes)
[*blank*]	Editorial comment
~~Aaaa~~	Text crossed out
<u>Word</u>	Underlined in the text

BOOK OF ORDERS AND ACCOUNTS
BELONGING TO THE BOROUGH OF STOCKTON[1]

[*p. ii*] [*blank*]

[*p. iii*]
A Booke of Orders and Accompts for the Burrow of Stockton in the
County Palatine of Durham

[*p. iv*] [*blank*]

[*p. v*][2]

The Table[3]

A: A:

	folio
An account of money paid about the anchoridge lease	
anno 1620 at 9s. 2d. per burgage	9th
\ And for severall others the renewalls thereof se folio the	8th/
Atkinson John his account folios 48: 54: [*erasure*] 62.	

An account of disbursements & arrears about the anchoridge lease
folio 53:
An account of the arrears about renewing the charter: 57

---

1   This is the title on the vellum binding, in a hand probably of the eighteenth
    century; it is noticeable that it uses the modern spelling 'Borough'. Above the
    title in a later hand is the number '40'.
2   After the text on this page, there is a modern addition in pencil over three
    lines: '1922 / 1629 / 293'. This appears to be a calculation of the age of the
    volume, at its rediscovery in 1922 (though the earliest entry relates to 1616,
    not 1629 as in the calculation).
3   This and the next twenty pages constitute an alphabetical index, with tabs
    cut out down the right-hand side, two index letters per tab. There is a single
    entry for I/J and similarly for U/V. The top right corner of this first folio has
    been torn off. The table indexes names of the mayors only and was probably
    not updated after 1754 (see below, p. 167, William Sutton's accounts).

Atkinson William folios 88: 94: 143:
A particular account of all the debts discharged by the
waste ground in the Westrow Street &c.   156
Atkinson William Hart folio 167:
An account of the charge of the new cross by whom
disburst and how repaid   177:

[*p. vi*]

B: B:

Burdon Rowland his account folios: 25: 27: 31: 33: 43: 46:
Bunting John. folios: 39: 41:
Burdon James. folios: 102: 105: 133: 136: 139:
Bunting Ralph. folios: 159: 161: 179:
Bowlby Richard. folio 171:
Burgages folios 9 & 10.
Burdett John. folios 187: 189: 191: 221: 225: 226: 127:
Brown Henry 232: 233:
Burdett John 234:
Bunting Ralph 235
Brown Henry his accounts 267

[*p. vii*]

C: C:

Cooke James his account folios 23: 29: 66: 76:
Cooke James his son 76: 78: 109: 113: 129: 149:
Cook James the grandson, 163: 176:
Customs & rights about election of mayors 147 & 148
Cooke John 190: 192: 197: 198: 204: 207.
Cross the charge thereof 173.
A charter for our markett & faire granted by Toby lord bishop of
Durham dated 4th of June 1602 in which is recited a former charter
then produced by Nicholas Fleatham mayor dated the 11 of May
1310 granted by Anthony late patriark of Jerusalem & lord bishop of
Durham – see in the long black box.[4]

---

4   The 'long black box' has not been identified, nor has the editor encountered
    any other mentions of it in other Stockton sources.

Another charter thereof from John lord bishop of Durham dated 24 of Aprill 1666 to Robert Jackson mayor in which is recited both the aforesaid charters. See also in said box.

[*p. viii*]

D: D:

Certaine duties upon coals malt salt and deals folios 37: 39: 52: 43: 45: \See the mayor's account for metage causey money & burrow corne. folios 11: 13: 19:/
Dowthwaite David his accompt. 217. 223. 240:

[*p. ix*]

E: E:

[*p. x*]

F: F

Fleatham Nicholas his account folios: 70th: 74:
Fewler Christopher folio 1st
Finch John folios 227, 229.
Ferrand Richardson his accounts 283
Ditto   Ditto   284

[*p. xi*]

G: G:

Gibson William his account folios. 211th. 212. 214.

[*p. xii*]

H: H:

                                                              folio
Hart William his accompt. folio: 1st : 5th: 1st

[*p. xiii*]

J: J:

Jessep: John his account 6th: 7: 13: 15: 17: 19:
Jessop: Thomas his account 49: 50: 60: 64: 66:
Jackson Robert: 56: 58: 68: 80: 84: 125: 127:

[*p. xiv*]

K: K:

[*p. xv*]

L: L:

folio
1st

Lambert Thomas his accompt folio the 1st
Lee William his account 86: 87:

[*p. xvi*]

M: M:

Moone Ralph his account folio the 98th: 115: 117:
The mayor's oath folios 54: 81: 85: 87: 92: 96: 101: 104: 108: 112: 114:
116: 120: 122: 124: 126: 128: 131: 135: 138: 142: 145: 151: 157: 169: 182:
184: 187: 190: 196: 198: 201: 204:

[*p. xvii*]

N: N:

O: O:

Ogle Thomas 196: 199

[*p. xviii*]

O: O:

folios

An order for impowering the mayor to cause a distress
upon non payment for corne or other goods that come in
by shiping 3
An order of 2d per last of corne \or other goods/
imported. Laid upon straingers. 6
An order that none shall be a mayor above two years
fol. 71: 71
An order that no mayor disburse above 40s without
consent &c: 71: 71
And that every mayor perfect his accounts the next head
court day after he goes out on paine of 5li: \and to deliver
up his books seale & papers/ fol. 71

An order that every person bringing in any corne shall
pay 2^d per last more than formerly &c and shall pay for
ship^5 deals or wainscot boards 12^d per hundred and for
oake timber and planks 6^d per tunn, for great fir balks
4^s per hundred, for small balkes 2^s and for spars 6^d per
hundred   72:
An order that every free burgess shall have an abatement
of a 3^d part for timber and plannke   72:
An order that no strainger comeing to live in Stockton
shall use the trade of fishing in the river untill he pay
13^s 4^d to the mayor   75
And that none sell any corne or graine, beef or other flesh
before the bell be rung on pain 6^s 8^d 75:
An order that the sergent shall be the cheife measurer
of corne exported & shall have 3 deputies & none to be
exported but what they measure on paine of 39^s 11^d. And
that the antient all[owance] of 4^d per last be augmented
to 6^d whereof one moiety to the sergent the other to the
deputies   82
An order against makeing bricks &c without licence of
the mayor &c and for paying 5^{li} to Anthony Fleatham,
and buying a statute booke, and for setting rates or wages
for poarters   89
An order to get subscriptions for defraying the charge of
the clock   95
An order that Thomas Fowler shall keep the clock and
have 30^s per annum for the same   95
An order that William Claxton shall sett out stoals &c and
keep watch &c   95
An order for paying 6 13 1½ to Mr Webster resting due
for the clock-bell   97
An order to collect 5^s per burgage for renewing the
anchoridge lease   103
Another for 20^s per burgage for dischargeing of debts &c   106
Another that Mr Moone shall have interest for 21^{li} 10^s he
disburst in geting a free kaye &c   107
Another that Mr Cooke & Mr Atkinson shall have interest
for 33^{li} they disburst to prevent a free kaye at Portrack 118

5   MS 'shit'.

6 Between the house and the common sewer is meant: see below, pp. 122–3.
7 A brace between this and the previous folio number indicates that they
   should be reversed.

[*p. xxi*]

R: R:

[*p. xxii*]

S: S:

[*p. xxiii*]

T: T:

Troy Jonathan his account folios 264: 268
Ditto   Ditto   282

[*p. xxiv*]

V: U:

[*p. xxv*]

W: W:

Watson Thomas his account folios the 11th: 21: 35: 37: 45:49
Weatherill Giles folio the 15:
Wrangham Thomas folios 121: 123: 152:
Wells John folios 183: 186:
Whitley Ralph his accounts 275. 278

[*The verso and the following six folios are blank, except for 'The xi daie of' at the head of the folio preceding p. 1, below.*]

[p. 1]
Burrow of Stockton. The xi[th] daie of October anno domini 1616[8]

Memorandum that Thomas Lambart, being maior, hath received the daie and yeare above written the summe of five poundes twelve shillinges eight pence to the towne's use, and he hath made his accompte and all thinges are discharged and so their remaines – 5[li] 12[s] 8[d]

[col. 1] Ch[risto]ph[e]r Fewster, Rowland Weatherill, Anthony Harperley, Richard Harperley, Henry Burdon,[9] Willm. Fewler, Roger Fewler, Christofer Reade, Thomas Watson
[col. 2] William Burdon, clarke, John Coates, Gregory Hurwouth, Roger Baynbridge, John Osbourne, Ralfe Welfeut, Thomas Rawe.

William Harte[10] maior of Stockton hath made his accompt the xix[th] daie of October anno domini 1625 and hath remainyng in his hand xix[s] i[d] and all thinges dischar[g]ed.

Rowland Weatherill,[11] Thomas Watsonn, Ch[risto]ph[e]r Fewster, John Thompson, Tho. Rawe, Anthony Storie,* Brian Cottes.*

[p. 2] [blank]

---

8   Despite Sowler dating the book's start to 1620 (History, pp. 465–79), the date of this entry is not in doubt (see Figure 1).
9   The Burdons had deep roots in Stockton and feature repeatedly as mayors. According to Richmond, Robert Burdon in 1495 was the first person recorded as mayor of Stockton (Richmond, Local Records, p. 18). Sowler (History, p. 425) has a Richard Maunce as mayor in 1380 but, while taking all profits from the borough, he was a burgess, not necessarily acting on behalf of all burgesses: VCH Durham III, p. 354.
10   A William Harte died in 1627, but elsewhere it is claimed William Harte was mayor in 1627 to 1629 (Sowler, History, p. 426; Bayley, 'Genealogical Additions', p. 80). A William Harte, alderman, was buried in 1658: Surtees, History, p. 174, which gives a footnoted list of mayors.
11   Rowland Weatherill took the lease from the bishop, for anchorage, plankage and metage, in 1620 (Richmond, Local Records, p. 31). In that year he was also granted a messuage, croft, and an oxgang and a half from Thomas Burdon (Surtees, History, p. 174).

[p. 3]

An order made concluded and agreed upon by Thomas Watson, maior of Stockton, and the most parte of the burrough men whose names are hereunder written the 16th day of March anno regni regis Jacobi Anglie &c xxi° et Scotiae lvii° annoque domini 1623 in manner following viz:–

Whereas an anncyent custome hath bene and yet is used in Stockton aforesaid, that every burrough man may have a quantyty of corne or other commodyty out of every shippe or other vessell arriving within the porte of Stockton aforesaid, paying for the same att such reasonable tyme or tymes, as the maior of Stockton aforesaid for the time being shall give commandement to his officers for the collecting thereof; and whereas many inconveniences have happened and arisen by the negligences of divers of the said burrough men in deferring and delaying their payments, it is now therefore for the preventing of such inconveniences, fully agreed upon and condiscended unto by the above said maior and burrough men, that what burrough men soever shall take upp any corne or grane or other comodyties in right of their said burrough, forth of any shippe or other vessell arriving within the said porte, refusing to pay for the same att such reasonable time or tymes as the then maior shall thinke convenyent for the payment thereof, that then it shall and may be lawfull to and for the said maior and the serjants his officers to distreane the goods and chattels of those soe refusing to pay for their commodityes. And the distresse soe taken to sell, therewith to pay for their said commodityes the remainder if anie be, to be restored to the owners therof. And it is alsoe further agreed upon by the said maior and burrough men, that if anie burrough man lett his burgage to any other he the said burrough man shall be bound to performe the order abovsaid himselfe.

Thomas Watsonn, maior, Row. Weatherill, John Harperley, Thomas Lambert, William Hart [p. 4] Henry Burdon* his mark, Thomas Hart* his mark, William Fowler* his mark, Cristofer Readd* his mark, Roger Bainbridg* his mark, William Bainbridg" his mark, Anthony Storye* his mark, John Bainbridge* his mark, Thomas Fletham* his mark, Anthony Fleatham, Thomas Rawe, John Buntinge,[12] John

---

12   The Bunting family was said to have been, along with the Cookes and Burdons, one of the most important families in the borough from the days of Elizabeth I: Bayley, 'Genealogical Additions', p. 82.

Thompson, Gregory Hurworth* his mark, John Jeckkell* his mark,
Mathew Heron* his mark, William Lambart* his mark in the behalf
of Raph Fewler, William Fewler \senior/* his marke, Raph Welfoote*
his marke, Ch[risto]ph[e]r Fewster senior, George Swanston,[13] John
Fewler* the wever his [mark], Raiphe Lambaert, John Fewler junior*
his marke, Roger Fewler sinnior*[14] his mark, John Osburne* his
marke, John Osburne* his mark.

[p. 5]
20th of October 1629

Received of Mr Alderman Watson in full upon
satisfatcktion of his account by me William Hart mayor
the some of the &c   8ˢ 4ᵈ

I say received by me William Hart* mayor his mark   8ˢ 4ᵈ

John Thompson, Thomas Rawe.

20th of October 1629

Received of Robart Kitchin \34ˢ 4ᵈ/ in part of pament of
his account of pament of [£]2 5[s.] 4ᵈ being sarjant   34ˢ 4ᵈ

20ᵗʰ of October 1629

Received of Thomas Raw sarjant of his account the some
of xxiiijˢ ijᵈ   1ˡⁱ 4ˢ 2ᵈ

19ᵗʰ of October 1630

An account maid by Mr William Hart and all thing is
discharged except xviiiˢ xᵈ dew to be paid by him the
towen to the aforsaid Mr William Hart   xviiiˢ xᵈ

13 William Swainston was mayor in 1622. Bayley mentions two sons, John and
    Anthony, but not a George (Bayley, 'Genealogical Additions', p. 76). George,
    Anthony and Thomas appear as burgage holders in 1636, but John Swainston
    not until 1664 (below, pp. 43–4, 59).
14 The Fewler family was said to have been 'one of the most numerous families
    in the town': Bayley, 'Genealogical Additions', p. 77.

Recived \the same day/ by Mr Giles Weathereild[15] mayor
the some of five shillings for causey mony   v[s]

Witnesses herof,
William Hart* his mark, Thomas Watson, Tho: Rawe.

[p. 6]
The 15th off October 1633

Memorandum that I John Jessepp maior of Stockton haith
maid up my account and ther remanes in my hand three
pound seavetene shilling   3[li] 17[s]

per me John Jessepp, maior.

Witnes hereof John Lambert, William Hart* mark, Christopher Read*
mark, John Fewler* weaver his mark, Brian Cottes* his mark, John
Jeckell* his mark, John Thompson.

Stockton
An order made concluded & agreed upon by John Jessep maior of
Stockton & the most part of the burrow men 18th day of October 1633.

That whereas ~~whereas~~ there hath beene much occasion for corne to
supply the wants of the contrey by which dayly trade hath bene the
decay of the causeyes & hywayes about the burrow, it is ordred ~~by~~
that every last of corne or other goods imported into the saide towne
of Stockton by straingers shall pay two pence \a/ last toward the
repaire of the said causies & hywayes.

John Thompson, sarjeant.

[p. 7]
The 14th off October 1634

Memorandum that I John Jessepp maior off Stockton haith maid my
account to Thomas Watson maior for this yeare next folowing & the

---

15   Son of Rowland Weatherill, mayor in 1619–20: Bayley, 'Genealogical
     Additions', p. 75.

rest of neighbours & haith paid to Thomas Watson maior for the use of the towne x^{li} xviij^{s}

Rests upon an account by Mr Jessepp to the town ~~as by~~ for monyes received in lew of burrow ~~witnesses~~ corne as by note of partickulars doth appere viij^{s} ij^{d} which eight shillings and ij^{d} is paid to Mr William Hart in part of pament of xviii^{s} dew to him by our towne.

More paid in full satisfacktion of the some above named
to Mr William Hart   x^{s} x^{d}

Witnesses
Tho: Rawe, Anthony Fleatham, Rowland Burdon, John Osburne, Christopher Read* his mark, John Thompson.[16]

[p. 8]
An account of what money hath been paid for certaine renewalls of the anchoridge lease[17]

	li	s	d
Paid for the fine anno 1612 as appears by the mayor's accompt upon the file	20	0	0
Fees &c	2	12	4

And what was collected for the same anno 1620 see this book folio 9th and 10th

| Anno 1635. See the mayor's account on the above said file where is mentioned for the 1st and 2nd payment at 3^{li} apiece | 6 | 00 | 0 |

Anno 1663. See the mayor's account on same file where is charged paid to Mr James Cook for his assignment of that

lease	28	00	0
fees and charges	03	07	6
Anno 1676. Paid for the lord bishopp's fine	20	00	0
fees and charges	03	10	0

16 Below the signatures is written 'Ressing in mtr'.
17 The entries on this page are in an early eighteenth-century hand.

Anno 1687. Paid		13	06	8
fees and charges		03	5	6
Anno 1703. Paid		30	00	0
fees and charges		03	00	0

August the 24 Anno 1715. Paid for the fine by John Wells
Esq. mayor   13 19 6
And for the secretary's fee 2[li] 3[s] 0[d] and for inrolment &
other fees 6[s] 4[d] tot' inde   02 09 4

[p. 9]
~~14th of October 1634~~
regestred this 13th of October 1634

A note of the names of those burrow men that paid ther
monyes to the lease of ankaridg ~~and~~ planke and mettaig
the 30th of November 1620.[18]   li   s   d

Imprimis Anthony Dossey[19]	1 burgage	0	9	[2]
Item Rowland Weathereild	1 burgage	0	9	[2]
Item Mistress Lambart	3 burgages	1	7	[6]
Item Thomas Lambart	1 burgage	0	9	[2][20]
Item John Lambart	1 burgage	0	9	2
Item Raphe Lambart elder	1 burgage	0	9	2
Item Christopher Wetherild	1 burgage[21]	0	9	2
Item William Burdon	1 burgage	0	9	2
Item Roger Fewler elder	1 burgage	0	9	2
Item Roger Fewler younger	1 burgage	0	9	2
Item John Thompson elder	1 burgage	0	9	2
~~John Johnson~~ \\Item James Cooke//[22]	1 burgage	0	9	2

18   There is damage to the right-hand margin of this page, and hence some
     missing text, which has been interpolated based on what is obviously a
     standard rate per burgage plot.

19   Reading uncertain (could read 'Cossey') but the list of burgage holders in
     Stockton in 1602 (see below, Appendix 6, p. 314) includes John Dossey.

20   Damage down the top right-hand edge of the page has caused loss of the
     pence column; figures have been assumed, based on the standard rate of
     9s. 2d. per burgage.

21   This entry has been altered either from or to two burgages at 18s. 4d. The
     sequence of alteration is not clear from the text.

22   The Cooks were described as a 'very considerable' merchant family in the
     borough, who owned the mansion at the south end of the town, near the site
     of Stockton Castle: Bayley, 'Genealogical Additions', p. 81.

Raphe Welfoote	1 burgage	0	9	2
John Jeckell	1 burgage	0	9	2
Item Thomas Watson	1 burgage	0	9	2
Item Thomas Raw	2 burgages	0	18	4
Item John Osburne elder	2 burgages	0	18	4
Item Robart Bainbridg elder	1 burgage	0	9	2
Item John Bainbridg	1 burgage	0	9	2
Item John Harperlay	1 burgage	0	9	2
Item ~~John Cottes~~ \\Roger Coates 1//	~~1 burgage~~	0	5[23]	0
Item Thomas Hart	1 burgage	0	9	2
Item John Fewler elder	1 burgage	0	9	2
Item John Fewler younger	2 burgages	0	18	4[24]
Item John Harplay	1 burgage	0	9	2
Item Thomas Fletham	1 burgage	0	9	2
Item Gregory Hurworth	1 burgage	0	9	2
Item Rowland Burdon	1 burgage	0	9	2
Item Elsabeth Alleson	1 burgage	0	9	2
Item ~~Widdow~~ \John/ Bunting	1 burgage	0	5	0
Item William Bainbridg	1 burgage	0	9	2
	Total 37[25]	16	14	[0][26]

[p. 10]

Item Mathew Heron	1 burgage	0	9	2
Item Christopher Read	1 burgage	0	9	2
Item Mr John Jessop	1 burgage	0	9	2
\John Jenkins	1 burgage	0	9	2/
Item George Swainston	1 burgage	0	9	2
Item John Osburne younger	1 burgage	0	9	2

Item Roger Fewler third part of one burgage for Thomas Merchant

	burgage	0	1	0

---

23 It is not clear whether '0' has been changed to '5' or vice versa. The reason for some burgages paying 5s. rather than 9s. 2d. is unclear.

24 The figure '1' has been overwritten '2' and the sum changed from 9s. 2d. to 18s. 4d.

25 The subtotal of thirty-seven burgages appears to include both John Cottes' burgage, which was struck through, the two burgages (increased from one) of John Fewler the younger and both of Christopher Wetherill's burgages, which were reduced to one, as noted above.

26 The subtotal appears to read £16 14s. [–]d., though the paper is damaged. If the assumptions above are correct, the total should be £16 15s. 10d.

Item John Fewler weaver	1 burgage[27]	0	9	2
Item Marmaduke Wilson	1 burgage	0	9	2
Item William Fewler younger	1 burgage	0	9	2
Item William Hart	3 burgages	1	7	6
Item Francis Carter	1 burgage	0	9	2

A note of all them that paid 6s 8d to the maior   s d

[–]th [Oct]ober [1]636[28]

Item Anthone Swainstone	1 burgage	0	6	8
Item Thomas Swainstone	1 burgage	0	6	8
Item George Denham	1 burgage	0	6	8
Item Anthone Fleatham	1 burgage	0	6	8
Item Bryand Coates	1 burgage	0	6	8
Item Raphe Fewler	1 burgage	0	6	8
Item Nycholas Hull	1 burgage	0	6	8
Item Roberte Kitchin for Mr Lowerance Sayer for				
	1 burgage	0	6	8
Item for Alien Askew	1 burgage	0	6	8
Thomas Wetherill for Mr Sayer	1 burgage	0	6	8
Isbell Welfoot for the like	1 burgage	0	6	8
October 1649 16th[29]				
Mr John Jenkings	5 burgeses	1^{li}	13	4
Thomas Gouldsbrough	1 burgage	0	6	8
Thomas Gouldsbrough & Margrett Bainbridge for 2				
thirds of one burgage		0	4	6

Tot' inde	31	11 18 08[30]
On the other side	37	16 14 00
Total	68	28 12 08[31]

---

27   The figures appear to have been altered from three burgages at £1 7s. 6d. to
     one burgage at 9s. 2d.
28   Damage has caused loss of text from left margin.
29   Change of hand.
30   The individual sums appear to total £11 18s. 11d.
31   The three lines of totals are in a later hand, probably of c.1700.

[p. 11]
The 20th of October 1635.

Memorandum that I Thomas Watson alderman hath maid
my account to John Jessepp maior for this yeare ~~next~~
~~folowing~~ last past and haith paid to John Jessepp maior

for the use off[32] the burjesses the some off mettage	xi^{li} x^{s}
paid for causie mony	vij^{s}
& the remainder off the last yeare account	iiij^{s} vi^{d}
more paid in lew off burow corne	x^{li} iiij^{s}
More received of William Lambart for Mr Davison for this yeare account in lew of burrow corne	15^{s} 10^{d}
more for metaig paid by William Lambart	11^{s} 2^{d}

Witnesses of this account
John Jessepps, William Hart,* Tho: Rawe, Rowland Burdon, Anthony
Fleatham, John Buntinge, John Lambert.

[p. 12] [*blank*]

[p. 13]
The 12th of October 1636

Memorandum that I John Jessepp maior haith maid my
account and ~~there rests in in my hand~~ and paid to the

towne for mettaig monyes	25^{li}		
more paid in lew of burrow corne	18^{li} 6^{s}		
	43	6	0
Resting for mettaig in my hand	2^{li}	3^{s}	1^{d}
Resting in my hand in lew of burrow corne	13	14	0
Resting more in my hand	00	17	6
Resting in total	16	14	7

Rowland Weatherill, Thomas Watson, John Harperley, Rowland
Burdon, Anthony Fleatham

Mr John Jessopp rests as above	£16 14	7

---

32 MS: 'off' repeated.

Per causey m[oney]s received of James Cooke[33] and John Welfoot	£0	2	0
Per received of Raph Fewler for his freedom in the lease	£0	6	8
Per received of John Waselbye	£0	5	0
Per received of Clem' Angells	£0	7	6
	£17	15	9

Mr Jessopp hath disburst for:			
particular charges as per his note	£5:	19	10
Restes posted to the next m[ayo]r	£11	15	11
	£17	15	9

[p. 14] [*blank*]

[p. 15][34]
17th off October 1637

Memorandum that I \Mr/ John Jessepp ~~maior~~ haith maid
my account to Mr Giles Weatherield maior for the lew of
borrow corne & haith \paid/ the soom of   24li 2s 3d

\\Mr John Jessopp hath paid to Mr Gyles Wetherell in full
of what rested in his hands the last yeare   £11 15 11//

17 Oct. Memorandum more received of Mr John Jessepp
by Mr Giles Weatherield for mettaig monyes the some of   14li 16s 1d

Paid out of these somes above written to Mr Thomas
Watson by Mr Maior for charges in a sut in answering
John Fewer[35]   3li 3s 6d

---

33 James Cooke would be a major player and eventually leave the most
     substantial surviving will in seventeenth-century Stockton and Norton, if we
     exclude Sir Thomas Davison of Blakiston Hall. James Cooke's son, James,
     and grandson, John, all feature heavily in the commerce of the town. Cooke's
     first mention in the Exchequer Port Books is from about this time, though
     there are large gaps in the records. That he was already collecting causey
     money suggests he was already established in the community.
34 The page number '14' has been overwritten '15' at top left; '15' is repeated
     at top right. There has been renumbering and removal of pages early in the
     life of the book. Here and below, this transcript uses the updated (latest)
     handwritten page numbers.
35 Reading of surname uncertain.

paid out of thes moones & that was charges   3   7 10
devided amongst the borrowmen after 12^s per burgiss   36 12   0

Resting in Mr Maire his hand and all things discharged   7 10   0
More resting for repairing the causes in Mr Maior hands
per 2^d per last   4   7   7
John Jessepp, Thomas Watson, Ri: Sutcliff, James Cooke.

The 6th of November 1638
Memorandum \disburst/ by Mr Giles Weath[er]eild laite
maior deceased the some of   3^{li} ii^s 6^d

More paid by Mrs Weathereild to Mr John Jessepp maior
the some of   3^{li} 18^s 6^d

Memorandum disburst by me John Thompson for
causeies and other things the some of   3^{li} 2^s 8^d

more paid to Mr John Jessepp maior by me John
Thompson the some of   1^{li} 4^s ii^d

[p. 16] [*blank*]

[p. 17]^{36}
The 6th of November 1638

An account maid by Mr John Jessepp maior

And hath paid to the borowmen in lew of borow corne that
is paid ech burgage the som of 00 – 5^s which amonts to   15^{li} 5^s
which was duw to the borow for and in lew of burow
corn the some of 16–3–4^d wherof ther doth rest in my
hands the some of eighteen schelings fower pens of the
said moenes   18^s 4^d

mor I have resting in my hands that is due to the town for
the mending of caueses and other things about the borow
the some of eight pownds three schelings five penses   8^{li} 3^s 5^d

36   Originally numbered '16' and overwritten.

and more that is resting to the borow in my hands
dew for the ankerch leas and metage the some of twelf
pownds feveften schelings and sex pens   12 15   6

Per me John Jessepp, Thomas Watson, John Harperley, John Buntinge,
Rowland Burdon, Antho: Fleatham, John Thompson.

[p. 18] [*blank*]

[p. 19]
October the 18th 1639

Memorandum that Mr Jessepp late maior hath maide upp
his accounts and there is resting in his hand which he
stayes in his hand for the freight of his shipp to Barwick[37]
15^{li} which moneyes is dew to the towne which he doth
promise to ~~pay~~ use meanes to recover and he hath
delivered in to Mr Watson's hand which is due to the
towne being 2^d per last for causey money eleaven pounds
~~five~~ three shillings and fower pence.   11^{li} 3^s 4^d

Delivered more in to Mr Watson's hand which is resting
uppon account for and in lew of burrow corne and
mettage money.   4^{li} 2^s[0^d]

John Jessepp,[38] Tho: Rawe, Rowland Burdon, Antho: Fleatham,
Anthony Swainston, John Thompson.

[p. 20] [*blank*]

[p. 21]
October the 20th 1640

Memorandum that Mr Thomas Watson \ould maior/ hath
maid up his accounts to the towne and hath paid into the
hand \of/ James Cook now maior the sum of six pounds
and seaventene shillings in full of all ~~which is~~ accounts due
by him. In witnesse whereof we say received   06^{li} 17^s 00^d

---

37   Probably Berwick-upon-Tweed.
38   John Jessop was buried 25 May 1640: Surtees, *History*, pp. 173–4.

Witnesse heareof
James Cooke maior, Tho: Rawe, John Harperley, John Bunting,
Rowland Burdon, Antho: Fleatham.

[p. 22]
Memorandum that Sir William Allison \of Yorke/ is
behind for the burrow ~~dewes~~ duties for 12 laste of malt
the 19th October 1641 the sume of twelve shillings. I say
the some of   00 12 00

[p. 23]
Stockton October the 19th 1641

Memorandum that James Cooke \late/ maior hath made
upp his account the day above written to the inhabitants
of the ~~towne~~ burrow of Stockton and hath paide into
Rowland Burdon hand now maior the summe of eleaven
pounds seaventene shillings & seaven pence.
I say received in full   11 17   7
Witnesse our hands
Rowland Burdon maire, Thomas Watson alderman, William Hart
alderman, John Buntinge, Nicholas Fleatham, Tho: Rawe, Antho:
Fleatham, John Harperley.

[p. 24] [*blank*]

[p. 25]
October 19th 1642

Memorandum that I Rowland Burdon latte maior of
Stockton haith mayd up his account the daye above
written to the inhabetants of the borrowe of Stockton
and haith cleared all accounts and demandes what so
evere and haith \paid/ the full sume of fourtye nyne
poundes seaventen shilings tow pence. More nowe resting
in my hand being nowe elected mayor for this presen[t]
yeare 1642 the sume six poundes fiftene shilings eighte
pennce: I say   6^{li} 15^s 08^d
John Lambert, Raiph Hart, Tho: Rawe, Antho: Swainston, John
Buntinge, John Thompson, William Fewler.

[p. 26] [*blank*]

[p. 27]
October the 24th 1643

Memorandum that Rowland Burdon hath mad up his
account (beinge maior the last yeare) the day and yeare
above written to the inhabitants of the burrow of Stockton
and hath cleared all accounts and demaunds whatsoever
and hath paid in to the burrow the sume of eleaven
pounds three shillings six pence \whereof there is/
~~Memor~~ restinge in the hands of James Cooke now maior
the day abovesaid the sume of five \pounds/ thirteene
shillings. I say   5^{li} 13^s 0^d
James Cooke, Thomas Watson, John Lambert, Nicholas Fleatham,
Antho: Fleatham, Roger Coats* his mark.

[p. 28] [*blank*]

[p. 29]
~~October the 17th 1648~~
October the 3th 1644

Memorandum that James Cooke hath made up his
account beinge maior the last yeare the day & yeare
above written to the inhabitants of the burrow of
Stockton & hath cleared all & evry accounts & demaunds
whatsoever & the town is indebted to him the sume of   3^{li} 4^s 5^d.
Paid unto Mr Cooke by the town the sume of   3^{li} 4^s 5^d
Per me Ja: Cooke
John Buntinge, Thomas Watson, Row: Burdon, Wm Hart,* Ri: Sutcliff.

[p. 30] [*blank*]

[p. 31]
October the 7th 1645

Memorandum that Rowland Burdon maior hath made
up his accounts (being maior this yeare above written[)]
to the inhabitants of the burrow of Stockton and hath
cleared all accounts & demaunds & hath resting in his
hands   3^{li} 2^s 6^d
Received by the towne of Rowland Burdon   3   2   6

John Bunting, Thomas Watson, Thomas Jessepp, Antho: Fleatham, Ja: Cooke.

[p. 32] [*blank*]

[p. 33]
Stockton October the 20th 1646

	li	s	d

Memorandum that Rowland Burdon hath made up his account beinge maior for this yeare above written to the inhabitants of the burrow and hath cleared all accounts & demaunds whatsoever & rests in his hands the summe of fowerteene shillings & 2d

| | 00 | 14 | 2 |

Paide in full to the town the sum of   00 14 2

John Buntinge, Thomas Watson, Thomas Jessepp, Ja: Cooke, Nicholas Fleatham.

[p. 34] [*blank*]

[p. 35]
October the 8th 1647

Memorandum that Thomas Watson hath made up his accounts he being maior for this & yeare above written for the inhabitants of Stockton burrow and hath cleared all accounts and demaunds whatsoever & rests in his hands   11^{li} 17^s 8^d.
Paide in full of this account to the towne   11 17 8

Ja: Cooke, Row. Burdon, John Buntinge, Nicholas Fleatham, Thomas Jessepp.

[p. 36]³⁹
October 26 1648

Paid by Antony Fleatham in parte which was due to the towne the sume of   1^{li} 5^s 10^d
Witnes: Row: Burdon, Nicholas Fleatham.

---

39   Pages 36 and 37 were originally numbered 35 and 36 and those numbers were overwritten.

[p. 37]
October the 17th 1648

Memorandum that Thomas Watson hath maid up his
account & he beinge maior for this year above written
to the inhabitants of the burrow of Stockton and hath
cleared all accounts and demaunds whatsoever & there is
restinge in Anthony Fletham's hands (being serjant) the
sum of eleven pounds five shillings & nyne pence. I say 11^{li} 5^s 9^d
which he hath promised to pay to John Buntinge now
maire for the use of the burrowmen within 28 days time.

Debts restinge now to the town as follows	li	s	d
John Moone Sheelds pro 15 chalder cooles	0	5	0
William Buncle for salte & cooles	0	4	4
John Barwicke Wells pro 9 lasts malte	0	4	6
Robert Webster pro 31 wee[40] salte	0	10	4
William Chapman pro 47 wee salte	0	15	8
William Paule Sunderland pro 129 wee salte	2	3	0
Mr Thomas Davison pro 9 chalder cooles	0	3	0
Mr Hollis of Hull 13^{li} 7^s 5^d rye	0	6	6
Richard Willson pro compasition[41] pro dayls	1	0	0
sume is	5	12	4

John Buntinge maior, Ja: Cooke, William Harte* his mark, Thomas
Jessepp, John Harperley.

Received by John Buntting maiore for
Thomas Weitherilt borgidge 6^s 8^d
Allin Asquie[42] house 6^s 8^d
Wedow Welfoute house 6^s 4^d

[p. 38] [blank]

---

40   i.e. 'weigh', a measure. In all of these and similar entries (p. 53), salt is 4d. per
      weigh.
41   Composition: agreement to pay a given sum in return for exemption from
      assessment.
42   i.e. Alien Askew, see above, p. 44.

[p. 39]
The 16th of October 1649

Memorandum that John Buntinge maior hath made his
account the day and yeare above written for this yeare
and hath cleared all his accounts exeptinge eleven
pounds six shillings & eight pence which remaines
in Mr Maior's hand & the sarjeant's which must be
accounted for the next yeare   11^{li} 06^s 08
paide unto Thomas Gouldsbrough the same day   00 02 06
Nett restinge   11 04 02

Debts restinge for this yeare 1649
John Moore for 15 chalder of coales   00 05 00
John Barwick of Wells pro 9 last malt   00 04 04
Robert Webster pro 31 weigh of salt   00 10 04
William Chapman pro[43] Sheiles pro 47 weigh salt   00 15 08
William Paule Sunderland 129 weight salt   02 03 00
Mr Thomas Davison pro 9 chalder coales   00 03 00
Richard Wilson pro comp[osition] m[ade][44] pro dales[45]   01 00 00
                                                     05 01 04

Thomas Watson, Row: Burdon, Nicholas Fleatham, Thomas Jessepp,
Tho: Rawe, John Harperley, Antho: Swainston.

[p. 40] [blank]

[p. 41]
October the 15 1650

Memorandum that the day and yeare abovesaid Mr John
Buntinge late maior of this corporacion hath given in his
accompt and hath paid into the hands of Mr Rowland
Burdon present maior in full of all his accompts the
sume of eleven pounds thirteene shillings and nyne
pence. I say   11^{li} 13^s 9^d

43 'of' is perhaps meant.
44 Expansion of abbreviation uncertain.
45 Dales (also 'deals', 'dayles') were sawn timber planks, usually of softwood
    e.g. fir or pine.

per Row: Burdon maior, Thomas Watson alderman, Tho: Rawe, Antho: Fleatham, John Atkinson, Thomas Jessepp.

[p. 42] [*blank*]

[p. 43]
October the 18th 1653

Memorandum that Rowland Burdon late maior hath made his account to inhabitants of the burrow of Stockton the day & yeare above written & cleared all debts & demaunds whatsoever
And paid into Mr Thomas Watson's hand now maior the
summe of   00 04 02
Rest due to Anthony Fleatham serjeant to be paid by the
burrow the summe of   01 01 11
Due to the burrow by Cristopher Crosley for mettage of
19 chalder of coales the summe of   00 06 04
More due to the burrow by Robert Guy for two yeares
rent due at Michelmas 1653   02 00 00
Thomas Watson, William Hart*mark, Tho: Raw, Nicholas Fleatham, Francis Carter, John Johnson* his marke, Geo: Denam* his marke, John Osburn junior* his marke, Leonard Fewler* his marke, Antho: Fleatham serjeant.

[p. 44] [*blank*]

[p. 45]
October the xviith 1654

Memorandum that Thomas Watson late mayor of the
borrow of Stockton hath maid his account unto the
inhabitants theirof, the day and yeare above written and
hath paid to Mr Rowland Burdon lately elected mayor
in full of all accounts unto the borrow due from the 4th
of October 1653 untill the 3th of October 1654 \and of all
other accounts whatsoever/ the some of eight shillings
on[e] halpenny.   00^{li} 08^s 00½^d
Memorandum the 8^s ½^[d] in this account above written is by consent allowed to Anthony Fleatham in part of more money due to him.
In testimony whereof we have subscribed our names as under written:

Row. Burdon maire,[46] John Bunting, Tho: Rawe, John Atkinson, Nichollas Flleatham, John Johnson, William Storye,* Robert Guy* his mark, Antho: Fleatham.

Memorandum the borrow and the inhabitants theirof
is resting \the day and yeare abovesaid/ to Anthony
Fleatham sargaint the some of   00 07 06½
As alsoe the said Anthony Fleatham is content to rec[eive]
upon Mr Rowland Burdon now mayor in part of the
abovesaid some being due for dailes resting upon account
in his hand   00 05 00
soe their is resting only to Anthony Fleatham   00 02 06½
Memorandum of certaine debts resting to the inhabitants of the
borrow of Stockton
viz.   John Clark for 10 chalder of coles   00 03ˢ 04ᵈ
           John Ward for 6 chalder of coles   00 02 00

[p. 45][47] [blank]

[p. 46]
October the xiiij[th] 1656

Memorandum that Mr Rowland Burdon \late maior/
hath made up his accounts (for the burrow of Stockton) to
Mr Thomas Watson[48] now maior for the 2 last yeares 1654
& 1655 & part of 1656 and the burrow rests indebted to
Mr Burdon the summe of fouer shillings. I say   00 04 07
More indebted to the burrow by Robert Guy for the
rent of his shopp for 3 halfe yeares the summe of thirty
shillings   001 10 00.
Thomas Watson maior, John Bunting, John Atkinson, Nichollas Flleatham, John Johnson* his marke, William Hart* his marke, Tho: Hart* his marke,[49] Antho: Fleatham serjeant.

46 Rowland Burdon was buried 13 May 1657: Surtees, History, p. 174.
47 Two successive pages are numbered 45, the second being blank.
48 Thomas Watson, later an alderman, was buried 16 October 1672: Surtees, History, p. 174.
49 The names of William Hart and Thomas Hart are written to the right of the other witnesses.

[p. 47]
December the 5th 1657

Memorandum that Thomas Watson late maior of the
burrow of Stockton hath this day made up his account
to this burrow and hath paid in good moneye thirteene
pounds and twelve shillings. I say   13^{li} 12^s [00]
out of which they have returned him back for payinge a
yeare and a halph rent to the lord for the ankoridge lease 4^{li} 10^s
Soe heare is restinge in money and put into the hands of
John Atkinson present mayor the sume of nyne pounds
and two shillings; I say   9^{li} 2^s
witnesse our hands the day and yeare first above written:
John Atkinson, John Bunting, Nichollas Flleatham, Tho: Hart* his
mark, William Hearon, John Osburne seny[o]r* \marke/, Christ.
Coots*, A C.*⁵⁰

[p. 48]
October the 22th 1658

Memorandum that Mr John Atkinson late maior of the
burrow of Stockton hath made upp his account to this
burrow & hath paide in good money thirty pounds
seaventene shillings & five pence whereof ~~Resting in his~~
~~account~~ Thomas Jessopp's \hand/ now maior ten pounds
seaventeane shillings & five pence for defraying the
burrow's charges. I say   10^{li} 17^s 5^d
Memorandum that the other twenty pounds is left in the hands of
Thomas Jessepp now maior for which he hath given securitie to
Mr James Cook & John Buntinge aldermen for the use of the burrow.
In witnesse whereof we have sett to our hands this day and yeare
above written.
Thomas Jessepp maior, Ja: Cooke, John Bunting, Francis Carter,
Antho: Fleatham.

---

50   Written below the signatures; probably the mark of Anthony Coates (see
     Appendix 5).

[p. 49]
October the 25 1659

Memorandum that this day Thomas Jessepp late maior
of this corporation hath ~~this~~ made up his account and
hath ~~given~~ paid to the neighboures 10s. an house for 69
burgages is   34^{li} 10^s
and there is left in hands this day   11^{li} 17^s 1½^d
and all other charges whatsoever are[51] discharged to this day as
witnesse our hands heare under the day and yeare first above
written:
Thomas Watson, John Atkinson, John Bunting, Leonard Calvert,
Nichollas Flleatham, Tho: Raw, William Storye, Robt Dale* his
marke, Antho: Fleatham, Tho: Ward* his marke.

[p. 50]
October the 20th 1660

Memorandum that Mr Thomas Jessepp late maior hath
this day maid up his accounts before Mr William Peers
now maior with the rest of his neighbours & hath paid
into his hands the sum of ~~one pound~~ twelve pounds &
five pence; we say received   12^{li} 00^s 5^d
More ~~left~~ \resting/ in Mr James Cook's hands due to the
~~towne~~ burrow for the yeare last past which he refuseth to
pay the summ of one pound & ten shillings eleaven pence
halfe penny   1^{li} 10^{s}11½^d
Per me Thomas Watson & per Thomas Jessepp
John Bunting, Leonard Calvert, Tho: Raw, Robt Jackson, Nichollas
Flleatham,[52] Antho: Fleatham.

[p. 51] [blank]

---

51   MS: 'and'.
52   Nicholas Fleatham was said to own a mill at or near Stockton in 1660: Bayley,
      'Genealogical Additions', p. 85.

[p. 52]
October the 14: 1662

Memorandum that this day William Peares late maior
of this corporacion hath th̶ made his accounte and
discharged all, and hath paid into the hands of Ralph
Eden[53] present maior the some of sixteene pounds fower
shillings and six pence. I say   16^{li} 4^s 6^d
Witnesse our hands Ralph Eden.
Mr James Cooke is restinge to the burrow of Stockton for
compo[sition] for 2000 of firr deales and for mettedge of
twentie six lastes of rye at 4d. per last the sume of   001^{li} 8^s 9^d
Tho: Watson, Jo: Atkinson, Thomas Jessopp, Tho: Raw, Jo: Lambert,
Antho: Fleatham junior.

[p. 53]
The names of those burow men that have not paid 10s. a house to
purchace the leace of ankoridge and mettadge in the yeare 1663, Ra:
Eden then mayor, are as follows:
H̶o̶m̶f̶r̶e̶y̶ ̶J̶e̶n̶k̶i̶n̶g̶s̶   3̶ ̶b̶u̶r̶g̶a̶g̶e̶s̶ D. per Robert Jackson.[54]

John Osburne	1 burgage
Thomas Raw	1 bur[gage]
Leonard Fewler	1
John Coates	1
John Lambert[55]	

August 15 1664
Received of the parties under mentioned and paid to Mr Samuell
Hartlib[56] who is imployed at London upon the burrowe's accounte,
which is to be repaid them the first moneyes that comes into the
burrowe's stock by generall consent these soumes foll[owing]:
        of Mr Thomas Watson twenty shillings is   1$^{[li]}$

---

53   Ralph Eden's father was also Ralph Eden: Surtees, *History*, pp. 173–4.
54   'D' is perhaps for 'discharged'.
55   A John Lambert had four hearths in 1666: Green, *Hearth Tax*, p. 40.
56   Samuel Hartlib was the son of the more famous Samual Hartlib, and was
       an excise officer for Berwick and solicitor for the Merchant Adventurers
       of Newcastle upon Tyne. He was a drinking companion of Samuel Pepys
       and would later be dismissed for corruption in collecting Hearth Tax, and
       flee the country having been accused of seditious speeches and libel: see
       M. Greengrass, 'Samual Hartlib 1600–1662', *ODNB*.

of Mr James Cooke twenty shillings is	1
of Mr William Peares twenty shillings	1
of Mr Thomas Jessep twenty shillings is	1
of John Atkinson then maior 20s	1
of Mr Robert Jackson twenty shillings	1
of Thomas Swainston twenty shillings	1
of William Thomson twenty shillings is	1
of John Jessep twenty shillings is	1
of John Swanston twenty shillings is	1

   paid him all October 15th 1672[57]

October the 19th 1675 paid every man above, then the remaining some of 10s. a peice per the above disburs[ments] by I James Cooke then mayor out of the 5s. per burges that were in a lease about the market towne got by Robert Jackson when he was mayor.[58]

[p. 54]
October the 18th 1664

Memorandum that this day Mr John Atkinson late mayor
hath made up his account to Mr Robert Jackson now
maior the some of nine shilengs & foure peence. I say the
some of   00[li] 09[s] 4[d]
As wittnes our hands:
Robert Jackson, Tho: Watson,[59] Thomas Jessepp.

October the 14th 1664
The coppy of the oth of Robert Jackson then elected maior for the b[o]rough of Stockton tooke before the lord bishopp &c.
I Robert Jackson shall truth and faith beare to our soveraigne lord the King's Majestie his heires & sucesers & to the Lord Bishopp of Durham & to his sucessers bishopps of Durham & all such acts & orders as I shall consent & agree unto to be made shall be according to my skill & knowledge for the common welth & the benefit & the

---

57 The mark 'X' has been written twice against each of these amounts, indicating a checking procedure. From the hand and the ink used, these do not seem to relate to the entry below, which was added eleven years later.

58 Added in a different hand, apparently eleven years after the main entry.

59 Thomas Watson was buried 13 May 1672: Surtees, *History*, pp. 173–4. He may have been the Thomas Watson senior who had seven hearths in 1666: Green, *Hearth Tax*, p. 41.

profit of the b[o]rough of Stockton & the freemen and inhabitance thereof & I shall at noe time or times heare after while I am mayor of this b[o]rough attempt or goe aboute to make any orders against the royalties or priviledges of the Bishopp of Durham nor for the only profit of my selfe nor of any other privit person or persons or consent & agree to the same; soe helpe me god & by the contents of this booke.[60]

wittnis: Miles Stapelton exa'[61]

[p. 55] [*blank*]

[p. 56]
October the 17th 1665

Memorandum that this day Robert Jackson late mayor of Stockton hath made his accompt to the borrow, & there is rising due from the burgers to the said Robert Jackson as appears by the account the some of   01[li] 19[s] 00[d]
as wittnes our hands: John Atkinson, Thomas Jessepp, Nicholas Fleatham, Jo: Johnson junior.*

[p. 57]
October the 16th 1666

A note of the names of all those that hath not paid their 5s. per burgis for the geting of the charter renewed for a markit towne.

		li	s	d
Imprimis Mr James Cooke 2 burgages[62]	X[63]	0	10[64]	0
	\\these paid October 19//			
Widdow Coots paid per Ant. Coots	X	0	5	0

---

60   This is the first of thirty-three mayoral oaths recorded between 1664 and 1721 (indexed under 'O', above, p. 31). The next two such oaths, Robert Jackson and William Lee (below, pp. 61, 69), use the phrase 'liege people', which is not used thereafter. After p. 71 the oaths have not been transcribed in full but refer to Robert Jackson's oath on p. 59 as an exemplar. Minor spelling variations are not noted. The main textual variant is that some oaths include 'according to my skill and knowledge' and some do not.

61   Probably *examinatur*, 'examined'.

62   James Cooke had five hearths in 1666, presumably in his own residence, one of three burgages which he held: Green, *Hearth Tax*, p. 40.

63   As explained at the foot of the list, the 'X's represent payment.

64   Altered from '05' to '10'.

John Osburne		0	5	0[65]
Robert Banbridge		0	3	4
Mr William Males \\& Jessepp d[66] 5^s & Thomas Hope paid 5^s //				
	XX	0	10	0
Mrs Burdon \\paid per hir son George//	X	0	5	0
Elizabeth Fleatham & William Story	X	0	5[67]	0
Thomas Raw daughter		0	5	0
John Coats	X	0	5	0
Mr Lambert \\Ja Lees paid it//	X	0	5	0
\\Robert Jackson per Lambert//	X	0	5	0
Leonard Fuller				
Robert Fuller	X	0	5	0
Mr Ogle	X	0	5	0
Mr John Atkinson \\paid per his son William//	X	0	10	0
Elizabeth Calvert		0	5	0
Thomas Harte		0	5	0
Mary Browne		0	5	0
William Herin marriner		0	5	0
Osburne house \\paid per J. Raisbecke//	X	0	5	0
John Herrin		0	5	0
J. Askew \\paid per R. Jackson//	X	0	5	0
J. Litster \\paid per Ed: Cooke//	X	0	5	0
William Johnson		0	5	0
Roger Wilson \\per M Stoory//	X	0	5	0
		£6	12s	04d

October 19th 1675 Received then of severall above that is crost then the some of 3^{li} 17^s 6^d when J. Cooke was mayor.

[p. 58]
October the 16th 1666

Memorandum that this day Robert Jackson late mayor of
this corporation of Stockton hath given in his accompts
to the borrow & there doth rist due to the said Robert
Jackson from the bur[ges]ses the some of two poundes
eighteene shilengs & eleven pence. I say   2^{li} 18^s 11^d

---

65   In right margin by this entry '(75)'.
66   'd': perhaps for 'died' or 'deceased'.
67   This appears to have been '4', overwritten '5'.

Thomas Jessepp present maior, Nichollas Flleatham, James Kitchinge, J: Jessepp, Antho: Fleatham junior, Jo: Atkinson.[68]

[p. 59] [*blank*]

[p. 60]
1667 October the first

Memorandum that this day Thomas Jessepp late maior of this corporation of Stockton hath given in his accompt to the burrow and their doth rest dew to the sayd Thomas Jessepp for his disbursement for the sayd burrow [*erasure*] thirtty two shelings eight pence which the sayd burrow is ingaged to reemburce him againe by sese[69] or so soune as any monyes come into town's purse.   1^{li} 12^s 08^d
Seen and allowed. W[itnes]s:
Jo: Atkinson, Ja: Cooke, Robt Jackson, Tho: Swainston,[70] Antho: Fleatham, J: Jessepp, Wm Thompson, George Burdon, Robert Fewler, Jo: Swainston.

[p. 61] [*blank*]

[p. 62]
October 6th [16]68

Memorandum that this day John Atkinson late maior of Stockton haith given in his account to the borrow & paid unto the hands of Mr Jessepp now maior the sume of four pounds three shillings two pence   04^{li} 03^s 02^d
Seane & allowed by us:
Thomas Jessopp maior, Ja: Cooke, Robt Jackson, Tho: Swainston, Antho: Fleatham, George Burdon, Wm Thompson, J: Jessepp, Jo: Swainston.

[p. 63] [*blank*]

---

68   John Atkinson had three hearths in 1666: Green, *Hearth Tax*, p. 41.
69   Reading uncertain but perhaps 'sese' for 'sess', meaning assessment, tax or rates.
70   The previous year the Hearth Tax returns record Thomas Swainston as having four hearths: Green, *Hearth Tax*, p. 41.

[p. 64]
October 19th 1669

Memorandum that this day Thomas Jessepp late maior of
the corporation of Stockton haith given in his account to
the borrow & paid into the hands of James Cooke present
maior the sume four pounds one shilling: 04^{li}01^{s} 00^{d}.
Seane & allowed by us:
Ja: Cooke maior, Jo: Atkinson, Robt Jackson, Antho: Fleatham, Tho:
Swainston, J: Jessepp, George Burdon.
Memorandum that though the above said Thomas
Jessepp haith paid the said sume above written yett their
is due unto him when he was maior in the yeare 67 the
sume of one pound twelfe shillings eight pence   01^{li} 12^{s} 08^{d}
Wittnes: William Cuthbert sarjant

[p. 65] [*blank*]

[p. 66]
October the 18th 1670

Memorandum Mr James Cooke this day late maior of
the borrough of Stockton hath given in his accompt to
the borrowmen and paid into the hands of Mr Thomas
Jessop present maior the sume of seventeen pounds and
seventeen shillinges seven pence by us.   17^{li} 17^{s} 7^{d}
Seen and allowed by us:
Nicholas Fleatham, Antho: Fleatham, George Burdon, Will: Atkinson,
Robert Nicholson* his marke, Willyam Johnson, Francis Carter,
Antho: Coates,* Thom. Ward.*

October the 17th 1671
Memorandum that this presentt day and yeare above[71]
written Thomas Jessopp late maior of the burrow of
Stockton hath given in his accompt to Mr Robertt Jackson
present maior and the rest of the burrow men and paid
into the hands of the now presentt maior the sum of
twenty one pounds two shilings three pence farthing to
witt   21 02   3¼

---

71   MS: 'abovof'.

Seen and allowed by us underwritten:
[*col. 1*] Nicholas Fleatham, Thomas Swainston, George Burdon, Christopher Coats* marke, Anthony Coats* marke
[*col. 2*] Willyam Johnson, Robert Nicholson* marke, Antho: Fleatham.

[p. 67] [*blank*]

[p. 68]
October the 15ᵗʰ 1672

Memorandum that this present day Robert Jackson late
major of this burrough of Stockton, hath given in his
accompt to Mr Nicholas Fleatham, the present major
and the rest of the burgesses & upon that accompt
there rested in his hands foureteene pounds foureteene
shillings & six pence halfe penny which is payd over
to the sayd Mr Nicholas Fleatham the present major &
allowed on by us   14ˡⁱ 14ˢ 6ᵈ ob.⁷²
Nicholas Fleatham maior, Thomas Jessopp, James Cooke, Tho'
Swainston, Will Atkinson, Tho: Harperley, Ja: Kitchinge, Antho:
Fleatham, George Burdon, Jno Wells,⁷³ William Cuthbert searjant.

[p. 69] [*blank*]

[p. 70]
October the 14th 1673

Memorandum that this day Mr Nicholas Fleatham the
present major having bene alsoe major for the yeare
before made & passed his accounts to the burgesses of
this burrough & upon that account (which was seene &
allowed) there rested due to the said Mr Major from the
said burrough the summe of six pounds ~~three~~ \thirteen/

---

72   'ob', for *obolus*, a halfpenny.
73   John Wells, a regular signatory from 1672, is perhaps to be identified with John Wells senior (d. 27 January 1709), whose house was certificated as a public meeting place for Protestant dissenters in 1706, by Thomas and Nicholas Swainston: Thomas Richmond, *History of Protestant Nonconformity and of the Society assembling in the Old Meeting-House, High-Street, Stockton* (Stockton-on-Tees, 1856), pp. 11, 18.

shillings six pence which wee agree shall be repaid him in
the next yeare's proffitt   06^{li} 13^s 06^d
Robt Jackson, Thomas Jessopp, Ja: Cooke, Thomas Swainston, George
Burdon, Will Atkinson, Jno Eden, Tho: Harperley, Raiph Buntinge
sargent.

[p. 71]
At the court held the 20th of October 1674

It is ordered by & with the consent & assent of Mr James Cooke the
present major & the cheife burgesses of the the burrough of Stockton
that from hence forth noe person or persons shalbe elected or chosen
to serve as major for this burrough for above the tyme & terme of two
yeares togeather. [*In left margin:*] vide fol. 134.[74]

It is likewise ordered by the like consent that noe person or persons
which shall hereafter serve as major for this burrough shall disburse
any particuler summe of money out of the towne's stock exceeding
forty shillings without the consent of the cheife burgesses of the said
burrough in common councell first thereunto had & obteyned & an
order of court for that purpose made & entered.

It is likewise ordered by the like consent that if any major shall
hereafter neglect or refuse to make & perfect his accounts of his
majoralty the first head court day \next/ after hee shall goe out of
his office being the called the accounting day upon payne of \hee/
forfeiting \the summe of/ five pounds to the lord of this burrough for
the tyme being & shall alsoe under the like penalty then deliver upp
the bookes, seale & papers belonging to this burrough.

[*col. 1*] Ja: Cooke maior, Thomas Jessopp, Robt Jackson, Nicholas
Fleatham, Edwd Cooke, Tho: Swainston, Ja: Raisbeck, Ja: Peers, Tho:
Harperley, William Welford
[*col. 2*] Will Atkinson, Antho: Fleatham, the marke of Anthony
Coates,* the marke of Robert Nicholson,* the marke of Thomas
Ward,* the marke of Thomas Fewler,* George Burdon, the marke of
Thomas Murshant,* William Story
[*col. 3*] William Johnson, the marke of Chr: Coates,* Raiph Buntinge
sargent.

74   See below, p. 92.

[p. 72]
At the court held the 20th of October 1674.

It is ordered by & with the consent & assent of Mr James Cooke
present major & the cheif burgesses of the burrough of Stockton that
from hence forth all & every person & persons that shall import or
bring in any corne into this burrough or port shall pay to the major of
this burrough for the tyme being two pence for every last ~~for repaire
of the~~ over and above what is now paid which said two pence a last
shall be imployed towards the repairing of the common causewayes
within the said burrough & that all & every person & persons that
shall bring in ~~any~~ or import any slit dayles or waynescote boards
shall pay to the major for the tyme being for the use of the burgesses
of the said burrough the summe of twelve pence for every hundered
and soe proportionably after that rate & shall alsoe pay six \pence/
per tunn for oak tymber \& plankes/ & shall alsoe pay for great firr
balkes fower shillings a hundered for middle balkes three shillings a
hundered & for small balkes two shillings a hundered & for sparrs
six pence a hundered.
[*col. 1*] Ja: Cooke maiore, Robt Jackson, Nicholas Fleatham, Will
Atkinson, Edw Cooke, Antho: Fleatham, George Burdon, Thomas
Swainston, Ja: Raiesbeck
[*col. 2*] Tho: Harperley, Ja: Peers, Antho: Coats,* Robt Nicholson,*
Willyam Johnson, Tho: Marchant,* Tho: Ward,* Tho: Fewler.*

16th of October 1677
Ordered by the major & burgesses in open court that from henceforth
every free burges of this burrough shall have an abatement of one
full third part of the towne dutyes imposed upon timber \& planks/
by the above written order \imposed upon them as well as strangers/
but to pay for dales as formerly.
[*col. 1*] Robt Jackson mayor, Thomas Jessopp, Ja: Cooke, Nicholas
Fleatham, Jno: Wells, Wm Webster
[*col. 2*] Wm Lee, George Burdon, Ralph Moone, Nicho: Milburne,
Will Atkinson
[*col. 3*] Ja: Raesbeck.

[p. 73] [*blank*]

[p. 74]
October the 20th 1674

Memorandum that this day Mr Nicholas Fleatham the
late major made & perfected his accounts to Mr James
Cooke the present major & the cheife burgesses of this
burrough & upon that account (which was seene &
allowed) there rested due from the said Mr Fleatham to
the said present major & cheife burgesses the summe of
eighteene pounds nyneteene shillings & two pence which
hee the said Mr Fleatham here in open court paid over to
the said Mr James Cooke the said present major.   18^{li} 19^{s} 2$^{d.}$

Ja: Cooke maior, Robt Jackson, Tho: Harperley, Ja: Peers, George
Burdon, Will Atkinson, Antho: Fleatham.

[p. 75]
19° Oct 1675

Ordered by the major & burgesses in open court that noe forreigner
or stranger that comes to live in Stockton that is not owner or farmer
of a burrough house shalbe admitted \or permitted/ to fish or use
the trade of fishing in the River of Tease untill such person have first
paid thirteene shillings & foure pence to the major of this burrough
for the tyme being for the use of the burgesses aforesaid said major
for the tyme being.

Ordered that noe person or persons shall sell any corne or expose to
sale any corne or grayne in the market att Stockton before the toll bell
be rung upon payne of forfeiting the summe of six shillings & eight
for every default to be imployed for the use of the major & burgesses
of the said burrough.

It is alsoe ordered that noe person or persons shall sell or expose to
sale in the Shambles in the market place at Stockton aforesaid \on
the market dayes/ any beefe mutton veale or any other deade flesh
before the said toll bell be rung upon payne of forfeiting six shillings
& eight pence for every defence up to be imployed for the use of the
said major and burgesses.

[*col. 1*] Tho: Harperley, Jno. Wells, Will Atkinson, the marke of
Thomas Hope,* Robert Nicklson

[*col. 2*] Ja: Cooke major, Thomas Jessopp, Robt Jackson, Nicholas Fleatham, James Raiesbeck, Antho: Fleatham, Wm Webstar, Ja: Peers, George Burdon, Marke Stainese, Raiph Bunting, shargent.

[p. 76]
October the 19th 1675

Memorandum that this day Mr ~~mr~~ James Cooke the
present major made & perfected his accounts to the
burgesses of this burrough & upon that account which
was seene & allowed there rested due from the said
Mr Cooke to the said burgesses the summe of fifty &
six pounds twelve shillings & seaven pence which still
remaynes in his hands being elected major again for the
yeare following.   56^{li} 12^s 7^d

[*col. 1*] Will Atkinson, Jno. Wells, Marke Stainese, Robert Nicklson
[*col. 2*] Thomas Jessopp, Robt Jackson, Nicholas Fleatham, Wm Webstar, Antho: Fleatham, James Peers, Tho: Harperley, George Burdon, Raiph Bunting, shargent.

[p. 77] [*blank*]

[p. 78]
October the 19th 1676

Memorandum that this day Mr James Cooke the late
major made and perfected his accounts to Mr Robert
Jackson the present major & the cheife burgesses of this
burrough and upon that account (which was seene and
allowed) there restes due from the said Mr Cooke to the
said present major and cheife burgesses the summe of
twenty three pounds one shilling & eight pence which
hee the said Mr Cooke here in open court paid ~~out~~ over
to the said Mr Robert Jackson the said present major   23^{li} 1^s 8^d
Thomas Jessopp, Jno: Wells, Nicholas Fleatham, Ja: Peers, George Burdon, Edwd Cooke, Nicho: Milburne, Ra: Moone, Raiph Bunting sargen.

[p. 79] [*blank*]

[p. 80]
October the 16th 1677

Memorandum that this day Robert Jackson Esq. the
present major made and perfected his accounts to the
cheife burgesses of this burrough & upon that account
(which was seene and allowed) there rested due from
the said major to the said burgesses the summe of eight
pounds seaven shillings and one penny which the said
major hath in his hands.   08^{li} 07^s 01^d

Thomas Jessopp, Nicholas Fleatham, Ja: Cooke, Wm Lee, Jno: Wells,
Wm Webstar, George Burdon, Will Atkinson, Ralph Moone.

[p. 81]
Burrough of Stockton upon Tease. I Robert Jackson Esq. major of the
said burrough doe sweare that I will faith & truth beare to our soveraigne lord the King's Majestie his heires & successors and to the Lord
Bishop of Durham and to his successors bishopps of Durham and all
such acts and orders as I shall consent and agree unto to be made
shalbe according to my skill and knowledge for the good benefitt and
profitt of his majesties leige people and of the burrough of Stockton
aforesaid and the burgesses freemen and inhabitants thereof. And
I will not at any time or times hereafter whilest I am major of the
said burrough attempt or goe about to make any orders against the
royalties or priviledges of the Lord Bishop of Durham nor for the
only profitt of my selfe nor of any other private person or persons
or consent or agree to the same; soe helpe me God & the contents of
this booke.
Robt Jackson maior.

Burrough of Stockton upon Teaze.
I William Lee Esq. major of the said burrough doe sweare that I
will faith & truth beare to our soveraigne lord the King's Majestie
his heires and successors and to the Lord Bishop of Durham and to
his successors bishopps of Durham and all such acts and orders as I
shall consent and agree unto to be made shalbe according to my skill
and knowledge for the good benefit & proffitt of his majestie's leige
people and of the burrough of Stockton aforesaid and the burgesses
freemen and inhabitants thereof. And I will not at any time or times
hereafter whilest I am major of the said burrough attempt or goe
about to make any orders against the royalties or priviledges of the

Lord Bishop of Durham nor for the onely profitt of my selfe nor of any other private person or persons or consent or agree to the same; soe helpe me God & the contents of this booke.
Wm Lee mayor.

Juratus apud Stockton decimo quinto die Octobris anno tricesimo Caroli secundi regis Anglie &c coram me.[75]

[p. 82]
Whereas there was auntiently allowed unto the serjeant of this burrough the summe of fower pence for the mettage of every last of corne or grayne sent & exported out of this river either to any place in this kingdome or elsewhere. And whereas the trade of exportacion of corne & grayne from this port hath of late very much increased soe that the same cannot be measured & attended by the serjeant himselfe as formerly. In consideracion whereof & for the preventing of abuses & mistakes in measuring thereof for the future, it is this day thought fitt & soe ordered by the worshippfull major the aldermen & burgesses of this burrough that from henceforth the serjeant of this burrough for the time being shalbe the chiefe sworne measurer of all corne & grayne exported & sent from & out of this port & that hee shall likewise, for the more ready dispatch of the said busines, have & keepe three deputy measurers to be allowed of & sworne by the major of this burrow for the time being, which said measurers & deputyes shall duely measure all corne & grayne whatsoever sent & exported from this port in sealed bushells to be allowed of & kept in the toll booth as common towne bushells for the purpose aforesaid. And it is hereby further ordered that noe person or persones whome-soever shall export or send any corne or grayne from this port but such as shalbe duely measured by the said sworne measurer or some of his deputyes as aforesaid, upon paine of forfeiting thirty nine shillings & eleaven pence to the lord bishop of Durham for the time being for every offence, and in respect that the said serjeant is constrayned to give more attendance & to imploy more deputyes then heretofore was accustomed. It is alsoe thought fit & soe ordered that the antient payment of fower pence per last be from henceforth augmented & increased to six pence per last whereof the said three deputyes are to have one moyety amongst them & the serjeant the other moyety who is hereby injoyned to keepe a booke of accounts

---

75   Sworn at Stockton, 15 October, 30 Charles II 'in my presence'.

of all corne & grayne measuered aboard any ship & exported from hence & by whome it was shipped or put aboard.

[col. 1] Will Atkinson, Ra: Moone, Jno: Wells, Nicho: Milburne
[col. 2] Robt Jackson, Nicholas Fleatham, Wm Webster
[col. 3] Wm Lee mayor, Thomas Jessopp, Ja: Cooke.

[p. 83]
[col. 1] James Peers, Ja: Kitching, George Burdon, George Jefferson, the marke of Anthony Coates,* Tho Ward* his marke.
[col. 2] The marke of Leonard Fewler,* John May* his marke, John Jeckell* his marke, William Storye, Robt Nicholson* his marke, Tho Fewler* his marke, the marke of Thomas Marchant.*

[p. 84]
October the 15th 1678

Memorandum that this day Mr Robert Jackson ~~being the present~~ \late/ maior made & perfected his accounts to William Lee Esq. present major & the cheife burgeses of this burrough & upon that account (which was seen and allowed) there rested due from the burrough to the said
Mr Jackson the summe of two pounds & nine pence   02li 00s 09d
& alsoe twenty shillings due to Mr Milburne   01li 00s 00d

[col. 1] Will Atkinson, Ja: Kitchginge, Ja: Peers, Ra: Moone
[col. 2] Wm Lee mayor, Thomas Jessopp, Ja: Cooke, Nicholas Fleatham, Jno: Wells, Wm Webstar.

[p. 85]
I William Atkinson major of Stockton doe declare & beleive that it is not lawfull ~~for~~ upon any pretence whatsoever to take armes against the king, and that I doe abhore that trayterous position of takeing armes by his authority against his person or against those that are commissioned by him.   Soe helpe me God.

I William Atkinson major of Stockton do declare that I hold that theire lyes no obligation upon me or any other person from the oath comonly called the Solempe Leage and Covenant. And that the same was in itselfe an unlawfull oath & imposed upon the subjects of the same against the knowne lawes & liberties of the kingdome.   W. A.

I shall truth & faith beare [*mayoral oath as above, p. 59*]
Memorandum that the sixth day of October 1680 William Atkinson
Esq. elected major for the burrough of Stockton did before the
takeing of the oath of majoralty contained in the said burrough take
the oath of allegiance & supremacy[76] as alsoe did take the oath &
subscribe the declaration within written. And then tooke the said
oath of mayoralty.
In presentia n[ost]ru[m]   Before me N[icolas] D[uresme]

Memorandum that these ut supra are true coppies of what the said
Mr Major was sworne to before the said bishopp of Durham In the
said sixth day of October \\1680// in Durham Castle in the presence
of Mr Thomas Mascall[77] notary public & me John Porret[78] senescal as
may apeare by the originall paper. \\Anno 1680//.

[p. 86]
October the 14th 1679

Memorandum that this day William Lee Esq. the present
major made and perfected his accounts to the cheife
burgesses of this burrough & upon that account which
was seen & allowed there rested due from the said major
to the said burrough the summe of eight pounds nineteen
shillings & six pence which the said major hath in his
hands   08^{li} 19^{s} 06^{d}

Thomas Jessopp, Robt Jackson, Will Atkinson, Nicho: Milburne,
Ralph Moone, Thome Fewler* \signum/, Ric[ard]i Wilson* \signum/,
Raiph Buntinge sargent.

---

76   The Act of Supremacy, introduced in 1535 by Henry VIII, required any
     person taking public or church office to swear loyalty to the monarch as the
     head of the church. The Oaths of Allegiance and Supremacy were mandated
     by the Corporation Acts of 1661 and the Test Act of 1673 with similar intent.
     These requirements, inhibiting Roman Catholics and Protestant noncon-
     formists, were refreshed, enforced or strengthened at various times, as after
     the Jacobite Rebellion of 1715.
77   Thomas Mascall of Durham, attorney, was mayor of Durham in 1666:
     Mackenzie and Ross, *Durham*, vol. 2, p. 425.
78   John Porrett served as steward for over half a century, until shortly before his
     death at the age of seventy-nine on 12 October 1732. He was described as 'late
     recorder' on his tombstone: Brewster, *History*, p. 322.

[p. 87]
October the 19th anno domini 1680

Memorandum that this day William Lee late mayor
made & presented his accounts to William Atkinson Esq.
present mayor and cheife burgesses of this burrow, and
upon that account (which was seen & allowed) their
rested due from the burrow to the said Mr Lee the sume
of twenty pounds five shillings & five pence   20^{li} 5^s 5^d

Will Atkinson major, Thomas Jessepp, Robt Jackson, Nicholas
Fleatham, James Raiesbeck, Geo: Burdon, Edwd Cooke, Ja: Dunning,
Raiph Buntinge.

Burrough of Stockton upon Tease
I William Atkinson Esq. mayor of this burrough of Stockton doe
swear [*mayoral oath as above, p. 59*].
Juratus in curia capitalis cum visu franciplegii &c locatus in et pro
burgo de Stockton predicto xviij° die Octobris anno xxxiij° Caroli
secundi regis Anglie &c. Coram me Johanne Porrett senescallo.[79]

[p. 88]
October the 18th anno domini 1681

Memorandum that this day William Atkinson Esq. major
made & perfected his account to the cheif burgesses of
this borrough and upon that account (which was seen
and allowed), there rested dewe in the hands of the
said Mr Mayor ~~hands~~ the summe of nine pounds fower
shillings \and/ ~~by~~ there is twelve pounds one shilling
six pence which is standing oute in debts, which were
received: ~~There rested~~ [——] \the/ said Mr Mayor ~~hands~~
does promiss to bring into a new account   9^{li} 4^s

Thomas Jessopp, Nicholas Fleatham, Wm Lee, Jno: Wells, Wm
Webstar, Tho: Swainston, Ra: Moone, Nicho: Milburne, Ja: Dunning,
George Jefferson, Antho: Cootes,* Jno: Maynerd.*

---

79   Sworn in head court, 18 October, 33 Charles II (1681); John Porrett, steward.

[p. 89]

Burgus de Stockton. Ad curiam capitalem cum visu franciplegii reverendi in Christo patris Nathaniel domini episcopi Dunelm' tenta ibidem xviij° die Octobris anno regni regis Caroli secundi nunc Anglie &c xxxiii° annoque domini 1681. Coram Willielmo Atkinson armigero mayore et Johanne Porret generoso senescallo.[80]

Ordered in the said court by the said mayor steward aldermen and burgesses of the said burrough that noe person or persons shall dig or make any bricke in the West Row or in any other waist ground within the burrough of Stockton without the licence of the major of Stockton for the time being nor in any such place nor other quantity of brickes but such as the grand jury for the time being shall set out and appointe; and that all & every person or persons that shall ~~procure~~ make or procure such bricke to be made shall pay to the major six pence per thousand for the same \for the use of the lord bishopp of Durham/ before the ground be diged or opened, and if such person or persons make more brickes, or in any other place then shall be appointed or set out by the jury as aforesaid, or shall sell or any way dispose of the same (otherwise then to his or their owne proper use in building within the said burrough), then to pay after the rate of six shilling eight pence per thousand to the major as aforesaid for soe many as such person or persons shall soe make, sell or dispose of, over and besides the said six pence per thousand ~~the money soe raised to be all imployed for the use of the major and burgesses.~~

Ordered likewise that the said major shall pay unto Anthony Fleatham of Stockton draper the sum of five pounds (out of the money that is oweing to the said burrough) in full of what the said Anthony paid or disburst about chimney or hearth money for the said burrough when he was sergient, or at any other time.[81]

---

80   Head court with view of frankpledge (i.e. court leet), 18 October, 33 Charles II (1681). William Atkinson, mayor, and John Porrett, steward.

81   Hearth Tax was collected between 1662 and 1689 based on the number of hearths/chimneys in a dwelling. In Stockton and Norton most houses were single hearth, but that in itself was not an indicator of poverty. The number of exemptions was quite high, which was more indicative: see Chris Husbands, 'Hearths, wealth and occupations: an exploration of the Hearth Tax in the later seventeenth century', in Kevin Schürer and Tom Arkell (eds), *Surveying the people: The interpretation and use of document sources for the study of population in the later seventeenth century* (Oxford, 1992), pp. 65–77. Hearth

It is likewise ordered that the said major shall buy a statute booke out of the moneys that is oweing to this burrough and that the same booke shall alwayes remaine with the major of this burrough for the time being.

Whereas severall inconveniencies have happened and been as well to the marchants, tradesmen and other inhabitants as alsoe to the watermen poarters and laborers within this burrough, for want of a set and certaine forme or order of rates and wages for poarters and laborers; it is this day thought fit and soe ordered [p. 90] in the said court by consent as aforesaid that Mr Alderman Jessopp, Mr Alderman Jackson, Mr Alderman Cooke, Mr Alderman Lee, Mr John Wells, Mr William Webster, and Mr Ralph Jackson or any four or more of them shall set appointe and make, such raites wages and orders \thereupon/ as they in their judgments shall thinke fit and convenient, to be had paid observed and performed, within the said burrough.

Will Atkinson major, Jo: Porrett senescall', Thomas Jessopp, Ja: Cooke, Wm Lee, Robt Jackson,[82] Nicho: Milburne, Ja: Dunning, George Jefferson, the marke of John Maineard,* the marke of Rob' Nicholson,* the marke of Christofer Denneham,* the marke of Anth: Coates,* Thomas Hodgson, the marke of Tho: Fowler,* William Storye, the marke of Joseph Davison.*

[p. 91] [blank]

[p. 92]
Burrough of Stockton in the County of Durham.
I Ralph Moone Esq. major of this burrough of Stockton, doe swere [mayoral oath as above, p. 59]   Ra: Moone mayor

Juratus in curiam capitalem, cum visu franciplegii &c tenta in & pro burgo superdicto xvij° die October anno xxxiiij° Caroli secundi nunc regis Anglie &c. Coram me Jo: Porrett senescallo curie predicti.[83]

Tax returns for Stockton survive for 1666 and 1674: see Green, *Hearth Tax*, and John Little, 'Merchants, mariners and yeomen: what does the Hearth Tax tell us about early modern Stockton?', *Cleveland History*, 105 (2014), pp. 3–32.
82 Followed by space before next signature.
83 Sworn in head court, 17 October, 34 Charles II (1682); John Porrett, steward.

[p. 93] [*blank*]

[p. 94]
October the 17th anno domini 1682.

Memorandum that this day William Atkinson late major
of this burrough of Stockton made & perfected his
accounts to Ralph Moone Esq. present major and to the
aldermen and cheife burgesses of this burrough, and
upon that account (which was seen and allowed) their
rested due from the said late mayor to the said present
mayor \aldermen/ & cheife burgesses of this burrough
the sume of four pounds & ten shillings which the said
late mayor hath in his hands & doth promise to pay the
same to the said present mayor, provided he be freed
from all incumbrances that shall happen about the clocke
late erected within or upon the towle booth.   04^{li} 10^s 00^d

Ra: Moone mayor, Robt Jackson, Ja: Cooke, Wm Lee, Ja: Burdon, Ja:
Dunning, Wm Thompson, Tho: Wrangham, Raiph Buntinge, Tho:
Swainston, George Jefferson, Thomas Hodgson.

[p. 95]
Burgus de Stockton. Ad curiam capitalem cum visu franciplegii
reverendi in Christo patris Nathaniel domini episcopi Dunelm' tenta
ibidem decimo septimo die October anno regni regis Caroli secundi
nunc Anglie &c tricesimo quarto annoque domini 1682. Coram
Radulpho Moone armigero major & Johanne Porret generoso senescallo ibidem.[84]

Ordered in the said court by the said mayor steward aldermen
and burgesses of the said burrough that Mr Alderman Jackson,
Mr Alderman Cooke, Mr James Burdon, Mr Thomas Swainston,
Mr William Webster, Mr William Thompson, Mr James Dunning &
Mr Nicholas Milburne goe about the burrow betwixt this and the
next court to get what subscriptions & money they can towards the
raiseing of a sume of m\o/ny money for defraying of the charge
about the clocke late erected in or upon the towle-booth, and alsoe

---

84   Court leet, 17 October, 34 Charles II (1682); Ralph Moone, mayor, and John
      Porret, steward.

to cal in & gather the moneys remaineing in arrear upon the ould subscriptions about the same concerne, and that they give an account thereof to the said Mr Mayor at the said next court.

Burgus de Stockton. February the 13th anno domini 1682.
Ordered then in the court barron by Ralph Moone Esq. mayor of the said burrow & by the aldermen and cheife burgesses of the said burrow that Thomas Fowler of shall keep the clocke in the towle booth and the said major & his successors shall pay yearely at or before the counting day the yearely sum of thirty shillings to the said Thomas for doing of the same.

Burgus de Stockton. By the mayor aldermen & burgess of the said burrow in the court leet held there the 16th day of Aprill anno domini 1683.

It is ordered that William Claxton shall ~~henceforth~~ set out all the stoals or booths in the market every market day after the first of May next, and shall keep watch for this burrow & towne for one yeare, and shall have for the same one new coate and thre pounds in money over & besides 2s 6d now paid in hand as earnest.[85] And if he neglect his duty in any respect, Mr Mayor \for the time being/ is to be the sole judge in the matter and may deduct what he thinks fit out of the said 3li for such neglect.

[p. 96]
Burgus de Stockton in Comitatu Dunelm'
I James Burdon major of this burrough of Stockton, doe s\w/eare,
[*mayoral oath as above, p. 59*]   Ja: Burdon Esq. major

Juratus in curia capitale cum visu franciplegii &c tenta in et pro burgo superdicto xvj° die Octobris Anno 35° Caroli secundi nunc regis Angliae &c annoque domini 1683. Coram me Jo: Porrett senescallo.[86]

[p. 97]
Burgus de Stockton. Curia capitalis cum visu franciplegii reverendi in Christo Patris Nathaniel domini episcopi Dunelm' tenta ibidem

---

85 Reading uncertain; 'earnest' meaning 'in advance' or 'part payment' would be appropriate here.
86 Sworn in head court, 16 October, 35 Charles II (1683); John Porrett, steward.

xvj° die Octobris anno domini 1683. Coram Jacobo Burdon armigero majore et Johanne Porrett senescallo ibidem.[87]

Ordered in the said court by the mayor aldermen & chiefe burgesses of the said burrow that the six pounds thirteen shillings and thre halfe pence resting due to Mr William Webster for the clocke-bell shall be paid him as soone as the money can be raised.

October the 14th [16]84. Memorandum that the abovesaid sum of 6^{li} 13^{s} $1\frac{1}{2}^{d}$ is paid by Mr Major to Mr Webster.

[p. 98]
October the 16th anno domini 1683.

Memorandum that this day Ralph Moone late major
of this burrough of Stockton made and perfected his
accompts to James Burdon Esq. present major and to the
aldermen and chiefe burgesses of this burrough. And
upon that accompt (which was seen and allowed) there
rested due unto the said Ralph Moone alderman the full
& just sum of ten pounds & twelve shillings by the said
burrough 10^{li} 12^{s} 00^{d}
And 46^{s} $10\frac{1}{2}^{d}$ more which he hath paid to Mr William
Webster towards the clocke-bell 2^{li} 06^{s} $10\frac{1}{2}^{d}$
                                                   Total 12^{li} 18^{s} $10\frac{1}{2}^{d}$

Ja: Burdon major, Thomas Jessupp, Robt Jackson, Ja: Cooke, Wm Lee, Will: Atkinson, J: Dunning.

[p. 99] [*blank*]

[p. 100]
Burgus de Stockton. Curia barronis reverendi in Christo Patris Nathaniel domini episcopi Dunel' tent ibidem tricesimo die Septembris anno regni regis Caroli secundi nunc Anglie &c tricesimo sexto annoque domini 1684.[88]

---

87   Head court, 16 October, 35 Charles II (1683); John Burdon, mayor, and John
      Porrett, steward.
88   Court baron, 30 September, 36 Charles II (1684).

[p. 101]

Burgus de Stockton in Comitatu Dunelm.

I James Burdon mayor of this burrow of Stockton doe sweare
[*mayoral oath as above, p. 59*]   Ja: Burdon major

Juratus in curia leet'[89] &c tenta in et pro burgo predicto 30° die
Septembris anno 36° Caroli secundi nunc regis Anglie &c annoque
domini 1684, coram me Jo:ᵉ Porrett senescallo.[90]

[p. 102]

October the 14ᵗʰ anno domini 1684.

Memorandum that this day James Burdon Esq. present
major made and perfected his accompts to the cheife
burgesses of this burrow, and upon that accompt which
was seen and allowed there rested due to the said
Mr Mayor from the burrow the full & just sum of eight
pounds eight shilings and three halfpence.   8ˡⁱ 8ˢ 3½ᵈ
More which Mr Mayor hath now paid to Mr Webster
eleaven shillings & a halfe penny which is in full for the
money due to Mr Webster for the bell.   11ˢ   ½ᵈ
                                                                8ˡⁱ 19ˢ 2ᵈ

Thomas Jessopp, Robt Jackson, Ja: Cooke, Wm Lee, Nicholas
Fleatham, Will Atkinson, Ra: Moone, Tho: Swainston, Wm Webstar.

[p. 103]

October the 14ᵗʰ anno Domino 1684.

Ordered then in full court by James Burdon Esq. mayor of this burrow
of Stockton and the aldermen & cheife burgesses that the sum of five
shillings of lawfull English money be assessed levied & gathered
of every owner or owners of every burgage within this burrow for
renewing of the ankhoridge lease of my lord bishopp of Durham
or his successor for the use of the owners of the said burgages as
formerly and that the said sum of five shillings a burgage shall be
paid to the said James Burdon Esq. upon or before the eleaventh day

89   Written over 'barron'.
90   Court leet, 30 September, 36 Charles II (1684); John Porrett, steward.

of November next upon the forfeiture of ~~ten shillings~~[91] double the value to be forfeited by every one that shall faile in \such/ payment which said forfeiture shall be to the said James Burdon Esq. for the generall use of the said burgages.

George Jefferson per Jon: Bainbridge

Tho: Jessopp, Robt Jackson, Ja: Cooke, Nicholas Fleatham, Wm Lee, Will Atkinson, Tho: Swainston, Wm Webstar, Thomas Wrangham, George Swainston, Geo Swainston,[92] Anthony Coates junior, the marke of Anth. Coates senior,* the marke of John ~~Bainbridge~~ \Maineard senior/,* the marke of Tho Ward.*

[p. 104]
I James Cooke major of Stockton doe declare and beleive that it is not lawfull upon any pretence whatsoever to take armes against the king, and that I doe abhore that trayterous position of takeing armes by his authority against his person or against those that are comissioned by him.   J. C.

I James Cooke major of Stockton doe declare that I hold that there lyes no obligation upon me or any other person from the oath commonly called the Solumne Leage & Covenant and that the same was in it selfe an unlawfull oath and imposed upon the subjects of the same against the knowne lawes and liberties of the kingdome.
                                                                    James Cooke

I James Cooke major of Stockton shall truth & faith beare [*mayoral oath as above, p. 59*]

Memorandum that the seaventh day of October 1685. James Cooke Esq. elected major for the burrough of Stockton did before the takeing the oath of majoralty contained in the said burrow take the Oath of Allegiance & Supremacie, as alsoe did subscribe the declarations above written and then tooke the said oath of majoralty.

Durham Castle, October 7. [16]85   Before me N[icholas] D[uresme]

---

91   Followed by a further illegible word, crossed through.
92   The two consecutive George Swainston signatures are in different hands.

Memorandum that these ut supra are true coppies of what the said Mr Major was sworne to & did signe before the said bishopp of Durham the said seaventh day of October in Durham Castle in the presence of me Jo: Porrett, notarius publicus et seneschallus de Stocktone.

[p. 105]
October the 20th anno domini 1685

Memorandum that this day James Burdon late major of
this burrow of Stockton made and perfected his accompts
to James Cooke Esq. present major and to the aldermen
& cheife burgesses of the said burrow, and upon that
accompt (which was seen and allowed) theire rested due
to the said James Burdon late major from the said burrow
the full & just sume of five pounds & two pence halfpenny
over & besides the sum of eight pounds nyneteen
shillings and two pence resting due to him as appears by
the last yeare's account, soe that the totall is   13li 19s 4½d

James Cooke, Thomas Jessopp, Robt Jackson, Nicholas Fleatham, Wm Lee, Will Atkinson, Ra: Moone, Ja: Dunning, Jno: Wells, Tho: Swainston, Anthony Coates, Geo Swainston, Raiph Bunting, Tho Wrangham, George Swainston.

October the 15th anno 1689 Received in payment £0 19s 2d from of Mr Ralph Moone late major the sume of ninetene shillings and two pence per me Ja: Burdon.

[p. 106]
Burgus de Stockton October the 20th anno 1685.

Ordered the day abovesaid in full courte that Whereas there is severall sums of money due to severall persons who have disburst the same upon severall accompts for the use of the said burrow, and by reason there is no money in the town's stocke to defray the same. And whereas alsoe the yearely revinue & profits of the said burrow are not sufficient to defray the said debts already contracted upon the account of the said burrow & to maineteine the necessary charge & expence of the same, wee the major aldermen and burgesses of the said burrow now assembled in full court doe hereby order and appointe that every owner of a burrow-right within the said burrow

shall & doe paye to James Cooke Esq. the present major the sume of
twenty shillings per burgag for every burrow right & soe after that
rate for every ~~greater~~ \burrow right/ or lesser part for payment of
the aforesaid debts & other disbursements incident & necessary; the
same to be paid in manner as aforesaid upon or before the first day
of January next.

[*col. 1*] Ja: Dunning, Tho Wrangham, John Maynard senior*
[*col. 2*] Ja: Cooke, Thomas Jessopp, Robt Jackson, Nich Fleatham, Wm
Lee, Will Atkinson, Ra: Moone, Ja: Burdon, Jno: Wells.

[p. 107]
Burgus de Stockton. Curia capitalis cum visu franciplegii reverendi
in Christo patris Nathaniel domini episcopi Dunelm' tenta ibidem
vicessimo septimo die Aprilis anno regni regis Jacobi secundi nunc
Anglie &c secundo annoque domini 1686. Coram Jacobo Cooke
armigero majore & Johanni Porret generoso senescallo ibidem.[93]

Memorandum that it is this day in full court ordered by a generall
& unanimus consent of the said Mr Mayor & all the aldermen &
burgages here present that Mr Alderman Moone shall upon \or
before/ the counting day yearely (to wit) upon or before Tuesday
\fortnight/ yearely \next/ after Michelmas Day in every yeare \have
& receive from the major for the time being/ the full sume of twenty
five shilling & nyne pence for the use or interest money of the just
& full sume of twenty one ~~shilling & ten pence~~ pounds and ten
shillings \untill the same be paid in/ which he the said Mr Moone
paid for obtaineing & geting a free kea made within ~~the~~ this burrow,
as alsoe the interest money \now/ due for the same from the 14th day
of October 1684, as test' my hand the day & yeare first above written.
                                                      Jo: Porrett steward

[p. 108]
Burgus de Stockton in Comitatu Dunelm'
I James Cooke mayor of ~~Stockton~~ this burrow of Stockton, doe
sweare, [*mayoral oath as above, p. 59*][94]   Ja: Cooke

93   Head court, 27 April, 2 James II (1686); James Cooke, mayor, and Jonathan
     Porett, steward.
94   This and the following oath omit the phrase 'according to my skill and
     knowledge'.

Juratus in curia leet &c tenta in et pro burgo predicto quinto die Octobris anno regni regis Jacobi secundi nunc Anglie &c secundo annoque domini 1686. Coram me Jo: Porrett senescall'.[95]

[p. 109]
October the 19th anno domini 1686

Memorandum that this day James Cooke Esq. major of this burrow of Stockton made & perfected his accompts to the aldermen and cheife burgesses of this burrow, and upon that accompt which was seen & allowed there rested due to the said Mr Major from the burrow, the full & just sum of nyne pounds nyneteen shillings & thre pence halfe penny   9li 19s 3½d

Thomas Jessopp, Ni Fleatham, Will Atkinson, Ra: Moone, Ja: Burdon, Tho: Swainston, Ja: Dunning, Richd Jackson, Anthony Coates junior, George Jefferson, Geo: Swainston.

[p. 110]
I [blank] major of Stockton doe declare and beleive that it is not lawfull upon any pretence whatsoever to take armes against the king and that I doe abhore that trayterous position of takeing armes by his authoryty against his person or against those that are commissioned by him.

I [blank] major of Stockton doe declare that I hold that there lyes no obligation upon me or any other person from the oath commonly called the Solemne League & Covenant. And that the same was in itselfe an unlawfull oath & imposed upon the subjects of the same against the knowne lawes & liberties of the kingdome.

[p. 111] [blank]

[p. 112]
Burgus de Stockton in Comitatu Dunelm'
I Ralph Moone major of this burrow of Stockton doe sweare [mayoral oath as above, p. 59]   Ra: Moone

Juratus in curia leet & curia capitalis adjurnatus usque ad hanc diem videlicet quarto diem Octobris anno regni regis Jacobi secundi

95   Sworn in court leet, 5 October, 2 James II (1686).

nunc Anglie &c tertio annoque domini 1687. Coram me Jo:^{nn} Porrett senescallum.[96]

[p. 113]
October the 18th anno domini 1687.

Memorandum that this day James Cooke late major of this burrow of Stockton made & perfected his accompts to ~~the said~~ Ralph Moone Esq. present major and to the aldermen & cheife burgesses of the said burrow and upon that accompt (which was seen & allowed) there rested due to the said James Cooke late major, from the said burrow the full & just summe of thirty pounds four shillings & two pence halfe penny ~~resting due to him~~ as appears by ~~the last~~ this last yeare's account & this which is to be allowed him   30^{li} 4^{s} 2½^{d}

Ra: Moone mayor, Thomas Jessopp, Robt Jackson, Wm Lee, Nicholas Fleatham, Will Atkinson, Ja: Dunning, George Swainston, Wm Webster, Tho: Swainston, Anthony Coates junior.

October the 16th anno 1688.
Received then the summe of 8^{li} 11^{s} 11^{d} in part of 18^{li} 12^{s} 8^{d} which I disburst about renewing the anchoridge lease, being included in the above said sume of 30^{li} 4^{s} 2½^{d}. I say received the same as above by me Ja: Cooke.

                                                        Test'[97] Jo: Porrett

October the 15th 1689
Received more of Mr Moone late major 21s 9d by me Ja Cooke.

                                                        Test' Jo: Porrett.

October the 14th 1690
Allowed him by Thomas Wrangham Esq.   4^{li} 18^{s} 6^{d}
Oct^{o} 20 1692 of Mr Thomas Wrangham   4 00 06
Sum   £18 12   8 cl[98]

---

96   Sworn in court leet and head court adjourned to 4 October, 3 James II (1687); John Porrett, steward.
97   *testimonium*, 'witness'.
98   Probably *clarus* ('clear'), as the sum is balanced by the receipts listed immediately afterwards.

Oct° 20 1692. Received these severall sums being together
eighteen pounds twelve shillings eight pence.   8 11 11
                                                             1 01 09
                                                             4 18   6
                                                             4 [0] 6
                              Total   £18 12   8⁹⁹
                                                            Ja: Cooke

[p. 114]
I Ralph Moone major of Stockton doe declare and beleive that it is
not lawfull upon any pretence whatsoever to take armes against the
king, and that I doe abhore that traterous position of takeing armes
by his authority against his person or against those that are commissioned by him. Soe helpe me God.   Ra: Moone.

I Ralph Moone major of Stockton shall truth & faith beare [*mayoral
oath as above, p. 59*]   Ra: Moone

Memorandum that the third day of October 1688, Ralph Moone
Esq. elected major for the burrow of Stockton did before the takeing
the oath of majoralty contained in the said burrow take the Oath of
Allegiance and Supremacie, as alsoe did take the oath above written
& then tooke the said oath of majoralty.   Before me N. Duresme
Durham Castle Oct 3ʳᵈ 1688 in presence [of] Jo: Porrett notarius
publicus.

Memorandum that these ut supra are true coppies of what the said
Mr Major was sworne to & did signe before the said bishopp of
Durham the said 3rd day of October in Durham Castle in the presence
of me Jo: Porrett notarius publicus et seneschallus de Stockton.

[p. 115]
October the 16ᵗʰ anno 1688

Memorandum that this day Ralph Moone Esq. major of this
burrow of Stockton made & perfected his accounts to the

---

99 The page has been added to at various dates and calculation/reckoning
    carried out by James Cooke, accounting for receipt of money he had paid out
    for anchorage and plankage rights from the bishop on behalf of the borough.
    It shows that the money he handed over included backdated payments from
    Moone and Wrangham made before the date of entry.

aldermen and cheife burgesses of this burrow and upon that
account which was seen & allowed there rested due to the
said Mr Major from the burrow the full & just summe of
twenty three pounds ten shillings ten pence halfe penny   23^{li} 10^{s}10½^d

Thomas Jessopp, Ja: Cook, Wm Lee, Will Atkinson, Jno: Wells,
Thos Swainston, Ja: Dunning, Wm Thompson, Richd Jackson, Roger
Coates, Wm Webstar.

[p. 116]
Burgus de Stockton in Comitatu Dunelm
I Thomas Wrangham major of this burrow of Stockton doe swear
[*mayoral oath as above p. 59*]   Tho Wrangham

Juratus in curia leet adjurnata usque ad hanc diem videlicet primum
diem Octobris anno domini 1689, coram me Jo: Porrett senescall'.[100]

[p. 117]
October the 15th anno domini 1689

Memorandum that this day Ralph Moone gentleman late
major of this burrow of Stockton made & perfected his
accompts to Thomas Wrangham Esq. present major and
to the aldermen & cheife burgesses of the said burrow
and upon that accompt which was seen and allowed there
rested due to the said Mr Moone from the burrow the full
& just sume of nyne pounds nyne shillings & a penny,[101]
which is to be allowed \& paid/ him in his course   09^{li} 09^s ½^d.

Tho Wrangham mayor, Tho: Jessopp, Robt Jackson, Ja: Cooke, Wm
Lee, Will Atkinson, Nich Fleatham, Ja: Burdon, Wm Thompson, Tho:
Swainston, Jno: Wells, Ja: Dunning, Richd Jackson, George Jefferson,
Roger Coates, Thomas Hodgson.

	li	s	d
Received of Mr Atkinson of Yarme	2	5	6
of Mr William Webster	1	3	0
of Mr Witeley	0	18	0
Total	4:	6:	6

---

100 Sworn in court leet adjourned to 1 October 1689; John Porrett, steward.
101 Thus in text, despite figure in the right-hand column reading £9 9s. ½d.

Item more of Robert Corney	0	10	0
And of Mr Webster	0	04	2
Total	5	00	8

Soe rests due to me only 4^{li} 8^s 3½^d of the abovesaid sume of 9^{li} 9^s ½^d

Ra: Moone

[p. 118]
Burgus de Stockton. Curia capitalis cum visu franciplegii reverendi in Christo patris Nathaniel domini episcopi Dunelm' tenta ibidem decimo quinto die Octobris anno domini 1689. Coram Thome Wrangham armigero majore & Johanne Porrett generoso senescallo ibidem.[102]

Memorandum that it is this day in full court ordered by & with a generall & unanimus consent of the said Mr Mayor & all the aldermen & burgesses present that Mr Alderman Cooke & Mr Alderman Atkinson upon or before the counting day yearely (to wit) upon or before Tuesday fortnight yearely next after Michaelmas Day in every yeare \shall/ have & receive from the major of this place for the time being the summe of thirty nyne shillings and seaven pence for the use or interest of the just summe of thirty & three pounds untill the principall summe be paid in, the which the said Mr Cooke & Mr Atkinson paid for obtaneing \disburst/ in & about defending the right of this burrow touching one free key and preventing a free key to be made at Portrack by Sir Thomas Stringer and others concerned in the lands there, as witness our hands the day & year abovesaid.

Tho Wrangham major, Tho: Jessopp, Robt Jackson, Wm Lee, Ra: Moone, Nich Fleatham, Ja: Burdon, Wm Thompson, Thos Swainston, Jno: Wells, Ja: Dunning, Richd Jackson, George Jefferson, Roger Coates, Thomas Hodgson.

[p. 119] [blank]

[p. 120]
Burgus de Stockton in Comitatu Dunelm.
I Thomas Wrangham Mayor of this Burrow of Stockton doe sweare [mayoral oath as above, p. 59]   Tho Wrangham

---

102 Head court, 15 October 1689; Thomas Wrangham, mayor, and John Porrett, steward.

Juratus in curia leet adjurnata usque ad hanc diem videlicet tricesimum diem Septembris anno domini 1690, coram me Jo: Porrett senescall'[103]

[p. 121]
October the 14th anno domini 1690

Memorandum that this day Thomas Wrangham Esq. ~~present~~ mayor of this burrow of Stockton made & perfected his accounts to the aldermen & chiefe burgesses of this burrow and upon that account which was seen & allowed there rested due to the said Mr Mayor from the burrow the full and just summe of twenty four pounds four shillings & two pence which is to be paid and allowed him in course   24[li] 4[s] 2[d]

Tho: Jessop, Robt Jackson, Nich° Fleatham, Will Atkinson, Ra: Moone, Ja: Dunning, Jno: Wells, Wm Webstar, Wm Coatsworth, George Swainston, John Truitt, Roger Coates, Thomas Hodgson.

[p. 122]
I Robert Jackson mayor of Stockton shall truth & faith beare [*mayoral oath as above, p. 59*]   Robert Jackson

Memorandum that the seaventh day of October anno domini 1691 Robert Jackson Esq. elected mayor for the burrow of Stockton did before the takeing the oath of majoralty contained in the said burrow, take the oathes appointed by act of parliament made anno primo Guilielmi & Marie intituled an Act for the Abrogateing of the Oaths of Supremacy & Allegiance & appointeing other oaths, and then tooke also the said oath of majoralty.

Before me N[icholas] Duresme.
Vera copia originalis examinatur per me Jo: Porrett seneschallum & notarium publicum.[104]

---

103 Sworn in court leet adjourned to 30 September 1690; John Porrett, steward.
104 'True copy of the original as examined by me, John Porrett, steward and notary public.'

[p. 123]
October 20th 1691

Memento. That this day Mr Thomas Wrangham late major
of this burrough of Stockton made and perfected his
accounts to the aldernmen Robert Jackson Esq. the present
major the aldermen & chiefe burgesses of this burrow and
upon that account which was seen and allowd by them
there rested due to the abovesaid Mr Thomas Wrangham
from the burrough aforesaid the full and just summ of
seven pounds twelve shillings & nine pence which is to be
paid and allowd him in course   £7 12 09.

Robt Jackson mayor, Ja: Cooke, Nich° Fleatham, Will Atkinson, Ja:
Burdon, Wm Coatsworth, Tho: Swainston, John Truitt, Roger Coates,
Anthony Coates, Thomas Hodgson, Ja: Dunning, Jno. Maynard
senior.

[p. 124]
I Robert Jackson mayor of Stockton shall truth & faith beare [*mayoral
oath as above, p. 59*]   Robert Jackson mayor

Memorandum that the fifth day of October anno domini 1692 Robert
Jackson Esq. elected major for the burrow of Stockton did before
the takeing the oath of majoralty contained in the said burrow
take the oaths appointed by act of parliament made anno primo
Gulielmi et Marie intituled an Act for the Abrogateing of the Oaths
of Supremacie and Allegience and appointeing other Oaths, and then
took alsoe the said oath of majoralty.
                                    Before me N Duresme
Vera copia originalis examinatur per me Jo: Porrett senescallum.

[p. 125]
October the 18th anno domini 1692

Memorandum that this day Robert Jackson Esq. mayor
of this burrow of Stockton made & perfected his accounts
to the aldermen and cheife burgesses of this burrow, and
upon that account which was seen & allowed there rested
due to the said mayor Mr Mayor from the burrow the full
& just summ of twenty five pounds eleaven shillings &
six pence which is to be paid and allowed him in course 25li 11s 6d

Thomas Jessop, Ja: Cooke, Will Atkinson, Ra: Moone, Tho: Swainston, Robt Sayer, Jno: Wells, John Mayles, John Maynerd,* William Story.

[p. 126]
Burgus de Stockton in Comitatu Dunelm'.
I James Cooke major of this burrow of Stockton doe sweare [*mayoral oath as above, p. 59*][105]   Ja: Cooke

Juratus in curia leet adjurnata usque ad hanc diem videlicet tertium diem Octobris anno domini 1693, coram me Jo: Porrett senescallo.[106]

[p. 127]
October the 17th anno domini 1693

Memorandum that this day \Mr/ Robert Jackson late major of this burrow of Stockton made and perfected his accompts to James Cooke Esq. present major and to the aldermen and cheife burgesses of the said burrow, and upon that accompt which was seen and allowed there rested due to the said late mayor from the burrow the full & just summe of three & fifty shillings & four pence halfe penny (over & above what rested due to him by the last year's account) to be paid & allowed him in course   02li 13s 4½d

James Cooke major, Will Atkinson, Ja: Burdon, Tho Wrangham, Jno: Wells, Ja: Dunning, Robt Sayer, Jno: Moone, Roger Coates, Willm Houltby junior.

[p. 128]
Burgus de Stockton in Comitatu Dunelm'.
I James Burdon mayor of this burrow of Stockton doe sweare [*mayoral oath as above, p. 59*][107]   Ja: Burdon

Juratus in curia leet adjurnata usque ad hanc diem videlicet secundum diem Octobris anno domini 1694, coram me Jo: Porrett.[108]

---

105 Omits the phrase 'according to my skill and knowledge'.
106 Sworn at court leet adjourned to 3 October 1693; John Porrett, steward.
107 The phrase 'according to my skill and knowledge' has been inserted as an afterthought.
108 Sworn in court leet adjourned to 2 October 1694 before John Porrett.

[p. 129]
October the 16th anno domini 1694

Memorandum that this day Mr James Cooke late mayor
of this burrow of Stockton made & perfected his accompts
to James Burdon Esq. present major and to the aldermen
& cheife burgesses of the said burrow, And upon that
accompt which was seen & allowed there rested due to
the said late major from the burrow the full & just summe
of one & forty shillings a penny halfepenny (over and
above \Li s d/ what remaines due to him upon his former
accompts) to be paid & allowed him in course   02^{li} 01^s 1½^d

Tho: Jessop, Robt Jackson, Ja: Dunning, Antho: Coats, Roger Coates,
Will: Houltby, Thomas Maynard, Anthony Story, William Fewler.

[p. 130]
Burgus de Stockton. Curia capitalis cum visu franciplegii reverendi
in Christo patris Nathaniel domini episcopi Dunelm' tenta ibidem
decimo sexto die Octobris anno regnorum Willelmi & Marie nunc
regis & regine Anglie sexto annoque domini 1694. Coram Jacobo
Burdon armigero majore et Johanne Porrett generoso senescallo
ibidem.[109]

Memorandum that it is this day ordered & agreed in full court that
Mr John Howell shall have liberty to erect a litle swine-coate or
hen house upon the street or common ground within this burrow
adjoyneing to the meeting house gate att the north end of the
bowleing-green, so as the same be not prejudiciall to their majesties'
subjects nor stop any passage. And that the same erection be not
longer continued then during the pleasure of Mr Mayor of Stockton
aforesaid for the time being, for which shall \be/ paid xij^d per annum
at Easter court to the said mayor during the continuance of such
erection.

                                              Ja: Burdon mayor

109 Head court, 16 October, 6 William and Mary (1694); James Burdon, mayor,
     and John Porrett, steward.

[p. 131]
Burgus de Stockton in Comitatu Dunelm'
I James Burdon mayor of this burrow of Stockton doe sweare
[*mayoral oath as above p. 59*]   Ja: Burdon

Juratus in curia leet adjurnata usque ad hanc diem videlicet primum
diem Octobris anno domini 1695. Coram me Jo: Porrett senescallo.[110]

[p. 132] [*blank*]

[p. 133]
October the 15th anno domini 1695

Memorandum that this day James Burdon Esq. mayor of
this burrow of Stockton made & perfected his accompts
to the aldermen and cheife burgesses of the said burrow,
and upon that accompt which was seen and allowed
there rested due to the said Mr Mayor from the burrow
the full & just summe of ten pounds thirteen shillings &
a halfe penny which is to be allowed him in course (over
and besides the former arrears)   10^{li} 13^s ½^d

Robt Jackson, Will Atkinson, Ja: Dunning, James Dale, Roger Coates,
Will: Houltby, Christipher Barnat, Thomas Hodgson, William Fewler,
Thomas Manard.

Burgus de Stockton. Curia capitalis vis franciplegii reverendi in
Christo patris Nathaniel domini episcopi Dunelm' tenta ibidem
vicesimo.[111]

[p. 134]
October the 6th anno 1696.

Whereas by an order made the 20th day of October 1674, no person or
persons shall be elected or chosen to serve as mayor for this burrow
of Stockton for above the time or terme of two years together, it is
now thought fit that the same be nuld & made voide. And the same
order is hereby, by & with the consent & assent of James Burdon Esq.

---

110 Sworn in court leet adjourned to 1 October 1695; John Porrett, steward.
111 Head court held on 20 [October 1695].

present mayor and the cheife burgesses of this burrow, absolutely nuld set-aside and made voide, the said sixth day of October 1696.

Thomas Jessopp, Robt Jackson, Ja: Cooke, Thos Wrangham, Jno: Wells, Tho: Swainston, Wm Raisbeck,[112] John Mayles, Thomas Hodgson, John Watson, John Bainbridge, Ja: Dunning, Wm Coatsworth.

[p. 135]
I James Burdon mayor of the burrow of Stockton, do sweare [*mayoral oath as above, p. 59*][113] So help me God & by the contents of this booke
Ja: Burdon mayor.

Memorandum that the eight day of October anno domini 1696 James Burdon Esq. elected mayor for the abovesaid burrow of Stockton did before the takeing the oath [*illegible deletion, 2 lines in length*] of majoralty contained in the said burrow take the oaths appointed by act of parliament made anno primo Gulielmi et Marie intituled an Act for the Abrogateing of the Oaths of Supremacy & Allegiance and appointeing other Oaths, and then tooke also the said oath of majoralty.
Before me N[icholas] Duresme.
Vera copia originalis examinetur per me Jo: Porrett.

[p. 136]
October the 20th anno domini 1696

Memorandum that this day James Burdon Esq. mayor of
this burrow of Stockton made & perfected his accompts
to the aldermen & chiefe burgesses of the said burrow,
and upon that accompt which was seen & allowd there
rested due to the said Mr Major from the burrow the full
& just summe of six pounds seventeen shill[ings] 6d ¼
(over and above what remaines due to him upon his
former accompts) to be paid & allowed him in course   06li 17s 6¼d

Tho: Jessopp, Robt Jackson, Will Atkinson, Ja: Dunning, Hen: Burdon, James Dale, William Raisbeck, John Watson, Roger Coates, Thomas Hodgson, William Fewler, Will: Houltby.

112 William Raisbeck was a merchant from Newcastle: Bayley, 'Genealogical Additions', p. 97.
113 The oath is to 'our sovereign King William' rather than 'his King's Majestie'.

[p. 137]
Burgus de Stockton. Curia capitalis cum visu franciplegii reverendi in Christo patris Nathaniel domini episcopi Dunelm' tenta ibidem vicesimo die Octobris anno regni domini Willielmi tertii nunc regis Anglie &c octavo annoque domini 1696. Coram Jacobo Burdon armigero majore et Johanne Porrett generoso senescallo ibidem.[114]

Memorandum that it is this day agreed in full court that the incroachment formerly made by Mr Robert Sayer at the west end of a certaine house in Dove Coate Laine adjoyning to the West Row, now belonging to William Southgate, may be freely enjoyed by the said William Southgate his heirs & assignes for ever, without molestation for the future, and that all fines or presentiments which have been in the court about the same are hereby absolutely discharged.

Jo: Porrett senescallus

[p. 138]
Burgus de Stockton In Comitatu Dunelm
I William Atkinson mayor of this burrow of Stockton do sweare
[*mayoral oath as above, p. 59*]   Will Atkinson

Juratus in curia leet adjurnata usque ad hanc diem videlicet quinto diem Octobris anno domini 1697. Coram me Jo: Porrett senescallo[115]

[p. 139]
October the 19th anno domini 1697

Memorandum that this \day/ James Burdon alderman
late mayor of this burrow of Stockton made & perfected
his accompts to William Atkinson Esq. present mayor and
to the aldermen & cheife burgesses of the said burrow,
and upon that account which was seen and allowed there
remaind in the hands of the said late mayor the sume of
thirteen shillings & a halfepenny which he is to pay to the
present mayor   00^li 13^s 0½^d

114 Head court, 20 October, 8 William III (1696); James Burdon, mayor, and John Porrett, steward.

115 Sworn in court leet adjourned to 5 October 1697; John Porrett, steward.

Will Atkinson major, Thomas Jessopp, Robt Jackson, Thos Wrangham,
Jno: Wells, Ja: Dunning, Ja: Dale, Jno: Moon, Tho: Swainston, Richd
Jackson, Wm Raisbeck, Jon Watson, Roger Coates, James Raisbeck,
Thomas Manard, William Fewler, Thomas Sparrow.

[p. 140]
Burgus de Stockton. Curia capitalis cum visu franciplegii reverendi
in Christo patris Nathaniel domini episcopi Dunelm' tenta ibidem
17° die May anno regni domini Willielmi tertii nunc regis Anglie &c
decimo annoque domini 1698. Coram Willelmo Atkinson armigero
major et Johanne Porrett generoso senescallo ibidem.[116]

Memorandum it is this day ordered in full court by a unanimous
consent that the summe of three shillings per burgage be collected
& paid to the said William Atkinson present mayor on or before the
24th day of June next for defraying the charge of altering the clocke
in the toole bo[o]th in such manner as the said Mr Mayor shall thinke
most proper so as the same face the marketplace and that he also
have what contributions as can be procured of other inhabitants for
the same purposs.

[*col. 1*] Ja: Dale, Ja: Dunning, Tho: Readman, Jno: Moone
[*col. 2*] Thomas Jessopp, Robt Jackson, James Cooke, Thos Wrangham,
Tho' Swainston, Wm Coatsworth, Wm Raisbeck, Ja: Raisbeck, John
Mayles, Anth. Coats,* Tho: Hodgson, Will: Houltby, Chris: Barnett*
his mark, Simon Fowler, Thomas Maynard, Rich. Wilson* his marck.

[p. 141] [*blank*]

[p. 142]
I James Cooke mayor of the burrow of Stockton do sweare [*mayoral
oath as above, p. 59*]   Ja: Cooke

Memorandum that the fifth day of October anno domini 1698 James
Cooke Esq. elected mayor for the abovesaid burrow of Stockton did
before the taking the oath of majoralty contained in the said burrow,
take the oathes appointed by act of parliament made anno primo
Gulielmi & Marie intituled an Act for the Abrogating of the Oaths of

116 Head court, 17 May, 10 William III (1698); William Atkinson, mayor, and John
     Porrett, steward.

Supremacy & allegiance and appointing other oaths, and then tooke the said oath of mayoralty.

Before me N[icholas] Duresme

Vera copia originalis examinetur per me Jo: Porrett.

[p. 143]
Burgus de Stockton. Curia capitalis cum visu franciplegii reverendi in Christo patris Nathaniel domini episcopi Dunelm' tenta ibidem 18° die Octobris anno regni domini Willelmi tertii nunc regis Anglie &c decimo annoque domini 1698. Coram Jacobo Cooke armigero majore & Johanne Porrett generoso senescallo ibidem.[117]

Memorandum that this day William Atkinson alderman late mayor of the said burrow made and perfected his accompts to James Cooke Esq. present mayor and to the aldermen & cheife burgesses of the said burrow, and upon that accompt which was seen and allowed there remaind nothing in his hand nor any thing due to him. So ballanced & cleared all accounts save what is due to him upon a former accompt or order.

[col. 1] Wm Raisbeck, Ja: Dunning, Simon Fewler, Is. Jefferson, Jno: Watson, Wm Coatsworth, Jno: Moone, Ja: Dale

[col. 2] James Cooke mayor, Thomas Jessopp, Robt Jackson, Thos Wrangham, Jno: Wells, Hen: Burdon, Richd Jackson, Robert Thompson, Wm Heron, Roger Coates, Thomas Sparrow, William Fewler.

[p. 144]
Burgus de Stockton. Curia capitalis cum visu franciplegii reverendi in Christo patris Nathaniel domini episcopi Dunelm' tenta ibidem vicesimo quinto die Aprilis anno regni domini Willielmii tertii nunc regis Anglie &c undecimo annoque domini 1699. Coram Jacobo Cooke armigero majore et Johanne Porrett generoso senescallo ibidem.[118]

Memorandum that it is this day ordered in full court by a unanimous consent that James Cooke Esq. present mayor shall erect three or four rows of butcher stoals well coverd with tyles within twelve months,

---

117 Head court, 18 October, 10 William III (1698); James Cooke, mayor, and John Porrett, steward.

118 Head court, 25 April, 11 William III (1699); James Cooke, mayor, and John Porrett, steward.

at some convenient place in or neare the marketplace in this burrow, and pave about twenty yards at the south-end of the pavement in the market-place all the breadth of the old pavement; and in consideration thereof he shall have all the benefitt of the stoaleidge of the whole market for the terme of eight years, from Tuesday next after Michaelmas Day next, commonly called the election day, and that at the end of the said terme of eight years, the benefitt of all the said stoalidge and shamles shall redound or be to the benefitt of the mayor aldermen and burgesses of this burrow in generall, and not applyd to the mayor in particular.

[*col. 1*] Jno: Wells, Hen: Burdon, Anthony Coates,* Roger Coates, Robart Thompson, Wm Heron, Thomas Hodgson, William Coats, John Mayles, Thomas Sparrow, John Coates* mark, William Fewler, Simon Fewler, Thomas Maynard
[*col. 2*] Tho: Jessopp, Robt Jackson, Will Atkinson, Ja: Burdon, Thos Wrangham,[119] Tho: Swainston, Hen Wilkinson, Tho: Readman, Ja: Dale, Wm Raisbeck, John Watson, James Raisbek, Wm Coatsworth.

[p. 145]
I Thomas Wrangham mayor of the burrow of Stockton do sweare
[*mayoral oath as above, p. 59*]   Tho Wrangham

Memorandum that the fourth day of October anno domini 1699 Thomas Wrangham Esq. elected mayor for the abovesaid burrow of Stockton did before the takeing the oath of mayoralty contained in the said burrow take the oathes appointed by act of parliament made anno primo Gulielmi & Marie intituled an Act for the Abrogating of the Oaths of Supremacy and Allegiance and appointeing other Oaths and then tooke also the said oath of mayoralty.
                                        Before me N[icholas] Duresme.
Vera copia originalis examinetur per me Jo: Porrett.

[p. 146] [*blank*]

[p. 147]
Burgus de Stockton. Curia capitalis cum visu franciplegii honoratissimi ac reverendi in Christo patris Nathaniel domini Crew domini episcopi Dunelm' tenta ibidem decimo septimo die Octobris anno

---

119 Gap of *c.*3 lines between this and the following signature.

regni domini Willielmi tertii nunc regis Anglie &c undecimo annoque domini 1699. Coram Thome Wrangham armigero majore et Johanne Porrett generoso senescallo ibidem.[120]

Whereas divers controversies or debates have lately happened touching the electing of mayors to serve for this burrow: to prevent the like differances for the future, and that the antient rights and customs thereof may be the better understood and preserved amongst us; itt is hereby declared and unanimusly agreed, in the said court that the antient customes and rights of election were and yet are as follows (viz):

1. That every man above the age of one and twenty years which hath a whole burgage within this burrow by inheritance or for terme of life in his owne right or in right of his wife, after a fine thereof taken according to the custome of this court, is duly qualified to give his voate to the electing a mayor to serve for this burrow.

2. That where a burgage shall decend to coheirs their husbands may voate, after this manner (to wit) the eldest sister's husband the first yeare, the second sister's husband the next yeare, and so by course according to the number and seniority of the coheirs married.

3. That where parcell of a burgage is sold of or conveyd, and no particular reservation or grant made of of the burrow-right, the purchaser or other owner thereof may voate the first yeare.

4. That where severall parcells are sold \or conveyd/ of to divers persons, the first purchaser or owner may voate the first yeare, the second purchasor or owner the next yeare, and so by course according to their priorities of purchas or estates.

5. That where a burgage is divided into severall parts by distinct names, as a moyety to one person, a quarter to another person & an eight to another person, such persons or owners may voate according to their respective parts (to wit) he that hath the moyety every other yeare, hee that hath the fourth every fourth yeare and he

---

120 Head court, 17 October, 11 William III (1699); Thomas Wrangham, mayor, and John Porrett, steward.

that hath the eighth, the eight yeare, and so in course according to such his proportion of the whole burgage.

[p. 148]
6. Item that where two or more are joynt purchasors or owners, the first person mentioned in the deed may voate the first year, the second person mentioned therein the next yeare, and so in course according to their place & number, if they have a whole burgage, but if they have but halfe, or any other part of a burgage, then may voate onely in course according to such their part of the burgage. And if they have as many burgages as they are owners then they may all voate, but if they have any less, as if three persons have but two burgages or two & a halfe, then they must voate in course according to their places & parts as above.

7. That if the person whose right by course it is to voate shall refuse or neglect to voate, then the next in course and faileing him any other owner of any part of the same burgage may voate, the party in course being alwayes preferd before the other, and the party & parties so refusing or neglecting, not to voate till in course againe after all the rest.

8. That there can be but one voate for any one burgage (except that of the mayor's for the time being, and he may give two voats) nor can any person though he hath severall burgages give more then one voate; except the said Mr Mayor and hee cannot exceed his said number of two in the whole.

9. That any may either grant or reserve the burrow-right, or right of election, to, or with, any part of the burgage. And where the same is so granted or reserved the with any sellor or purchasor cannot voate for the remainder of that burgage.

10. That where an estate is conveyd to trustees, not the trustees, but the person for whose use they stand seized in fee or for life shall voate.

11. That no person whatsoever is or can be qualified to voate before a fine taken of the premisses according to custome of this court and he sworne to the fealty.

[p. 149]
[———]¹²¹ written James Cooke alderman late mayor of
this burrow of Stockton made & perfected his accompts
to Thomas Wrangham Esq. present mayor and to the
aldermen and cheife burgesses of the said burrow,
and upon that account which was seen & allowd there
remained due to the said late mayor from the said
burrow to be paid him in course, (besides what may
appeare by any former account) the sume of nyne
shillings & two pence   00ˡⁱ09ˢ 2ᵈ

Thos Wrangham mayor, Tho: Jessopp, Robt Jackson, Will Atkinson,
Ja: Burdon, John Metcalf, Tho: Readman, Ant. Story, Jno: Wells, Is:
Jefferson, Hen Wilkinson, Henry Burdon, Ra: Bunting, Roger Coat,
Thomas Maynard, Robart Thompson, Thomas Hodgson, Wm Coats.

[p. 150] [*blank*]

[p. 151]
Burgus de Stockton in Comitatu Dunelm'
I Thomas Wrangham mayor of this burrow of Stockton do sweare
[*mayoral oath as above, p. 59*]   Tho Wrangham major

Juratus in curia leet adjurnata usque ad hanc diem videlicet primum
diem Octobris anno domini 1700. Coram me Jo: Porrett senescallo.¹²²

[p. 152]
Burgus de Stockton. Curia capitalis cum visu franciplegii honer-
atissimi ac reverendi in Christo Patris Nathaniel domini Crew
domini episcopi Dunelm' tenta ibidem decimo quinto die Octobris
anno regni domini Willelmi tertii nunc regis Anglie &c duodecimo
annoque domini 1700. Coram Thome Wrangham armigero mayore
et Johanne Porrett genersoso senescallo ibidem.¹²³

Memorandum that this day Thomas Wrangham Esq.
mayor of this burrough made & perfected his accompts to

---

121 Damage, four or five words in length.
122 Sworn at court leet adjourned to 1 October 1700; John Porrett, steward.
123 Head court, 15 October, 12 William III (1700); Thomas Wrangham, mayor,
     and John Porrett, steward.

the aldermen and chiefe burgesses of the said burrough
and upon that accompt, which was seen & allowed there
rests due to the said Mr Mayor from the said burrough
the full & just summe of eight pounds and eleven pence
halfepenny (over and above what remaines due to him
upon his former accompts) to be paid and allowd him in
course   08^{li}00^{s}11½^d

[*col. 1*] Hen: Burdon, Wm Raisbeck, Wm Heron, Thomas Hodgson,
Roger Coates, Simon Fewller, James Hope
[*col. 2*] Tho: Jessopp, Robt Jackson, Ja: Cooke, Will Atkinson, Ja:
Burdon.

[p. 153]
Burgus de Stockton. Curia capitalis cum visu franciplegii honoratissimi ac reverendi in Christo Patris Nathaniel domini Crew domini
episcopi Dunelm' tenta ibidem decimo quarto die Octobris anno
regni domini Willielmi tertii nunc regis Anglie &c decimo tertio
annoque domini 1701. Coram Radulpho Bunting armigero mayore
et Johanne Porrett generoso senescallo ibidem.[124]

Whereas the said lord bishop of Durham lord of this burrow
hath (upon the peticion and effectuall solicitacion of Mr Alderman
Wrangham (then mayor of this place) together with us the \present/
mayor aldermen and burgesses or some of us, on behalfe of ourselves
and rest of the burgesses of the said burrow) granted, or consented to
be granted unto us a certaine parcell of waste ground in the West-Row
Street within this burrow adjoyning to the West-Row Close extending
from Meetinghouse Gate to Rams Lane, and hath also authorised his
steward of this court to convey the same unto us, or some three or
more of us by fine, in trust for the use of us & our successors for ever.
And whereas it was always intended that the same ground should
be apply'd towards discharging of such debts as were and yet are
due to the severall persons hereafter named, who (as appears by
severall orders and accompts entered in this book) have disburst the
same for necessary expenses in and about defending and supporting
the antient rights priviledges & honours of our said burrow, and
procuring some improvements to the same; which said debts do in

124 Head court, 14 October, 13 William III (1701); Ralph Bunting, mayor, and
   John Porrett, steward.

the whole amount unto the full and just summe of two hundred and eight pounds two shillings and five pence farthing. And for as much as the annuall rent or profitts of the said ground is of very little or no value at present, and never likely to defray interest for the said money; nor can that ground come neare to the satisfying & paying of the said debt of two hundred and eight pounds two shillings and fivepence farthing any other way than by saile; neither (in truth) is it now, or ever (without great expense) likely to [p. 154] be worth near that summe in true value, yett forasmuch as the parties to whome the said summe of two hundred eight pounds two shillings and fivepence farthing halfe penny is (bona fide) due as hereafter expressed (to wit) to Mr Alderman Jackson 28^{li}: 04^s 10½^d; to Mr Alderman Cooke 30^{li} 10^s 10^d; to Mr Alderman Atkinson 16: 10: 00; to Mrs Frances Moone widow and administratrix of Mr Alderman Moone deceased 62^{li} 08^s ½^d; to Mr Alderman Burdon 30^{li} 09^s 9¼^d; due to the said Mr Alderman Wrangham 39^{li} 17^s 11^d; are all willing to accept of the said parcell of ground amongst them in full satisfaction of all their said debts so as the same ground be convey'd unto them their heirs and assignes for ever, proportionably according to their said respective debts. Therefore wee the mayor aldermen and burgesses of the said burrow doe hereby in full court unanimously consent agree and order as followeth (viz.) that Mr Alderman \Jessop/, Mr Thomas Swainston, Mr William Coatsworth and Mr Thomas Sutton \of/ this burrow or any three of them shall or may accept and take from the said steward a fine, according to custome of this court, of such a parcell of the said wast ground, as it is hereafter mentioned (to witt) of all that parcel of wast ground, containeing in length one hundred and twenty yards or thereabouts, abutting or lying on the east side of the said West-Row Close and a litle house next Meetinghouse Gate called Elizabeth Hawell's Henhouse, soe as to bring the said wast ground into a stright line, leaveing a way betwixt itt and the said litle house, into the said West-Row Close, all the breadth of that part of the same close, and the common street at the east side of the said wast ground sixteen yards wide, and at the north end other sixteen yards at the least. To have and to hold the said one hundred and twenty yards of wast ground which is limitted & boundered as aforesaid, unto the said Thomas Jessop, Thomas Swainston, William Coatsworth and Thomas Sutton their heirs and assignes for ever, in trust for the uses intents and purposes hereafter mentioned and expressed concerneing the same, that is to say, for the use benefitt and behoofe of the said Alderman Jackson, Alderman Cooke, Alderman Atkinson, Mrs Frances Moone, Alderman Burdon and Alderman Wrangham their heirs and assignes for ever;

and that they the said trustees and their heirs shall and will upon
request and at the charges in the law of the said Mr Jackson, Mr Cook,
Mr Atkinson, Mrs Moone, Mr Burdon and Mr Wrangham their heirs
or assignes (after a division by them made & agreed upon of the said
wast ground for their respective shares of the same, in proportion to
their said respective debts) grant and convey the same premisses unto
them, their heirs and assignes for ever or otherwise howsoever as they
or their councell shall reasonably advise, in pursuance and according
to the purport and true intent of this order, and in full satisfaction and
discharge of their respective debts aforesaid amounting in the whole
to the said summe of two hundred eight pounds two shillings and
fivepence halfepenny farding.

[p. 155]
It is likewise ordered that the mayor of this burrow shall not after
this day have any allowance for his charges in going or attending at
the Assizes or Sessions[125] to be held in this county, but for the future
shall beare the same at his owne expence.

Memorandum the signing this order doth as well relate to the order
on the two last pages as to that on this side.[126]

Thomas Jessopp, Robt Jackson, Ja: Cooke, Will Atkinson, Ja: Burdon,
Tho Wrangham, Tho: Swainston, Tho: Readman, Wm Raisbeck,
Tho: Sutton, Wm Heron, Robart Thompson, John Mayles, Thomas
Sparrow, Tho: Hodgson, John Fewler, Richd Mawer, Nich: Cockfield,
Tobias Ansley, Walter Marchell, Roger Coates, George Simson* his
marke.

[p. 156]
Memorandum that the summe of 208[li] 2[s] 5¼[d] mentioned in the within
written order made the 14 of October 1701 became due unto the
severall persons therein named in manner following viz:

	li	s	d
To Mr Moone the 16th of Oct 1683	12	18	10½
16 of Oct 1688	23	10	10½
15 Oct 1689	09	09	0½
tot' inde	45	18	9½

125 MS: 'Sesessions'.
126 This sentence is in a different hand from the body of the order.

Whereof paid as in folio 117[th][127]	05	00	8
So remained due to him then	40	18	0½

And about geting a free key made	21	10	0	
In all	62	08	0½	Sume:
62 08 0½[128]				

To Mr Burdon the 14th of Oct 1684	08	19	2
20 Oct 1685	05	00	2½
15 Oct 1695	10	13	0½
20 Oct 1696	06	17	6¼
	31	09	11¼

Whereof paid by Mr Moone the				
15 of October 1689	00	19	2	
So remained due	30	10	9¼	Sume: 030 10 9¼

To Mr Cooke the 19 of Oct 1686	09	19	3½
18 Oct 1687	20	04	11
16 Oct 1694	02	01	01½
7 Oct 1699	00	09	02
	32	13	06

Whereof paid as in fol. 113[129]	18	12	8	
So remained due	14	00	10	
And about preventing a free key at Portrack				
as in fol. 118[130]	16	10	00	
In all	30	10	10	Sume: 30 10 10
To Mr Wrangham 14 of Oct 1690	24	04	02	
27 Oct 1691	07	12	9½	
15 Oct 1700	08	00	11½	
In all	39	17	11	Sume: 39 17 11
To Mr Jackson 18th Oct 1692	25	11	6	
17 Oct 1693	02	13	4½	
In all	28	04	10½	Sume: 28 04 10½

127 Above, p. 86.

128 This and the following totals of the amounts due to each individual form a separate column, each sum written to the right of brackets grouping the calculations relating to the lender.

129 Above, p. 84.

130 Above, p. 87.

And to Mr Atkinson about preventing
a free key at Portrack as in the said
fol. 118   16 10 00   Sume: 16 10 00
                    Totall   208 02   5½

[p. 157]
Burgus de Stockton in Comitatu Dunelm'.
I Ralph Bunting mayor of this burrow of Stockton doe swear [*mayoral
oath as above p. 59*]   Ra: Bunting.

Juratus in curia leet adjurnata usque ad hanc diem videlicet vi° diem
Octobris anno domini 1702. Coram me Jo: Porrett senescallo.[131]

[p. 158] [*blank*]

[p. 159]
Burgus de Stockton. Curia capitalis cum visu franciplegii honoratissimi & ac reverendi in Christo patris Nathaniel domini episcopi
Dunelm' Dom' Crew tenta ibidem vicesimo die Octobris anno
regni domine Anne nunc regine Anglie &c primo annoque domini
1702. Coram Radulpho Bunting armigero majore et Johanne Porrett
generoso senescallo ibidem.[132]

Memorandum that this day Ralph Bunting Esq. mayor
abovesaid made & perfected his accompts to the
aldermen and chiefe burgesses of the said burrough and
upon that accompt which was seen & allowd there rested
due to the said aldermen & burgesses, from the said
Mr Mayor the full & just summe of thirty nyne shillings
& seven pence – which he hath in his hands   01^li 19^s 6^d

Thomas Jessopp, Will Atkinson, Ja: Burdon, Tho: Readman, Wm
Raisbeck, Tho: Sutton, Wm Heron, Robart Thompson, Tho: Hodgshon,
Is: Jefferson, John Fewler, Richd Mawer, John Mayles, Ja: Dunning.

[p. 160] [*blank*]

131 Sworn at court leet adjourned to 6 October 1702; John Porrett, steward.
132 Head court, 20 October, 1 Anne (1702); Ralph Bunting, mayor, and John
    Porrett, steward.

[p. 161]
Burgus de Stockton. Curia capitalis cum visu franciplegii honoratissimi ac reverendi in Christo patris Nathaniel domini episcopi
Dunelm' dom' Crew tenta ibidem decimo nono die Octobris anno
regni domine Anne nunc regine Anglie &c secundo annoque domini
1703. Coram Jacobo Cooke armigero majore et Johanne Porrett
generoso senescallo ibidem.[133]

Memorandum that this day Ralph Bunting alderman late
mayor of this burrow made and perfected his accompts
to James Cooke Esq. present mayor and to the aldermen
and cheife burgesses of the said burrow, and upon that
accompt which was seen and allowd there remained
in the hands of the said late mayor for his last year's
account ending the fifth of October instant, the sume of
four pounds seven shillings \seven/ pence three fardings
which with one pound nyneteen shillings & six \pence/
due by him in his former accountt make in all the full &
just sume of six pounds seven shillings & a penny three
farthings – all which he hath this day paid into the hands
of the said present mayor 6^{li} 7^s $1\frac{3}{4}^d$

Ja: Cooke major

[*col. 1*] Tho: Readman, Tho: Sutton, Wm Coatsworth, Robart
Thompson, John Mayles, Thomas Hodgshon, Richd Mawer, John
Truit, Thomas Sparrow, Will: Houltby
[*col. 2*] Thomas Jesop, Will Atkinson, Ja: Burdon, Ja: Dunning, Jno:
Wells, Wm Dowthwaite,[134] Is: Jefferson, Nic: Swainston.

[p. 162]
Burgus de Stockton. Curia capitalis cum visu franciplegii honorat-
issimi ac reverendi in Christo patris Nathaniel domini episcopi
Dunelm' Dom' Crew tenta ibidem novo die Maii anno regni domine
Anne nunc regine Anglie &c tertio annoque domini 1704. Coram

133 Head court, 19 October, 2 Anne (1703); James Cooke, mayor, and John
Porrett, steward.
134 William Dowthwaite (d. 1718) was collector of the customs from 1680, when
the customs house was moved from Hartlepool to Stockton, taking over from
Samuel Hodgkins: Richmond, *Local Records*, p. 46.

Jacobo Cooke armigero majore et Johanne Porrett generoso senescallo ibidem.[135]

Whereas the above named James Cooke Esq. hath at our request
lately procured the anchoridge lease of the River Tease appertaineing
to this burrow to be renewd by the said lord bishop of Durham for
the benefitt of us and the rest of the burgesses of this said burrow
and hath actually disburst the full and just summe of three & thirty
pounds for and about the same; it is therefor unanimusly agreed in
full court and hereby orderd that the said summe of three &thirty
pounds and interest for the same from the eighth day of October
last shall be paid unto him or his assignes by the mayor of this
burrow for the time being in manner following, that is to say: so
much money as shall happen to be in the present mayor's hand at
the next counting day (for which he shall or may be accomptable to
the aldermen & burgesses of this burrow) he shall & may detaine
towards the satisfaction of the said debt & interest or either of them;
and that every succeeding mayor shall (out of the like profitts) pay
what shall so remaine in his or their hands every counting day
unto the said James Cooke his executors administrators or assignes
untill the said principall summe or remainder thereof and interest
aforesaid be fully paid & discharged. And that for better securing
the same payments the said lease shall not onely continue & remaine
in the custody of the said James Cooke his executors administrators
or assignes but that he or they shall or may upon request have such
assignement thereof from the lessees in the same lease named as
councell shall reasonably devise & require.

[*col. 1*] Tho: Sutton, Robart Thompson, Roger Coates, John Mayles,
Richard Mawer, Thomas Sparrow
[*col. 2*] Wm Coatsworth, Tho: Hodgson
[*col. 3*] Ja: Cooke major, Thomas Jessopp,[136] Will Atkinson, Ra:
Bunting, Ja: Dunning, Hen: Burdon, Wm Dowthwaite.

---

135 Head court, 9 May, 3 Anne (1704); James Cooke, mayor, and John Porrett,
   steward.
136 A Thomas Jessop was a member of the Nonconformist church and died
   27 June 1704. He is thought to have been 'of the same family as John Jessepp,
   mayor in 1632, and who married a sister of Rowland Burdon; and Thomas
   Jessopp, mayor in 1658': Richmond, *Nonconformity*, p. 17.

[p. 163]
Burgus de Stockton. Curia capitalis cum visu franciplegii honer-
atissimi ac reverendi in Christo patris Nathaniel domini episcopi
Dunelm' Dom' Crew tenta ibidem decimo septime die Octobris anno
regni domine Anne nunc regine Anglie &c tertio annoque domini
1704. Coram Thome Readman armigero majore et Johanne Porrett
generoso senescallo ibidem.[137]

Memorandum that this day Mr James Cook alderman
late mayor of this burrow made and perfected his
accompts to Thomas Readman Esq. present mayor and
to the aldermen & cheife burgesses of the said burrow,
and upon that accompt which was seen and allowd
there remained due to the said late mayor from the said
burrow the full and just summe of thirty five pounds
sixteen shillings & tenpence halfepenny to be paid
as usuall with interest for 26 12 1½ [—] thereof that
remaines due to him about the anchoridge lease   35[li] 16[s]10½[d]

And it is also agreed & hereby orderd that in all causes to be tryd
notice shall be given on Saturday \next/ before that court day at
fordest[138] to the defendant ~~or his attorney~~ or his baile.

[col. 1] Jo: Porrett senescallus, Nic: Swainston, Wm Dowthwaite, Wm
Raisbeck, Roger Coates, Robart Thompson
[col. 2] Tho: Readman major, Will Atkinson, Ra: Bunting, Ja: Dunning,
Hen: Burdon, Wm Coatsworth, Tho: Sutton, John Atkinson, Wm
Fleatham, Is: Jefferson.

[p. 164] [blank]

[p. 165]
Burgus de Stockton. Curia capitalis cum visu francplegii honer-
atissimi ac reverendi in Christo patris Nathaniel domini episcopi
Dunelm' Dom' Crew tenta ibidem decimo sexto die Octobris anno
regni domine Anne nunc regine Anglie &c quarto annoque domini

---

137 Head court, 17 October, 3 Anne (1704); Thomas Readman, mayor, and John
     Porrett, steward.
138 i.e. 'furthest'.

1705. Coram Thome Readman armigero majore & Johanne Porrett generoso senescallo ibidem.[139]

Memorandum that this day Thomas Readman aforesaid Esq. present mayor made & perfected his accompts to the aldermen and cheife burgesses of this said burrow, and upon that account which was seen and allowd there remaind ~~there was~~ due unto them by the said Mr Mayor the full & just sume of six pounds ten shillings a[nd] three halfe pence which at their request he hath actually paid unto Mr Alderman Cooke before the signeing here of in part of 26^{li} 12^{s} 1½^{d} resting due about the anchoridge lease & 1^{li} 11^{s} 9½^{d}[140] interest thereof for one yeare, so remaines due thereupon to Mr Cooke 21^{li} 13^{s} 9^{d} besides 9^{li} 4^{s} 9^{d} due to him upon other accounts which is to be paid him in course.   06^{li} 10^{s} 1½^{d}

[*col. 1*] Leo^{d} Dale, Wm Gibson, John Burdett, Tho: Middleton, Robart Thompson, Richd Mawer, Thomas Hodgson, Thos Sparrow, John Berdon
[*col. 2*] Ra: Bunting, Ja: Cooke, Wm Dowthwaite, Hen: Burdon, Wm Raisbeck. William Hart Atkinson.

[p. 166]
Burgus de Stockton. Curia capitalis cum visu franciplegii honoratissimi ac reverendi in Christo patris Nathaniel domini episcopi Dunelm' Dom' Crew tenta ibidem decimo quinto die Octobris anno regni domine Anne nunc regine Anglie &c quinto annoque domini 1706. Coram Willelmo Hart Atkinson armigero majore et Johanne Porrett senescallo ibidem.[141]

Memorandum that this day Mr Thomas Readman alderman late mayor of this burrow made and perfected his accompts to William Hart Atkinson Esq. present mayor and to the aldermen and cheife burgesses of the said burrow and upon that account which was seen

---

139 Head court, 16 October, 4 Anne (1705); Thomas Readman, mayor, and John Porrett, steward.
140 The number of pence has been changed from '4' to '9'; the halfpenny has been deleted.
141 Head court, 15 October, 5 Anne (1706); William Hart Atkinson, mayor, and John Porrett, steward.

and allowd there remained due to the said late mayor from the said
burrow the full and just summe of two pounds ten shillings & two
pence which is to be paid him in course.

William Hart Atkinson, Ra: Bunting, Ja: Cooke, Wm Dowthwaite,
Tho Middleton, Tho: Dunning, Jno: Wells, Hen: Burdon, Tho: Sutton,
Wm Coatsworth, John Metcalf,[142] Robart Fewler, John Burdett,
Leo[d] Dale.[143]

[p. 167]
Burgus de Stockton. Curia capitalis cum visu franciplegii honer-
atissimi ac reverendi in Christo patris Nathaniel domini episcopi
Dunelm' Dom' Crew tenta ibidem decimo quarto die Octobris anno
regni domine Anne nunc regine Magne Britanie &c sexto annoque
domini 1707. Coram Richardo Bowlby amigero majore & Johanne
Porrett generoso senescallo ibidem.[144]

Memorandum that this day William Hart Atkinson[145]
alderman late mayor of this burrow made & perfected his
accompts to Richard Bowlby Esq. present mayor and to
the aldermen & cheife burgesses of this burrow and upon
that accompt which was seen & allowed there remained
due to the said late mayor from the said burrow to be
paid him in course the full summe of eight pounds four
shillings & six pence To be allowed him in course   08[li] 4[s] 6[d]

[col. 1] Nic: Swainston, Jno: Wells seneior, Wm Dowthwaite, Hen:
Wilkinson
[col. 2] Richd Bowlby mayor, Ra: Bunting, Ja: Cooke, Hen: Burdon,
Tho: Middleton, Tho: Dunning, Richd Jackson, Wm Coatesworth,
Rob. Dale, Tho: Sutton.

142 Reading of surname uncertain.
143 On 4 February 1706, James Cooke, Thomas Readman, Nicholas Swainston,
     Nicholas Cockfield, John Benton, Henry Burdon, Richard Jackson and Henry
     Wilkinson signed an agreement, as burgage holders adjoining the river side,
     for a highway along the river side, acknowledging that there had been an
     ancient highway there: Richmond, *Local Records*, p. 53.
144 Head court, 14 October, 6 Anne (1707); Richard Bowlby, mayor, and John
     Porrett, steward.
145 William Hart Atkinson was a descendant of William Hart, mayor in 1627:
     Surtees, *History*, pp. 173–4.

[p. 168] [*blank*]

[p. 169]
Burgus de Stockton in Comitatu Dunelm'

I Thomas Sutton mayor of this burrough of Stockton do swear
[*mayoral oath as above, p. 59*][146]   Tho: Sutton
Juratus in curia leet adjurnata usque ad hanc diem videlicet quinto
die Octobris anno domini 1708 Coram me. Jo: Porrett senescallo.[147]

[p. 170] [*blank*]

[p. 171]
Burgus de Stockton. Curia capitalis cum visu franciplegii honoratissimi ac reverendi in Christo patris Nathaniel domini episcopi
Dunelm Dom' Crew tenta ibidem decimo nono die Octobris anno
regni domine Anne nunc regine Magne Britanie &c septimo annoque
domini 1708: coram Thomas Sutton armigero majore et Johanne
Porrett generoso senescallo ibidem.[148]

Memorandum that this day Mr Richard Bowlby alderman
late mayor of this burrow made & perfected his accompts
to Thomas Sutton Esq. present mayor and to the
aldermen & cheife burgesses of this burrow, and upon
that accompt which was seen and allowd there remained
in his hand the full and just summe of thirty nyne pounds
fourteen shillings & ten pence thre farthings, which he is
to pay as followeth, to witt, to Mr Alderman Cooke for
his debt due from the burrow   33 10   0
To Mr Alderman Readman for his debt   02 10   2
And to Mr Alderman Atkinson in part of his debt   03 14   8¾
                                                      39 14 10¾
which they have accepted as paid and so he hath cleard his said
accompt.

146 The oath is the first to name Anne as Queen of Great Britain, following the
     Act of Union in 1707.
147 Sworn in court leet adjourned to 5 October 1708; John Porrett, steward.
148 Head court, 19 October, 7 Anne (1708); Thomas Sutton, mayor, and John
     Porrett, steward.

Item it is this day ordered in full court that the said present mayor may either repair or make a new cross in the markett place in such manner as he shall & the aldermen or the majority of them shall thinke fit and to be reimburst out of the money to become due to the this burrow.

[*col. 1*] Wm Coatesworth, Wm Fleatham, Tho: Middleton, Jno: Burdett, John Mayles, Wm Dowthwaite
[*col. 2*] Hen: Burdon, Jno: Wells, Richd Jackson
[*col. 3*] Tho: Sutton mayor, Ra: Bunting, Ja: Cooke, Tho: Readman, Wm Hart Atkinson, Richd Bowlby.

[p. 172] [*blank*]

[p. 173]
Burgus de Stockton. Curia capitalis cum visu franciplegii honoratissimi ac reverendi in Christo patris Nathaniel domini episcopi Dunelm' Dom' Crew tenta ibidem decimo octavo die Octobris anno regni domine Anne regine Magne Britanie &c octavo annoque domini 1709, coram Thoma Sutton armigero majore et Johanne Porrett generoso senescallo ibidem.[149]

Memorandum that this day Thomas Sutton Esq. mayor
of this burrow made and perfected his accounts to the
aldermen and cheife burgesses of the said burrow, and
upon that account which was seen and allowed there
remained due to the said Mr Mayor from the burrow the
full and just sume of thirty eight pounds, nyne shillings
and five pence halfe penny. two farthings And to
Mr Alderman Bunting, Mr Alderman Cook, Mr Alderman
Readman, Mr Alderman Atkinson, the above named
John Porrett and also to John Cook, Richard Jackson,
Henry Burdon, Henry Wilkinson, Nicholas Cockfield
and Thomas Ogle gents the sume of fifty five pounds
makeing in all the full and just sume of nynety three
\pounds/ nyne shillings & five pence halfe penny, which
hath been by them lately lent or advanced in manner
following for and about the building of the new cross

---

149 Head court, 18 October, 8 Anne (1709); Thomas Sutton, mayor, and John Porrett, steward.

(to witt) by the said Mr Mayor the said sume of thirty
eight pounds 9s 5½d. And by the eleven other persons
above named the severall and respective sumes of five
pounds apeice, all and every of which said sumes so
~~and~~ due unto ~~you~~ \them/, amounting in the whole to
the said sume of nynety three pounds nyne shillings
& 5½d, wee do hereby unanimously agree in full court
and hereby order shall be paid them their respective
executors administrators and assignes and interest for
the same from this time, by the respective mayors of this
place for the time being as the same can be raised \by/
and out of the profitts ariseing to this burrow before any
other debt now oweing, and that the present mayor and
his successors mayors of this place shall pay the same
accordingly or so much thereof as he or [p. 174] they
can yearly, on or before every counting day before his
accounts be allowed, and shall pay the same to the said
persons their respective executors administrators \or
assignes/ as they amongst themselves shall agree. And in
default of such agreement as the mayor for the time being
shall think fitt, untill all the said sume of nynety three
pounds nyne shillings & 5½ᵈ ~~be full~~ and interest thereof
be fully paid and discharged.   93ˡⁱ 09ˢ 5½ᵈ

[*col. 1*] Wm Dowthwaite, John Fewler
[*col. 2*] Tho: Sutton mayor, Ra: Bunting, Ja: Cooke, Tho: Readman, Wm
Hart Atkinson, Nich: Cockfield, Richd Jackson, Wm Coatesworth,
Tho: Middleton, Ja: Dunning, Wm Gibson, John Mayles, Robart
Thompson, Richd Mawer, Tho: [S]parrow, John Wells, Will: Houltby,
William Marshall, Thomas Hodgshon.
See the severall payments to them in folio 177¹⁵⁰

[p. 175]
Burgus de Stockton. Curia capitalis cum visu franciplegii honoratissimi ac reverendi in Christo patris Nathaniel domini episcopi
Dunelm' Dom' Crew tenta ibidem decimo septimo die Octobris anno
regni domine Anne nunc regine Magne Britanie &c nono annoque

150 Below, p. 116.

domini 1710 coram Jacobo Cooke armigero majore & Johanne Porrett generoso senescallo ibidem.[151]

Memorandum that this day Thomas Sutton alderman late mayor of this burrow made and perfected his accounts to the alderman and chiefe burgesses of the said burrow and upon that account which was seen and allowed there remained due to the towne thirty ~~one~~ pounds one shilling and a farthing which he hath paid as follows viz. five pounds ~~and~~ eleven \shillings/ & seven pence for interest of nynety three pounds nyne shillings & three pence; to his owne part thereof eight pounds nyne shillings & five pence halfe penny, to Alderman Atkinson five pounds, to Mr Henry Burdon five pounds & to Mr Henry Wilkinson five pounds in full of their respective debts or shares of the said nynety three pounds nyne shillings & three pence, and to the said present mayor twenty shillings in full of his account which this present mayor is to account for, as alsoe for two pounds & one shilling returned in arreare of the Shambles rent as by his said account   30^{li} 01^{s} ¼^{d}

[*col. 1*] Wm Dowthwaite, Tho Middleton, James Dunning, Wm Gibson, Jno: Burdett
[*col. 2*] Ja: Cooke mayor,[152] Ra: Bunting, Tho: Readman, Wm Hart Atkinson, Hen: Burdon, Nich: Cockfield.

[p. 176]
Burgus de Stockton. Curia capitalis cum visu franciplegii honoratissimi ac reverendi in Christo patris Nathaniel domini episcopi

---

151 Head court, 17 October, 9 Anne (1710); James Cooke, mayor, and John Porrett, steward.

152 This James Cooke was the son of James Cook, mayor in 1669, and the grandson of James Cooke, mayor from 1640 to 1643: Surtees, *History*, pp. 173–4. When James Cooke, Thomas Sutton and Ralph Bunting were present on 5 June 1710, when the foundation of the new church was laid (Richmond, *Local Records*, p. 54), Thomas Sutton was still mayor, as the mayoral elections were on the first Tuesday after Michaelmas (29 September). For the new church, see Tom Sowler, *The Parish Church of Stockton-on-Tees* (Stockton-on-Tees, 1990). It was consecrated on 21 August 1712, the Revd George Gibson being the first vicar: Richmond, *Local Records*, p. 56, Brewster, *History*, pp. 308–31, Surtees, *History*, p. 187.

Dunelm' Dom' Crew tenta ibidem decimo sexto die Octobris anno regni domine Anne nunc regine Magne Britanie &c decimo annoque domini 1711 Coram Radulpho Bunting armigero majore et Johanne Parrott generoso senescallo ibidem.[153]

Memorandum that this day James Cooke alderman late mayor of this burrow made and perfected his accounts to the aldermen and chiefe burgesses of the said burrow and upon that account which \was/ seen and allowed there remained due to the towne the sume of ten pounds two shillings and three \pence three/ farthing. Ten pounds whereof was paid to Mr Alderman Sutton in part of thirty pounds and the remainder being two shillings \3d/ and three farthings to the present mayor in full of the said last mayor's account, which said two shillings three pence and three farthings as alsoe thirty shillings returned in arreare by Thomas Scadlock and George ~~John~~ Harrison the present mayor is to account for 10^{li} 2^s $3\frac{3}{4}^d$

[col. 1] James Dunning, Tho Middleton, Wm Gibson, John Wells junior, John Wells senior, John Mayles, Richd Mawer, Thomas Hodgshon, Robart Thompson, Walter Marshall
[col. 2] Ra: Bunting mayor, Tho: Readman, Wm Hart Atkinson, Tho: Sutton, Tho: Ogle.

[p. 177]
I do hereby confess & agree that the new erection which I have made to Mr Rowland Burdon's house wherein I dwell adjoyneing to the street & Mrs Wrangham's[154] house (to wit) that part wherein I have my office or studdy, is an incroachment so farr as it raingeth further into the street than the said Mrs Wrangham's house & Mr Hendry's and the permiting itt to stand unpresented as such by the jury, I do acknowledge as a favour only to myselfe, for which I am obliged to the neighbourhood in general, and that it is & may at any time hereafter be lyable to be presented and proceeded against as an incroachment. And whilst I enjoy the same peaceably I am willing to pay an acknowledgement for it of six pence per annum to the mayor

153 Head court, 16 October, 10 Anne (1711); Ralph Bunting, mayor, and John Porrett, steward.
154 Perhaps the widow of Thomas Wrangham (d. 1704): DULASC, DPRI/3/1704/B80/1–2.

of this burrow for the time being every counting day if requested.
Witness my hand the 16 of October 1711.   Jo: Porrett

Memorandum there is due to Mr Alderman Sutton & others about
the cross as in folio 173[155] the severall sumes following viz.

	li	s	d
To said Mr Sutton	38	09	5½
Mr Bunting	05	00	0
Mr Cooke	05	00	0
Mr Redman	05	00	0
Mr Atkinson	05	00	0
Mr Porrett	05	00	0
Mr John Cooke	05	00	0
Mr Jackson	05	00	0
Mr Henry Burdon	05	00	0
Mr Wilkinson	05	00	0
Mr Cockfield	05	00	0
and Mr Thomas Ogle	05	00	0
Total	93	09	5

whereof paid as follows

	li	s	d
To Mr Sutton as in fol. 175	08	09	5½
To Mr[156] Atkinson	05	00	0
To Mr Burdon	05	00	0
and to Mr Wilkinson	05	00	0
more to Mr Sutton in fol 176	10	00	0

October the 14th anno 1712 \paid/ as in fol 179[157]

to Alderman Cooke	05	00	0
To Mr John Cooke	05	00	0
To Mr Ogle	05	00	0
To myselfe John Porett	05	00	0

October the 20th anno 1713 as in fol. 180[158]

Paid to Alderman Sutton	10	00	0
To Alderman Bunting	05	00	0

---

155 Above, p. 112.
156 'Mr' repeated in MS.
157 Below, p. 117.
158 Below, p. 118.

And to Mr Cockfield   05 00   0
Total inde   73 09   5½

October the 19th anno 1714

paid to Mr Alderman Sutton as in   10 00 00
To Alderman Readman   05 00 00
And to Mr Richard Jackson   05 00 00
Total   93 09 05½

Besides interest.[159]

Memorandum the whole charge of building the crose (as appears by Mr Sutton's account anno 1709) amounted to the summe of 107^{li} 08^s 11^d.

[p. 178] [*blank*]

[p. 179]

Burgus de Stockton. Curia capitalis cum visu franciplegii honoratissimi ac reverendi in Christo patris Nathaniel domini episcopi Dunelm' Dom' Crew tenta ibidem decimo quarto die Octobris anno regni domine Anne nunc regine Magne Britanie &c undecimo annoque domini 1712. Coram Thoma Readman armigero majore et Johanne Porrett generoso senescallo ibidem.[160]

Memorandum that this day Ralph Bunting alderman late mayor of this burrow made & perfected his accounts to Thomas Readman Esq. present mayor and to the aldermen & cheife burgesses of this burrow, and upon that account which was seen & allowd there remained due unto them from the said late mayore the full & just sume of twenty pounds fifteen shillings seven pence ¾d which he hath paid as followeth viz. twenty pounds thereof to Mr Alderman Cooke, Mr John Cooke, Mr Ogle & Mr Porrett at 5^{li} a peice and 15^s 7¾^d which is the balance to the said present mayor and hath returned an arrear of debt as by his account of 5^{li} 16^s 0^d which the present mayor is to receive   20^{li} 15^s 7¾^d

---

159 This phrase is written somewhat adrift of, and below, the column, but in the same hand as 'Total' in the line above.

160 Head court, 14 October, 11 Anne (1712); Thomas Readman, mayor, and John Porrett, steward.

Tho: Readman major, Ja: Cooke, Tho: Sutton, Hen: Burdon, Wm
Fleatham, Tho: Ogle, Tho: Middleton, John Burdett, John Wells
senior, Robart Thompson, Will: Houltby, Walter Marshall, Anthony
Coates, Thomas Sparrow.

[p. 180]
Burgus de Stockton. Curia capitalis cum visu franciplegii honer-
atissimi ac reverendi in Christo patris Nathaniel domini episcopi
Dunelm' Dom' Crew tenta ibidem vicesimo die Octobris anno regni
domine Anne nunc regine Magne Britanie &c duodecimo annoque
domini 1713. Coram Johanne Wells armigero majore et Johanne
Porrett generoso senescallo ibidem.[161]

Memorandum that this day Thomas Readman[162]
Alderman late mayor of this burrough made and
perfected his accompts to John Wells Esq. present
mayor and to the aldermen and cheife burgesses of this
burrough, and upon that accompt which was seen and
allowd there remained due unto them from the said late
mayor the full & just sume of twenty pounds 14ˢ 4¾ᵈ
which he hath paid as followeth (viz.) to Alderman
Sutton ten pounds, to Alderman Bunting five pounds,
to Mr Nicholas Cockfield five pounds; and fourteen
shillings 4¾ᵈ which is the ballance of his said account to
the present mayor and hath returned an arrear of debts
as by his account of 4ˡⁱ 4ˢ 6ᵈ which the present mayor is to
receive.   20ˡⁱ 14ˢ 4¾ᵈ

[*col. 1*] Tho Middleton, Wm Gibson, Tho Ogle, John Burdett, Tho:
Harperley, John Wells senior, Robart Thompson, William Coats
[*col. 2*] John Wells mayor, Ra: Bunting, Ja: Cooke, Tho: Sutton, Nich:
Cockfield, Wm Dowthwaite, James Dunning.

[p. 181] [*blank*]

---

161 Head court, 20 October, 12 Anne (1713); John Wells, mayor, and John Porrett,
     steward.
162 Thomas Readman died 1715 and was buried in Stockton St. Thomas
     churchyard: Brewster, *History*, p. 322 gives the inscription.

[p. 182]
Burgus de Stockton in Comitatu Dunelm'
I John Wells mayor of this burrough of Stockton do sweare [*mayoral oath as above p. 59*]   John Wells mayor

Juratus in curia leet adjurnata usque ad hanc diem videlicet quinto die Octobris anno domini 1714 Coram me Jo: Porret senescallo.[163]

[p. 183]
Burgus de Stockton. Curia capitalis cum visu franciplegii honoratissimi ac reverendi in Christo patris Nathaniel domini episcopi Dunelm' Dom' Crew tenta ibidem decimo nono die Octobris anno regni domini Georgii nunc regis Magne Britanie &c primo annoque domini 1714. Coram Johanne Wells armigero majore et Johanne Porrett generoso senescallo ibidem.[164]

Memorandum that this day John Wells Esq. mayor of this burrow made and perfected his accompts to the aldermen and cheife burgesses of the said burrow and upon that accompt which was seen & allowed there remained due unto them from the said mayor the full and just sume of twelve pounds three shillings & three pence halfe penny in cash received besides twenty pounds nyne shillings & five pence & halfe halfe penny which are returnd in arrear as by his said accountt makeing in all   32^{li} 12^s 9^d

Ra: Bunting, Ja: Cooke, Tho: Sutton, Richd Jackson, Wm Dowthwaite, Tho: Middleton, John Burdett, Wm Gibson, Tho: Ogle, Tho: Harperley, John Wells senior, Robart Thompson, Richd Mawer, John Mayles, Thomas Sparrow.

[p. 184] [*blank*]

[p. 185]
Burgus de Stockton in Comitatu Dunelm'
I John Burdett mayor of this burrough of Stockton do sweare [*mayoral oath as above, p. 59*]   John Burdett

163 Sworn in court leet adjourned to 5 October 1714; John Porrett, steward.
164 Head court, 19 October, 1 George I (1714); John Wells, mayor, and John Porrett, steward.

Juratus in curia leet adjurnata usque ad hanc diem videlicet quartum diem Octobris anno domini 1715. Coram me Jo: Porrett senescallo.[165]

[p. 186]
Burgus de Stockton. Curia capitalis cum visu franciplegii ~~reverendi~~ honoratissimi ac reverendi in Christo patris Nathaniel domini episcopi Dunelm' Dom' Crew tenta ibidem decimo octavo die Octobris anno regni domini Georgii nunc regis Magne Britanie &c secundo annoque domini 1715. Coram Johanne Burdett armigero majore & Johanne Porrett generoso senescallo ibidem.[166]

Memorandum that this \day/ John Wells alderman late
mayor of this burrough made and perfected his accompts
to John Burdett Esq. present mayor and to the aldermen
and cheife burgesses of \this/ burrough, and upon that
accompt which was seen and allow'd there remained due
unto them from the said late mayor the full & just summe
of thirty eight pounds two shillings ~~& six~~ \nyne/ pence
which he hath paid ~~as followeth (viz)~~ this day to the
hands of the said present mayor   38^li 02^s 9^d

John Burdett mayor, Ra: Bunting, Ja: Cooke, Tho: Sutton, Tho: Middleton, Tho: Ogle, Tho: Harperley, John Wells senior, John Mayles, Will: Houltby, Richd Mawer, Thomas Sparrow, John Fewler, Anthony Coates, Nich: Cockfield, Wm Gibson.

[p. 187]
Burgus de Stockton in Comitatu Dunelm'
I John Burdett mayor of this burrough of Stockton do sweare [*mayoral oath as above, p. 59*]   John Burdett mayor

Juratus in curia leet adjurnata usque ad hanc diem videlicet secundum diem Octobris anno domini 1716 coram me Jo: Porrett senescallo.[167]

[p. 188] [*blank*]

---

165 Sworn in court leet, adjourned to 4 October 1715; John Porrett, steward.
166 Head court, 18 October, 2 George I (1715); John Burdett, mayor, and John Porrett, steward.
167 Sworn in court leet adjourned to 2 October 1716; John Porrett, steward.

[p. 189]
Burgus de Stockton. Curia capitallis cum visu franciplegii honoratissimi ac reverendi in Christo patris Nathaniel domini episcopi
Dunelm' Dom' Crew tenta ibidem decimo sexto die Octobris anno
regni domini Georgii nunc regis Magne Britanie &c tertio annoque
domini 1716. Coram Johanne Burdett armigero majore & Johanne
Porrett generoso senescallo ibidem.[168]

Memorandum that this day John Burdett Esq. mayor of this burrough
made and perfected his accounts to the aldermen and cheife burgesses
of the said burrough and upon that account which was seen and
allowed there remained due unto them from the said mayor the full
and just sume of eleaven pounds twelve shillings and two pence which
is the ballance R of the said account. Besides sixty six pounds disbursed
about the act of parliament about the wast ground[169] allowed him in
the said account which he must account for when received.

[col. 1] Ra: Bunting, Ja: Cooke, Tho: Sutton, John Wells, Wm
Coatesworth, John Wells senior, James Raisbeck, John Wayres, Will:
Houltby, Tho: Hodgshon
[col. 2] Nich: Cockfield, Wm Gibson, Tho: Middleton.

[p. 190]
Burgus de Stockton in Comitatu Dunelm'
I John Cooke, mayor of this burrough of Stockton do swear [*mayoral
oath as above, p. 59*]   John Cooke

Juratus in curia leet adjurnata usque ad hanc diem videlicet primum
diem Octobris anno domini 1717 coram me Jo: Porrett sensecallo.[170]

[p. 191]
Burgus de Stockton. Curia capitallis cum visu franciplegii honer-
atissimi ac reverendi in Christo Patris Nathaniel domini episcopi
Dunelm' Dom' Crew tenta ibidem decimo quinto die Octobris anno

168 Head court, 16 October, 3 George I (1716); John Burdett, mayor, and John
     Porrett, steward.
169 This was the Act of 1 George I (1714), subsequent to Stockton becoming
     a separate parish in 1711, which allowed the vicar to rent out waste land
     between the Almshouses and William Peacock's house: for the text, see
     Brewster, *History*, Appendix I, No. V, pp. 471–2.
170 Sworn in court leet adjourned to 1 October, 1717; John Porrett, steward.

ibidem domini Georgii nunc regis Magne Britanie et tertio annoque
domini 1717 coram Johanne Cooke armigero majore & Johanne
Porrett generoso senescallo ibidem.[171]

Memorandum that this day John Burdett alderman late
mayor of this burrough made and perfected his accounts
to John Cooke Esq. present mayor and to the aldermen
and cheife burgesses of this burrough and upon that
account which was seen and allowed there remained due
unto them from the said late mayor the full and just sume
of thirty seven pounds ten shillings & four pence which
he hath paid to this day to the hand of the said present
mayor. And there yet remaines due to the burrow upon
Mr Walker's account thirty pounds & twelve shillings the
remainder of 66^{li} mention in the said Mr Burdett's last
account.   37^{li} 10^s 4^d

And itt \is also/ ordered this day in full court that the present mayor
and everey succeeding mayor for this burrough for the time being
shall have an allowance of twenty shillings a time for every Sessions
and when he goes to take the oaths and thirty shillings at the Assizes
if he attends the same.

[col. 1] Wm Fleatham, Tho: Middleton, John Wells senior, Geo:
Corney, Will: Houltby
[col. 2] John Cooke, Ra: Bunting, Ja: Cooke, Tho: Sutton, John Wells,
Will: Grundy, Wm Gibson, Tho: Ogle.

[p. 192]
November the 5th 1717

Memorandum that \it is/ this day unanimously agreed by Mr Mayor
the aldermen and burgesses of this burrough (for incouraging the
inhabitants to or burgesses to inlarge the common pavements) that
whosoever for the future shall lay or make any new pavements in the
said burrough by the consent of the said Mr Mayor or his successors
mayors of Stockton this place shall not only be discharged from
repairing the same but the said mayor for the time being shall att the

171 Head court, 15 October, '3' [recte 4] George I (1717); John Cooke, mayor, and
     John Porrett, steward.

publick charge repair and maintain the same so as the same be not within 6 yardes[172] of ~~these~~ a dwelling house nor nearer to the house than the comon sewer or water course.

John Cook mayor, Ra: Bunting, Ja: Cooke, Tho: Sutton, John Burdett, Will: Grundy, Wm Fleatham, Tho: Middleton, John Wells senior, Richd Mawer, Tho: Hodgshon, Tho: Sparrow, Geo: Corney, Geo: Hendry, Wm Gibson.

[p. 193] [*blank*]

[p. 194]
Burgus de Stockton. Curia capitallis cum visu franciplegii honer-atissimi ac reverendi in Christo patris Nathaniell domini episcopi Dunelm' Dom' Crew tenta ibidem sexto die Maii anno [regni] domini nostri Georgii nunc regis Magne Britanie &c quarto annoque domini 1718 coram Johanne Cooke armigero majore & Johanne Porrett generoso senescallo ibidem.[173]

Whereas to the great disgrace of the town severall dunghills are laid in the streett; ~~therefore~~ for the better preventing of the like nusances \for the future/ and for making the streets more commodious it is \now/ unanimously agreed by Mr Mayor the aldermen and burgesses of this burrough that all the whole burrough from the common shammells shall be paved; and for effecting of the same the moneys which shall yearly come to the said burrough shall be paid out in the paving of the said burrough untill it be wholly done and finished, and that the mayor for the time being shall have the direction ~~fo~~ of the same; alwayes provided that the smith shop at and adjoyning to the tolbooth be first purchased for the use of the said burrough. And whereas Mr William Gibson hath at his own expences lately paved before his front itt is likewise agreed that the said present mayor shall give him such recompence out of the said money or publick stock as he shall think fitt.
                                                                    John Cook, mayor

[*col. 1*] Wm Heron, Tho: Hodgshon, Wm Peacock, Thomas Sparrow, Anthony Coates, Geo: Corney, James Raisbeck, Tho: Heringson* his mark, Tho: Swinbank* mark, the mark of George Simpson*

---

172 Space preceding '6' contains what appears to be a superscript 'o'.
173 Head court, 6 May, 4 George I (1718); John Cooke, mayor, and John Porrett, steward.

[*col. 2*], Ra: Bunting, Ja: Cooke, John Wells, John Burdett, Will Grundy, Wm Fleatham, Tho: Middleton, John Wells senior, Walter Marshall.

[p. 195] [*blank*]

[p. 196]
Burgus de Stockton in Comitatu Dunelm
I Thomas Ogle, mayor of this burrough of Stockton, do swear
[*mayoral oath as above, p. 59*]   Tho: Ogle

Juratus in curia leet adjurnata usque ad hanc diem videlicet trices-
simum diem Septembris anno domini 1718 coram me Jo: Porrett
senescallo.[174]

[p. 197]
Burgus de Stockton. Curia capitallis cum visu francplegii honer-
atissimi ac reverendi in Christo patris Nathaniel domini episcopi
Dunelm' Dom' Crew tenta ibidem decimo quarto die Octobris anno
regnis domini nostri Georgii nunc regis Magne Britanie &c quinto
annoque 1718 coram Thome Ogle armigero majore & Johanne Porrett
generoso senescallo ibidem.[175]

Memorandum that this day John Cooke alderman late mayor of this
burrough of Stockton made and perfected his accounts to Thomas
Ogle Esq. present mayor and to the aldermen and cheife burgesses
of this burrough and upon that account which was seen and allowed
there remained due unto ~~them from~~ the said late mayor the full
& just sume of eight and twenty pounds and six pence which ~~he
hath~~ \is to be/ paid by the ~~hand of the~~ said present mayor or his
successors as money shall come in.

Tho: Ogle mayor, Ra: Bunting, Ja: Cooke,[176] John Wells, John Burdett,
Wm Gibson, Wm Fleatham, Tho: Middleton, Wm Heron, John Wells,

---

174 Sworn in court leet adjourned to 30 September 1718; John Porrett, steward.
175 Head court, 14 October, 5 George I (1718); Thomas Ogle, mayor, and John
     Porrett, steward.
176 In this year James Cooke was assessed, along with everyone else in the town,
     for his worth, which was house £60, land £48, stock £45 and cash £4 8s. 7d.
     (SRL, OOP 1718). He was probably the grandson of the James Cooke who
     was mayor in the 1640s. John Cooke was his brother (Bayley, 'Genealogical

Richd Mawer, Walter Marshall, Tho: Sparrow, Wm Peacock, Robt Fewler.

[p. 198]
Burgus de Stockton in Comitatu Dunelm'
I John Cook Esq. mayor of this burrough of Stockton do swear
[*mayoral oath as above, p. 59*]   John Cook

Juratus in curia leet adjurnata usque ad hanc diem videlicet sextum diem Octobris anno domini 1719 coram me Jo: Porrett senescallo.[177]

[p. 199]
Burgus de Stockton. Curia capitalis cum visu franciplegii honorat-issimi ac reverendi in Christo patris Nathaniel domini episcopi Dunelm' Dom' Crew tenta ibidem vicesimo die Octobris anno regni domini nostri Georgii nunc regis Magne Britanie &c sexto annoque domini 1719 coram Johanne Cook armigero majore & Johanne Porrett generoso senescallo ibidem.[178]

Memorandum that this day Thomas Ogle alderman late mayor of this burrough of Stockton made and perfected his accompts to John Cooke Esq. present mayor and to the aldermen and cheif burgesses of this burrough and upon that accompt which was seen and allowed there remains due unto the said late mayor the full and just sume of seventy five pounds fourteen shillings & four pence which is to be paid by the said present mayor or his successors as money shall come in.

John Cooke mayor

[*col. 1*] Tho: Sutton, Da^d Dowthwaite, Wm Gibson
[*col. 2*] Ra: Bunting, John Wells, John Burdett, Tho: Ogle, Tho: Middleton, John Wells senior, Wm Heron, James Raisbeck, Walter Marshall, Richd Mawer, Wm Peacock, Anthony Coates.[179]

Additions', p. 81) and in the same assessment was worth house £40, stock £35 and cash £2 5s. 2d.

177 Sworn in court leet adjourned to 6 October 1719; John Porrett, steward.
178 Head court, 20 October, 6 George I (1719); John Cooke, mayor, and John Porrett, steward.
179 The previous year's assessment gives the worth of the signatories James Raisbeck (house £30, stock £10 and cash 18s. 9d.) and William Dowthwaite (house £59): SRL, OOP 1718.

[p. 200]

Whereas an order of court was made the sixth day of May 1717 to impower the mayor for the time being to pave the burrough, itt is now by experience found that the late mayors have disbursed more in the said pavement than the income of the burrough. Wee therefore impower the present \mayor/ John Cooke Esq. mayor or any of his successors to continue the said pavement and to make two wells or pumps for the conveniency of the neighbours and that what is more disbursed shall be from time to time as the town dues become due be paid him or them with legall interest for the same. And further \whereas/ itt is found by experience that the frequent rejoycings are charged exorbently exorbitantly wee therefore limitt the said present mayor and his successors not to exceed thirty shillings at any one rejoycing.[180]

John Cooke mayor.

[*col. 1*] Tho: Sutton, Da[vi]d Dowthwaite, Wm Gibson

[*col. 2*] Ra: Bunting, John Wells, John Burdett, Tho: Ogle, Tho: Middleton, John Wells senior, Wm Heron, Walter Marshall, the mark of Thomas Sparrow,* Wm Peacock, Tho: Hodgshon, Anthony Coats.

[p. 201]

Burgus de Stockton in Comitatu Dunelm'.

I William Raisebeck mayor of this burrough of Stockton do swear [*mayoral oath as above, p. 59*]   Wm Raisbeck

Juratus in curia leet adjurnata usque ad hanc diem videlicet quartum diem Octobris anno domini 1720 coram me Jo: Porrett senescallo.[181]

[p. 202]

Burgus de Stockton in Comitatu Dunelm'. Curia capitalis cum visu franciplegii honoratissimi ac reverendi in Christo patris Nathaniel domini Crew episcopi Dunelm' Dom' Crew tenta ibidem decimo

---

180 It is not clear exactly what prompted this order. It may have been celebrations on completion of the paving of the High Street, to which the text refers. The corporation, like many others, would in future hold public celebrations at coronations, after famous victories such as Culloden and at civic events such as the visit of the duke of Wellington. Such rejoicings might take the form of public dinners, floating burning rafts on the river, and processions: for examples, see Heavisides, *Annals*, pp. 19, 56, 134, 186, 190, 193.

181 Sworn in court leet adjourned to 4 October 1720; John Porrett, steward.

octavo die Octobris anno regni domini nostri Georgii nunc regis Magne Britanie &c septimo annoque domini 1720 coram Willielmo Raisebeck armigero majore & Johanne Porrett generoso senescallo ibidem.[182]

Memorandum that this day John Cook alderman late mayor of this burrough of Stockton made and perfected his accompts to William Raisbeck Esq. present mayor and to the aldermen and cheife burgesses of this burrough and upon that accompt which was seen and allowed there remaines due unto the said late mayor the full and just sume of two hundred and thirty six pounds thre shillings and \ten pence/ which is to be paid by the said present mayor or his successors as money shall come in with legall interest for the same.

Item whereas there has been time beyond memory paid certain rates for deales, timber and other merchandize which from time to time have been imported into the River Tease as a due, duty and perquisite belonging to this antient burrough of Stockton and collected by the mayor for the times being or his officer. And whereas some persons who are burrough holders and freemen of the said burrough contrary to all reason and good nature and even to the duty and respect they owe to the said burrough as members thereof endeavour to infring the antient rights dutyes and privilidges thereof by refusing to pay the said dutyes and dues for such merchandizes so imported as aforesaid notwithstanding such persons importers and their ancestors have all along hithertofore paid the same. Wee therefore the mayor aldermen and burrough holders of the said antient burrough do hereby unanimously agree resolve and declare that wee and every of us respectively will to the utmost of our ability assert maintain and support our antient ~~port~~ burrough in these and all its just rights dues and privilidges and every [p. 203] particular branch thereof against all and every such person or persons whomsoever that doe or shall endeavour to invade and break the same or refuse to pay the same or any part thereof.

Item it is also hereby ordered and agreed that the smith's shop at the back of the tollbooth and the ground thereunto belonging mentioned in the lease thereof from the said lord bishop of Durham which is

---

182 Head court, 18 October, 7 George I (1720); William Raisbeck, mayor, and John Porrett, steward.

now taken in the name of Alderman John Cook, who hath sold the same unto us for the use of the burrough and is willing to assigne his whole interest therein unto us at our request or ~~and~~ to declare his trust therein for us accordingly, be inclosed or railed out at the pleasure of the present mayor.

Wm Raisbeck mayor

[*col. 1*] Wm Heron, Tho: Middleton, James Raisbeck, John Wells, Richd Mawer, Wm Peacock, Thomas Sparrow, Tho: Hodgshon, Mich^ll Paxton, the mark of George Simpson,* the mark of Thomas Harrison,* I C*,[183] the mark of Robert Catchaside*
[*col. 2*] Ra: Bunting, John Burdett, John Cook, Tho: Ogle, Tho: Sutton, Wm Gibson.

[p. 204]
Burgus de Stockton in Comitatu Dunelm
I John Cooke mayor of this burrough of Stockton do swear [*mayoral oath as above, p. 59*]   John Cooke

Juratus in curia leet vicessimo sexto die Octobris anno domini 1721 Coram me Jo: Porrett, senescallo[184]

[p. 205] [*blank*]

[p. 206]
Burgus de Stockton. Curia franciplegii sive curia leett honeratissimi ac reverendi in Christo patris Willielmi domini episcopi Dunelm' tenta ibidem vicesimo sexto die Octobris anno regni domini nostri Georgii nunc regis Magne Britanie &c octavo annoque domini 1721. Coram Johanne Cooke armigero majore & Johanne Porrett generoso senescallo ibidem.[185]

Memorandum that this day William Raisebeck alderman late mayor of this burrough of Stockton made and perfected his accompts to John Cooke Esq. present mayor and to the aldermen and cheif burgesses of this burrough and upon that accompt which seen was

---

183 Probably the mark of John Carter (see Appendix 5).
184 Sworn in court leet, 26 October 1721; John Porrett, steward.
185 Court leet, 26 October, 8 George I (1721); John Cooke, mayor, and John Porrett, steward.

seen and allowed there remained due to \from/ the said late mayor the full & just sume of twenty seaven pounds fourteen shillings and eight pence halfpenny which he hath this day paid to the said John Cooke Esq. present mayor in part of a debt of one hundred thirty six pounds thre shillings & tenn pence mentioned in foll. [*blank*]

John Cook mayor

[*col. 1*] Wm Heron, Tho: Middleton, John Wells, James Raisbeck, Richd Mawer, Walter Marshall, Tho: Hendry senior, Wm Peacock, Tho: Hodgshon, John Smurfit, John Turner, Richd Haw, John Fewler
[*col. 2*] Ra: Bunting, John Burdett, Tho: Ogle, Wm Raisbeck, Wm Gibson.

[p. 207]
Burgus de Stockton. Curia franciplegii sive curia leet honoratissimi ac reverendi in Christo patris Willielmi domini episcopi Dunelm' tenta ibidem decimo sexto die Octobris anno regni domini nostri Georgii nunc regis Magne Britannie &c nono annoque domini 1722. Coram Willielmo Gibson armigero majore & Johanne Porrett generoso senescallo ibidem.[186]

Memorandum that this day John Cook alderman late mayor of this burrough of Stockton made & perfected his accompts to William Gibson Esq. present mayor and to the aldermen & cheife burgesses of this burrough and upon that account which was seen & allowed there remains due to the said late mayor the full and just summe of one hundred & fifty two pounds eight shillings & 11¾ᵈ which is to be paid by the said present mayor or his successors as money shall come in with legall interest for the same.

Wm Gibson, mayor

[*col. 1*] Joh Turner, John Carter, Hy Dewer, Tho: Hodshon, John Fewler, Robt Catchasides
[*col. 2*] Ra: Bunting, John Burdett, Tho: Ogle, John Cook, William Raisbeck, Tho: Sutton, Wm Heron, Tho: Middleton, John Wells, Richd Mawer, Wm Peacock, James Hope, Ricd Haw, William Polwer,[187] Walter Ma[r]shell.

---

186 Court leet, 16 October, 9 George I (1722); William Gibson, mayor, and John Porrett, steward.
187 Reading uncertain.

[p. 208] [*blank*]

[p. 209]
Burgus de Stockton. Curia capitalis cum visu franciplegii honoratissimi ac reverendi in Christo patris Willielmi domini episcopi
Dunelm' tenta ibidem septimo die Maii anno regni domini Georgii
nunc regis Magne Britannie &c nono annoque domini 1723 coram
Willielmo Gibson armigero majore & Johanne Porrett generoso
senescallo ibidem.[188]

Whereas the severall persons hereafter named viz: James Cooke Esq.,
Nicholas Swainston Esq., Ralph Buntinge, John Burdett, William
Raisebeck, Thomas Ogle[189] aldermen, John Porrett, John Hendry,
Thomas Watson, David Dowthwaite, John Peacock and William Heron
gentlemen have (att the request of the present mayor) advanced &
paid unto John Cooke alderman the severall summs of tenn pounds
apeice for & towards reimburseing the said Alderman Cooke the
summe of 152^{li} 8^s 11¾^d (which by his account made to the said mayor
aldermen & other burgesses of this place the sixteenth day of October
~~next~~ last) appears to be justly due unto him from the burrough
holders. Itt is hereby unanimously agreed this day in full court and
hereby ordered that all and every of the said severall summes of
tenn pounds shall be paid unto the said severall persons who have
disburst the same as aforesaid or to their respective executors administrators or assignes & interest for the same ~~as aforesaid~~ from this
time by the respective mayors of this place for the time being as the
same as can be raised by & out of the profitts ariseing to the burrow
next & imediately after the remainder of the said debt of 152^{li} 8^s 11¾
be paid and discharged to the said Alderman Cooke. And whereas
the said present mayor in consideracion thereof hath promist to
disburse money for sinkeing & makeing a common draw well or
pump at or towards the north end of this burrow & doth not expect
to be reimburst the same till all the present debts of the burrow be
discharged itt is hereby likewise agreed and ordered that after the
aforesaid debts & another debt of 105^{li} 05^s which this day appears to
be also due to the said Alderman Cooke \\about the well// be all paid
with interest, then the said present mayor shall be likewise paid next

---

188   Head court, 7 May, 9 George I (1723); William Gibson, mayor, and John
    Porrett, steward.
189   Appears to be underlined in a different ink.

in course (what att the next counting day shall appear to be due unto him) with interest also for such his disbursements.

William Gibson, mayor

[*col. 1*] Thomas Hodshon, John Smurfit, Jas: Claxton
[*col. 2*] Ra: Bunting, Wm Raisbeck, John Hendry, Wm Heron, Tho: Middleton, John Wells, Richd Mawr, Wm Peacock, Walter Marshell, Jno: Vevers.

[p. 210] [*blank*]

[p. 211]
Burgus de Stockton. Curia capitalis cum visu franciplegii honer-atissimi ac reverendi in Christo patris Willielmi domini episcopi Dunelm' tenta ibidem decimo quinto die Octobris anno regni domini nostri Georgii nunc regis Magne Britannie &c decimo annoque domini 1723. Coram Willielmo Gibson armigero majore & Johanne Porrett generoso senescallo ibidem.[190]

Memorandum that this day William Gibson Esq. present mayor made and perfected his accompts to the aldermen and cheife burgesses of this burrow and upon that accompt which was seen and allowed there remained [......][191] in his hands the summe of twenty five pounds four shillings and threepence which he hath this day paid to John Cooke alderman in part of a greater summe.

Ra: Bunting, John Burdett, John Cook, Wm Raisbeck, Dad Dowthwaite, Tho: Middleton, John Wells, Edward Woodmast, Walter Marshell, Richard Haw, John Benton, John Turner, Wm Peacock, Tho: Sutton.

[p. 212]
Memorandum that this one & twentieth day of Aprill anno domini 1724 William Gibson Esq. present mayor hath this day delivered in an account under his hand of fifty two pounds five shillings & seven pence three farthings which he hath disbursed in or aboutt sinking of the north well which wee do agree shall be paid him in course with interest for the same from Michaelmas last.

---

190 Head court, 15 October, 10 George I (1723); William Gibson, mayor, and John
      Porrett, steward.
191 Ink blot.

Ra: Bunting, John Cook, Wm Raisbeck, Da^d Dowthwaite, Tho: Middleton, John Smurfutt, Richd Mawer, Wm Peacock, Walter Marshell, Jno: Turner, John Benton, Tho: Hodshon.

[p. 213] [*blank*]

[p. 214]
Burgus de Stockton. Curia capitalis cum visu franciplegii honora-tisimi ac reverendi in Christo patris Willielmi domini episcopi Dunelm' tenta ibidem vicesimo die Octobris anno regni domini nostri Georgii nunc regis Magne Britanie &c[192] annoque domini 1724 coram David Douthwaite armigero majore & Johanne Porrett generoso seneschallo ibidem.[193]

Memorandum that this day William Gibson alderman late mayor of this borough of Stockton made and perfected his accompts to David Douthwaite Esq. present mayor and to the aldermen and cheife burgesses of this burrough and upon that account which was seen and allowed there remained in his hands the summe of ten shillings and ~~ninepence~~ \\ten pence ha'penny// which he hath paid to the said present mayor.

[*col. 1*] Fra: Barker, Henry Brown, Geo: Sutton
[*col. 2*] David Dowthwaite mayor, Ra: Bunting, John Burdett, John Cook, Wm Raisbeck, Geo: White, Jon: Finch, Tho: Middleton, Wm Sutton, Edward Woodmats, Wm Peacock, John Smurfut, Wm Rayn, Tho: Hodshon, Richd Haw, Anthony Coates, John Benson.[194]

Memorandum that in the said last late Mr Mayor's account this day he hath paid to Alderman Cooke 17^li 4^s 8¾^d the ballance of his 152^li 8^s 11¾^d mentioned in folio 209,[195] and all interest due for the same.

Furthere was 110^li of it paid by eleven other persons at 10^li each as in folio 209. And said late mayor Mr Gibson paid as in his former account 25^li 04^s 03^d. But there is yet due & oweing to the said

---

192 The regnal year is missing.
193 Head court, 20 October, [11] George I (1724); David Dowthwaite, mayor, and John Porrett, steward.
194 Reading uncertain: could be 'Benton'.
195 Above, p. 130.

Alderman Cooke as in \said/ folio 209 the summe of 105^{li} 05^s 00^d about the well.[196]

[p. 215]
Whereas it is this twentieth day of October anno domini 1724 ~~if~~ in full court agreed by the mayor aldermen and cheife burgesses of this burrow of Stockton [*remainder of page blank*].

[p. 216] [*blank*]

[p. 217]
Burgus de Stockton. Curia capitalis cum visu franciplegii honer-atissimi ac reverendi in Christo patris Willielmi domini episcopi Dunelm' tenta ibidem decimo nono die Octobris anno regni domini nostri Georgii nunc regis Magne Britanie &c duodecimo annoque domini 1725 coram David Douthwaite armigero majore & Johanne Porrett generoso senescallo ibidem.[197]

Memorandum that this day David Douthwaite Esq. present mayor made and perfected his accompts to the aldermen and chiefe burgesses of this burrow and upon that account which was seen and allowed there remained due to him ~~the fulle sume of upon that accompt which was seen and allowed~~ the full summe of nine pounds three shillings and five pence halfe penny which is to be paide him in course.[198]

Wm Sutton

Ra: Bunting, John Burdett, Wm Raisbeck, Wm Gibson, Geo: White, John Hendry, Henry Brown, Tho: Middleton, William Wayn, Wm

---

196 In the margin, the calculation: '110–00–0 / 25–04–3 / 17–04–8¾ / 152–08–11¾'.
197 Head court, 19 October, 12 George I (1725); David Dowthwaite, mayor, and John Porrett, steward.
198 An indenture in 1725 between the bishop and David Dowthwaite and other key burgesses (Ralph Bunting, John Burdon, William Raisbeck, William Gibson, Alderman James Cooke, Alderman Nicholas Swainston, Robert Wilton, John Henry, George White, merchant, Francis Barker, merchant, James Dunning, mariner, John Peacock, mariner, Henry Brown and Thomas Middleton, barber) conferred River Tees conservancy rights. The bishop had now largely lost his Palatine powers, but not his conservancy of the River Tees: Sowler, *History*, pp. 303–4.

Heron, Edward Woodmast, Jon: Finch, Wm Peacock, John Smurfutt, Gilbert Cutts.

[p. 218] [*blank*]

[p. 219]
Burgus de Stockton. Curia capitalis cum visu franciplegii reverendi in Christo patris Willielmi domini episcopi Dunelm' tenta ibidem tertio die Maii anno regni domini nostri Georgii nunc regis Magne Britanie &c duodecimo annoque domini 1726. Coram Davido Dowthwaite armigero majore et Johanne Porrett generoso seneschallo ibidem.[199]

Whereas by an order in this book dated ~~that~~ the seaventh day of May 1723 it appears that this burrough was then indebted unto Mr John Cooke alderman now deceased a considerable summe of money which he disbursed for the said burrough and whereas it is now alledged that fifty pounds sixteen shillings and ~~eight~~ \nine/ pence thereof was money due to John Parkinson the paver for worke done for the burrough, & Nicholas Swainston Esq. and William Scarbrough gentleman administrators of the said Mr Cooke being willing that the said 50^li 16^s 9^d or what is due to the said John Parkinson shall be paid unto him in the first place out of the said summe so due to the said Mr Cooke, it is hereby agreed in full court that the said money or so much thereof as shall appeare due to the said Parkinson upon staiteing their accounts shall be paid to him or his assigns accordingly as the same can be raised in course out of the profitts ariseing out of the said burrough he or they procureing proper discharges for the same from the said administrators.

Da^d Dowthwaite mayor

[*col. 1*] Geo: White, John Hendry, Tho: Middleton, Jno: Finch, Wm Heron, Richd Marr, Wm Peacock, Edward Woodmats, Gilbert Cutts, Ralph Wayare
[*col. 2*] John Smurfut, John Turner, Thos Alderson, John Carter
[*col. 3*] Wm Gibson, Jno: Peacock, Jo: Porrett.

[p. 220] [*blank*]

---

199   Head court, 3 May, 12 George I (1726); David Dowthwaite, mayor, and John Porrett, steward.

[p. 221]
Burgus de Stockton in Comitatu Dunelm'
I John Burdett mayor of this burrough of Stockton do swear [*mayoral oath as above p. 59*]   John Burdett

Juratus curia leet adjurnata usque ad hanc diem videlicet quartum diem Octobris anno domini 1726 coram me Jo: Porrett senescallo.[200]

[p. 222] [*blank*]

[p. 223]
Burgus de Stockton. Curia capitalis cum visu franciplegii honoratissimi ac reverendi in Christo patris Willielmi domini episcopi Dunelm' tenta ibidem decimo octavo die Octobris anno regni domini nostri Georgii nunc regis Magne Britanie &c decimo tertio annoque domini 1726 coram Johanne Burdett armigero majore et Johanne Porrett generoso senescallo ibidem.[201]

Memorandum that this day David Douthwaite alderman late mayor of this burrough of Stockton made and perfected his accompts to John Burdett Esq. present mayor and to the aldermen and cheife burgesses of this burrough and upon that accompt which was seen and allowed there remained in the said late mayor's hand the summe of fifteen pounds and four pence halfe penny over and above fifty pounds sixteen shillings and nine pence which said fifteen pounds and four pence halfepenny is now paid into the present mayor's hands and the said fifty pounds sixteen shillings and nine pence is to be lodged in his hands and paid to John Parkinson upon proper discharges from the administrators of Alderman Cooke deceased pursuant to former orders.

                                  John Burdett, mayor

[*col. 1*] Fra: Barker, Henry Brown, John Finch, Tho: Middleton, Gilbert Cutts, Thos Alderson, John Turner
[*col. 2*] Ra: Bunting, Wm Raisbeck, Wm Gibson, Jno: Peacock, Ja: Dunning, John Hendry, Wm Sutton.

---

200 Sworn in court leet adjourned to 4 October 1726; John Porrett, steward.
201 Head court, 18 October, 13 George I (1726); John Burdett, mayor, and John Porrett, steward.

[p. 224]
November the 8th anno domini 1726

Whereas severall merchants and masters of ships or other vessels and certaine other persons have of late refused to pay anchorage & plankgage and other antient duties due unto us or this our burrow of Stockton for importation of cornes deals timber and other merchandizes into this River Tease it is hereby unanimously agreed and order'd in full court that the said Mr Mayor \for the time being/ doe cause the money so due from such offenders (or to become due) from \them or/ any other the like offenders to be demanded of them and upon refusall that he forthwith cause the person and persons so refuseing to be prosecuted for the same as he shall be advised by councell; and the better to enable him to proceed herein wee doe hereby promise that he shall be thankfully reimbursed all his just or reasonable expences in and about the recovering & defending these our just rights dues or priviledges. Witness our hands the day and year above said.

John Burdett, mayor

[col. 1] Fra: Barker, Henry Brown, Tho: Middleton, John Finch, Gilbert Cutts, Thos Alderson, John Turner
[col. 2] Ra: Bunting, Wm Raisbeck, Wm Gibson, Da^d Dowthwaite, Jno: Peacock, Ja: Dunning, John Hendry, Wm Sutton.

[p. 225]
Burgus de Stockton in Comitatu Dunelm'.
I John Burdett mayor of this burrough of Stockton do swear [*mayoral oath as above p. 59*]   John Burdett

Juratus in curia leet adjurnata usque ad hanc diem videlicet tertium diem Octobris anno domini 1727 coram me Jo: Porrett senescallo.[202]

[p. 226]
Burgus de Stockton. Curia capitalis cum visu franciplegii reverendi in Christo patris Willielmi domini episcopi Dunelm' tenta ibidem decimo septimo die Octobris anno regni domini nostri Georgii secundi nunc regis Magne Britanie &c primo annoque domini 1727.

---

202 Sworn in court leet adjourned to 3 October 1727; John Porrett, steward.

Coram Johanne Burdett armigero majore et Johanne Porrett generoso senescallo ibidem.[203]

Memorandum that this day John Burdett Esq. present mayor made and perfected his accounts to the aldermen and cheife burgesses of this burrow and upon that account which was seen and allowed there remained in his hands seventeen pounds one shilling and eight pence three farthings ten pounds whereof he is to pay to Mr John Peacock's executrix or administratrix and the remainder to keep in his hands 'till the next accompting day.

Wm Sutton, Wm Raisbeck, Wm Gibson, Da^d Dowthwaite, John Hendry, Geo: Sutton, Edwd Woodmast, John Finch, Wm Peacock, Wm Wayn, Gilbert Cutts, Joseph Claxton, Wm Preston, Thos Alderson, Ralf Waire, Richd Haw.

[p. 227]
Burgus de Stockton. Curia capitalis cum visu franciplegii honoratissimi ac reverendi in Christo patris Willielmi domini episcopi Dunelm' tenta ibidem decimo quinto die Octobris anno regni domini nostri Georgii secundi nunc regis Magne Britanie &c secundo. Coram Johanne Finche armigero \deputy/ majore et Johanne Porrett generoso senescallo ibidem.[204]

Memorandum that this day John Burdett alderman late mayor of this burrough of Stockton made and perfected his accompts to John Finch Esq. present mayor and to the aldermen and cheife burgesses of this burrough and upon that accompt which was seen and allowed there remained in the said late mayor's \hands/ the summe of thirty nyne pounds eighteen shillings and six pence halfe penny which he hath now paid into the hands of the \said/ present mayor out of which said Mr Mayor is to pay to James Cooke Esq. ten pounds and to Mr Scarborough what interest appeares to be due to him as executor \or administrator/ to Mr John Cooke \late/ alderman deceased.

John Finch

[*col. 1*] William Cutts, Joseph Claxton

---

203 Head court, 17 October, 1 George II (1727); John Burdett, mayor, and John Porrett, steward.
204 Head court, 15 October, 2 George II (1728); John Finche, mayor, and John Porrett, steward.

[*col. 2*] Wm Raisbeck, Wm Gibson, Da[d] Dowthwaite, Geo: White, Henry Brown, John Henry, Tho: Raisbeck, Geo: Sutton, Wm Sutton, Wm Heron, Wm Preston, Edwd Woodmast, Thos Alderson, Gilbert Cutts.

Memorandum his oath is upon the file.[205]

[p. 228] [*blank*]

[p. 229]

Burgus de Stockton. Memorandum that this 25th day of November anno domini 1729 Mrs Ann Finch widow and executrix of John Finch Esq. deceased our late mayor of this burrough of Stockton made up & perfected his accompts to William Sutton Esq. present mayor, and to the aldermen and cheife burgesses of this burrough, and upon that accompt, which was seen and allowd, there remained in the said deceased mayor's hands, the summe of £12 11s. which she his said widow hath now paid into the hands of the said present mayor.

Wm Sutton mayor,[206] Wm Raisbeck, Da[d] Dowthwaite, John Burdett, Henry Brown, Wm Barker, Geo: Sutton, Wm Heron, Marmad[uke] Swainston, Tho: Middleton, Wm Preston, Thos Alderson, Gilbert Cutts.

[p. 230]

Burgus de Stockton. Memorandum that this 4th day of May anno 1731 William Sutton Esq. present mayor made & perfected his accompts to Michaelmas last, to the aldermen and cheife burgages of this burrough and upon that accompt which is now seen & allowd there remaines due \to/ him seven pounds three shillings and eleven pence which is to be paid him in course which besides seventy which was borrowd of Alderman Dowthwaite, Mr Henry Brown, Mr George Sutton, Mr William Barker, Mr George White, Mr Thomas Troy and Mr Mayor himselfe at ten pounds each, which is likewise agreed to be paid to them in course with interest, which summe was advanced towards the building the custom house.[207]

---

205 Written in bottom left-hand corner of the page.

206 William Sutton was the son of Thomas Sutton, mayor in 1708: Surtees, *History*, p. 174.

207 'which summe … custom house' added in a different hand.

The abovesaid 7–3:– 8^d being to be carryed to his next year's accompt.

Ra: Bunting, Wm Raisbeck, Wm Gibson, Da^d Dowthwaite, Marma^d Swainston, Tho: Middleton, Wm Heron, Thomas Alderson, John Carter, William Cutts, Wm Preston, Richd Haw, Ralph Ware, Joseph Claxton.

[p. 231]
Burgus de Stockton. Memorandum that this nyneteenth day of October anno domini 1731 William Sutton alderman late mayor of this burrough of Stockton made [&] perfected his accompts to Henry Brown Esq. present mayor and to the aldermen and cheife burgesses of this burrough and upon that accompt which was seen and allowed there remained in the said late mayor's hand the sum of 45^{li} which he hath now ~~paid~~ \transferd/ to the said present mayor ~~Besides~~ the same^{208} being included in three bills from Mr David Dowthwaite 37–0–2½, from James Cooke Esq. 10^{li} 11^s 2¼^d & from Mr James Dunning 5–14–1½, makeing together the sum of 53^{li} – 5 – 6¼ being so much allowd to them by the burrow on account of the workhouse for which the overseers of the poore are to give security to the present mayor. Out of which when received Mr Mayor is to pay to the said late mayor 8^{li} 5^s 6^d.

Henry Brown mayor, Ra: Bunting, Wm Raisbeck, Wm Gibson, Marma^d Swainston, Wm Barker, Tho: Middleton, Wm Heron, William Cutts, Richd Haw, Gilbert Cutts, Joseph Claxton, Wm Preston, Thos Alderson, John Carter, John Gowland.

[p. 232]
Borough of Stockton. The court leet with the view of frankpledge of the right reverend father in God Edward lord bishop of Durham held at Stockton on the seventeenth day of October in the sixth year of the reign of King George the second and in the year of our Lord 1732 before Henry Brown Esq. mayor and John Porrett ~~Gent~~ gentleman steward.

Memorandum that this day Henry Brown Esq. present mayor made and perfected his accounts to Michaelmas last to the aldermen and cheif burgesses and upon that accompt which was seen and allowed

---

208 Change of hand from 'same' to end of paragraph.

there remained due to him the summe of thirteen[209] ~~nine~~ pounds seventeen shillings and [ten][210] pence which is to [be] allowed in his next year's accompt.
13 – 17 – 10[211]

Ra: Bunting, William Gibson, Wm Sutton, Marma^d Swainston, Tho Middleton, Wm Heron, Joseph Claxton, Gilbert Cutts, Ralph Ware* mark, John Gowland, Wm Preston, Thomas Wright, Thos Alderson, Jacob Talor, John Carter, James Marshal, Wm Barker.

[p. 233]
Borough of Stockton. The court leet with the view of frankpledge of the right reverend father in God Edward lord bishop of Durham held at Stockton the sixteenth day of October in the seventh year of the reign of King George the second and in the year of our Lord 1733. Before John Burdett Esq. mayor and Edmund Bunting gentleman steward.[212]

This day Henry Brown alderman late mayor of this burrough of Stockton made and perfected his accompts to John Burdett Esq. present mayor and to the alderman and cheife burgesses of this burrough and upon that accompt which was seen and allowed there remained due to him the summe of one pound eleven shillings and ninepence farthing which must be paid in course.

John Burdett mayor, Ra: Bunting, William Gibson, Wm Sutton, Marma^d Swainston, Tho: Middleton, Wm Heron, Wm Preston, Joseph Claxton, Gilbert Cutts, Ralph Ware *mark, John Gowland, Thomas Wright, Thos Alderson, John Carter, Jacob Talor, James Marshal, Wm Barker, Geo: Sutton.

[p. 234]
Borough of Stockton. The court leet with the view of frankpledge of the right reverend father in God Edward lord bishop of Durham

---

209 Changed from 'thirty'.
210 The figure has been changed from 'eight', though 'ten' (the reading suggested by the marginal entry) is far from clear.
211 Unusually, this amount is written in the left margin.
212 Edmund Bunting, a solicitor, was appointed bishop's steward in 1732, succeeding John Porrett, and apparently serving until 1764: Richmond, *Local Records*, p. 61; Bayley, 'Genealogical Additions', p. 84.

held at Stockton the fifteenth day of October and continued by adjournment to the fifth day of November in the year of our Lord one thousand seven hundred and thirty four before Ralph Bunting Esq. mayor and Edmund Bunting gentleman steward.

This day John Burdett alderman late mayor of this borough of Stockton who in the year of his mayoralty removed to the City of London did by letter request that his accounts might be passed to the satisfaction of the present mayor and to the aldermen and cheif burgesses of this borough and upon that account which was seen and allowed and there remained due to borough the sum of two pounds seventeen shillings and nine pence which sum was agreed to be allowed him for his extraordinary expences.

Ra: Bunting mayor, Wm Sutton, Henry Brown, Marma^d Swainston, Wm Heron, Tho Middleton, John Gowland, John Carter, Joseph Claxton, James Marshal, Jacob Taylor, Thomas Wright, Wm Preston.

[p. 235]
Borough of Stockton. The court leet with the view of frankpledge of the right reverend father in God Edward lord bishop of Durham held at Stockton the fourteenth day of October in the ninth year of the reign of King George the second and in the year of our Lord 1735 before David Dowthwaite Esq. mayor and Edmund Bunting gentleman steward.

This day Ralph Bunting[213] alderman late mayor of this borough of Stockton made and perfected his accounts to David Dowthwaite Esq. present mayor and to the aldermen and chief burgesses of this borough and upon that account which was seen and allowed the ballance to the borough appeared nine pounds eighteen shillings and ten pence which is ordered by the court to be paid to Mr William Scarborough for in part of interest due to him and which was accordingly paid to Mr Edmund Bunting for his use.

David Dowthwaite, mayor

---

213 Ralph Bunting died in 1745, aged eighty-six, and was buried in Stockton St. Thomas churchyard with his wife Anne and other family members: Brewster, *History*, p. 322 (which gives the inscription). Surtees states that he and Anne (who died in 1746) were married for sixty-two years and had eleven children, of whom only one survived them: Surtees, *History*, p. 185.

[*col. 1*] Joseph Claxton, Richd Haw, Thos Alderson, Thomas Wright [*col. 2*] Wm Gibson, Wm Sutton, Henry Brown, Wm Barker, Marma^d Swainston, Tho: Middleton, Jno: Richmond, Gilbert Cutts, Wm Preston, Jame[s] Marshal, John Carter.

[p. 236]
Borough of Stockton. The court of the right reverend father in God Edward lord bishop of Durham held there by adjournment the ninth day of March in the ninth year of the reign of King George the second and in the year of our Lord one thousand seven hundred and thirty five before David Dowthwaite Esq. mayor and Edmund Bunting gentleman steward.

Whereas the said lord bishop of Durham lord of this borough did by indenture of lease under his common seal bearing date on or about the first day of September in the sixth year of his said present Majesty's reign for himself and his successors devise and grant unto Henry Brown Esq. then mayor, Ralph Bunting alderman and others therein named their executors administrators and assignes for the use and benefit of the cheif officers and the rest of the burgesses of Stockton aforesaid for the time being all that smith's shop situate in Stockton aforesaid adjoining to the tollbooth there and also all that peice or parcell of waste ground thereunto adjoining containing from east to west sixteen yards or thereabouts and from north to south twelve yards or thereabouts together with all and singular profitts commodities advantages and appurtenances thereunto belonging for and during the term of twenty one years from thenceforth next ensuing at and under the yearly rent of fourpence payable as in the said lease is mentioned. And whereas the said smith's shop being ruinous and decayed and of small yearly value and no advantage hath been made of the adjoining ground hitherto tho' when the same was purchased it was with an intent to be built in such manner as to be ornamental to the said borough as well as an advantage to the inhabitants thereof, but the borough at present having no publick [p. 237] money in bank and the said burgesses for the advantage of the said borough being desirous to have the said ground built upon, are willing to accept proposals for that ende. And whereas David Dowthwaite Esq. present mayor, William Sutton and Henry Brown aldermen, Edmund Bunting and William Barker[214] gentlemen have

214 William Barker, corn merchant, was one of the merchants who funded the construction of the Town House: see Tom Sowler, *Town House, Stockton-on-Tees*

proposed to take down the said smith's shop and to advance and lay
out a considerable sum of money in erecting and building a dwell-
inghouse for the sergeant, with convenient cellars and a place for
setting the markett stalls in, which now stand exposed in the street,
and also to make several convenient shops and above them a large
room for the entertainment of the mayor aldermen and burgesses,
as they shall have occasion suitable to a plan now produced in court
which will be very uniform and ornamental to the said borough and
also at their own charge will renew the lease of the said lord bishop
of Durham and his successors as occasion shall require, and at the
end of twenty one years deliver up to the said burgesses in court
the said lease and peaceable possession of all the said premises or
assign the same in such manner as councell shall advise for the
use and benefit of the mayor aldermen and burgesses of the said
borough, provided they the said David Dowthwaite, William Sutton,
Henry Brown, Edmund Bunting and William Barker their executors
administrators or assignes may have the liberty to renew the said
lease in their own names or in the name of any other person or
persons in trust for them and to hold and enjoy the said premises
so to be erected and built for the said term of twenty one years and
receive the rents and profitts thereof to their own uses and benefitts
without any account to be given for the same to the said burgesses.
Therefore it is hereby in full court unanimously consented to and
agreed upon and wee do order that the said David Dowthwaite,
William Sutton, Henry Brown, Edmund Bunting and William [p. 238]
Barker their executors administrators or assignes have full power
and authority to surrender up the present lease and may apply for
and renew the same for twenty one years in their own names or in
the name of any person or persons in trust for them and hold and
enjoy the same accordingly towards reimbursing the money to be
laid out in building and the charges of renewing the said lease as
occasion shall require and for their trouble and hazard in and about
the same and take down the said smith's shop and erect and build

for an account of the Town House's development, and Brewster, *History*,
pp. 233–5 and 428–30 for comments on the court order, financing and design
and structure. In 1740, Barker was embroiled in popular unrest in the town,
sparked by grain shortages and high prices following a bad winter. There
was also unrest in other ports. His windows had been broken, he had feared
for his life, and his boatload of wheat was seized. The incident was ended
when a large contingent of troops was brought in: Richmond, *Local Records*,
p. 63.

in such manner as before mentioned or in some other uniform and convenient manner and lett and demise the same as they shall think proper during the said term of twenty one years and receive the rents issues and profitts thereof to their own uses without any account to be given to the said burgesses of the said borough for the same. And it is also unanimously agreed upon and ordered for their security, and that the cellars may be dugg and the building carryed on with greater expedition, that untill this present lease can be renewed the same for the residue of the term therein mentioned and the several persons therein mentioned. And the several persons therein named as lessees shall be in trust and hold the same to and for the several uses intents and purposes before mentioned and to and for no other use intent or purpose whatsoever.

David Douthwaite, mayor

[col. 1] Jas Raisbeck, Willm Fowler, Jacob Taylor* his mark, John Carter* his mark, Thomas Wright, Francis Eden serjeant
[col. 2] William Sutton, Ed: Bunting, Marmad Swainston, Tho Middleton, John Richmond, Thomas Alderson, Ralf Ware* his mark, Wm Preston, Ricd Haw, Joseph Claxton, Gilbert Cutts
[col. 3] Henry Brown, Wm Barker.

[p. 239] [blank]

[p. 240]
Borough of Stockton. The court leet with the view of frankpledge of the right reverend father in God Edward lord bishop of Durham held at Stockton the nineteenth day of October in the tenth year of the reign of King George the second and in the year of our Lord 1736 before James Raisbeck Esq. mayor and Ralph Bradley[215] deputy of Edmund Bunting gentleman steward.

This day David Dowthwaite alderman late mayor of this borough of Stockton made and perfected his accounts to James Raisbeck Esq. present mayor and to the aldermen and cheif burgesses of this borough and upon that account which was seen and allowed

215 If this is Ralph Bradley (1717–88), a solicitor who specialised in conveyancing, he would have been nineteen years old when he became the steward's deputy: see Richmond, Local Records, p. 88; Brewster, History, pp. 359–66; Surtees, History, p. 196.

the ballance to the borough appeared one pound eighteen shillings which was paid to the said present mayor accordingly.

Ja^s Raisbeck mayor[216]

[*col. 1*] Tho: Raisbeck, Wm Barker

[*col. 2*] Ra: Bunting, William Gibson, Wm Sutton, Henry Brown, Marma^d Swainston, Tho Middleton, Jno: Richmond, Wm Preston, Gilbert Cutts, Joseph Claxton, Richd Haw, James Marshal, Thos Alderson.

[p. 241]
Borough of Stockton. The court leet with the view of frankpledge of the right reverend father in God Edward lord bishop of Durham held at Stockton the eighteenth day of October in the eleventh year of the reign of King George the second and in the year of our Lord 1737 before Thomas Raisbeck Esq. mayor and Edmund Bunting gentleman steward.

This day James Raisbeck alderman late mayor of this borough of Stockton made and perfected his accounts to Thomas Raisbeck Esq. present mayor and to the aldermen and chief burgesses of this borough and upon that account which was seen and allowed the ballance to the borough appeared thirteen shillings and sevenpence which was paid to the said present mayor accordingly.[217]

Thos Raisbeck, mayor

[*col. 1*] Thomas Wright, the mark of Augustine Perkin,* Jacob Harrison

[*col. 2*] Ra: Bunting, Wm Sutton, Henry Brown, Marma^d Swainston, Tho Middleton, Jno: Longhorn,[218] John Richmond, Richd Haw, James Marshal, John Carter, Wm Preston, George Coser, Thos Alderson, Ralf Ware.

---

216 James Raisbeck and Thomas Raisbeck, who was mayor the following year, were both sons of William Raisbeck, mayor in 1720: Surtees, *History*, pp. 173–4.

217 Richmond (*Local Records*, p. 62) states that in this year 1737 a payment of £2 10s. was made to James Marshal for 'lettering books' and that this was the earliest evidence for a bookseller in the town. It also suggests that there were more detailed borough accounts that have not survived.

218 John Longhorn (d. 1758, aged seventy-three) was a merchant and trustee of the nonconformist meeting house: Richmond, *Nonconformity*, p. 12.

[p. 242]
Borough of Stockton. The court le\e/t with the view of frankpledge of the right reverend father in God Edward lord bishop of Durham held at Stockton the seventeenth day of October in the twelfth year of the reign of King George the second and in the year of our Lord 1738 before Thomas Raisbeck Esq. mayor and Edmund Bunting gentleman steward.

This day Thomas Raisbeck Esq. present mayor made and perfected his accounts to Michaelmas last to the aldermen and chief burgesses and upon that account which was seen and allowed there remained ballance due in his hands thirty pounds twelve shillings and five pence farthing including a bill drawn by Mr James \Dunning/ upon the overseers for the poor of Stockton for the sum of sixteen pounds yet undischarged.

[*col. 1*] Jacob Harrison, George Coser, Joseph Claxton
[*col. 2*] Ra: Bunting, Wm Sutton, Henry Brown, Jas Raisbeck, Marma^d Swainston, Tho Middleton, Jno Longhorn, Wm Preston, Thos Alderson, John Carter, Ralf Ware, Austin Parkin,* Richd Haw.

[p. 243]
17th October 1738

It \is/ this day unanimously agreed in full court that for the future every mayor of this burrough upon making up his accounts shall if he entertains at his court days in the publick room be allowed for such entertainments the sum of fifteen pounds if otherwise to have the former allowances.

Tho: Raisbeck mayor, Ra: Bunting, Wm Sutton, Henry Brown, Jas Raisbeck, Marma^d Swainston, Tho Middleton, Jno: Longhorn, Wm Preston, Thos Alderson, John Carter, Ralf Ware, Austin Parkin, Jacob Harrison, Rich Haw, Joseph Claxton, George Coser.

[p. 244]
Borough of Stockton. The court leet with the view of frankpledge of the right reverend father in God Edward lord bishop of Durham held at Stockton the twenty third day of October in the thirteenth year of the reign of King George the second and in the year of our Lord 1739 before Jonathan Troy Esq. mayor and Edmund Bunting gentleman steward.

This day Thomas Raisbeck alderman late mayor of this borough of Stockton made and perfected his accounts to Jonathan Troy Esq. present mayor and to the aldermen and chief burgesses of this borough and upon that account which was seen and allowed the ballance to the borough appeared twenty three pound nineteen shillings and eight pence which was paid to the present mayor accordingly.

[*col. 1*] Jacob Harrison, George Coser
[*col. 2*] Wm Gibson, Wm Sutton, Henry Brown, Jas Raisbeck, Marma^d Swainston, Tho Middleton, Jno Richmond, Wm Preston, John Gowland, Richd Haw, Thos Alderson, John Carter* his mark, Ralf Ware* his mark, Austin Parkin* his mark.

[p. 245]
23rd October 1739

Whereas David Dowthwaite of Stockton aforesaid merchant and one of the aldermen of this borough hath for several years last past refused to pay the ancient and accustomed dutys due unto us or this our borough of Stockton for the importation of timber and other merchandize into the port of Stockton aforesaid and we being resolved to maintain and support this ancient borough in all its just rights dues privileges and perquisites to the utmost of our power, it is therefore hereby unanimously agreed and ordred in full court that Mr Mayor for the time being do cause the said David Dowthwaite to be prosecuted for the same as the said Mr Mayor shall be advised by councel in order to compel the said David Dowthwaite to pay what is so strictly due and unjustly detained. And the better to enable the said Mr Mayor to proceed therein we do hereby promise that he shall be thankfully reimbursed out of the perquisites of the said borough all costs damages and expences that he shall be put unto or that shall be ~~occasioned~~ occasioned in and about the recovering and defending these ~~un~~ just and undoubted rights dutys and priviledges. As witness our hands the day and year above said.

[*col. 1*] Jonath' Troy, Ra: Bunting, Wm Sutton, Henry Brown, Jas Raisbeck, Thos Raisbeck
[*col. 2*] Marma^d Swainston, Tho Middleton, Jacob Harrison, Wm Preston, Jno Richmond, Rich Haw, John Gowland, Jno: Longhorn, George Coser.

[p. 246]
Burrough of Stockton. The court leet with the view of frankpledge of
the right reverend father in God Edward lord bishop of Durham held
at Stockton aforesaid the fourteenth day of October in the thirteenth
year of the reign of King George the second and in the year of our
Lord 1740 before Jonathan Troy Esq. mayor and Peter Dunning
deputy of Edmund Bunting steward.

This day Jonathan Troy Esq. present mayor made and perfected his
accounts to Michaelmass last and upon that account which was seen
and allowed there remained ballance due in his hands the sum of
twenty two pounds seventeen shillings.

[*col. 1*] Edwd Woodmast, John Benton, George Coser, the mark of
Ralph Ware,* John Carter* his mark.
[*col. 2*] Wm Sutton, Ra: Bunting, Henry Brown, Jas Raisbeck, Thos
Raisbeck, Marma^d Swainston, Tho Middleton, Jno Richmoned, Wm
Preston, Anthony Coates, John Gowland, Jno: Longhorn, William
Fowler.

[p. 247]
Burrough of Stockton. The court leet with the view of frank pledge of
the right reverend father in God Edward lord bishop of Durham held
at Stockton aforesaid the fourteenth day of April in the year of our
Lord 1741 before Jonathan Troy Esq. mayor and Edmund Bunting
gentleman steward.

Whereas several masters of ships have of late refused to pay the
ancient dues of anchorage and plankage, it is this day agreed in full
court that a demand be made of all such persons as are in arrear
and such as deny to pay shall be prosecuted as councel shall advise
and we will chearfully and thankfully reimburse the present or any
future mayor all such sum or sums of money as shall be expended in
the support of these ancient and indisputable rights of this burrough.

As witness our hands

Jonath' Troy mayor
[*col. 1*] Wm Preston, John Benton, John Carter, George Coser
[*col. 2*] Ra: Bunting, Henry Brown, Jas Raisbeck, Marma^d Swainston,
Tho Middleton, John Richmond, Anthony Coates, Jno: Longhorn,
Gilbert Cutts, Ralph Ware,* John Gowland.

[p. 248]
Burrough of Stockton. The court leet with the view of frank pledge of the right reverend father in God Edward lord bishop of Durham held at Stockton aforesaid the twentieth day of October in the fifteenth year of the reign of King George the second and in the year of our Lord 1741 before William Sutton Esq. mayor and Edmund Bunting gentleman steward.

This day Jonathan Troy alderman late mayor of this burrough of Stockton made and perfected his accounts to William Sutton Esq. present mayor and to the aldermen and chief burgesses of this burrough and upon that account which was seen and allowed the ballance to the burrough appeared to be sixteen pound nine shillings and nine pence which was paid to the present mayor accordingly.

William Sutton mayor

[*col. 1*] Jno: Cottingham, Tho Middleton, John Richmond, Anthony Coates, William Fowler, John Benton, Gilbert Cutts, John Gowland, Jno: Longhorn, Edwd Woodmast, Jacob Harrison, John Carter, Ralph Ware
[*col. 2*] Henry Brown, Jas Raisbeck, Thos Raisbeck.

[p. 249]
Burrough of Stockton. The court leet with the view of frank pledge of the right reverend father in God Edward lord bishop of Durham held at Stockton aforesaid the nineteenth day of October in the year of our Lord 1742 before James Raisbeck Esq. mayor and Edmund Bunting gentleman steward.

This day William Sutton alderman late mayor of this burrough of Stockton made and perfected his accounts to James Raisbeck Esq. present mayor and to the aldermen and chief burgesses of this burrough and upon that account which was seen and allowed the ballance to the burrough appeared to be fifteen pounds nineteen shillings and seven pence which was paid to the present mayor accordingly.

James Raisbeck mayor, Ra: Bunting, Wm Gibson, Henry Brown, Thos Raisbeck, Jonath' Troy, Wm Metcalf, John Benton, Joseph Claxton, Isaac Todd.

[p. 250]

Burrough of Stockton. The court leet with view of frank pledge of the right reverend father in God Edward lord bishop of Durham held at Stockton aforesaid the eighteenth day of October in the year of our Lord 1743 before William Sleigh Esq. mayor and Mr Ralph Bradley deputy of Edmund Bunting gentleman steward.

This day James Raisbeck alderman late mayor of this burrough of Stockton made and ~~performed~~ perfected his accounts to William Sleigh Esq. \present/ mayor and to the aldermen and chief burgesses of this burrough and upon that account which was seen and allowed there remained or appeared to be due to him \the said James Raisbeck/ the sum of twenty four pounds seven shillings and one penny which must be paid in course.

W: Sleigh, mayor

[*col. 1*] The mark of John Carter*
[*col. 2*] Wm Sutton, Henry Brown, Thos Raisbeck, Jonath: Troy, Isaac Todd, John Richmond, Thos Ware, William Fowler, George Coser, Christopher Tweedy, Robt Deighton, Gilbert Cutts, Richd Haw, John Benton, Ralph Ware.

[p. 251] [*blank*]

[p. 252]

Burrough of Stockton.

The court of the right reverend father in God Edward lord bishop of Durham held there by adjournment this thirty first day of January in the seventeenth year of the reign of King George the second and in the year of our Lord one thousand seven hundred and forty three before William Sleigh Esq. mayor and Edmund Bunting gentleman steward.

WHEREAS at a court held the ninth day of March in the ninth year of the reign of King George the second and in the year of our Lord one thousand seven hundred and thirty five, it was amongst other things in full court unanimously consented and agreed unto by the mayor aldermen and burgesses for the improveing and beautifying the said burrough of Stockton aforesaid and for the errecting and building a dwelling house for the serjeant and a large room for the use of the mayor aldermen and burgesses as often as occasion requires AND WHEREAS the burrough at that time not haveing any publick

money in bank it was therefore consented and agreed unto by the said
burgesses that David Douthwaite Esq. then mayor, William Sutton
and Henry Brown aldermen, Edmund Bunting and William Barker
gentleman according to proposalls then made shou'd have the sole
management and charge of the said building and advance and lay out
of their own proper money respectively such sums of money as was
necessary for building and carrying on the same AND WHEREAS
the said David Douthwaite, William Sutton, Henry Brown, Edmund
Bunting and William Barker did accordingly advance and lay out
severall sums of money in errecting and building the said house room
and shops to the amount of five hundred and thirteen pounds eleven
shillings and three pence AND WHEREAS for the reimbursing and
discharging the said severall sums so by them advanced and laid out
it was agreed that the said David Douthwaite, William Sutton, Henry
Brown, Edmund Bunting and William Barker their [p. 253] executors
administrators or assignes should hold and enjoy the said premisses
with the appurtenances for the term of twenty one years, and at their
charge to renew the lease of the said premisses of the said lord bishop
of Durham and his successors as often as occasion required and to take
and receive the rents and profitts thereof to their own uses and benefits,
without any account to be given for the same to the said burgesses,
as by the said order reference being thereunto had may and do more
fully appear AND WHEREAS the said David Douthwaite and William
Barker being dead and their executors unwilling to advance or lay out
any further sum and it being the design and intention of the mayor
aldermen and burgesses to rebuild the other part called the toll booth
and to make greater improvements, IT is hereby consented unto and
agreed upon that the said mayor alderman and burgesses do take the
same into their hands and pay of or secure to be paid as hereinafter
is mentioned the severall sums due to the said William Sutton, Henry
Brown and Edmund Bunting and to the executors of the said David
Douthwaite and Bi William Barker, and that the mayor aldermen and
burgesses shall at the expense of the said burrough renew the said
lease for the term of twenty one years therein to be named and that
the lessees, after the same is so renewed, shall assign the said lease
for the term therein to be named to some person or persons in trust
in the first place for securing to the said William Sutton Henry Brown
and Edmund Bunting, and to the executors and [p. 254] administrators
of the said David Douthwaite and William Barker respectively, the
payment of the sum of eighty eight pounds seventeen shillings and
three pence for with legall interest for the same from the eleventh day
of November last past till the same is paid of and discharged, and after

payment thereof then in trust for the mayor aldermen and burgesses of Stockton aforesaid. As witness our hands

W. Sleigh, mayor

[*col. 1*] The mark of Ralph Ware,* Robt Wilkinson, Christopher Tweedy, George Coser
[*col. 2*] Wm Sutton, Henry Brown, Thos Raisbeck, Ed: Bunting, Isaac Todd, Thos Ware, William Fowler, Jno: Benton, Jno: Carter* his mark, Richard Haw, Robt Deighton, Gilbert Cutts.

[p. 255]
Burrough of Stockton.
The court of the right reverend Father in God Edward lord bishop of Durham held there by adjournment this twenty sixth day of June in the eighteenth year of the reign of King[219] George the second and in the year of our Lord one thousand seven hundred and forty four before William Sleigh Esq. mayor and John Gibson deputy of Edmund Bunting gentleman steward.

WHEREAS by an order of this court made the ninth day of March in the ninth year of his present Majesty's reign for the errecting and building a dwelling house for the serjeant and a room for the entertaining of the mayor aldermen and burgesses and other erections and improvements then intended upon a parcell of ground behind the toll booth held by lease under the bishop of Durham on part whereof a smiths shopp then stood, it was amongst other things ordered and agreed that David Douthwaite Esq. then mayor, William Sutton and Henry Brown aldermen and Edmund Bunting and William Barker gentlemen should take down the said smiths shop and erect and build as is therein and thereby mentioned and agreed and hold and enjoy the premisses so to be errected for the term of twenty one years and receive and take the rents and profitts thereof to their own uses and benefitts without any account to be given for the same to the said burgesses AND WHEREAS the said David Douthwaite, William Sutton, Henry Brown, Edmund Bunting and William Barker did in pursuance of the said agreement lay out and expend in the errecting and building the said house and long room and severall shops below the same the sum of five hundred and thirteen pounds eleven shillings and three pence and the said David Douthwaite and William Barker are both since dead

---

219 Written over 'our sovereign & lord'.

AND WHEREAS it has been since found necessary and advantagious for the burrough [p. 256] to make some alterations in and aditions to the new errections and to take down and rebuild the toll booth, and the representatives of the said David Douthwaite and William Barker not being willing to advance any further sums of money for that purpose, it was agreed that the said William Sutton Henry Brown and Edmund Bunting and the legall representatives of the said David Douthwaite and William Barker should come to an account touching their said disbursments and the rents by them received forth and out of the said new errections, and on the ballance of the said account there appeared to be due to each and every of them the sum of eighty eight pounds seventeen shillings and three pence AND by one other order of this court made the thirty first day of January now last past it was consented and agreed upon that the mayor and burgesses should take into their hands the said new errections and pay of or secure to be paid the said severall sums then due to the said William Sutton, Henry Brown and Edmund Bunting and the executors of the said David Douthwaite and William Barker, and renew the said lease and assign the same for securing to the said William Sutton, Henry Brown and Edmund Bunting and to the executors and adminstrators of the said David Douthwaite and William Barker respectively the payment of the said eighty eight pounds seventeen shillings and three pence, with legall interest from the eleventh day of November then and now last past, and after payment thereof then in trust for the mayor aldermen and burgesses as by the said order said severall orders relation being thereunto respectively had more fully may appear AND WHEREAS in pursuance of the said last mentioned order the said lease has been renewed by and in the names of William Sleigh Esq. mayor, William Sutton, Henry Brown, James Raisbeck, Thomas Raisbeck, Jonathan Troy aldermen and Edmund Bunting gentleman steward [p. 257] and the said intended additions and alterations in the said new errections are proceeded in and now carrying forwards and the said toll booth taken down and rebuilding, and Wiliam Sleigh Esq. now mayor having paid of and discharged the said debt due to the executor of the said William Barker, and there being a considerable debt oweing to the burrough from the said David Douthwaite at the time of [*illegible deletion, ¾ line in length*] his death and still resting due the demands of the said executors or other legall representatives of the said David Douthwaite touching the premisses are not yet settled and adjusted, NOW for the raising money for the carrying on and finishing the said buildings and improvements it is hereby ordered consented and agreed unto by the mayor aldermen and burgesses of this corporation that the sum of four hundred pounds shall and may be advanced and borrowed upon a mortgage of the said new ~~erected~~ errections and all other the premisses comprized in the said last mentioned lease, and paid into the hands of Mr Mayor to be by him applyed and disposed of for and towards the makeing and finishing the said improvements AND it is hereby ordered and agreed that as well the said new errected toll booth and buildings above the same as the premisses comprized in the said lease shall stand and be a security for the said sum of four hundred pounds and interest AND for as much as the said William Sleigh William Sutton Henry Brown and Edmund Bunting have agreed to joyn in the said mortgage and that the premisses shall stand charged with the said four hundred pounds and interest in the first place NOW it is hereby ~~ordered~~ further ordered consented and agreed unto that not only the said last \mentioned/ premisses (subject to the payment of the said four hundred pounds and interest) but also all other the rights and revenues of this burrough (except what arises [p. 258] from anchorage and plankage) shall stand and be a security for and charged and chargeable with the said severall sums of eighty eight pounds seventeen shillings and three pence a peice to the said \William Sleigh/ William Sutton Henry Brown and Edmund Bunting their executors adminstrators and assignes with legall interest for the same, to be computed from the said eleventh day of November now last past AND for the further and better secureing the payment of the said severall sums of money and interest it is hereby further ordered and agreed that Mr Mayor for the time being shall cause the sum of eight hundred pounds to be insured upon the said severall new errections comprized in the said lease and shall in his account have the expence thereof allowed by this burrough from time to time.

W: Sleigh, mayor

[*col. 1*] Isaac Todd, Thos Ware, Richd Haw, Jno: Benton, Robert Wilkinson, Anthony Coates, George Coser, John Carter* his mark, Gilbert Cutts, Ralph Ware* his mark, Robt Deighton, Thos Mawre [*col. 2*] Wm Sutton, Henry Brown, Jas Raisbeck, Thos Raisbeck.

[p. 259]
Burrough of Stockton. The court \leet with view of frank pledge ~~of~~/ of the right reverend father in God Edward lord bishop of Durham held at Stockton aforesaid the twenty third day of October in the year of our Lord one thousand seven hundred and forty four before William Sleigh Esq., mayor, and Edmund Bunting gentleman, steward.

This day William Sleigh Esq. present mayor made and perfected his accounts to Michaelmas last to the aldermen and chief burgesses and upon that account which was seen and allowed there remained due \\to him// a ballance seventy three pounds sixteen shillings and five pence three farthings which will be allowed and paid in course.

[*col. 1*] Isaac Todd, Tho Ware, John Benton, Anthony Coates, Wm Preston, the mark of Ralph Ware*, Richd Haw, Robt Deighton, the mark of John Carter*, George Coser, John Richmond
[*col. 2*] Wm Sutton, Henry Brown, Jas: Raisbeck, Thos Raisbeck, Jonath: Troy.

[p. 260]
Burrough of Stockton.
The court of the right reverend father in God Edward lord bishop of Durham \held/ here by adjournment this fourth day of December in the eighteenth year of the reign of our sovereign lord George the second by the grace of God of Great Britain France and Ireland king defender of the faith and so forth and in the year of our Lord one thousand seven hundred and forty four before William Sleigh Esq. mayor and \John Gibson deputy of/ Edmund Bunting gentleman steward.

WHEREAS there is due and oweing from the mayor aldermen and burgesses of Stockton aforesaid to James Dunning of the same place merchant for timber and deals used in and about the errecting and improveing the Town House the sum of seventy seven pounds AND WHEREAS the said James Dunning is willing to advance and lend unto the said mayor aldermen and burgesses to be applyed towards discharging the expence of building the said Town House the further sum of forty three pounds, which together with the sum of seventy seven pounds so due and oweing as aforesaid make together the sum of one hundred and twenty pounds, AND WHEREAS there is due to Edmund Bunting gentleman steward of this court for money disbursed and charges in equity against the late Mr Douthwaite and Mr Peirse for recovering the town dues the sum of twenty pounds over and above the sum of twenty one pounds nineteen shillings and two pence he received in part, being the said Mr Douthwaite's share of the Town House rents, and which will be discounted by the said burrough with the said Mr Douthwaite's executors. IT is therefore hereby unanimously agreed this day in full court and hereby ordered that the said severall sums of one hundred and twenty pounds [p. 261] and twenty pounds shall be paid to the said James Dunning and Edmund Bunting respectively or to their respective executors administrators and assignes with legall interest for the same from this time by the mayor of this place for the time being, as the same can be raised by and out of the profitts ariseing to the said burrough next after such debts as are already due and oweing and antecedent thereto. In witness whereof we have hereunto sett our hands the day and year first before written.

W. Sleigh mayor

[col. 1] Isaac Todd, John Benton, Thos Ware, Gilbert Cutts, the mark of John Carter,* Jno: Longhorn, John Richmond, Robt Deighton, the mark of Ralph Ware,* Wm Preston
[col. 2] Wm Sutton, Henry Brown, Jas: Raisbeck, Jonath: Troy.

[p. 262]
Burrough of Stockton
The court of the right reverend father in God Edward lord bishop of Durham held at Stockton aforesaid the thirtieth day of April in the year of our Lord one thousand seven hundred and forty five before William Sleigh Esq. mayor and Peter Dunning deputy of Edmund Bunting gentleman steward.

WHEREAS by several orders heretofore made by this court it has been ordered and agreed upon that several alterations and additions should be made in and to the sergeant's house and Long Room and the toll booth & court room taken down and rebuilt, and that the sum of four hundred pounds should be raised for that purpose and secured by and out of certain branches of the revenues of this burrough as therein is mentioned which said sum of four hundred pounds has been advanced and lent by Mr Mathew Waistal AND WHEREAS the said sum of four hundred pounds is not sufficient to pay of and discharge all the debt owing for and on account of the said buildings and alterations and there is now due and owing on account thereof the further sum of two hundred pounds, one hundred pounds whereof is to be advanced and lent by the said Matthew Waistal and [—][220] one hundred pounds [—][221] other part thereof by John Beckwith NOW it is hereby ordered consented and agreed

220 Illegible; word deleted.
221 Illegible; word deleted.

unto by the mayor aldermen and burgesses of this corporation that the said two several sums of one hundred pounds apiece so agreed to be advanced and [p. 263] lent by the said Mr Waistal and John Beckwith shall be paid into the hands of William Sleigh Esq. present mayor to be by him paid applyed and disposed of for and towards the discharging of the debts contracted for and on account of the said several alterations and additions in and about the sergeant's house and Long Room and the pulling down and rebuilding of the said toll booth. And we the said mayor aldermen and burgesses do hereby order and appoint that all and every the revenues of this burrough shall stand and be a security for and charged and chargeable with the payment as well of the said sum of one hundred pounds to the said Mathew Waistal his executors administrators or assigns with legal interest for the same as of the said sum of one hundred pounds to the said John his executors administrators or assigns together with legal interest for the same In witness whereof we have hereunto set our hands the day and year before written.

W. Sleigh mayor

[*col. 1*] Isaac Todd, Thos Ware, Richd Haw, Gilbert Cutts, Anthony Coates, Wm Preston, the mark of John Carter,* Robt Deighton, John Benton, the mark of Ralph Ware*
[*col. 2*] Wm Sutton, Henry Brown, Jas: Raisbeck, Thos Raisbeck, Jonath: Troy, Ed: Bunting.

[p. 264]
13 May 1745

Received then of William Sleigh Esq. mayor of Stockton the sum of twenty six pounds ten shillings in full discharge of twenty pounds and all interest thereon formerly lent by David Douthwaite late of Stockton aforesaid merchant deceased, and also received of the said Mr Sleigh the further sum of one hundred and eighteen pounds thirteen shillings and six pence which with twenty seven pounds eight shillings and ten pence formerly received by the said Mr Douthwaite makes together the sum of one hundred and forty six pounds two shillings and four pence, in full for all sum and sums of money advanced and lent to the said corporation or burrough of Stockton aforesaid towards repairing or rebuilding the Town House there or renewing the lease thereof, and in full for all rent or interest or otherwise due and oweing from the said corporation or burrough to the said David Douthwaite. I say received the same by me as surviving executor of the last will and testament of the said David Douthwaite.

T. Wright

Witnesse Thomas Topcliff.

[p. 265]
Burrough of Stockton.
The court leet with view of frank pledge of the right reverend father in God Edward lord bishop of Durham held at Stockton aforesaid the fifteenth day of October in the nineteenth year of the reign of our sovereign lord George the second by the grace of God of Great Britain France and Ireland king defender of the faith and so forth and in the year of our Lord 1745 before Henry Brown Esq. mayor and Edmund Bunting gentleman steward.

This day William Sleigh alderman late mayor of this burrough of Stockton made and perfected his accounts to Henry Brown Esq. present mayor and to the aldermen and chief burgesses of this burrough and upon that account which was seen and allowed there remains due to the said William Sleigh to ballance the sum of two pounds and three pence three farthings which sum was paid him by the said mayor.

Henry Brown mayor

[*col. 1*] The mark of John Carter,* Gilbert Cutts, Thos Brown
[*col. 2*] Jas: Raisbeck, Thos Raisbeck, Jonath: Troy, Isaac Todd, John Benton, the mark of Ralph Ware,* Thos Ware, Jacob Harrison, the mark of Thomas Mitchell,* George Coser, R: Deighton, Richd Haw
[*col. 3*] Wm Sutton.

[p. 266]
Burrough of Stockton. Att the court held the said fifteenth day of October in the year of our Lord 1745 before Henry Brown Esq. mayor and Edmund Bunting gentleman steward.

It is ordered by the mayor aldermen steward and burgesses in full court that the serjeant or who ever for the future shall farm the markett after every markett day shall constantly clear the street and remove all the stalls with the utensills and implements thereunto belonging within the butchers' Shambles and for every neglect of this order such person farming the markett shall forfeit five shillings to be paid to the mayor for the time being upon request and to be by him accounted for yearly as an additionall rent of the said markett.

Henry Brown mayor

[*col. 1*] Wm Sutton
[*col. 2*] Jas: Raisbeck, Thos Raisbeck, Jonath: Troy, W. Sleigh.

[p. 267]
Burrough of Stockton. The court leet with view of frank pledge of the right reverend father in God Edward lord bishop of Durham held at Stockton aforesaid the fourteenth day of October in the twentyeth year of the reign of King George the second and in the year of our Lord 1746 before James Raisbeck Esq. mayor and Edmund Bunting gentleman steward.

This day Henry Brown alderman late mayor of this burrough of Stockton made and perfected his accounts to James Raisbeck Esq. present mayor and to the aldermen and chief burgesses of this burrough and upon that account which was seen and allowed the ballance due to the burrough appeared to be fourteen pounds sixteen shillings and six pence which was paid to the present mayor accordingly.

Jas: Raisbeck mayor

[*col. 1*] Anthony Coates, Thom Mitchell,* Ferdinando Simpson, William Maston, Nich⁵ Rutlidge
[*col. 2*] Wm Sutton, Thos Raisbeck, Jonath: Troy, W: Sleigh, Isaac Todd, Gilbert Cutts, Thos Ware, Jacob Harrison, Richd Haw, the mark of John Carter,* George Coser, Rᵗ Deighton.

[p. 268]
Burrough of Stockton.
The court leet with view of frank pledge of the right reverend father in God Edward lord bishop of Durham held at Stockton aforesaid the twentyeth day of October in the twenty first year of the reign of our King George the second and in the year of our Lord 1747 before Thomas Raisbeck Esq. mayor and Edmund Bunting gentleman steward.

This day James Raisbeck alderman late mayor of this burrough of Stockton made and perfected his accounts to Thomas Raisbeck Esq. present mayor and to the aldermen and chief burgesses of this burrough and upon that account which was seen and allowed the ballance due to the burrough appeared to be fourteen pounds nineteen shillings and ten pence which was paid to the present mayor accordingly.

Thos Raisbeck mayor

[col. 1] Isaac Todd, Richd Haw, Gilbert Cutts, Thos Ware, the mark of Thomas Mitchell,* John Richmond, Ferdinando Simpson, Rt Deighton, Georg Coser, Thomas Wright, Jacob Harrison, Georg Ware, John Benton, the mark of John Carter*
[col. 2] Wm Sutton, Henry Brown, Jonath: Troy, W: Sleigh.

[p. 269]
Burrough of Stockton. The court leet with view of frank pledge of the right reverend father in God Edward lord bishop of Durham held at Stockton this twentyeth day of October in the twenty first year of the reign of King George the second and in the year of our Lord 1747 before Thomas Raisbeck Esq. mayor and Edmund Bunting gentleman steward.

Whereas by an act of parliament passed in the year of our Lord one thousand seven hundred and forty six, intitled an Act for the better Preservation of Havens Roads Channells and Navigable Rivers in that part of Great Britain called England, it is enacted that if any master or owner or any person acting as master or owner of any pink crayer lighter keil boat or other vessell whatsoever shall throw out or unload, or if at any time there shall be cast thrown out or unloaden from or out of any such ship or vessell being within any port road channel or navigable river any ballast rubbish gravell earth stone wreck or filth, but only upon the land where the tide or water never flows or runns, in such case any of his Majesty's Justices of the Peace may upon the information of one witness levy upon such person so offending the sum of five pounds, one half to be paid to the informer and the other to the poor of the parish where such conviction is prosecuted.

It is therefore this day ordered by the present mayor and the chief burgesses of the said burrough that for the preservation of the River Teese all such [p. 270] offenders for the future shall be punished as the law directs and any person that will inform the mayor of this corporation for the time being of such illicit practices will receive upon the conviction of every such offender the sum of ten shillings over and above the sum of two pounds ten shillings which he will receive by virtue of the said act of parliament in witness whereof we have hereunto sett our hand the day and year first before written.

Thos Raisbeck mayor, Wm Sutton, Henry Brown, Jas: Raisbeck, Jona: Troy, W: Sleigh, Isaac Todd, Gilbert Cutts, Richd Haw, Thos Ware, Jno: Richmond, the mark of Thomas Mitchell,* Thomas Wright, Rt Deighton, Jacob Harrison, Georg Coser, Georg Ware, John Benton, Ferdinando Simpson, the mark of John Carter.*

[p. 271]
Burrough of Stockton. The court leet with view of frank pledge of the right reverend father in God Edward lord bishop of Durham held at Stockton aforesaid the third day of May in the year of our Lord 1748 before Thomas Raisbeck Esq. mayor and John Gibson deputy of Edmund Bunting gentleman steward.

Whereas several master of ships \merchants and others/ have of late refused to pay the antient dues for importing of corn it is this day agreed in full court that a demand be made on all such persons [as] are in arrear and such as deny to pay to shall be prosecuted as councell shall advise and we will chearfully and thankfully reimburse the present or any future mayor all such sum and sums of money as shall be expended in the support of the antient and indisputable rights of this burrough.

As witness our hands
                                        Thos Raisbeck mayor
[col. 1] Ferdinando Simpson, the mark of John Carter,* Anthony Coates
[col. 2] Wm Sutton, Henry Brown, Jonath. Troy, W: Sleigh, Isaac Todd, Gilbert Cutts, Thos Ware, Jno Richmond, the mark of Thomas Mitchell,* Thomas Wright, R: Deighton, Jacob Harrisson, George Coser, George Ware.

[p. 272]
Burrough of Stockton. The court leet with view of frank pledge of the right reverend father in God Edward lord bishop of Durham held at Stockton aforesaid the twenty fifth day of October in the year of our Lord one thousand seven hundred and forty eight before Ralph Whitley Esq. mayor and Edmund Bunting gentleman steward.

This day Thomas Raisbeck alderman late mayor of this burrough of Stockton made and perfected his accounts to Ralph Whitley Esq. present mayor and to the aldermen and chief burgesses of this burrough and upon that account which was seen and allowed the ballance due to the said Thomas Raisbeck three shillings and five pence three farthings which was paid accordingly.

R. Whitley mayor

[col. 1] Isaac Todd, Gilbert Cuttes, Thos Ware, Jno Richmond, Ferdinando Simpson, George Ware, George Coser, Rt Deighton, Thomas Wright, Jacob Harrison, John Carter mark,* Thomas Mitchell* [col. 2] Henry Brown, Jonath: Troy.

[p. 273] [blank]

[p. 274]
Burrough of Stockton. The court leet with view of frank pledge of the right reverend father in God Edward lord bishop of Durham held at Stockton aforesaid the sixth day of December in the year of our Lord 1748 before Ralph Whitley Esq. mayor and Edmund Bunting gentleman steward.

WHEREAS severall masters of ships merchants and others have of late refused to pay the antient and accustomed dues and dutys due to this our burrough of Stockton for importation of timber \deals/ and other merchandize into the port of Stockton aforesaid and we being resolved to maintain and support this antient burrough in all its rights dues dutys priviledges and perquisites to the utmost of our power IT is therefore unanimously agreed and ordered in full court that a demand be made of all such person or persons as are in arrear and such as refuse to pay upon such demand made shall be prosecuted for the same as the mayor for the time being shall be advised by councell in order to compell such person or persons to pay what is so strictly due and unjustly detained and the better to enable the said mayor to proceed therein we do hereby promise that he shall be thankfully reimbursed out of the perquisites of the said burrough all costs charges damages and expences that he shall be putt unto or that shall be occasioned in and about the recovering and defending these just and undoubted rights dutys and priviledges as witness our hands.

R. Whitley mayor

[*col. 1*] Isaac Todd, Gilbert Cutts, Jno Richmond, Thos Ware, Thos Wright, Jno: Longhorn, Ferdinando Simpson, Robt Deighton, G[e]orge Ware, G[e]orge Coser, the mark of John Carter,* the mark of Thos Mitchell*
[*col. 2*] William Fowler
[*col. 3*] Henry Browne, Thos Raisbeck, W: Sleigh.

[p. 275]
Burrough of Stockton. The court leet with view of frank pledge of the right reverend father in God Edward lord bishop of Durham held at Stockton aforesaid the seventeenth day of October in the year of our Lord one thousand seven hundred and forty nine before Ralph Whitley Esq. mayor and Edmund Bunting gentleman steward.

This day Ralph Whitley Esq. Alderman late\present/ mayor of this burrough of Stockton made and perfected his accounts to Michaelmas last to the aldermen and chief burgesses and upon that account which was seen and allowed the ballance due to the burrough appeared to be twenty one pound eighteen shillings and four pence ¾d which will be accounted for and paid in course.

[*col. 1*] Isaac Todd, Jno: Longhorn, Gilbert Cutts, John Gowland, Jno Richmond, Thos Ware, the mark of John Carter,* Ferdinando Simpson, Jacob Harrison, Thomas Wright, George Ware
[*col. 2*] Wm Sutton, Henry Brown, Jas: Raisbeck, Thos Raisbeck, Jonath: Troy, W: Sleigh.

[p. 276] [*blank*]

[p. 277]
Burrough of Stockton. The court leet with view of frank pledge of the right reverend father in God Edward lord bishop of Durham held at Stockton aforesaid this eighth day of May in the year of our Lorde one thousand seven hundred and fifty before Ralph Whitley Esq. mayor and Edmund Bunting gentleman steward.

Whereas three parts of the ferry boat, boat house, bake house, three closes and three shops with the appurtenances in Stockton held by lease for three lives under the bishop of Durham are advertised to be sold, it is hereby ordered by the mayor aldermen and burgesses in open court that the partys impowered to sell the same be treated with about the purchase thereof for the use and benefitt of this burrough and that

Ralph Whitley Esq. the present mayor and alderman and \the/ steward of this court or any three they shall nominate do treat for the same or part thereof accordingly, who are to make their report at the next adjournment of this court and if the terms are then approved on the same to be carryed into execution and the purchase money to be raised in such manner as shall be then agreed upon. As witness our hands

R. Whitley mayor

[*col. 1*] Isaac Todd, Thos Ware, Ferdinando Simpson, Jacob Harrison, Robt Deighton, John Gowland, Thomas Wright, the mark of Jno: Carter,* the mark of Thos Mitchell,*
the mark of Chris: Garbutt*[222]
[*col. 2*] Wm Sutton, Henry Brown, Jas: Raisbeck, Jonath: Troy, W: Sleigh.

[p. 278]
Borough of Stockton 25th October 1750.

Then Ralph Whitley Esq. late mayor of this burrough of Stockton made and perfected his accounts to Jonathan Troy Esq. present mayor and to the aldermen and chief burgesses of this burrough and upon that account which was seen and allowed the balance due to the burrough appeared to be twenty five pounds ten shillings and nine pence which was paid to the present mayor accordingly.

Jonath. Troy mayor

[*col. 1*] George Ware, Ferdinando Simpson, John Gowland, the mark of John Carter,* the mark of Tho: Mitchell,* the mark of Chris: Garbutt,* Jona: Garbutt
[*col. 2*] Wm Sutton, Henry Brown, Thos. Raisbeck, Jas: Raisbeck, W: Sleigh, Gilbert Culls, John Richmond, Thos Ware, Rt Deighton, Jacob Harrison.

[p. 279] [*blank*]

[p. 280]
Burrough of Stockton.
The court leet with view of frank pledge of the right reverend father in God Joseph lord bishop of Durham held at Stockton aforesaid

---

222 This is written between the two columns of signatures.

this thirtyeth day of Aprill in the year of our Lord one thousand seven hundred and fifty one. Before Jonathan Troy Esq. mayor and Edmund Bunting gentleman steward.

Whereas there is due and owing from the mayor aldermen and burgesses of Stockton aforesaid to William Sleigh of the same place esquire the sum of eighty pounds principall money and the said William Sleigh being desireous to have the same paid in, Mrs Sarah Hutchins of Stockton aforesaid widow hath agreed to advance and lend the same. It is therefore hereby unanimously agreed this day in full court and hereby ordered that the said sum of eighty pounds shall be paid to the said Sarah Hutchins her executors administrators and assignes with legall interest for the same from this time by the mayor of this place for the time being as the same can be raised by and out of the profitts arising to the said burrough next after such debts as are due and oweing and antecedent thereto. In witness whereof we have hereunto sett our hands the day and year first above written.

[*col. 1*] W: Sleigh, John Gowland, Thomas Wright, George Ware, the mark of John Carter,* the mark of Thos. Mitchell,* the mark of Wm Brown,* John Walker
[*col. 2*] Wm Sutton, Henry Brown, Jas: Raisbeck, Thos Raisbeck, Isaac Todd, Thos Ware, Rt Deighton, Ferdinando Simpson, Jacob Harrison.

[p. 281]
6th November 1751. Received then of Richardson Ferrand Esq. mayor of Stockton the sum of twenty pounds principall money and one pound sixteen shillings and seven pence for interest and which said sum of twenty pounds was advanced and lent by Thomas Topcliff late officer of excise deceased to William Sleigh Esq. late mayor of the burrough of Stockton aforesaid and we do acknowledge the same to be in full of all accounts debts dues and demands due and oweing unto us from the said burrough as administratixes to the said Thomas Topcliff deceased.

The mark of Averell Swainston*
The mark of Hannah Smith*

N.B. Administration was granted to Averell wife of Peter Swainston and Hannah Smith spinster as administratixes to Thomas Topcliff deceased.

[p. 282]

Burrough of Stockton. The court leet with view of frank pledge of the right reverend father in God Joseph lord bishop of Durham held at Stockton this twenty second day of October in the year of our Lord 1751 before Richardson Ferrand Esq. mayor and Edmund Bunting gentleman steward.

Then Jonathan Troy Esq. late mayor of this burrough of Stockton made and perfected his accounts to Richardson Ferrand Esq. present mayor and the aldermen and chief burgesses of this burrough and upon that account which was seen and allowed the ballance due to the burrough appeared to be twenty three pounds one shilling and ten pence which was paid to the present mayor accordingly.

Richardson Ferrand mayor.

[col. 1] Thomas Wright, George Ware, the mark of John Carter,* Wm Thrush, John Gowland, Jacob Harrison

[col. 2] Wm Sutton, Henry Brown, Jas: Raisbeck, W: Sleigh, Isaac Todd, Anthony Coates, Thos Ware, Jno Richmond, Rt. Deighton, Ferdinando Simpson.

[p. 283]

Borough of Stockton. 31st October 1752.

Then Richardson Ferrand Esq. present mayor of this burrough of Stockton made and perfected his accounts to Michaelmas last to the aldermen and chief burgesses and upon that account which was seen and allowed the ballance due to the burrough appeared to be seventeen pounds one shilling and eleven pence[223] which will be accounted for and paid in due course.

[col. 1] John Richmond, Anthony Coates, John Gowland, George Ware, Ferdinando Simpson, Wm Thrush, John Carter,* Thomas Mitchell*

[col. 2] Wm Sutton, Henry Brown, Jas: Raisbeck, Thos Raisbeck, W: Sleigh.

---

223 Followed by a space filler.

[p. 284]
Borough of Stockton. The court leet with view of frank pledge of the right reverend father in God Richard lord bishop of Durham held at Stockton aforesaid this sixteenth day of October in the year of our Lord one thousand seven hundred and fifty three before William Sutton Esq. mayor and Edmund Bunting gentleman steward.

Then Richardson Ferrand Esq. late mayor of this borough of Stockton made and perfected his accounts to William Sutton Esq. present mayor and to the aldermen and chief burgesses of this borough and upon that account which was seen and allowed the ballance due to the borough appeared to be one \two/ pound one shilling and nine pence halfpenny which was paid to the present mayor accordingly.

[*col. 1*] John Gowland, Robt Deighton, Geo[r]ge Ware, the mark of John Carter,* Wm Thrush, Wm Kaye, Edmd Harvey, Thomas Wright, Thos Ware
[*col. 2*] Wm Sutton, Henry Brown, Jas: Raisbeck, Thos Raisbeck, Jonath. Troy, W: Sleigh, R. Whitley, Nath Wetherell, Gilbert Cutts, Jno: Barker, John Rayne, Jno Richmond, Ferdinand Simpson.

[p. 285]
Burrough of Stockton. The court leet with view of frankpledge of the right reverend father in God Richard lord bishop of Durham held at Stockton aforesaid this fifteenth day of October in the year of our Lord one thousand seven hundred and fifty four before William Sleigh Esq. mayor and Edmund Bunting gentleman steward.

This day William Sutton Esq. late mayor of this burrough of Stockton made and perfected his accounts to William Sleigh Esq. present mayor and to the aldermen and chief burgesses of this burrough and upon that account which seen and allowed the ballance due to the said William Sutton appeared to be seventy five pounds one shilling and five pence which will be raised and paid by the present mayor accordingly out of money to be borrowed on security of the borough.
                                                            W: Sleigh mayor

[*col. 1*] Edmd. Harvey, Ferdinand Simpson, John Gowland, Thos. Ware, George Ware, Jno Longhorn, Thomas Wright, the mark of John Carter,* the mark of Thomas Mitchell,* W. Kaye [*col. 2*] Henry Brown, Jas: Raisbeck, Thos. Raisbeck, Jona: Troy, R. Whitley, Rich'dson Ferrand, Jno. Barker, Gilbert Cutts, Robt Deighton.

[p. 286]
Burrough of Stockton. The court leet with view of frank pledge of the right reverend father in God Richard lord bishop of Durham held at Stockton aforesaid by adjournment this twenty ninth day of October in the year of our Lord one thousand seven hundred and fifty four before William Sleigh Esq. mayor and Edmund Bunting gentleman steward.

WHEREAS it appears on the other side that William Sutton Esq. late mayor of this burrough made and perfected his accounts to William Sleigh Esq. present mayor and to the aldermen and chief burgesses of the said burrough then present and that the said William Sutton had disbursed and laid out severall sums of money in raising and repairing the Customs House Key and other things done in and for the said burrough, whereby it appeared upon settling and ballanceing the said account that there was due from the said mayor aldermen and burgesses to the said William Sutton the sum of seventy five pounds one shilling and five pence, which was agreed should be borrowed by the said present mayor and paid to the said William Sutton in discharge of his said debt AND therefore the present mayor hath borrowed of Thomas Cowper of Billingham in the said County of Durham, butcher, the sum of eighty pounds, the receipt whereof the said present mayor doth hereby acknowledge and out of which the said sum of seventy five pounds one shilling and five pence is acknowledged by the said William Sutton \to be paid and discharged/ NOW it is hereby ordered consented and agreed unto by the mayor aldermen and burgesses of this corporation that the said sum of eighty pounds so borrowed as aforesaid shall be paid to the said Thomas Cowper his executors adminstrators and assignes with legall interest for the same from the day of [p. 287] the date hereof by the mayor of this corporation for the time being as the same can be raised by and out of the profitts arising to the said burrough next after such debts as are already due and owing and antecedent thereto. In witness whereof we have hereunto sett our hands the day and year first within written.

W: Sleigh mayor

[*col. 1*] Jno. Barker, Gilbert Cutts, Robt. Deighton, Edmd. Harvey, Ferdinando Simpson, Jno Richmond, John Gowland, Thos Ware, Wm Kaye, George Ware, Thomas Wright, the mark of John Carter,* the mark of Thomas Mitchell*
[*col. 2*] Wm Sutton, Rich'dson Ferrand, Thos. Raisbeck, R. Whitley, Jonath. Troy, Jas: Raisbeck.

[p. 288]
Borrough of Stockton. The court leet with view of frank pledge of the right reverend father in God Richard lord bishop of Durham held at Stockton aforesaid by adjournment this twenty eighth day of October in the year of our Lord one thousand seven hundred and fifty five before Henry Brown Esq. mayor and Tomlinson Bunting,[224] deputy of Edmund Bunting gentleman steward.

This day William Sleigh Esq. late mayor of this borrough of Stockton made and perfected his accounts to Henry Brown Esq. present mayor and to the aldermen and chief burgesses of this borrough and upon that account which was seen and allowed the ballance due to the said William Sleigh appeared to be twenty one pounds one shilling and eight pence which will be raised and paid accordingly and we do hereby consent and agree that in order for the raising of money for the above ballance and also the further sum of thirty two pounds eight shillings and eight pence for the fines and fees of the anchorage and plankage lease & the lease of the Town House now renewed there be advanced and borrowed the sum of fifty pounds upon the credit of the revenues of this borough and to be charged upon and payable thereout with interest and that this court be adjourned to Tuesday the twenty fifth day of November for that purpose.

[*col. 1*] Jacob Harrison, Gilbert Cutts
[*col. 2*] Jno. Barker, John Richmond, Robt. Deighton, John Gowland, Thos. Ware, Geo[r]ge Ware, Thomas Wright, the mark of John Carter,* the mark of Thomas Mitchell*
[*col. 3*] Henry Brown, Wm Sutton, Jas: Raisbeck, Thos. Raisbeck, Jonath: Troy, Rich'dson Ferrand, Nath Wetherell.

---

224 Tomlinson Bunting was son of Edmund Bunting from his second marriage, to Dorothy, daughter of John Tomlinson of York (Bayley, 'Genealogical Additions', p. 84), and acted as assistant to him in the role of steward.

[p. 289]

Borrough of Stockton. The court of the right reverend father in God Richard lord bishop of Durham held at Stockton aforesaid by adjournment the twenty fifth day of November in the year of our Lord one thousand seven hundred and fifty five before Henry Brown Esq. mayor and Tomlinson Bunting deputy of Edmund Bunting gentleman steward.

WHEREAS at a court held by adjournment the twenty eighth day of October last William Sleigh Esq. late mayor of this borrough made and perfected his accounts to Henry Brown Esq. present mayor and to the aldermen and chief burgesses of the said borrough in which account which was seen and allowed there appeared to be a ballance due from the said borrough to the said William Sleigh of twenty one pounds eight shilling and eight pence AND it was then consented and agreed by the said mayor aldermen and burgesses that in order for the raising of money for the payment of the above ballance and also of the further sum of thirty two pounds eight shillings and eight pence for the fines and fees of renewing the anchorage and plankage lease and the lease of the Town House, there should be advanced and borrowed the sum of fifty pounds upon the creditt of the revenues of the said borrough and to be charged upon and payable thereout with interest AND THEREFORE the said Henry Brown Esq. mayor hath borrowed of George Illingworth of Aclam in the County of York yeoman the said sum of fifty pounds the receipt and payment whereof the said present mayor doth hereby acknowledge NOW it is hereby consented and agreed unto by the mayor aldermen and burgesses of this corporation that the said sum of fifty pounds so borrowed as aforesaid shall be paid to the said George Illingworth his executors adminstrators and assigns with legall interest for the same from the day of the date hereof by the mayor of this corpo-ration for the time being as the same can be raised by and out of the revenues [p. 290] arising to the said borrough next after such debts as are due and owing and antecedent thereto ~~in witness whereof we have hereunto sett our hands the day and year first before written and the said Thomas Raisbeck doth hereby declare and agree that~~ And[225] it is hereby declared that the sum of fifty pounds secured in and by the deed of agreement bearing even date herewith whereby the said leases are assigned to Strickland Hill for securing several

225 Change of hand at this point.

sums therein mentioned and amongst the rest the sum of fifty pounds to Thomas Raisbeck is the same sum of fifty pounds herein mentioned and secured to the said George Illingworth and the said Thomas Raisbeck doth hereby declare that his own name is made use of in trust only for him the said George Illingworth. In witness whereof we have hereto set our hands the day and year first before written.

[*col. 1*] Thos. Ware, Thos Wright, the mark of John Carter,* Jno. Barker, Jno Longhorn, Wm Thrush, the mark of Thomas Mitchell,* the mark of John Carr*
[*col. 2*] Henry Brown, Wm Sutton, Thos. Raisbeck, Jonath: Troy, W: Sleigh, Rich'dson Ferrand, John Richmond, Robt: Deighton, John Gowland.

[p. 291] [*blank*]

[p. 292]
Borrough of Stockton. The court leet with view of frank pledge of the right reverend father in God Richard lord bishop of Durham held at Stockton by adjournment the twenty second day of October in the thirtieth year in the reign of King George the second and in the year of our Lord one thousand seven hundred and fifty six before James Raisbeck Esq. mayor and Tomlinson Bunting deputy of Edmund Bunting gentleman steward.

This day Henry Brown Esq. late mayor of this borrough of Stockton made and perfected his accounts to James Raisbeck Esq. present mayor and to the aldermen and chief burgesses of this borrough and upon that account which was seen and allowed the ballance appeared to be due to the said Henry Brown is twenty one pounds six shillings and five pence which will be raised and paid by the present mayor accordingly.

Jas: Raisbeck mayor

[*col. 1*] Jacob Harrison, Thos Haw,[226] Jno: Longhorn

226 Thomas Haw was a shipbuilder in Stockton from 1782 to 1800, when he passed his shipyard on to his son Thomas, junior. He built twenty-four vessels between 1782 and 1790 with Mark Pye, and a further fifty-six after that: Richmond, *Local Records*, p. 89; Heavisides, *Annals*, pp. 55–6. See also Betteney, *Shipbuilding*, p. 13.

[*col. 2*] Wm Sutton, Thos. Raisbeck, W: Sleigh, R. Whitley, Nath Wetherell, Gilbert Cutts, John Richmond, R. Deighton, John Gowland, Thos. Ware, George Ware, Edmd. Harvey, Thomas Wright, I. C.*[227]

[p. 293]
Borrough of Stockton
The court leet with view of frank pledge of the right reverend father in God Richard lord bishop of Durham held at Stockton by adjournment this third day of May 1757 before James Raisbeck Esq. mayor and Tomlinson Bunting deputy of Edmund Bunting gentleman steward.

Memorandum. It is hereby d agreed that the purchase \agreement/ for \3 fourths parts of/ all that piece or stripe of ground being parcel of a field belonging to Mr Ashenden adjoining on the West Row and entred into by James Raisbeck Esq., William Sutton Esq. and Thomas Raisbeck gentleman for the use of this borough is hereby confirmed and shall be carried into execution at the expence of this borough and the mayor for the time being is hereby authorised to treat and agree for the purchase of the remaining fourth part thereof.

Jas: Raisbeck mayor

[*col. 1*] Henry Brown, Thos. Raisbeck, W: Sleigh, Rich'dson Ferrand, Gilbert Cutts, John Richmond, John Gowland, Tho. Ware
[*col. 2*] George Ware, the mark of John Carter,* Jacob Harrison, Fra⁵: Eden, Jno Jackson, Willm: Harrison, Richd: Thompson.

[p. 294]
Borough of Stockton. The court leet with view of frank pledge of the right reverend father in God Richard lord bishop of Durham held at Stockton by adjournment the tenth day of November in the year of our Lord one thousand seven hundred and fifty seven before Thomas Raisbeck Esq. mayor and Edmund Bunting gentleman steward.

This day James Raisbeck Esq. late mayor of this borough of Stockton made and perfected his accounts to Thomas Raisbeck present mayor and to the aldermen and chief burgesses of this borough and upon that account which was seen and allowed the balance due to the said borough appeared to be thirty five pounds seven shillings and

---

227 The mark of John Carter (see Appendix 5).

ten pence which was paid to the present mayor accordingly James Raisbeck appeared to be thirt fifty seven pounds nine shillings and eight pence wh which is to be raised and paid by the present mayor accordingly.

Thos. Raisbeck mayor

[*col. 1*] Jno. Barker, Thos Rudd, Robt. Deighton, Jno Jackson, Thos Ware, John Gowland, Thos. Haw, John Cock, Thomas Wright, Jacob Harrison, George Ware, John Carter* mark
[*col. 2*] Wm Sutton, Henry Brown, W: Sleigh.

[p. 295]
Borough of Stockton. The court leet with view of frankpledge of the honorable and right reverend father in God Richard lord bishop of Durham held at Stockton aforesaid the seventeenth day of October in the year of our Lord one thousand seven hundred and fifty eight before Ralph Whitley Esq. mayor and Tomlinson Bunting deputy of Edmund Bunting steward.

This day Thomas Raisbeck Esq. late mayor of this borough of Stockton made and perfected his accounts to Ralph Whitley Esq. present mayor & to the aldermen & chief burgesses of this borough and upon that account which was seen and allowed, the ballance due to the said Thomas Raisbeck appeared to be forty two pounds twelve shillings and sixpence halfpenny which is hereby agreed to be secured and paid out of the money arising from the revenues of this borough together with legal interest for the same.

R. Whitley mayor

[*col. 1*] Robt Deighton, Thomas Wright, John Gowland, Geo[r]ge Ware, John Cock, Thos Bartram, Jas: Weir, Jo: Smith, Willm Burrell
[*col. 2*] Wm Sutton, Henry Brown, Jas: Raisbeck, W: Sleigh, Rich'dson Ferrand, Jno. Barker, Thos Haw, Fra: Eden.

[p. 296]
Borough of Stockton. The court leet with view of frankpledge of the honorable and right reverend father in God Richard lord bishop of Durham held at Stockton aforesaid the twenty ninth day of April one thousand seven hundred and sixty before George Sutton Esq. mayor and Tomlinson Bunting deputy of Edmund Bunting steward.

This day Ralph Whitley Esq. late mayor of this borough of Stockton made and perfected his accounts to George Sutton Esq. present mayor & to the aldermen and chief burgesses of this borough and upon that account which was seen & allowed, the ballance due to the said Ralph Whitley appeared to be three pounds fourteen shillings and five pence three farthings.

Geo: Sutton mayor

[*col. 1*] Thos. Bartram, John Beckwith, John Smith, John Cock, Ra Vipond

[*col. 2*] Wm Sutton, Henry Brown, Jas: Raisbeck, Thos. Raisbeck, W: Sleigh, Rich'dson Ferrand, Jno. Barker, Rt. Deighton, Jno Jackson, Geo Ware.

[p. 297]
Borough of Stockton. The court leet with view of frankpledge of the honorable and right reverend father in God Richard lord bishop of Durham held at Stockton aforesaid the fourteenth day of October in the year of our Lord one thousand seven hundred and sixty before George Sutton Esq. mayor and Tomlinson Bunting deputy of Edmund Bunting steward.

This day George Sutton Esq. mayor of this borough of Stockton made and perfected his accounts to the aldermen and \chief/ burgesses of this borough and upon that account which was seen and allowed, the ballance due to the said George Sutton appeared to be seven pounds ~~seventeen~~ \sixteen/ shillings and sixpence to be carried to a new account.

[*col. 1*] Henry Dixon, John Smith, Thomas Wright, Ra Vipond, Willm Burrill

[*col. 2*] Wm Sutton, Jas: Raisbeck, Thos Raisbeck, W: Sleigh, Rich'dson Ferrand, Jno. Barker, R Deighton, Fras Eden, Thos. Bartram, George Ware, Jno Jackson, John Beckwith, John Cock.

[p. 298]
Borough of Stockton. The court leet with view of frankpledge of the honorable and right reverend father in God Richard lord bishop of Durham held at Stockton aforesaid the twentieth day of October in the year of our Lord one thousand seven hundred and sixty one \before William/ ~~George~~ Sutton Esq. mayor and Tomlinson Bunting deputy of Edmund Bunting gentleman steward.

This day George Sutton Esq. late mayor of this borough of Stockton made and perfected his accounts to William Sutton Esq. the present mayor and to the aldermen and chief burgesses of this borough and upon that account which was seen and allowed the ballance due to the said borough appeared to be twenty four pounds eight \shillings/ and ten pence ~~which is hereby agreed to be~~ twenty two pounds ten shillings, part of which sum, is hereby agreed to be paid to Mr Thomas Raisbeck alderman of the said borough in part satisfaction of the sum of forty two pounds ten shillings due and owing to the said Thomas Raisbeck & secured to be paid to him his executors administrators & assigns out of the monies arising from the revenues of the said borough.

[*col. 1*] George Ware, Thos. Moone, Jno Jackson, Henry Dixon
[*col. 2*] Wm Sutton, Henry Brown, Thos. Raisbeck, Jno. Barker,[228] Thos: Haw, Jno. Pickering, John Cock, Thos. Bartram, Jos. Smith, Willm. Burrell, Ra Vipond.

[p. 299]
Borough of Stockton. The court leet with view of frankpledge of the honorable and right reverend father in God Richard lord bishop of Durham held at Stockton aforesaid the twenty first day of October in the year of our Lord one thousand seven hundred and sixty two before Richardson Ferrand Esq. mayor & Tomlinson Bunting deputy of Edmund Bunting steward.

This day William Sutton Esq. late mayor of this borough of Stockton made & perfected his accounts to Richardson Ferrand Esq. the present mayor and to the aldermen and chief burgesses of this borough and upon that account which was seen and allowed, the balance due to the said borough appeared to be one pound two shillings and eleven pence.

Rich'dson Ferrand mayor

Henry Brown, Thos. Raisbeck, W: Sleigh, Geo: Sutton, Willm Burrell, John Beckwith, Ottivill Stoney, George Ware, Thomas Bartram, Ra. Vipond, John Cock, Jos: Smith, Thos. Moone, Thos. Haw, Jno Jackson, Henry Dixon, Jno. Pickering.

---

228 This and the following names form a separate column in the bottom right-hand corner of the page.

[p. 300]
Borough of Stockton. The court leet with view of frankpledge of the honorable and right reverend Father in God Richard lord bishop of Durham held at Stockton aforesaid the twenty fifth day of October in the year of our Lord one thousand seven hundred and sixty three before William Sleigh Esq. mayor and [———][229] John Stapylton Raisbeck,[230] deputy of Edmund Bunting gentleman steward.

This day Richardson Ferrand Esq. late mayor of this borough of Stockton made and perfected his accounts to William Sleigh Esq. the present mayor and to the aldermen and cheif burgesses of this borough and upon that account which was seen and allowed, the ballance due to the said borough appeared to be twenty six pounds four shillings and fourpence half penny.

W: Sleigh mayor

Wm Sutton, Henry Brown, Willm Burrell, John Beckwith, Ottivill Stoney, George Ware, Thos: Haw, Ra Vipond, Thos Wright, Thos Bartram, Jno. Cock, Jo: Smith, Peter Ovington, Jno. Pickering, Francis Peacock, John Gowland.

[p. 301]
Borough of Stockton. The court leet with view of frankpledge of the honorable and right reverend father in God Richard lord bishop of Durham held at Stockton aforesaid the sixteenth day of October in the year of our Lord one thousand seven hundred and sixty four before Thomas Fall Esq. mayor and John Stapylton Raisbeck deputy of Edmund Bunting gentleman steward.

This day William Sleigh Esq. late mayor of this borough of Stockton made and perfected his accounts to Thomas Fall Esq. the present mayor and to the aldermen and cheif burgesses of this borough and upon that account which was seen and allowed the ballance due to the said borough appeared to be forty one pounds eight shillings and fourpence.

Tho: Fall mayor

---

229 Deletion, about 5 cm in length.
230 J. S. Raisbeck, solicitor, was the son of Thomas Raisbeck, mayor in 1737: Surtees, *History*, pp. 173–4; Bayley, 'Genealogical Additions', p. 98.

[*col. 1*] Thomas Wright, Francis Peacock
[*col. 2*] Wm Sutton, Henry Brown, Thos. Raisbeck, Rich'dson Ferrand, Willm Burrell, Henry Dixon, [Geor]ge Ware, John Beckwith, Jno. Pickering, Peter Ovington, John Cock, Thos. Bartram, John Gowland, Thos: Haw, Jo: Smith.

[p. 302]
Borough of Stockton. The court leet with view of frankpledge of the honourable and right reverend father in God Richard lord bishop of Durham held at Stockton aforesaid the fifteenth day of October in the year of our Lord one thousand seven hundred and sixty five before Thomas Fall Esq. mayor and John Stapylton Raisbeck gentleman steward.

This day Thomas Fall Esq. mayor of this borough of Stockton made and perfected his accounts to the aldermen and cheif burgesses of this borough and upon that account which was seen and allowed there appeared to be a ballance due to the said Thomas Fall of five pounds three shillings and five pence halfpenny to be carried to a new account.

[*col. 1*] John Gowland, John Smith, George Ware, John Cock, Francis Peacock, Thomas Wright
[*col. 2*] W: Sleigh, Rich'dson Ferrand, G. Sutton, R. Deighton, John Beckwith, John Rudd, Robert Spark, Jno. Pickering, Thos: Haw, John Jackson.

[p. 303]
Borough of Stockton. The court leet with view of frankpledge of the honourable and right reverend father in God Richard lord bishop of Durham held by adjournment at Stockton aforesaid the eighth day of November in the year of our Lord one thousand seven hundred and sixty five before Thomas Fall Esq. mayor and John Stapylton Raisbeck gentleman steward.

FOR AS MUCH AS the lord bishop of Durham hath lately renewed the three leases of the Town House, anchorage and plankage and the West Row, and granted the said new leases to Thomas Fall Esq. the present mayor and to the cheif burgesses of this borough and to John Stapylton Raisbeck steward of this court on trust for the mayor and burgesses of this borough in such manner as therein is severally mentioned NOW it is hereby unanimously consented and agreed unto that the said two several leases of the said Town House, anchorage and plankage be immediately assigned and transferred to Strickland Hill Esq. his executors administrators and assigns upon trust for the securing raising and paying of the several sums of money now due and owing \from/ to this borough to the several persons mentioned in an indenture of assignment now proposed for that purpose and made of the said several premises and bearing date herewith and executed amongst others by us whose names are severally hereunto set and subscribed AND FOR AS MUCH AS Mr Thomas Raisbeck alderman has advanced and paid for the fyne and fees of the said several leases now renewed and for sundry other expenses attending the renewing the said leases the sum of forty pounds,[231] IT is hereby consented declared and agreed that the said sum of forty pounds shall stand and be charged and chargeable upon the revenues of this borough with interest for the same to be computed from the thirty first day of October[232] now last past, after the rate of four pounds ten shillings by the hundred by the year, to the said Thomas Raisbeck his executors administrators and assigns and the mayor of this borough for the time being, is hereby desired and authorised to pay the same accordingly by and with the money that shall arise by and out of the revenues of this borough. Given under our hands the year and date above written.

Tho: Fall mayor

Wm Sutton, Henry Brown, Thos. Raisbeck.[233]

[p. 304]
Rich'dson Ferrand, G. Sutton, R. Leighton, John Beckwith, John Rudd, Jno. Pickering, Thos. Haw, John Cock, George Ware, John Gowland, Robert Spark, John Smith, Frances Peacock, John Fairfowl.

[p. 305]
Borough of Stockton. The court leet with view of frankpledge of the honourable and right reverend father in God Richard lord bishop of Durham held at Stockton aforesaid the sixth day of October in the year of our Lord one thousand seven hundred and sixty six before

---

231 Here and in the following clause, the sum has been entered in a blank space left for that purpose.
232 The day and month have been entered in blank spaces left for that purpose.
233 Thomas Raisbeck died in 1765 and is buried in Stockton St. Thomas churchyard: Brewster, *History*, p. 322.

John Wilkinson Esq. mayor and John Stapylton Raisbeck gentleman steward.

This day Thomas Fall Esq. mayor of this borough of Stockton made and perfected his accounts to the aldermen and cheif burgesses of this borough and upon that account which was seen and allowed there appeared to be a ballance due to the said Thomas Fall of nine pounds twelve shillings and three pence to be carried to a new account.

John Wilkinson mayor

[*col. 1*] Robert Spark, Thos. Sheraton, George Ware, John Cock, John Gowland, Thomas Wright, John Fairfowl, Wm Wray
[*col. 2*] W: Sleigh, Rich'dson Ferrand, John Rudd, Jno. Pickering, John Beckwith, Tho. Haw.

[p. 306]
Borough of Stockton. The court leet with view of frankpledge of the honourable and right reverend father in God Richard lord bishop of Durham held at Stockton aforesaid the twentieth day of October in the year of our Lord 1767 before John Wilkinson Esq. mayor and John Stapylton Raisbeck gentleman steward.

This day John Wilkinson Esq. mayor of this borough of Stockton made and perfected his accounts to the aldermen and cheif burgesses of this borough and upon that account which was seen and allowed there appeared to be a ballance due to the said John Wilkinson of twenty eight pounds three shillings and nine pence to be carried to a new account.

[*above the signatures in cols 1 and 2:*] Wm Sutton, W: Sleigh, G: Sutton, Tho: Fall.
[*col. 1*] John Gowland, Thomas Wright, John Fairful, Thos Sheraton
[*col. 2*] John Rudd, Jno. Pickering, Tho: Haw, John Cock, John Beckwith, Robert Spark, George Ware, Cuthbert Burrell, Wm Wray.

[p. 307]
Borough of Stockton. The court of the honorable and right reverend father in God Richard lord bishop of Durham held there by adjournment this tenth day of November in the year of our Lord 1767 before John Wilkinson Esq. mayor and John Stapylton Raisbeck steward.

WHEREAS the antient priviledge and custom of trying causes in this court for the recovery of small debts within this borough hath of late years been laid aside and neglected and the amercements imposed by this court upon the several persons who have been therein presented have not for some time past been levyed to the great prejudice of this borough and the encouragement of nusances and incroachments within the same AND WHEREAS it is the unanimous opinion of the mayor aldermen and chief burgesses the \whose/ names are hereto subscribed that it would be greatly for the benefit and advantage of this borough and of the inhabitants thereof that the said antient priviledge and custom should be revived and that the authority of the said court should be kept up and maintained in as full and ample a manner as at any \time/ heretofore NOW we the mayor aldermen and chief burgesses of the said borough whose names are hereunder written do hereby jointly and severally covenant declare and agree that we will from time to time \and at all times/ save defend and keep harmless and indemnifyed the said John Stapylton Raisbeck the present steward of this court of and from any prosecution or prosecutions which shall or may at any time be commenced against him by any person or persons whomsoever for or by reason or means of any warrant briefs or execution to be issued out of this court and of from and against all costs [p. 308] charges damages and expenses to be occasioned thereby. Witness our hands the day and year above written.

J: Wilkinson mayor, Wm Sutton, Henry Brown, W: Sleigh, G Sutton, Tho: Fall, John Rudd, Jno. Pickering, John Beckwith, Robert Spark, George Ware, Wm Wray, Thos: Haw, Thos Wright, Cuthbert Burrell, John Cock, John Gowland, Thos Sheraton, John Fiarfowl.

[p. 309] [*blank*]

[p. 310]
Borough of Stockton. The court leet with view of frankpledge and court baron of the honourable and right reverend father in God Richard lord bishop of Durham held within the borough aforesaid the tenth day of May 1768 before John Wilkinson Esq. mayor and John Stapylton Raisbeck gentleman steward.

Whereas the butchers' Shambles in this borough being found on examination to be in a ruinous condition and the roof thereof so rotten and decayed as not to admit of being repaired and whereas the covered cross within this borough erected in the year 1709 by reason of its size and the impropriety of its situation greatly incumbers the market place and spoils the regularity thereof, it is therefore judged expedient and necessary and it is hereby ordered and agreed by the mayor aldermen and chief burgesses of this borough whose names are hereto subscribed that the said butchers' Shambles shall be taken down and rebuilt upon such a plan as shall be approved of by the said mayor and aldermen and that the said covered cross shall also be taken down and a column erected in its stead.[234] But for as much as the want of a covered cross may be an [p. 312][235] inconvenience in rainy weather for people attending the market with butter eggs poultry &c, in order to remedy that inconvenience and to accomodate the inhabitants of this borough it is hereby further ordered and agreed that a piazza be erected on the north side of the Town's House and to adjoin thereto. And for the carrying these designs in execution it is agreed that the mayor for the time being shall raise such sums as shall be necessary for that purpose and that the money so raised shall be secured with interest by mortgage of the revenues of this borough. Given under our hand the day and year above written.

J: Wilkinson, mayor, Wm Sutton, Henry Brown, W: Sleigh, G. Sutton.

[p. 313]
Borough of Stockton. The court leet with view of frankpledge of the honourable and right reverend father in God Richard lord bishop of Durham held at Stockton aforesaid the twenty fifth day of October in the year of our Lord 1768 before George Sutton Esq. mayor and D'arcy Fowler[236] deputy of John Stapylton Raisbeck gentleman steward.

This day John Wilkinson Esq. late mayor of this borough of Stockton made and perfected his accounts to the aldermen and cheif burgesses of this borough and upon that account which was seen and allowed there appeared to be a ballance due to the said John Wilkinson of thirty one pounds eleven shillings and a half penny to be carried to a new account.

---

234 The Doric column in the High Street was erected by John Shout at a cost of £45: Richmond, *Local Records*, p. 74. Shout appears as a signatory in 1775 (below, p. 187).
235 Page 311 is blank.
236 D'Arcy Fowler was an eminent attorney in Stockton: Richmond, *Local Records*, p. 72.

W: Sleigh, Tho: Fall, John Rudd, Jno. Pickering, John Beckwith, Thos: Haw, Thos Sheraton, Cuthbert Burrell, George Ware, Jno: Cock, Thos Wright, Henry Dixon.

[p. 314]
Borough of Stockton. The court leet with view of frankpledge of the honorable and right reverend father in God Richard lord bishop of Durham held at Stockton aforesaid the thirty first day of October in the year of our Lord 1769 before John Stapylton Raisbeck mayor and Gascoign Finch Esq.[237] steward.

This day George Sutton Esq. late mayor of this borough of Stockton made and perfected his accounts to the aldermen and cheif burgesses of this borough and upon that account which was seen and allowed there appeared to be a ballance due to the said borough of seven pounds six shillings and five pence which was paid to the present mayor accordingly.

J. S. Raisbeck mayor

W: Sleigh, Tho: Fall, John Rudd, Jno. Pickering, John Beckwith, Tho: Haw, George Ware, Jno. Cock, Cuthbert Burrell, Thos Wright, Wm Stubbs, Thos Dumble, Thos Sheraton.

[p. 315]
Borough of Stockton. The court leet with view of frankpledge of the honorable & right reverend father in God Richard lord bishop of Durham held at Stockton aforesaid the sixteenth day of April in the year of our [Lord] 1771 before John Stapylton Raisbeck Esq. mayor and Gascoyne Finch Esq. steward.

This day John Stapylton Raisbeck Esq. mayor of this borough of Stockton made and perfected his accounts to the aldermen and chief burgesses of this borough and upon that account which was seen and allowed there appeared to be a balance due to the said John Stapylton Raisbeck of five pounds one shilling and a penny half penny to be carried to a new account.

W: Sleigh, G. Sutton, John Wilkinson, John Rudd, Jno. Pickering, John Beckwith, Thos: Haw, Wm Wray, Cuthbert Burrell, George

237 Gascoigne Finch was a solicitor: *ibid.*, p. 75.

Ware, Wm Stubbs, John Cock, Thos Sheraton, Thomas Wright, Thos Dumble, Robert Spark.

[p. 316]
Borough of Stockton. The court leet with view of frankpledge of the right reverend father in God John lord bishop of Durham held at Stockton aforesaid on Tuesday the fifteenth day of October 1771 before Robert Preston Esq. mayor and Gascoyne Finch Esq. steward.

This day John Stapylton Raisbeck late mayor of this borough of Stockton made and perfected his accounts to the aldermen and chief burgesses of this borough and upon that account which was seen and allowed there appeared to be a ballance due to the said borough of six pounds fifteen shillings & six pence halfpenny which was paid to the present mayor accordingly.

R: Preston mayor

John Rudd, Cuthbert Burrell, Jno. Pickering, Wm Wray.

[p. 317]
Borough of Stockton. The court leet with view of frankpledge of the right reverend father in God John lord bishop of Durham held at Stockton aforesaid on Tuesday the 20th day of October 1772 before Robert Preston Esq. mayor and Gas[coigne] Finch Esq. steward.

This day Robert Preston[238] mayor of this borough of Stockton made and perfected his accounts to the aldermen and chief burgesses of this borough and upon that account which was seen and allowed there appeared to be a ballance due to the said Robert Preston of sixteen pounds seventeen shillings.

W: Sleigh, J. S. Raisbeck, John Rudd, Jno. Pickering, John Beckwith, Thos: Haw, Wm Wray, George Ware, Cuthbert Burrell, Thos Dumble, Edward Fawcett, Jno. Cock, Thos Wright, Tho Sheraton, Wm Stubbs.

[p. 318]
Borough of Stockton. The court leet with view of frankpledge of the right reverend father in God John lord bishop of Durham held at the

238 A Robert Preston was Collector of the Customs from 1781 until his death in 1792: *ibid.*, p. 460.

usual place in and for the said borough on Friday the thirtieth day
of April one thousand seven hundred and seventy three before John
Carter gentleman,[239] steward, in the presence of the the Worshipful
Robert Preston Esq. mayor and the aldermen of the said borough.

Ordered by the court that the custom house within the said borough
be effectually repaired by the mayor and that the common quay
commonly called the Custom House Quay be repaired likewise by
the mayor so as the repairs of such quay do not exceed five pounds.
And it is further ordered that as well two several sums of forty
pounds and one hundred and forty pounds which by two former
orders, one dated the eighth day of November 1765 and the other
dated the tenth day of May 1768 together with interest for the said
two several sums as also a sufficient sum for completing the said
repairs shall be borrowed at interest upon the credit of the corporation estate.

R: Preston mayor

[*col. 1*] John Cock, Thos: Haw, Thos Wright, Wm Wray, Robert Spark
[*col. 2*] W: Sleigh, G. Sutton, J. S. Raisbeck, John Rudd, Jno. Pickering,
John Beckwith, Edward Fawcett, George Ware, Cuthbert Burrell,
Thos: Dumble.

[p. 319]
Borough of Stockton. The court leet with view of frankpledge and
court baron of the right reverend John lord bishop of Durham held
at the usual place in and for the said borough on Wednesday the
eighteenth day of May in the year of our Lord one thousand seven
hundred and seventy four before the worshipful William Sleigh Esq.
and mayor of the said borough and John Carter gentleman steward
by adjournment.

Adjourned from time to time to Tuesday the fourth day of October
one thousand seven hundred and seventy four at six o'clock in the
evening, by John Carter steward.

[p. 320]
Borough of Stockton. The court leet with view of frankpledge and
court baron of the right reverend John lord bishop of Durham held

239   John Carter was a solicitor: *ibid.*, p. 77.

at the usual place in and for the said borough on Tuesday the fourth day of October in the year of our Lord one thousand seven hundred and seventy four before the worshipful William Sleigh Esq. mayor of the said borough and John Carter gentleman steward at six of the clock in the evening, by adjournment.

We \the/ mayor aldermen and burgesses present do order direct consent and agree, as follow, that is to say

That all freehold leasehold or other estates belonging the said corporation shall be charged with and lyable to the payment of all sum and sums of money whatsoever at any time or times heretofore advanced or borrowed by us in our collective body or by any of us, separately for the use of the said corporation, together with interest for the same and that every further act requisite for the more effectual charging the same estates with the same sum and sums of money and interest shall be done by and at the expense of the said corporation.

That they every future mayor shall account annually for the whole revenues of the corporation and be allowed thereout the sum of thirty pounds only to defray the expense of his office; but it is not expected that any future mayor should give [p. 321] more than a supper at his election and a dinner at the Easter and Michaelmas court leet to the aldermen and jury, nor pay more than two shillings a piece for each juryman's dinner or supper.

W: Sleigh mayor, G. Sutton, John Wilkinson, J. S. Raisbeck, R: Preston, Jno. Pickering, Thos: Haw, Wm Wray, John Beckwith, Robert Spark, Cuthbert Burrell, Thos Sheraton, Thos Dumble, Geo[r]ge Ware, Thos Wilkinson, John Cock.

[p. 322]
Borough of Stockton. At the court leet and court baron with of view of frankpledge of the right reverend John lord bishop of Durham held at the usual place in and for the said borough, by adjournment this fifteenth day of November in the year of our Lord one thousand seven hundred and seventy four before the worshipful Benjamin Lumley Esq.[240] mayor and John Carter gentleman steward.

240 Benjamin Lumley was a banker, Justice of the Peace and Deputy Lieutenant: Bayley, 'Genealogical Additions', p. 104.

This day Robert Preston Esq. late mayor of this borough perfected his accounts to the aldermen and chief burgesses of the said borough and upon that account which was seen and allowed there appeared a ballance of seventy five pounds due to him which William Sleigh Esq. the ~~the~~ succeeding mayor has since paid. And at the same \time/ the said William Sleigh ~~Esq.~~ produced and perfected his accounts to the same aldermen and chief burgesses of the said borough and upon that account \which/ was allowed there remains a ballance due to the said William Sleigh of the sum of thirty four pounds thirteen shillings and six pence which we agree shall remain a charge upon the estates belonging to the said borough until payment.

Benj. Lumley mayor

[*col. 1*] Thos: Haw, Robert Spark, John Cock, Cuthbert Burrell, Thos Dumble, William Stubb, Alexr Hunter, Thos: Sheraton
[*col. 2*] W: Sleigh, G. Sutton, R. Preston, J. S. Raisbeck, Jno. Pickering, Wm Wray, John Beckwith, George Ware.

[p. 323] [*blank*]

[p. 324]
Borough of Stockton. The court leet and court baron of the right reverend John lord bishop of Durham holden at the Town House in and for the said borough on Tuesday the seventeenth day of October in the year of our Lord one thousand seven hundred and seventy five before the worshipful Benjamin Lumley Esq. mayor of the said borough and John Carter gentleman steward.

This day the said Benjamin Lumley mayor of the said borough for the last year, and since re-elected perfected his accounts to the aldermen and chief burgesses of the said borough and upon such accounts which were seen and allowed there remains a ballance of sixteen pounds thirteen shillings and one penny due ~~from~~ \to/ the said ~~Corporation~~ Benjamin Lumley ~~to~~ \from/ the said borough.

At the same court Ralph Whitfield signified his intention to quit the Town House stables Shambles tolls and other appurtenances in his occupation at May day next – therefore ordered that the notice be accepted and publick notice be given by the steward in the York and Newcastle papers for a tenant for the said premises.

Also order'd that in future the revenues of the said borough shall not be contributory to the repairs of the two publick pumps within the said borough.

[*col. 1*] Cuthbert Burrell, George Ware, Thos Dumble, Alexr Hunter, Wm Wray, Jno. Shout, Thos Simpson, John Claxton
[*col. 2*] W: Sleigh, G. Sutton, Jno. Pickering, John Beckwith, John Cock, Thos Sheraton.

[p. 325] [*blank*]

[p. 326]
Borough of Stockton. The court leet and court baron of the right reverend John lord bishop of Durham holden at the Town House ~~within~~ and for the said borough on Tuesday the twenty ninth day of October in the year of our Lord one thousand seven hundred and seventy six before George Hutchinson Esq. mayor and John Carter gentleman steward.

This day Benjamin Lumley Esq. late mayor of the said borough perfected his accounts to the mayor aldermen and chief burgesses of the said borough and upon such accounts which were seen and allowed there remains ~~of~~ a ballance of one shilling & ten pence halfpenny due to the said Benjamin Lumley from the said borough.

Geo. Hutchinson, W: Sleigh, G. Sutton, J: Wilkinson, J. S. Raisbeck, Jno. Pickering, Thos: Haw, John Beckwith, Cuthbert Burrell, Alexr Hunter, Thos Dumble, Wm Wray, Jno. Cock, Robert Spark, Thos Sheraton, Char^s Wharton, Thos. Perkins.

Note. At the same court it[241] was ordered that the corporation revenue should not in future be lyable to any expences in cleaning the Shambles or repairing the windows or furniture in the Town's House or for money given the publick ringers.

Witness: John Carter, steward.

---

241 MS: 'is'.

[p. 327]

Borough of Stockton. The court leet and court baron of the right ~~right honourable~~ reverend John lord bishop of Durham holden at the Town House in and for the said borough on Tuesday the thirteenth day of October in the year of our lord one thousand seven hundred and seventy seven before George Hutchinson Esq. mayor and John Carter gentleman steward.

This day the said George Hutchinson as mayor of the \said/ borough for the last year perfected his accounts to the chief burgesses of the said borough and upon such accounts, which were examined and allowed \there/ ~~ther~~ remains a ballance of thirty seven pounds eleven shillings and two pence three farthings due to the said borough to be carried to the next year's account.[242]

G. Sutton, J. S. Raisbeck, Benj. Lumley, Jno Pickering, Wm Wray, Thos Haw, John Beckwith, Jno. Cock, Cuthbt Burrell, Thos Dumble, Alexander Hunter, James Walker, Char^s Wharton, Thos Sheraton, Thomas Faith.

[p. 328]

Borough of Stockton

The court leet and court baron of the right reverend John lord bishop of Durham holden at the Town House in and for the said borough on Tuesday the twenty seventh day of October in the year of our Lord one thousand seven hundred and seventy eight before Jonathan Davison Esq. mayor and Timothy Smallwood deputy of Robert Preston gentleman steward.

This day George Hutchinson Esq. late mayor of the said borough for the last year perfected his accounts to the chief burgesses of the said borough and upon such accounts which were examined and allowed there remains a ballance \of/ sixty two pounds eight shillings and four-pence farthing which was paid to the present mayor accordingly.

Jona: Davison, mayor

---

242 'thirty seven pounds … next year's account' is in a different hand from the remainder of the entry.

[*col. 1*] Thos Sheraton, Thos Faith
[*col. 2*] G. Sutton, John Wilkinson, J. S. Raisbeck, Benj: Lumley, Jno. Pickering, Wm Wray, Thos Haw, John Beckwith, Jno. Cock, Cuthbt Burrell, Thos: Dumble, Alex^r Hunter, James Walton, Char^s Wharton.

[p. 329]
Borough of Stockton
The court leet and court baron of the right reverend John lord bishop of Durham holden at the Town House in and for the said borough on Tuesday the twenty fourth day of October in the year of our Lord one thousand seven hundred and eighty before Rowland Webster Esq. mayor and Robert Preston gentleman steward.

This day Jonathan Davison Esq.[243] as late mayor of the said borough for the last year perfected his accounts for the chief burgesses of the said borough and upon such accounts which were examined and allowed there remains a ballance of forty one pounds twelve shillings and nine pence which was paid to the present mayor accordingly.

G. Sutton,[244] R. Preston, Jno. Pickering, John Beckwith, Jno. Cock, Cuthbt Burrell, Thos Haw, Wm Brown, Thos Sheraton, Thomas Fall, Char^s Wharton, Wm Barker, Thos Dumble, John Woodhouse.

[p. 330]
Borough of Stockton. The court leet and court baron of the right reverend John lord bishop of Durham holden at the Town House in and for the said borough on Tuesday the twenty second day of October in the year of our Lord one thousand seven hundred and eighty two before Charles Sleigh Esq. mayor and Robert Preston the younger gentleman steward.

This day Rowland Webster Esq. as late mayor of the said borough for the last year perfected his accounts to the chief burgesses of the said borough and upon such accounts which were examined and allowed there remains a ballance of thirty five pounds thirteen shillings and three pence halfpenny which was paid to the present mayor accordingly.

243 Jonathan Davison held the post of Collector of the Customs from 1764 to 1781: Brewster, *History*, p. 191; Surtees, *History*, p. 176.
244 A name has been erased between this and the following signature.

G. Sutton, J. Davison, R. Preston, Jno. Pickering, John Beckwith, Jno. Cock, Cuthbt Burrell, Thos Haw, Wm Brown, Thos Sheraton, Thomas Fall, Char^s Wharton, Wm Barker, Thos Dumble, John Woodhouse.

[p. 331]
Borough of Stockton. The court leet and court baron of the right reverend John lord bishop of Durham holden at the Town House in and for the said borough on Tuesday the twenty eighth day of October in the year of our Lord one thousand seven hundred and eighty three before John Sutton Esq. mayor and Robert Preston the younger gentleman steward.

This day Charles Sleigh Esq. as late mayor of the said borough for the last year perfected his accounts to the chief burgesses of the said borough and upon such accounts, which were examined and allowed there remains a ballance of forty two pounds nine shillings and eleven pence which was paid to the present mayor accordingly.

G. Sutton, J. Davison, R. Preston, Jno. Pickering, John Beckwith, Jno. Cock, Cuthbt Burrell, Thos: Haw, Wm Brown, Thos Sheraton, Thomas Fall, Char^s Wharton,[245] Wm Barker, Thos Dumble, John Woodhouse.

[p. 332]
Borough of Stockton. The court leet and court baron of the right reverend John lord bishop of Durham holden at the Town House in and for the said borough on Tuesday the twenty sixth day of October in the year of our Lord one thousand seven hundred and eighty four before George Sutton Esq. mayor and Robert Preston the younger gentleman steward.

This day John Sutton Esq. as late mayor of the said borough for the last year perfected his accounts to the chief burgesses of the said borough and upon such accounts which were examined and allowed there remains a ballance of one hundred and two pounds five shillings and sixpence half penny which was paid to the present mayor accordingly.

[*immediately below*] J. S. Raisbeck, R. Preston, J. Wilkinson, Benj: Lumley, J. Davison

---

245 Charles Wharton was a customs officer: Ritson, *Stockton Jubilee*, p. 18.

[*at foot of page*] Thos Dumble, Wm Brown, John Beckwith, John Cock, Wm Wray, Wm Barker, Thos Haw, Thos: Fall, Geo Taylor, Ralph Beckwith, Cuthbt Burrell, Thos Sheraton.

[p. 333]
Borough of Stockton
Whereas there is now due and owing by and from the corporation of Stockton to George Sutton Esq. (the present mayor) the sum of ninety pounds principal money, it is hereby ordered and agreed by the aldermen and chief burgesses of this borough whose names are hereto subscribed and set that the said George Sutton do retain \out of the money in his hands belonging to the said corporation/ the said sum of ninety pounds and the interest attending the same in satisfaction and discharge of his debt so due to him as aforesaid. Given under our hands this first day of January one thousand seven hundred and eighty five.

J. S. Raisbeck, R: Preston, Benj: Lumley.

[p. 334]
Borough of Stockton. The court leet and court baron of the right reverend John lord bishop of Durham holden at the Town House in and for the said borough on Tuesday the eighteenth day of October in the year of our Lord one thousand seven hundred and eighty five before John Wilkinson Esq. mayor and Robert Preston the younger gentleman steward.

This day George Sutton Esq. as late mayor of the said borough for the last year perfected his accounts to the chief burgesses of the said borough and upon such accounts which were examined and allowed there remains a ballance of nine pounds ten shillings & seven pence halfpenny which was paid to the present mayor accordingly.

[*col. 1*] John Beckwith, Wm Wray, Cuthb. Burrell, Thos Dumble, Jno. Cock, Wm Brown, Thos: Haw, Ralph Beckwith, Jno Walker, Thos Sheraton, Char^s Wharton
[*col. 2*] J. S. Raisbeck.

[p. 335]
Borough of Stockton. The court leet and court baron of the right reverend John lord bishop of Durham holden at the Town House in and for the said borough on Tuesday the seventeenth day of October in the year of our Lord one thousand seven hundred and eighty

six before Christopher Smith Esq. mayor and Robert Preston the younger gentleman steward.

This day John Wilkinson Esq. as late mayor of the said borough for the last year perfected his accounts to the chief burgesses of the said borough and upon such accounts which were examined and allowed there remains a ballance of twenty eight pounds nine shillings \and six pence/ which was paid to the present mayor accordingly.

[p. 336] [*Crossed-out draft of rubric for court to be held 21 October 1788 (changed from 1787) with draft minute recording receipt of mayor's accounts but no financial amounts. The following entry covers both years.*]

[p. 337]
Borough of Stockton. The court leet and court baron of the reverend father in God Thomas lord bishop of Durham holden at the Town House in and for the said borough on Thursday the twenty first day of October in the year of our Lord one thousand seven hundred and eighty eight before John Stapylton Raisbeck Esq. mayor and Robert Preston the younger gentleman steward.

This day Christopher Smith Esq. as mayor for the two last years perfected his accounts to the chief burgesses of the said borough and upon such accounts which were examined and allowed there remains a balance of forty five pounds fourteen shillings & four pence halfpenny which was paid to the present mayor accordingly.

J. S. Raisbeck mayor

[*col. 1*] John Cock, Char^s Wharton, Ralph Beckwith, John Whitaker, Thos. Elstob, Jno. Walker junior, Thos. Middleton, Thos. Haw, Robt Rochford, Benjn Creary, Philip Hodgson, Wm Wray
[*col. 2*] G. Sutton, J. Wilkinson.

[p. 338]
Borough of Stockton. The court leet and court baron of the right reverend father in God Thomas lord bishop of Durham held at the Town House in and for the said borough on Tuesday the twenty seventh day of October in the year of our Lord one thousand seven hundred and eighty nine before Benjamin Lumley Esq. mayor and Robert Preston the younger gentleman steward.

This day John Stapylton Raisbeck Esq. as mayor for the last year perfected his accounts to the chief burgesses of the said borough and upon such accounts which were examined and allowed there remains a balance of sixty two pounds six shillings & 7½^d which was paid to the present mayor.

B. Lumley mayor

[*col. 1*] John Cock, Wm Wray, William Atkinson, John Metcalf, Ralph Beckwith, Thos. Elstob, Benjn Creary, Jno Walker, Wm Brown, Wm Barker, Char^s Wharton, John Peverall, John Jefferson junior
[*col. 2*] G. Sutton, Chris. Smith, J: Wilkinson.

[p. 339]
Borough of Stockton. Whereas there is now due and owing by and from the corporation of Stockton to ~~John~~ \Ann/ Oliver the sum of two hundred pounds and to Henry Stapylton Esq. the sum of two hundred and sixty pounds which two sums are now attended with interest after the rate of five pounds per centum per annum, it is hereby resolved and accordingly ordered that in case the said John Oliver and Henry Stapylton are not agreeable to accept henceforth four pounds ten shillings per centum per annum for the same sums they shall be immediately paid in. Given under our hands this twenty seventh day of October 1789.

B. Lumley mayor

[*col. 1*] John Cock, Wm Wray, William Atkinson, John Metcalf, Ralph Beckwith, Thos. Elstob, Benjn Creary, John Wasker,[246] Char^s Wharton
[*col. 2*] G. Sutton, J. S. Raisbeck, Chris Smith, J. Wilkinson.

[p. 340]
27th October 1789
Borough of Stockton. At a court held at the Town House the day and year ~~above~~ \before/ mentioned it was resolved and accordingly ordered that George Cragie be appointed to give a proper account of the names of the persons owners of the pigs that may be found at large ~~and that he~~ in the borough street and that he be allowed three pence on conviction of every offence or trespass by the corporation and one half of the fine \inflicted/ by the jury.

B. Lumley mayor

---

246 Signature in capital letters.

[*col. 1*] John Cock, Char^s Wharton, Wm Wray, William Atkinson, John Peverall, Ralph Beckwith, Jno Walker, Thos. Elstob, Benjn Creary, John Jefferson junior
[*col. 2*] J. S. Raisbeck, Wm Stephenson.

[p. 341]
Borough of Stockton. The court leet and court baron of the right reverend father in God Thomas lord bishop of Durham held at the Town House in and for the said borough on Tuesday the twenty sixth day of October in the year of our Lord one thousand seven hundred and ninety before William Sleigh Esq. mayor and Robert Preston the younger gentleman steward.

This day Benjamin Lumley Esq. as mayor for the last year perfected his accounts to the chief burgesses of the said borough and upon such accounts which were examined and allowed there remains a balance of eighty pounds three shillings and sixpence which was paid to the present mayor.

Wm Sleigh mayor

[*col. 1*] John Cock, J. Peacock, Cuthbert Burrell, Thos. Elstob, John Metcalf, Richd Moor, John Jefferson junior, Matthew Pibous, Wm Dale junior, Benjn Creary, Ralph Beckwith, Char^s Wharton
[*col. 2*] G. Sutton, J. Wilkinson.

[p. 342]
Borough of Stockton. The court leet and court baron of the honourable and right reverend father in God Shute lord bishop of Durham held at the Town House in and for the said borough on Tuesday the twenty fourth day of October in the year of our Lord one thousand seven hundred and seve ninety one before John Sutton Esq. mayor and John Stapylton Raisbeck gentleman steward.

This day William Sleigh Esq. mayor for the last year perfected his accounts to the chief burgesses of the said borough and upon such accounts which were examined and allowed there remains a balance of ninety nine pounds six shillings and six pence halfpenny which was paid to the present mayor.

John Sutton mayor

TEXT p. 344 195

[*col. 1*] John Cock, Wm Beckwith, Philip Hodgson, Willm Dale junior, Benjn Creary, Matthew Pibous, Thomas Kingston, William Stephenson, John Craggs, Matt: Wadeson, Char^s Wharton
[*col. 2*] G. Sutton, B. Lumley, J. Wilkinson, Chris Smith, Wm Sleigh.

[p. 343]
Borough of Stockton. The court leet and court baron of the honorable and right reverend father in God Shute lord bishop of Durham held by adjournment at the Town House in Stockton in and for the said borough on Friday the second day of ~~Oc~~ November in the year of our Lord one thousand seven hundred and ninety two before George Sutton Esq. mayor and John Stapylton Raisbeck gentleman steward.

This day the accounts of the late John Sutton Esq. mayor deceased were perfected to the chief burgesses of the said borough and upon such accounts which were examined and allowed there remains a balance of ~~two pounds and eleven pence half penny~~ nineteen pounds nineteen shillings and a halfpenny due to the personal representatives of the said John Sutton \now/ deceased and to be paid out of the first monies that shall arise \from/ ~~out of~~ the revenues of the corporation.

Chris Smith, John Cock, Matt: Wadeson, Philip Hodgson, Chas. Liddell, John Craggs, Matthew Pibous, Thos. Kingston, John Metcalf, Wm Beckwith, Ralph Taylor, Wm Walton, Wm Dale, Char^s Wharton.

[p. 344]
Borough of Stockton. The court leet and court baron of the honorable and right reverend father in God Shute lord bishop of Durham held at the Town House in and for the said borough on Tuesday the sixteenth day [of] April in the year of our Lord one thousand seven hundred and ninety three before George Sutton Esq. mayor and John Stapylton Raisbeck gentleman steward.

Whereas John Hayton schoolmaster hath occupied the schoolhouse belonging to this corporation at the yearly rent of two pounds ~~two shillings~~ and there will be due from him two years rent on the fifth day of July now next ensuing, it is hereby ordered that unless the said John Hayton shall pay the said rent on the said fifth day of July the steward of this borough do prosecute the said John Hayton for recovery of the said rent.

G. Sutton

[p. 345]
Borough of Stockton. The court leet and court baron of the honorable and right reverend father in God Shute lord bishop of Durham held by adjournment at the Town House in Stockton in and for the said borough on Tuesday the fifteenth day of October in the year of our Lord one thousand seven hundred and ninety three before Rowland Burdon Esq. mayor and John Stapylton Raisbeck gentleman steward.

This day the account of George Sutton Esq. mayor for the last year perfected his accounts to the chief burgesses of the said borough and upon which accounts which were examined and allowed there remains a balance of eight pounds nine shillings and four pence due to the said George Sutton to be paid out of the first monies that shall arise from the revenues of the corporation.

R. Burdon mayor[247]

B. Lumley, John Cock, Thos: Kingston, Matthew Pibous, Wm Walton, Ralph Taylor, Philip Hodgson, William Dale junior, Jno Craggs, John Metcalf, Chas. Liddell, Henry Beckwith, W. Beckwith.

[p. 346]
Borough of Stockton. The court leet and court baron of the honourable and right reverend and father in God Shute lord bishop of Durham held by adjournment at the Town House in Stockton in and for the said borough on Monday the third day of November in the year of our Lord one thousand seven hundred and ninety four before Rowland Burdon Esq. mayor and John Stapylton Raisbeck[248] gentleman steward.

This day Rowland Burdon Esq. mayor for the last year perfected his accounts to the chief burgesses were examined and allowed of the said borough and upon which accounts which were examined and allowed there remains a ballance of thirty nine pounds five shillings

---

247 In 1793, Rowland Burdon had presented to the House of Commons a petition, signed by 181 principal inhabitants of Stockton, for the abolition of the slave trade: Brewster, *History*, p. 437. This Rowland Burdon was the great-grandson of the Rowland Burdon who was mayor in the early 1640s: Surtees, *History*, pp. 173–4.

248 John Stapylton Raisbeck died suddenly on 4 December 1794, very soon after the entry above. Several notable people in the town died that winter: Tittler, *Two Weather Diaries*, p. 61.

& three pence \halfpenny/ due to the said \borough/.[249] ~~Rowland Burdon to be paid out of the first monies that shall arise from the revenues of the Corporation~~

[*col. 1*] Philip Hodgson, Thos: Kingston, George Newton
[*col. 2*] G. Sutton, John Cock, Matt Wadeson, Wm Dale junior, Matthew Pibous, Henry Beckwith, John Metcalf, Ra Taylor, Jno. Craggs.

[p. 347]
Borough of Stockton. The court leet and court baron of the honorable and right reverend father in God Shute lord bishop of Durham held ~~by adjournment~~ at the Town House in Stockton in and for the said borough on Thursday the twenty second day of October in the year of our lord one thousand seven hundred and ninety five before Robert Clarke[250] gentleman steward.

This day ~~George Sutton~~ \Rowland Burdon/ Esq. mayor for the last year perfected his accounts to the chief burgesses of the said borough and upon which accounts (which were examined and allowed) there remains a balance of one hundred pounds seven shillings and one penny due to the said borough.

[*col. 1*] John Cock, Wm Beckwith, Chris Potter, Henry Busby, Stephenson Ingrams, John Craggs, John Metcalf, Matt: Wadeson, Thos: Kingston, Chas Liddell, Ra Wear,[251] Henry Beckwith
[*col. 2*] G. Sutton, Chris Smith.

[p. 348]
Borough of Stockton. The court leet and court baron of the honorable and right reverend father in God Shute lord bishop of Durham held at the Town's House in Stockton in and for the said borough on Tuesday the twenty fourth day of April in the year of our Lord one thousand seven hundred and ninety eight before George Sutton Esq. mayor and Robert Clarke gentleman steward.

---

249 Details of the balance and the interlineation 'borough' are in a different hand from the rest of the entry.
250 Robert Clarke was a solicitor, appointed steward from 1794 to 1804. On stepping down, he presented the town with a new clock for the Town House, value £100: Richmond, *Local Records*, p. 94.
251 Reading uncertain.

At this court the accounts of Thomas Simpson Esq.[252] mayor of this borough for two years ending the first Tuesday after new Michaelmas Day last were produced to and examined by the present mayor and chief burgesses of the said borough, in which accounts appears a a charge of twenty pounds one shilling being Mr Raisbeck's bill for suing out a writ of mandamus for the election of a mayor of the said borough in Michaelmas term one thousand seven hundred and ninety five, which sum it is this day agreed shall not be allowed to the said Thomas Simpson but all the other articles in his said accounts were allowed and there remains (including the said sum of twenty pounds one shilling) a balance of thirty four pounds fourteen shillings and fourpence due from him to the said borough.

And it is this day also agreed that if the said Thomas Simpson shall refuse to pay the whole of the said sum of thirty four pounds fourteen shillings [p. 349] and four pence on or before the 12th day of May next proper measures shall be taken at the expence of the corporation of the said borough to compel him to pay the same.

[col. 1] John Cock, Wm Trenholm, Thos: Kingston, Henry Beckwith,[253] Thos: Foxton, Thos Coser, Wm Dale, Anthony Hall, Wm Beckwith, Jno. Craggs, Robt. Hodgson, Matt Wadeson
[col. 2] G. Sutton, Wm Sleigh, B. Lumley.

[p. 350]
Borough of Stockton. The court leet and court baron of the honorable and right reverend father in God Shute lord bishop of Durham held by adjournment at the Townshouse in Stockton in and for the said borough on Thursday the eighteenth day of October in the year of our Lord one thousand seven hundred and ninety eight before Robert Clarke gentleman steward (Christopher Smith Esq. mayor being absent).

---

252 On 29 December 1795, Thomas Simpson was elected mayor for a second time that year, his election on 6 October having been declared void, as he was not a burgess. The Court of the King's Bench authorised a new election: Richmond, *Local Records*, p. 95; Surtees, *History*, pp. 173–4; Brewster, *History*, pp. 145–8.

253 Henry Beckwith built a chapel in West Row for the Calvinist dissenters, who had been using a building in Green Dragon Yard: Richmond, *Local Records*, p. 98.

This day \the accounts of/ George Sutton Esq. mayor of this borough
for ~~two~~ \one/ year ending the first Tuesday after New Michaelmas
Day last were produced to and examined by us the undermentioned
burgesses then and there present upon which accounts there remains
a balance of fifteen pounds sixteen shillings and ten pence due to the
said borough.

[*col. 1*] John Cock, Wm Beckwith, Henry Beckwith, Thos Coser, Jno.
Craggs, Thos: Kingston, Robt. Hodgson, Wm. Dale, Martin Kirtley,
Wm Trenholm, Matt Wadeson, Thos Foxton
[*col. 2*] Henry Busby.

[p. 351]
Borough of Stockton. The court leet and court baron of the honorable
and right reverend father in God Shute lord bishop of Durham
held at the Town'shouse in Stockton in and for the said borough
(by adjournment) on Tuesday the twenty ninth day of October one
thousand seven hundred and ninety nine before Robert Wilkinson
Esq.[254] mayor and Robert Clarke gentleman steward.

This day the accounts of Christopher Smith Esq. late mayor of this
borough for one year ending the first Tuesday after New Michaelmas
Day last were produced to and examined by us the burgesses whose
names are hereunto subscribed and who were then and there present
upon which accounts there remains a balance of forty four pounds
thirteen shillings and three halfpenny due to the said borough.

Robt. Wilkinson mayor

[*col. 1*] John Cock, Wm Walton, Wm Lockey, Wm Carr, Thos Jennett,
Wm Trenholm, Jno Craggs, Henry Busby, Thos Foxton, Wm.
Beckwith, Matt^w Wadeson
[*col. 2*] Thos. Kingston, Jon^n Garbutt, Stephenson Ingrams.

[p. 352]
4th November 1800. Borough of Stockton.

The court leet and court baron of the honorable and right reverend
father in God Shute lord bishop of Durham held (by adjournment) at
the Townshouse in Stockton in and for the said borough on Tuesday

---

254 Robert Wilkinson was a banker: Tittler, *Two Weather Diaries*, p. 137.

the fourth day of November one thousand eight hundred before Robert Wilkinson Esq. mayor and Robert Clarke gentleman steward.

This day the accounts of Robert Wilkinson Esq. mayor for one year ending the first Tuesday after New Michaelmas Day last were produced to and examined by us the burgesses whose names are hereunto subscribed and who were then and there present upon which accounts there remains a balance of eighty three pounds sixteen shillings and eleven pence due to the said borough.

John Cock, Wm Walton, Martin Kirtley, Wm Beckwith, John Metcalf, Thomas Hubback, Henry Beckwith, Wm Trenholm, Matt^w Wadeson, Thos: Kingston, W: Richmond, Thos Coser, Stephenson Ingram.

[p. 353]
27th November 1801

Borough of Stockton. The court leet and court baron of the honorable and right reverend father in God Shute lord bishop of Durham held (by adjournment) at the Town House in Stockton in and for the said borough on Friday the twenty seventh day of November one thousand eight hundred and one before Richardson Ferrand Esq. mayor and Robert Clarke gentleman steward.

This day the accounts of Robert Wilkinson Esq. late mayor of this borough for one year ending the first Tuesday after New Michaelmas Day last were produced to and examined by us the burgesses whose names are hereunto subscribed and who were then and there present upon which accounts there remains a balance of twenty five pounds and one penny due to the said borough.

Rich^n Ferrand mayor

[col. 1] John Cock, Wm Beckwith, Henry Beckwith, Thomas Coser, Willm: Richmond, John Metcalf, Matt: Wadeson, John Craggs
[col. 2] Martin Kirtley, Thos Hubback, Wm Trenholm, Wm Walton, Richd Wright, Thos. Kingston.

[p. 354]
22nd October 1802

Borough of Stockton. The court leet and court baron of the honorable and right reverend father in God Shute lord bishop of Durham held (by adjournment) at the Town House in Stockton in and for the said borough on Friday the twenty second day of October one thousand eight hundred and two before Richardson Ferrand Esq. mayor and Robert Clarke gentleman steward.

This day the accounts of Richardson Ferrand Esq. mayor for one year ending the first Tuesday after New Michaelmas Day last were produced to and examined by us the burgesses whose names are hereunto subscribed and who were then and there present upon which accounts there remains a balance of fifty three pounds seventeen shillings and twopence halfpenny due to the said borough.

[*col. 1*] Matt^w Wadeson, W: Richmond, John Cock, Thomas Coser, Wm Walton, Henry Beckwith, Wm Beckwith, John Metcalf, Henry Busby, Thos. Kingston, Thos Hubback, Martin Kirtley, Richd Wright[255]
[*col. 2*] G. Sutton, Wm Sleigh.

[p. 355]
Borough of Stockton. The court leet and court baron of the honorable and right reverend father in God Shute lord bishop of Durham held by adjournment at the Town House in Stockton in and for the said borough on Friday the twenty second day of October one thousand eight hundred and two before Richardson Ferrand Esq. mayor and Robert Clarke gentleman steward.

WHEREAS the principal sum of one thousand seven hundred and thirty five pounds is due and owing from the mayor commonalty and burgesses of this borough to the several persons and in the sums herein after mentioned (that is to say)   £   s   d

	£	s	d
To Mr John Stonehouse of Oughton	320		
The Executors of Mr Lawrence Richardson late of Stockton	325		
Mrs Ann Robinson	310		
Henry Stapylton Esq. of Norton	260		
Mr Thomas Stonehouse	200		
Mr James Dunning of Sunderland	120		
Mr William Shadforth of Elwick	100		
Mr Robert Wilkinson of Norton	100		
	£1735		

255 In pencil in the bottom left margin three sets of initials '[..] H', 'W. T.', 'J. C.'.

AND WHEREAS it is essential to the interest of this borough that an annual saving should be made out of the revenues thereof to be applied towards the discharge of the said debt, to effect which purpose the mayors of this borough have some years past served the office of mayoralty without the [p. 356] allowance of thirty pounds in and by an order of this corporation bearing date the fourth day of October 1774 directed to be allowed to the mayor for the time being for the expences of his office, IT is therefore hereby agreed and ordered that henceforth until the sum of seven hundred and thirty five pounds part of the said sum of one thousand seven hundred and thirty five pounds shall be satisfied and discharged by the application of the revenues of this borough without borrowing further sums the said allowance of thirty pounds per annum shall be discontinued, and that Richardson Ferrand Esq. \the present/ mayor and every succeeding mayor until the said sum of seven hundred and thirty five pounds[256] be satisfied and discharged shall serve his office without any allowance whatever out of the revenues of this corporation. But in consideration thereof it is hereby also agreed that neither the present nor any future mayor of this borough shall be obliged to be at any expence during his mayoralty in entertainments at his election or on any other occasion for the burgesses jury or inhabitants of Stockton and its neighbourhood.

Rich[n] Ferrand mayor
Witness: Rt Clarke steward

[col. 1] John Cock, Anthony Hall, John Metcalf, Henry Busby, Thos Hubback, John Craggs, Richd Wright, W: Richmond, Wm Beckwith
[col. 2] Martin Kirtley, Wm Trenholm, Wm Walton, Matt[w] Wadeson, Thos. Kingston, Thomas Coser, Henry Beckwith
[col. 3] G. Sutton, Wm: Sleigh.

[p. 357]
Borough of Stockton. The court leet with view of frankpledge and court baron of the right reverend father in God Shute lord bishop of Durham held at the Townshouse in Stockton in and for the said borough on Tuesday the eleventh day of October one thousand eight hundred and three before John Carr Esq. mayor and Robert Clarke gentleman steward.

---

256 The sum of £735 is underlined in pencil and in the left margin is pencilled: '£995.1.0 was paid off in Decr 1818 and in [sic]'.

This day the accounts of Richardson Ferrand Esq. late mayor of this borough for one year ending the first Tuesday after New Michaelmas Day last were produced to and examined by us the burgesses whose names are hereunto subscribed and upon these accounts there remains a balance of one hundred and thirty nine pounds seventeen shillings and nine pence halfpenny due to the said borough, one hundred pounds of which we direct shall be applied in reduction of the debt due and owing from the mayor commonality and burgesses of the said borough.

John Carr mayor[257]

[*col. 1*] John Cock, Henry Beckwith, Stephenson Ingram, Martin Kirtley, Wm Walton, John Craggs, Wm Trenholm, Tho. Beckwith, Wm Beckwith, Thos. Kingston, Thos. Jennett
[*col. 2*] Matt^w Wadeson, Thomas Coser, Henry Busby.

[p. 358]
Borough of Stockton. The court leet with view of frank pledge and court baron of the right reverend father in God Shute lord bishop of Durham held at the Townshouse in Stockton in and for the said borough on Tuesday the thirtieth day of October one thousand eight hundred and four before John Carr Esq. mayor and Robert Clarke gentleman steward.

This day the accounts of John Carr Esq. mayor of this borough for one year ending the first Tuesday after New Michaelmas Day last were produced to and examined by us the burgesses whose names are hereunto subscribed, and upon these accounts there remains a balance of seventy eight pounds fifteen shillings and sixpence due to the said borough: fifty pounds of which we direct shall be applied in reduction of the debt due and owing from the mayor, commonality and burgesses of the borough.

John Carr mayor

[*col. 1*] Henry Beckwith, Wm Beckwith, Wm Walton, Martin Kirtley, William Carr, William Lockey, Willm. Gent, Joseph Pickering, John Craggs, Wm Trenholm
[*col. 2*] Matt^w Wadeson, Thomas Coser, Robt Hodgson, John Metcalf.

257 John Carr, from Ryhope, was Collector of the Customs from 1799 to 1817: Brewster, *History*, p. 191; Surtees, *History*, pp. 173–4, 176.

[p. 359]
Borough of Stockton. The court leet with view of frankpledge and court baron of the right reverend father in God Shute lord bishop of Durham held at the Town House in Stockton in and for the said borough on Tuesday the twenty second day of October one thousand eight hundred and five before George Hutchinson Esq. mayor & Leonard Raisbeck gentleman steward.

This day the accounts of John Carr Esq. late mayor of this borough for one year ending the first Tuesday after New Michaelmas Day last were produced to and examined by us the burgesses whose names are hereunto subscribed and upon these accounts there remains \ the sum/ of twenty eight pounds eighteen shillings. And we do order that as soon as the balance in hand shall amount to fifty pounds the same shall be applied in reduction of the debt due from the mayor commonality and burgesses of the borough.

George Hutchinson mayor

[*col. 1*] Richd Wright, Wm Walton, Willm. Dale, Matthew Davison, John Foster, William Lockey, Thos. Kingston
[*col. 2*] G. Sutton, Robt. Wilkinson, Matt\ Wadeson, W: Richmond, Thos. Jennett, Ralph Lodge, Thos Hubback, Thos. Fall, Thomas Coser, John Metcalf.

[p. 360]
Borough of Stockton. The court leet with view of frank pledge of the right reverend father in God Shute lord bishop of Durham held at the Town House in Stockton in and for the said borough on Friday the second day of May one thousand eight hundred and six before George Hutchinson Esq. mayor and Leonard Raisbeck gentleman steward.

At this court the declaration of the ancient rights and customs of election in the borough made in the court held on the 17th day of October 1699 and entered in folio 147 of this book[258] was read and unanimously agreed to and confirmed, and it is also hereby declared and unanimously agreed that according to the ancient custom within this borough no person is or can be qualified to be elected, or to serve as mayor for this borough unless he hath a whole burgage within

258 Above, pp. 98–9.

this borough and hath been admitted and been sworn to the fealty according to the custom of this court.

George Hutchinson mayor

[*col. 1*] Philip Hodgson, Joseph Pickering, Wm. Beckwith, Henry Beckwith
[*col. 2*] G. Sutton, Matt^w Wadeson, Richd. Dickson, Wm Trenholm, William Lockey, Willm. Gent, Thos. Farmer, John Craggs, Wm. Atkinson.

[p. 361]
Borough of Stockton. The court leet with view of frankpledge & court baron of right reverend father in God Shute lord bishop of Durham held at the Town House in Stockton in and for the said borough on Friday the seventeenth day of October one thousand eight hundred & six before George Hutchinson Esq. mayor & Leonard Raisbeck gentleman steward.

This day the accounts of George Hutchinson Esq. mayor of this borough for one year ending the first Tuesday after New Michaelmas Day last were produced to & examined by us the burgesses whose names are hereunto subscribed & upon these accounts there remains the sum of seventy nine pounds five shilling & eleven pence halfpenny due to the said borough, seventy pounds of which we direct shall be applied in reduction of the debt due & owing from the mayor, commonalty & burgesses of the said borough.

G. Sutton, Wm. Sleigh, Matt^w Wadeson, Thos. Jennett, Wm Walton, W Lockey, Thos. Kingston, Wm. Bradley, Thomas Fall, Thos. Catherick, Thomas Coser, Martin Kirtley, Ralph Lodge, W. Richmond, Thos Hubback.

[p. 362]
Borough of Stockton. The court leet with view of frankpledge & court baron of the right reverend father in God Shute lord bishop of Durham held at the Town House in Stockton in and for the said borough on Tuesday the twentieth day of October one thousand eight hundred and seven ~~George Hutchinson~~ \Watson Alcock/[259] Esq. mayor & Leonard Raisbeck gentleman steward.

259 Watson Alcock was an eminent surgeon as well as twice mayor, retiring to The Square in Stockton: Heavisides, *Annals*, p. 22.

This day the accounts of George Hutchinson Esq. late mayor of this borough for one year ending the first Tuesday after New Michaelmas Day now last past were produced to & examined by us the burgesses whose names are hereunto subscribed & upon these accounts there remains the sum of twenty six pounds two shillings and ten pence due to the said borough.

G. Sutton, Watson Alcock, Matt^w Wadeson, Richd. Dickson, W: Richmond, Thos. Jennett, Ra: Lodge, Thomas Coser, Wm Bradley, Thos. Catherick, Willm Dale, William Lockey, Wm. Atkinson, Robt. Hodgson.

[p. 363]
Borough of Stockton. The court leet with view of frankpledge and court baron of the right reverend father in God Shute lord bishop of Durham held at the Town House in Stockton in and for the said borough on Tuesday the twenty fifth day of October one thousand eight hundred and eight before Watson Alcock Esq. mayor & Leonard Raisbeck gentleman steward.

This day the accounts of Watson Alcock Esq. mayor of this borough for one year ending the first Tuesday after New Michaelmas Day last were produced to and examined by us the burgesses whose names are hereunto subscribed and upon these accounts there remains the sum of ninety three pounds twelve shillings and ten pence three farthings due to the said borough.[260]

Matt^w Wadeson, Richd. Dickson, Thos. Jennett, Thos. Hubback, Robt. Hodgson, Thos. Catherick, Willm. Dale, Thomas Kingston, Wm Walton, Wm. Bradley, Jon^n Garbutt, Richd Wright, Ra: Lodge, W: Richmond.

[p. 364]
Borough of Stockton. The court leet with view of frankpledge and court baron of the right reverend father in God Shute lord bishop of Durham held at the Town House in Stockton in and for the said borough on Tuesday the seventeenth day of October one ~~hundred~~ thousand eight hundred and nine before James Walker Esq. mayor & Leonard Raisbeck Esq. steward.

---

260 The sum has been added in a different hand, perhaps that of Matthew Wadeson, the first signatory.

This day the accounts of Watson Alcock Esq. late mayor of this borough for one year ending the first Tuesday after New Michaelmas Day last were produced to and examined by us the burgesses whose names are hereunto subscribed and upon these accounts there remains the sum of forty one pounds thirteen shillings and three pence three farthings which we direct shall be applied in reduction of the debt due and owing from the mayor comm[on]alty and burgesses of the said borough to Mr John Stonehouse.

James Walker mayor

Matt^w Wadeson, Chas. Engledow, W: Richmond, Ra: Lodge, Willm. Dale, Jona. Garbutt, Thomas Kingston, Richd Wright, Thos Hubback, Willm Walton, Henry Beckwith, Thos Catherick, Robt. Hodgson.

[p. 365]
Borough of Stockton. The court leet with view of frankpledge and court baron of the right reverend father in God Shute lord bishop of Durham held at the Town House in Stockton in and for the said borough on Friday the twenty sixth day of October one thousand eight hundred and ten before John Hutchinson Esq. mayor and Leonard Raisbeck gentleman steward.

This day the accounts of James Walker Esq. mayor of this borough for one year ending the first Tuesday after New Michaelmas Day last were produced to and examined by us the burgesses whose names are hereunto subscribed, and upon these accounts there remains a balance of fifty three pounds three shillings and eight pence halfpenny due to the said borough to be applied in reduction of the debt due and owing from the mayor commonalty and burgesses of the said borough to Mrs Margaret Shadforth.

Matt^w Wadeson, Wm Walton, Thomas Coser, Richd Wright, Thos. Catherick, George Howson, Willm Dale, Thos Hubback, Chas. Engledow, Robt. Hodgson, Ra: Lodge, Thos. Jennett, Thos. Fall, W: Richmond, Thomas Kingston.

[p. 366]
Borough of Stockton. The court leet with view of frankpledge and court baron of the honorable and right reverend father in God Shute lord bishop of Durham held at the Town House in Stockton in and for the said borough on Tuesday the twenty ninth day of October one thousand eight hundred and eleven before Leonard Raisbeck steward.

This day the accounts of John Hutchinson Esq. the late mayor of this borough for one year ending the first Tuesday after New Michaelmas Day last were produced and examined and upon these accounts there remains a balance of one hundred and fifteen pounds twelve shillings and four pence due to the said borough out of which we do hereby direct that one hundred pounds shall be paid to Mrs Margaret Shadforth in discharge of the debt due from to her from the mayor commonalty and burgesses of the said borough.

Matt^w Wadeson, Thos. Jennett, Rich. Dickson, Willm. Dale, Geo: Moss, John Appleton, Thomas Fall, Chas. Engledow, W: Richmond, Wm Walton, Robt. Hodgson, Thos. Catherick, Richd Wright, Thos Hubback, Thomas Coser.

[p. 367]
Borough of Stockton. The court leet with view of frankpledge and court baron of the honorable and right reverend father in God Shute lord bishop of Durham held at the Town House in Stockton in and for the said borough on Friday the sixteenth day of October one thousand eight hundred and twelve before Thomas Hutchinson Esq. mayor and Leonard Raisbeck gentleman steward.

This day the accounts of James Walker Esq.[261] the late mayor of this borough for one year ending the first Tuesday after New Michaelmas Day last were produced and examined and upon these accounts there remains a balance of forty nine pounds thirteen shillings and one penny due to the borough which we direct shall be applied in reduction of the debt due and owing from the mayor commonalty and burgesses of the said borough.

Thomas Hutchinson mayor

[col. 1] Matt^w Wadeson, Thos. Jennett, John Wilkinson, Richd Wright, Thomas Eeles, Willm. Dale, Chas. Engledow, W: Richmond, Thomas Fall, William Foxton, Geo: Rowntree, Thos. Catherick, Wm Walton, Robt Hodgson, Thomas Coser

261 James Walker was elected mayor after George Snowdon had been elected but declined to take office. The King's Bench intervened and ordered an additional court leet to be held, at which Walker was elected: Brewster, *History*, pp. 148–9. George Snowdon is perhaps to be identified as the joint proprietor, with Richard Morley, of Norton water-mill: Tittler, *Two Weather Diaries*, p. 63.

[*col. 2*] Watson Alcock alderman, G: Sutton.

[p. 368]
Borough of Stockton. The court leet with view of frankpledge and court baron of the honorable and right reverend father in God Shute lord bishop of Durham held at the Town House in Stockton in and for the said borough on Tuesday the twenty sixth day of October one thousand eight hundred and thirteen before George Sutton Esq. mayor and Leonard Raisbeck gentleman steward.

This day the accounts of Thomas Hutchinson Esq. late mayor of this borough for one year ending the first Tuesday after New Michaelmas Day last were produced and examined and upon these accounts there remains a balance of thirteen pounds two shillings and two pence halfpenny due to the borough which we direct shall be applied in reduction of the debt due and owing from the mayor commonalty and burgesses of the said borough.

Matt^w Wadeson, G. Sutton, Thomas Fall, Chas. Engledow, John Wilkinson, Thomas Eeles, Willm. Bradley, Thos Catherick, Wm Walton, William Dale, H. W. Foxton, Wm. Beckwith, Wm. Atkinson, Robt Hodgson.

[p. 369]
Borough of Stockton. The court leet with view of frankpledge and court baron of the honorable and right reverend father in God Shute lord bishop of Durham held at the Town House in Stockton in and for the said borough on Tuesday the twenty fifth day of October one thousand eight hundred and fourteen before Richard Dickson Esq. mayor and Leonard Raisbeck gentleman steward.

This day the accounts of George Sutton Esq.[262] late mayor of this borough for one year ending the first Tuesday after New Michaelmas Day last past were produced and examined and upon these accounts there appears to be a balance of three pounds three shillings and four pence half penny due from the said late mayor to the said borough

262 George Sutton, 'senior alderman', died 4 February 1817, aged eighty-one, leaving the bulk of his substantial property to his grand-nephew George Hutchinson, who took the name of Sutton. He was one of the town's wealthiest men: Richmond, *Local Records*, pp. 127–8; Tittler, *Two Weather Diaries*, p. 64.

to be paid out of the first money to be received from the revenues of the corporation.[263]

Richd. Dickson mayor

[*col. 1*] Matt[w] Wadeson, William Foxton, Thomas Eeles, Robt. Hodgson, Wm. Wolton, Thos Catherick, Wm: Atkinson, Willm. Dale, Thomas Fall, Chas. Engledow, Geo. Rowntree, W: Richmond, John Wilkinson, Thos Jennett
[*col. 2*] G. Sutton, Watson Alcock, J. Hutchinson.

[p. 370]
Borough of Stockton. The court leet with view of frankpledge and court of the honorable and right reverend father in God Shute lord bishop of Durham held at the Town House in Stockton in and for the said borough on Tuesday the seventeenth day of October one thousand eight hundred and fifteen before Richard Dickson Esq. mayor and Leonard Raisbeck gentleman steward.

This day the accounts of Richard Dickson Esq. mayor of this borough for one year ending the first Tuesday after New Michaelmas Day last past were produced and examined and upon these accounts there appears to be a balance of one hundred and twenty seven pounds six shillings and four pence halfpenny due to the said borough, which, or a sufficient part thereof, we direct shall be applied in renewing the leases from the bishop of Durham.

Richd. Dickson mayor

Wm Walton, Thos Jennett, T. Eeles, Wm Dale, G. Rowntree, John Dixon, W: Richmond, Jno Wilkinson, William Foxton, Wm. Atkinson, John Palmer, Wm Sleigh, Geo. Tweddell, Robt. Hodgson.

[p. 371]
Borough of Stockton. The court leet with view of frankpledge and court baron of the honorable and right reverend father in God Shute lord bishop of Durham held at the Town House in Stockton in and for the said borough on Friday the twenty fifth day of October one thousand eight hundred and sixteen before Henry Hutchinson Esq. mayor & Leonard Raisbeck gentleman steward.

---

263   The text 'to be paid out … corporation' is very faint and overwritten with a line of dots.

This day the accounts of Richard Dickson Esq. the late mayor of this borough for one year ending the first Tuesday after New Michaelmas Day last past were produced and examined and upon these accounts there appears to be a balance of seventy four pounds fifteen shillings and seven pence half penny due to the said borough which we direct shall be applied in reduction of the debt due and owing from the mayor commonalty and burgesses of the said borough.

H. Hutchinson (mayor)[264]

[*col. 1*] Matt^w Wadeson, Thos. Jennett, Robt. Wilson, John Dixon, John Wilkinson, R. Jordison, Willm. Dale, John Palmer, Danl. Pearson, W: Richmond, Wm. Sleigh, Henry Beckwith, Thomas Eeles, John Filiner [*col. 2*] ~~John Filiner~~, Watson Alcock, Richd. Dickson.

[p. 372]
Borough of Stockton. The court leet with view of frankpledge and court baron of the honorable and right reverend father in God Shute lord bishop of Durham held at the Town House in Stockton in and for the said borough on Friday the twenty fourth day of October one thousand eight hundred and seventeen before Henry Hutchinson Esq. mayor & Leonard Raisbeck gentleman steward.

This day the accounts of Henry Hutchinson Esq. mayor of this borough for one year ending the first Tuesday after New Michaelmas Day last past were produced and examined and upon these accounts there appears to be a balance of one hundred and twenty nine pounds four shillings and seven pence due to the said borough which we direct shall be applied in reduction of the debt due and owing from the mayor commonalty and burgesses of the said borough.

H. Hutchinson mayor

Mattw: Wadeson, W: Richmond, John Dixon, John Palmer, Thos. Jennett, Jno Wilkinson, Rob. Bald, Wm Musgrave, Wm Russell, Willm. Gent, Martin Kirtley, George Iley, Wm Trenholm, R. Jordison, Thomas Fall, Wm Beckwith.

[p. 373]
Borough of Stockton. At a meeting of the mayor aldermen and burgesses held at the Town House this 6th day of November 1817

264 Henry Hutchinson beat Thomas Jennet by seventeen to sixteen votes in the poll to elect the mayor: Surtees, *History*, pp. 173–4.

pursuant to due notice given to the several members of the corporation individually.

It is resolved that in order to remove the doubts which have for some time existed on the subject, a case shall be stated and the opinion of His Majesty's Attorney General obtained by Mr Raisbeck whether the record or entries of the burgesses' fines or admittances be liable to any and what stamp duty.

Also that William and Edward Fawell shall be forthwith required to restore to the corporation the ground belonging to them of which they \have/ wrongfully possessed themselves and part whereof they have converted into a garden and the residue whereof they have appropriated for scites for dwelling houses and other buildings lately erected by them; that the vacant ground between the above mentioned garden and the granary late belonging to Mr Sutton shall be forthwith let to the best advantage for any term not exceeding six years.

[*col. 1*] H. Hutchinson,[265] Mr Dickson [*in pencil; followed by space before the following signatures at the bottom of the page:*] Thomas Fall, Robt. Wilson, Joseph Pickering.
[*col. 2*] Mattw: Wadeson, Richard Walker, Wm Braithwaite, Willm Gent, W: Richmond, Rob. Bald, Jas Atkinson, Richd Wright, Thos Eeles, Thos Jennett, Willm. Watson, John Dixon, R. Jordison, [*blot*] Robinson.

[p. 374]
Borough of Stockton. At a meeting of the mayor aldermen and burgesses held at the Town House this twenty seventh day of November one thousand eight hundred and seventeen pursuant to due notice.

It is resolved

First that the Towns Hall and the stallage and dues of the market and Shambles be let by proposal for a term not exceeding three years

---

265 Henry Hutchinson convened public meetings to appoint special constables, due to persistent unrest and poor behaviour in the town: Sowler, *History*, pp. 140–2. A surviving poster from 1817 shows that he exhorted the townspeople to attend a public meeting and show support for public order: TA, U/ PG 5–14.

to commence at May Day 1818 and that a proper advertisement for letting the same be forthwith inserted in the provincial newspapers requiring separate proposals for each to be delivered sealed up to Mr Raisbeck on or before the eighth day of January next.

Secondly that the property belonging to the corporation shall on every future occasion be let by the mayor \aldermen/ and burgesses at a meeting regularly convened for that purpose.

Thirdly that a committee of seven persons be now appointed to enquire into the state of the market and the stallage and dues now paid and to report thereon to the first court to be held in and for the said borough after the twenty eighth day of November instant and that the following burgesses form such committee: William Richmond, Robert Bald, William Braithwaite, Richard Wright, James Atkinson, Thomas Hubback, William Watson.[266]

Fourthly that the jury to whom such report shall be made be requested to prepare a new [p. 375] rate of stallage and market dues agreeably thereto and do cause the same to be entered in the book of the corporation and do sign such entry.

Fifthly that these resolutions be entered in the order book of the corporation and be signed by the burgesses present.

[col. 1] Henry Hutchinson mayor, [in pencil, below mayor's signature: 'Wm Sleigh Esq.'], [lower down page:] Joseph Wel[c]h, Wm Atkinson [col. 2] Richd. Walker, Jas. Crowe, Wm Braithwaite, W: Richmond, Willm Watson, Richd Wright, Danl. Pearson, John Dixon, Wm Russell, Robt. Bald, Willm. Gent, Thomas Fall, John Wilkinson, Thos. Jennett, R. Jordison, Matt^w Wadeson, Jas. Atkinson, Thomas Coser, William Fawell, Wm. Sleigh silversmith, Thomas Walker, Thos. Eeles, Thos. Hubback, John Grant.

[p. 376]
Borough of Stockton. At a meeting of the mayor aldermen and burgesses held at the Town House this 15th day of January 1818 pursuant to due notice.

---

266 These are not signatures but written in the same hand.

The proposals received for the Town House and the stallage and dues of the market and Shambles having been laid before the meeting and considered, resolved unanimously that the property be let to Mr Henry Wade Foxton for three years from Mayday next at the rent of two hundred and forty pounds a year he paying all parliamentary and parochial taxes and assessments in respect of the premises and he and Mr William Richmond and Mr John Fox as his sureties giving a bond to secure the punctual payment of the rent.

Wm Braithwaite, Thos. Jennett, Richd Wright, John Grant, Danl Pearson, T. Hubback, Wm Gent, Robt. Bald, R. Jordison, Thomas Fall, W: Richmond.

Memorandum that at the above meeting William Sleigh Esq., Mr Henry Hutchinson, Mr John Hutchinson, Mr Watson Alcock and Mr Richard Dickson severally resigned the office of alderman.
                                        H. R. E. Wright, deputy steward.

[p. 377]
Borough of Stockton. The court leet with view of frankpledge and court baron of the honourable and right reverend father in God Shute lord bishop of Durham held at the Town House in Stockton on Tuesday the twenty seventh day of October one thousand eight hundred and eighteen before William Braithwaite Esq. mayor and Leonard Raisbeck gentleman steward.

This day the accounts of ~~William Braithwaite~~ \Henry Hutchinson/ Esq. mayor of this borough for one year ending the first Tuesday after New Michaelmas Day last past were produced and examined and upon these accounts there appears to be a balance of £59–13–7 due to the said borough which with the accruing half year's rents we direct shall be applied in reduction of the debt due and owing from the mayor commonalty and burgesses of the said borough.
                                        William Braithwaite mayor

Thos Jennett, Jno Wilkinson, Geo Moss, Wm Trenholm, Richd Wright, John Grant, Danl. Pearson, George Iley, Matt^w Wadeson, T. Hubback, Wm Gent, Robt Bald, Richd Jackson, Thomas Eeles, R. Jordison, Thomas Fall, W: Richmond.[267]

267 Pencilled numbers in left margin against the following signatures: Wm
    Trenholm ('1'); Danl Pearson ('2'); George Iley ('3'); T. Hubback ('4').

[p. 378]

At a meeting of the mayor aldermen and burgesses held at the Town House this 5ᵗʰ day of February 1819 pursuant to due notice.

Resolved unanimously that the yearly sum of twenty pounds be paid as a subscription out of the corporation funds to Mr Fowler Wilson as the master of the Grammar School[268] for the term of three years in case he shall so long continue to be the master of such school.

Also resolved that the lease to Mr Foxton be extended to the term of six years and the draught now read be approved and be forthwith engrossed – that this meeting be adjourned to Tuesday the ninth day of February instant and that the mayor aldermen and burgesses do meet at the Town House on that day \at ten o clock in the forenoon/ to execute such engrossment.

[*col. 1*] Wm Braithwaite mayor, John Metcalf, Jas. Crowe, Thos. Jennett, R. Jordison, Thomas Fall, Thos Hubback, John Dixon, Richd Jackson, Willm. Dale, Thomas Eeles, John Wilkinson, Wm. Barnes
[*col. 2*] Richd Wright, Wm Trenholm, James Atkinson junior, Wm Russell, Danl. Pearson, Willm. Gent, Willm Watson, William Sleigh, John Grant, Robt Seymour, Wm Musgrave, Robt Bald, W: Richmond, Wm Farmer
[*col. 3*] James Etherington, John F[os]ter.[269]

[p. 379]

At a meeting of the mayor aldermen and burgesses held at the Town House this 9th day of February 1819 pursuant to adjournment.

The lease to Mr Foxton of the Town House and the stables and shops held therewith and of the stallage and dues of the market and Shambles was sealed and executed.

Wm Braithwaite mayor, Richd. Jackson, Thos Jennett, Robt. Bald, John Grant, James Atkinson, junior, Willm. Gent, Willm. Dale, Thomas Fall.

---

268 Appointments of masters of the grammar school, established in 1785, do not appear in the book until this entry. Previous masters are listed in Brewster, *History*, p. 250.

269 Reading of surname uncertain.

[p. 380]

Copy

Report of the Committee appointed at a meeting of the mayor aldermen and burgesses regularly convened and held in the Town House the 27th day of November 1817.

In examining into the state of the market we particularly notice the necessity there is of affording some relief to that part called the Corn Market and recommend the adoption of the plan laid down below for the purpose of giving more room and convenience therein by laying down at equal distances stones of twelve or fourteen inches square as stands in direct lines for the purpose of exposing grain for sale so that the persons engaged in the buying and selling thereof may have a free communication with each other and thereby avoid the bustle and confusion which have hitherto prevailed in that part of the market.

We also beg leave to lay before them you the different stall rents and wharfage dues as per the annexed schedule which we have no doubt you will find adjusted in such proportions as to give satisfaction to all parties concerned, that a toll board be placed in the lobby of the Town House specifying all the rates and dues to be paid by order of the court.

We also suggest the necessity there is of adopting some plan for the general enlargement of the market place by removing one third part of the Shambles from the north to the south as the only effectual means of obtaining such enlargement.

In order to give effect to these improvements we particularly recommend the expediency of appointing annually a Committee of Repairs (along with the other officers of the court), consisting of five or seven, to take under their care [p. 381] property belonging to the corporation and to cause such improvements to be made and repairs to be done as upon due consideration shall be found necessary.

And lastly we think it is highly proper that auditors be also annually appointed for the purpose of investigating the corporation accounts.

[*Followed by schematic plan of Market Place; see Figure 6.*]

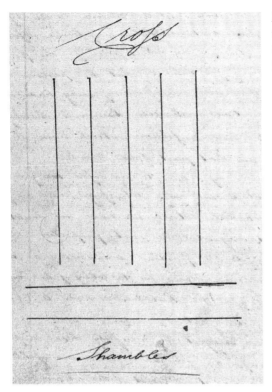

Figure 6   Proposed revision of layout of Corn Market, 1817 (p. 381 of MS).

Wm Braithwaite, W. Richmond, Robt Bald, James Atkinson, Thomas Hubback, Richd Wright, Willm Watson.[270]

[p. 382]
Rates of Stallage

	£	s	d
Butchers stalls per year for the use of the party taking and only and subject to the lessee for the time being of the market under the corporation having the privilege of letting the same on the days when the same are not actually occupied by the yearly tenant himself	3	0	0
Each butcher for stall for a Wednesday only		1	0
ditto for a Saturday only			6d

270 These are not signatures, all being in the same hand.

All stalls 8 feet in length and 4 feet in breadth except such
as afterwards mentioned covered   9d
ditto uncovered   6d
Stalls of greater dimensions in proportion
Standage on the ground for 12 feet by 6 feet for pots,
glass, wooden ware, baskets and furniture   6d
For brooms   1d
Hucksters and fruit stalls covered   6d
Ditto not covered   3d
Potatoe and fruit carts   3d

For standage of goods sold by auction

Furniture   1s 0d
Implements of husbandry & farming utensils   1s 0d
Horses, cows, pigs, sheep or other beasts for each lot   1s 0d
For each hawker's cart or wagon   2s 0d
Fish stalls of the above dimensions per day   4d
Caravans per day, small   9d
Middle size   1s 6d
Large ditto   2s 0d
On the 4 hiring days and at the races the dues and
stallages to be double.

[p. 383]
Custom House Quay
Quay dues for landing shipping merchandise   £   s   d
Admitted burgesses landing or shipping their own goods   Nothing
For all other goods whether landed or shipped by
admitted burgesses or other persons two thirds of the
average rates of wharfage taken for the time being by the
public wharfingers at Stockton and to be ascertained by
the mayor for the time being
Sand per ton   1^{d}

Ferry Boat Landing
All timber or deals to pay for landing or shipping per load   2^{d}

[p. 384]
Memorandum that the undersigned Fowler Wilson is appointed
the master of the Grammar School at Stockton for the term of three

years[271] to be computed from the seventh day of December last but subject to be removed for neglect of duty or other sufficient cause at the end of six months after notice from the mayor for the time being.

And it is agreed that during the time the said Fowler Wilson[272] shall continue in the said office he shall have the use of the building in the West Row in Stockton appropriated for a school room without paying any rent or other consideration for the same or being subject to the expence of repairs.[273]

And the said Fowler Wilson[274] on his part engages to act as such master and diligently to perform all the duties for the office for the said term of three years and not to resign his situation either at that period or at any subsequent time without giving six calendar months previous notice in writing of his intention to do so to the mayor for the time being.

Also to teach gratis in his school at all times during the term two[275] boys to be nominated by the mayor for the time being.

And also that a public examination of his scholars or pupils shall take place in the said schoolroom on the Tuesday immediately preceding the commencement of each midsummer and each[276] Christmas vacation at eleven o'clock [p. 385] in the forenoon and that proper notice of each \such/ intended examination shall be given at his expence to the principal inhabitants of Stockton at least three days previous thereto. Witness our hands this ninth day of February 1819.[277]

                              Wm Braithwaite mayor
                              Fowler Wilson

Memorandum that at the time of signing the above agreement it was stipulated and understood that the boys to be nominated by the mayor for the time being were to be received on condition of their

---

271 'three' underlined in pencil and 'one' written beside it; 'years' altered to 'year' in pencil.
272 Name underlined in pencil and initials 'G. H.' written above it.
273 'or … repairs' added in a different pen.
274 Again, underlined in pencil and 'G. H.' written above.
275 The word 'two' is underlined, and the figure '4' added above, in pencil.
276 'midsummer and each' underlined in pencil.
277 '34' pencilled above '19'.

being provided at his expence with necessary and proper books and being also neat and clean in their cloathing and persons and not being subject to perform any menial or other service for the master.

Wm Braithwaite mayor[278]

Fowler Wilson

[p. 386]

Borough of Stockton. The court leet with view of frankpledge and court baron of the honourable and right reverend father in God Shute lord bishop of Durham held at the Town House in Stockton on Thursday the twenty first day of October one thousand eight hundred and nineteen before Thomas Jennett Esq. mayor and Leonard Raisbeck gentleman steward.

This day the accounts of William Braithwaite Esq. mayor of this borough for one year ending the first Tuesday after New Michaelmas Day last past were produced and examined and upon these accounts there appears to be a balance of £369–13–1 due to the said ~~borough from~~ William Braithwaite which we do direct shall be paid to him out of the first money that shall become due to the corporation together with interest after the rate of five per centum per annum in the mean time for the same.

Thos Jennett mayor

W: Richmond, Robt. Jordison, Thomas Fall, John Wilkinson, Willm. Gent, Wm. Musgrave,[279] Thomas Eeles, John Grant, Wm. Bradley, Rob: Bald, W. Sadler, Geo. Moss, George Hay.

[p. 387][280]

At a meeting of the mayor aldermen and burgesses held at the Town House this 15th day of February 1820 pursuant to due notice.

---

278 William Braithwaite was elected mayor in 1818. He lived at 39 High Street and was a wholesale merchant. He was chief magistrate during a difficult time when the press was being suppressed and political imprisonment was rife, apparently acting in a 'very judicious and liberal manner': Heavisides, *Annals*, p. 25.

279 A William Musgrave owned a steam mill and warehouse which burnt down on 14 August 1828: Richmond, *Local Records*, p. 153. It prompted a public meeting and subscription to a third fire engine for the town.

280 This numbered page is preceded by two unnumbered blank pages with remains of sealing wax circles at top and bottom of the outer side of each

Resolved that a meeting of the mayor aldermen and burgesses shall be convened within twenty one days after Michaelmas Day in each year; that at such meeting the mayor's account of receipts and payments for the year preceding shall be submitted to inspection and a committee of repairs, and auditors of accounts for the year ensuing shall be elected.

At this meeting William Gent, William Watson, Daniel Pearson, John Grant, John Wilkinson, James Atkinson [and] Robert Bald were elected a committee of repairs for the current year which will expire on the first Tuesday next after the twenty ninth day of September next, and Richard Jackson, James Crowe [and] Thomas Walker were elected auditors of accounts for the same period.

[*col. 1*] Willm. Gent, Richd. Jackson, Jas. Atkinson junior, Wm Watson, Richd Wright, Danl. Pearson, John Grant, John Wilkinson
[*col. 2*] Jas. Atkinson, Rob Bald, Jas Crowe, Richd Walker senior, Thos Coser, Wm Bradley, W: Richmond, Thomas Walker.

[p. 388]
Borough of Stockton
At a meeting of the mayor aldermen and burgesses held this 21st day of October 1820 pursuant to due notice.

The accounts of Thomas Jennett Esq. late mayor of this borough for the year ending the first Tuesday after New Michaelmas Day now last past allowed by the auditors being produced and there appearing to be a balance of forty eight pounds eight shillings and six pence due to the said Thomas Jennett. We do direct that the same shall be paid to him with five percentum interest from this day out of the \first/ monies that shall be in hand or shall come in after the principal money and interest now remaining due to Mr William Braithwaite under or by virtue of the order made on the 21st day of October 1819 shall be fully satisfied and discharged.

We do also order and agree that the allowance to the jury at the Easter and Michaelmas courts shall be increased to four shillings a head; that the bellman shall attend every court which shall be

page. These would have prevented opening the blank pages, which had presumably been passed over in error.

held and shall be allowed henceforth one pound six shillings per annum to be paid quarterly as a compensation for such attendance and for his trouble in setting out the stalls for butter on the market days; that he shall also be provided with a cocked hat bound with white worsted lace and a blue cloth cloak faced with scarlet with a scarlet collar edged with white worsted lace to be worn by him when attending the court or acting as bellman but on no other occasions.

[p. 389]
We do further direct that specific stalls or seats in the pew belonging to the corporation in Stockton church shall be assigned and set out for the mayor and recorder and for each alderman and that the aldermen shall be placed according to seniority, and that no other person be allowed the use of the pew except His Majesty's naval or military officers or stranger gentlemen.

At this meeting John Grant, William Gent, William Watson, James Atkinson senior, William Bursey, William Richmond and Philip Hodgson were elected a committee of repairs for the current year which will expire on the first Tuesday next after the twenty ninth day of September next

and James Atkinson junior, Charles Barratt [and] Thomas Coser were elected auditors of accounts for the same period.
Wm. Skinner[281] mayor
[col. 1] Richd. Jackson, Thomas Walker, John Grant, J. Wilkinson, Willm Gent, Thomas Fall, Richd Wright, Robt. Bald, Joseph Pickering, James Atkinson, Rob: Jordison, John F … ter,[282] John Jackson
[col. 2] Wm. Braithwaite, Thos. Jennett,[283] Philip Hodgson, Thomas Coser, W. Richmond, Wm. Bursey, Willm. Watson, James Atkinson junior, Charles Barrett.

---

281 William Skinner was a banker in Stockton and his son William was mayor five times, including when the duke of Wellington visited. A William Skinner was president of the Mechanics' Institute from its formation in 1825 until 1835: Heavisides, *Annals*, pp. 24, 76.
282 Reading of surname very uncertain.
283 The signatures of Braithwaite, Jennett and the mayor are separated by a line from the remaining signatures in the right-hand column.

[p. 390]
Borough of Stockton. At a meeting of the mayor alderman and burgesses held this 25 day of May 1821 pursuant to due notice.

It being stated that Mr Thomas Fall, Mr James Atkinson senior and Mr Henry Wade Foxton who were duly appointed and sworn in flesh searchers at the court leet held in and for this borough on Tuesday the 24th day of October now last past for a year then next ensuing did in execution of their office on Wednesday the third day of January last seize a calf exposed to sale in open market on that day by Johnson Kemp as unwholesome meat and the same was thereupon condemned as such by the jury of the said court leet and was ordered by them to be publicly burned and that such order was carried into execution by the said officers and an action at the suit of the said Johnson Kemp has in consequence been commenced against them. Ordered that the said action be defended and that the said Thomas Fall, James Atkinson and Henry Wade Foxton[284] be indemnified out of the funds of the corporation.

Also Ordered that a committee be appointed to obtain plans and estimates for repairing and rebuilding the butchers' Shambles and to report the same with their opinion to a meeting of the mayor aldermen and burgesses to be held on Tuesday the third day of July next at six o'clock in the evening and that this meeting be adjourned to that time.

[p. 391]
That such committee consist of the following burgesses viz Mr William Braithwaite, Mr James Atkinson junior, Mr Robert Bald, Mr William Richmond, Mr Charles Barrett, Mr John Grant, Mr Robert Jordison, Mr William Watson and Mr John Wilkinson and that any five or more of them be competent to act.

Wm. Skinner mayor
Wm. Braithwaite

Wilfrid Sadler, W. Richmond, Thomas Fall, Thomas Eeles, Robt. Jordison, John Grant, James Atkinson junior, Charles Barrett, Jno. Wilkinson, Robt. Bald, Willm. Gent, Willm. Watson.

---

284 Henry Wade Foxton was originally a spirit merchant in Ramsgate, Stockton. He was for many years the town sergeant and also adjutant in the Stockton Volunteers: Heavisides, *Annals*, p. 25.

[p. 392]
Borough of Stockton. At a meeting of the mayor aldermen and burgesses held this third day of July 1821 pursuant to adjournment.

The report of the Committee for [*erasure*] \obtaining/ plans and estimates for repairing and rebuilding the butchers' Shambles having been take into consideration, ordered that on account of the great expense which would attend the putting the Shambles into complete repair the present Shambles be taken down and convenient new Shambles be erected.

That proper steps be taken by the recorder to ascertain whether the corporation be empowered to alter the scite of the Shambles and that he be authorised (if he think it necessary) to take counsel's opinion and that he report thereon to a general meeting to be held on the twenty eighth day of August next at six o clock in the evening.

Also Ordered that a committee be appointed to inquire and ascertain by what means the money requisite for defraying the expense of rebuilding the Shambles can be raised \and do report thereon to the said general meeting/. That such committee consist of the following burgesses viz: Mr John Wilkinson, Mr Thomas Jennett, Mr James Atkinson junior, Mr William Skinner junior, Mr Richard Jackson, Mr Thomas Walker, Mr John Grant, Mr Robert Bald and Mr William Richmond and that any five or more of them be competent to act.

That this meeting be adjourned to the said 28th day of August next at 6 o'clock in the evening and that public notice of such meeting be previously given.

Wm Skinner mayor

[*col. 1*] Wm[285] Russell, Thomas Eeles, Wilfred Sadler, Thomas Fall, Thomas Walker, Robt. Jordison, Joseph Pickering, William Watson
[*col. 2*] John Heaviside, Wm. Bursey, W: Richmond, Jno. Wilkinson, Willm. Gent, John Grant, James Atkinson junior, John Filiner
[*col. 3*] Richd. Jackson
[*col. 4*] Richd. Walker, Thos. Jennett, Jas. Atkinson, Rob: Bald, Thomas Coser, Wm Skinner junior.

---

285 Reading uncertain.

[p. 393]
Borough of Stockton. At a meeting of the mayor aldermen and burgesses held this eleventh day of July 1821 pursuant to due notice.

Ordered that such sum as shall be requisite to liquidate the debt due from the trustees of Stockton Bridge not exceeding forty two pounds five shillings shall be advanced as a donation from the funds of the corporation.

That the Committee for repairs appointed on the \twenty first/ day of October last do procure estimates of the value to be sold of \such part of/ the ground belonging to the corporation as has been built upon by Edward and William Fawell and of the value to let of such part as they have converted into a garden and do report the same to the meeting to be held on the 28th of next month.

Thos. Coser, Philip Hodgson senior

That the sum of ten pounds be subscribed towards a fund for providing beef and bread for the poor of Stockton on the day of His Majesty's coronation.

[*col. 1*] Wm Skinner junior deputy mayor, Thos Jennett, Richd. Jackson, Jno. Wilkinson, Thomas Walker, John Grant, Wilfred Sadler, James Atkinson junior, William Gent, James Atkinson, William Watson, Willm. Dale
[*col. 2*] Robt. Jordison, Robt. Bald, Thos. Fall, W: Richmond, John Filiner,[286] Jno. Heaviside.

[p. 394]
Borough of Stockton. At a meeting of the mayor aldermen and burgesses held this 28 day of August 1821 pursuant to due notice.

The recorder having reported his opinion that the corporation cannot legally extend the Shambles over any part of the public street but recommended the opinion of councel on the point being taken, ordered that the opinion of the recorder be acquiesced in and that no further opinion be obtained.

---

286 Reading of surname uncertain.

Also ordered that after payment of the principal money and interest now due from the corporation and of the expence of the repairs recommended to be done by the present Committee of Repairs, the surplus income of the corporation be placed on government security and that when a fund to the amount of one thousand pounds shall be accumulated the Shambles shall be rebuilt or erected in such a situation and on such a plan as shall be determined upon and approved by the mayor aldermen and burgesses at a meeting to be then held for the purpose of taking the same into consideration.

[*col. 1*] Thos. Jennett, J: Wilkinson, Willm. Dale, Thomas Coser, John Grant, Danl. Pearson, Bar[nar]d Unthank, James Atkinson, Richd Wright, Joseph Pickering, George Hay, John Jackson
[*col. 2*] Philip Hodgson senior, James Atkinson junior, William Watson, Willm. Bursey, Willm. Gent, W. Richmond, Thomas Fall, Jas. Crowe, J. Palmer, W. Sadler, Jno. Heaviside, John Proctor, Robt. Jordison.[287]

[p. 395]
Borough of Stockton. At a meeting of the mayor aldermen and burgesses held this 18th day of October 1821 pursuant to due notice.

Matthew Wadeson, Robert Claphan, Matthew Watson, Wilfred Sadler, William Skinner senior, Robert Jordison [and] William Gent were elected a committee of repairs for the current year which will expire on the first Tuesday next after the twenty ninth day of September next,

and Mr Thomas Fall, Thomas Eeles [and] Henry Beckwith, junior, were elected auditors of accounts for the same period

The accounts of William Skinner Esq. late mayor of this borough for the year ending the first Tuesday after New Michaelmas Day now last past allowed by the auditors being produced and there appearing to be a balance of one hundred and sixty three pounds six shillings & one penny due to the said William Skinner we do direct that the same shall be paid to him with five per cent interest from this

---

287 Pencilled ticks have been written beside the signatures in col. 1 and those in col. 2 as far as Thomas Fall. The names of the remaining signatories in col. 2 have been pencilled in before signature in ink.

day and that (with the consent of Mr Jennett whose claim remains undischarged) the rent to become due from Mr Foxton at Martinmas next shall be applied towards payment of the said balance and that the residue thereof with the interest shall be liquidated out of the first monies that shall [be] to hand after Mr Jennett's claim is satisfied.

Also Ordered that for the year ending at Michaelmas 1822 Mr Foxton shall be allowed two guineas for the use of rooms for the magistrates and at meetings of the corporation and their officers.

Also that the sum of twenty pounds be paid as a subscription to Mr Thomas Grey as the master of the Grammar School in case he shall perform the duties of that office to the satisfaction of the Mayor [p. 396] until the first Tuesday after the twenty ninth day of September next.

Also that in future no butcher's stalls shall be placed at the outside of the Shambles unless on occasions when all the stalls within the Shambles are occupied.

Also that an offer be made to William and Edward Fawell to accept the sum of six pounds as a compensation for eighty square yards \of land/ belonging to the corporation on which they have erected buildings on condition of their forthwith delivering up possession of the garden they occupy belonging to the corporation and that in default of their immediately acceding to this proposition an ejectment shall be commenced to recover the premises.

[*col. 1*] Richd Jackson mayor, Wm Braithwaite, Thos. Jennett, Wm. Skinner, Matt^w Wadeson, Jno: Christopher, Thos. Eeles, James Atkinson, John Grant, Willm Bursey, Willm Gent, Willm Watson, James Atkinson junior, Robt. Jordison, Wm Skinner senior, Robt Bald, John Filiner, W. Richmond, Thomas Fall, B. Unthank
[*col. 2*] Willm Dale, Philip Hodgson senior, the mark of John Hazelhurst,* Joseph Pickering, Danl. Pearson, Wilfred Sadler, Robt. Clephan, Matthew Webster, Wm [B]radly, John Foster, [*'Richd Wright' in pencil*], Henry Beckwith junior.

[p. 397]
Borough of Stockton. At a meeting of the mayor, aldermen and burgesses held this 21st day of June 1822 pursuant to due notice.

A proposition made on the part of William and Edward Fawell that the corporation shall pay the expence of erecting the wall of the garden claimed with interest and the cost of the ejectment and confirm their title to the houses and that they the said William and Edward Fawell shall relinquish to the corporation the said garden and the wall inclosing the same having been taken into consideration was unanimously rejected.

That a deputation of five burgesses be appointed to superintend the setting out so much of the ground belonging to the corporation as is required for the Stockton and Darlington Railway and to treat and contract for the sale thereof and that such deputation consist of the following persons viz. Mr James Atkinson junior, Mr Henry Beckwith junior, Mr Sadler, Mr Jordison and Mr William Watson any three of whom shall be competent to act.

That Mr John Wilkinson, Mr Matthew Watson, Mr William Watson, Mr James Atkinson junior and Mr Robert Bald be a committee to assist the mayor in the regulation of the market and that any two or more of them be competent to act and that in case of any opposition to the arrangements to be prescribed by them or of a refusal to pay the dues specified in the table heretofore agreed upon on demand the mayor be authorised to direct the proper legal steps to be taken to assert and recover the right and priviliges of the corporation.

That proper application be forthwith made for a renewal of the leases held under the bishop.

Richard Jackson mayor,[288] Thos Jennett
[*col. 1*] Matt^{w} Wadeson, Thomas Heaviside, Danl. Pearson, Matthew Watson, Henry Beckwith junior, Robt. Bald, Thos: Fall, William Watson
[*col. 2*] Robt Barker, James Atkinson, Wilfred Sadler, Thomas Eeles, John Wilkinson, W: Richmond, James Atkinson junior.

---

288 Richard Jackson was a currier (treater and finisher of tanned leather) and was elected mayor in 1821. His son Richard would later be mayor: Heavisides, *Annals*, p. 25.

[p. 398]
At the above meeting it was unanimously ordered that the bishop of Durham and his clergy be invited to dine at the corporation expence at the approaching confirmation at Stockton and that the mayor be authorised to invite any gentlemen he may think proper to meet them.

Also that ten guineas be subscribed towards procuring an additional fire engine for the use of the town and borough of Stockton.

By order of the meeting   Richd. Jackson mayor

Borough of Stockton. At a meeting of the mayor aldermen and burgesses held this 13th day of September 1822 pursuant to due notice.

The committee of the Stockton and Darlington Railway having signified that it is found necessary for them to purchase not only so much of the ground at Cottage Row as is requisite for the line of railway but also a sufficient plot or parcel of that ground to answer for landing and depositing the materials and other things requisite for their works and undertaking, resolved that all the proprietors of the said railway shall be accommodated with such a quantity of the said ground as is wanted for the purposes aforesaid and that Mr James Atkinson junior, Mr Jordison, Mr Sadler, Mr Henry Beckwith junior and Mr William Watson be deputed to set out and contract for the sale of the same. That any three of them shall be competent to act and that they shall be at liberty to consult with and obtain the opinion of any competent judges as to the value of the [p. 399] ground for their government.

                                              Richd. Jackson mayor

[col. 1] W: Richmond, Thos. Eeles, Robt. Bald, Willm. Gent, Wilfred Sadler, William Watson, Joseph Pickering, Thomas Coser
[col. 2] James Atkinson junior, Charles Barrett,[289] Robt. Jordison, Jno. Wilkinson, Thomas Fall.

---

289 In 1827, Charles Barrett, described as 'gentleman', was living in Park Row: P&W, p. 315.

Borough of Stockton. At a meeting of the mayor aldermen and burgesses held this 11th day of October 1822 pursuant to due notice.

William Skinner junior, William Richmond, Wilfred Sadler, Robert Bald, Thomas Eeles, William Gent and John Grant were elected a committee of repairs for the \current/ year which will expire on the first Tuesday next after the 29th day of September next.

Matthew Wadeson, James Atkinson junior and Henry Beckwith were elected auditors of account for the same period.

and John Grant, Matthew Watson, William Watson, James Atkinson junior [and] Robert Bald were elected a committee to assist the mayor in the regulation of the market and any two or more of them declared to be competent to act.

[p. 400]
The accounts of Richard Jackson Esq. late mayor of this borough for the year ending the first Tuesday after New Michaelmas Day now last past allowed by the auditors being produced and there appearing to be a balance of three hundred and thirty five pounds seven shillings and two \pence/ due to the said Richard Jackson, we do direct that the same shall be paid to him with five per cent interest from this day out of the first monies that shall become due to the corporation.

The mayor having stated the terms on which the appointment of Mr Thomas Gray as the master of the Grammar School has been renewed for the ensuing year, ordered that twenty pounds be paid as a subscription to him out of the funds of the corporation in case he shall perform the duties of his office to the satisfaction of the mayor until the first Tuesday after the twenty ninth \day/ of September next.

And it being communicated to the meeting that Robert Garbutt has refused to comply with the general regulations for placing the stalls in the market and that he and Charles Ratcliffe have both resisted the payment of the stallage due to the lessee of the corporation, ordered that a case be stated for the opinion of councel as to the right of the corporation to arrange the stalls and to demand the dues in question and the means of enforcing the same and on any other points on which the mayor and the committee for regulating the market may deem it necessary to obtain legal advice or direction.

Also ordered that the ejectment depending with William and Edward Fawell be brought to trial and that Mr Jennett, Mr Richmond, Mr Bald, Mr Beckwith junior, Mr Atkinson junior, Mr William Watson and Mr Sadler be a committee for conducting the prosecution of the claim of the [p. 401] corporation and procuring the necessary evidence in support thereof and that any three or more of them be competent to act.

[*col. 1*] John Wilkinson mayor, Wm Braithwaite, Thos. Jennett, Wm Skinner
[*col. 2*] Mattw: Wadeson, Wm Skinner junior, Thomas Fall, W: Richmond, W Sadler, Robt Bald Thomas Eeles, John Heaviside, John Grant, William Gent, Henry Beckwith, William Watson, J. S. Atkinson junior [*followed in pencil by* 'Jos^h Pickering', 'Robt Barker'].

Borough of Stockton. At a meeting of the mayor aldermen and burgesses held this 20th day of December 1822 pursuant to due notice.

Ordered that Mr Matthew Wadeson, Mr Robert Bald, Mr William Gent and Mr John Grant be added to the committee appointed to set out and contract for the ground which the Stockton and Darlington Railway Company have applied to purchase and that such committee be requested to obtain a plan and admeasurement of the ground required and do lay the same with a report of their sentiments as to the value and the terms it may be advisable to impose on the purchasers before the next meeting of the corporation.

And the mayor having exhibited a plan for the new Shambles and communicated [p. 402] to the meeting a prospective calculation of the income and resources of the corporation by which it appears practicable to undertake the proposed improvement, ordered that such plan and calculation be submitted to the investigation and consideration of a committee and that they be desired to report their opinion of the accuracy of the calculation and of the expediency of erecting new Shambles at this period with any observations and the plan they may recommend for adoption to the next meeting.

That such committee consist of Mr John Proctor, Mr William Richmond, Mr John Dixon, Mr Robert Bald, Mr Thomas Eeles, Mr Wilfred Sadler \and/ Mr James Atkinson junior and that any three or more of them may be competent to act.

That this meeting be adjourned and that the mayor aldermen and burgesses do meet again at the Townshouse on Friday the 27th of December instant at eleven o'clock in the forenoon.

[*col. 1*] John Wilkinson mayor, Wm: Sleigh, Jas. Crowe, Wm Braithwaite, Thos Jennett, Willm. Gent, James Atkinson, John Grant, John Heaviside, James Atkinson junior, Wilfred Sadler, John Dixon, W. Richmond, Robt. Bald
[*col. 2*] Mattw: Wadeson, Thomas Eeles, William Watson, Thomas Fall, John Proctor, Richard Walker, Thomas Coser, Richd. Walker, Thomas Coser.[290]

[pp. 403–4] [*blank*]

[p. 405]
Borough of Stockton. At a meeting of the mayor aldermen and burgesses held this 27th day of December 1822 pursuant to due notice.

The Stockton and Darlington Railway Company having signified their desire to purchase a greater quantity of the ground at Cottage Row, ordered that the committee appointed on the 20th instant be requested to meet the company's engineer to set out and treat for the ground now required and do report the results to a meeting of the corporation to be convened whenever they shall direct.

At this meeting the report of the committee deputed to investigate and consider the prospective income and resources of the corporation and the expediency of erecting new Shambles was taken into consideration and it being their opinion that the expence of the undertaking and also all the existing debt of the corporation may be redeemed in the course of eleven years and they having also strongly recommended new Shambles being erected, ordered that the measure shall be proceeded with under the sanction and direction of that committee with the addition of Mr Alderman Braithwaite, Mr Alderman Jennett, Mr Alderman Skinner, and Mr Alderman Jackson, and that any three or more of such increased committee shall be competent to act.

---

290 This appears to be the same Thomas Coser signing twice. He may have signed, then noticed the pencilled placeholder for his name and signed again.

Also Ordered that, as it appears to be requisite to enlarge the present market place, the new [p. 406] Shambles shall be erected further to the south if it be legal to do so but so as not to extend beyond the line of the point of the houses on the north side of Ramswiend.

Jno Wilkinson mayor, Wm Braithwaite, Thos Jennett, Wm Skinner, Richd Jackson, W. Sleigh,[291] Jas. Crowe, Willm. Gent, Jas Atkinson, John Grant, William Sleigh, John Heaviside, Wm Russell, Chas. Barrett, Robt. Jordison, Matt^w Wadeson, Thos. Fall, Thos: Heaviside, Thos. Eeles, Jas. Atkinson junior, Henry Beckwith junior, W: Richmond, Wm Skinner junior [*followed by 'Jno. Proctor', 'Thos. Walker' in pencil, not inked over*].

[p. 407]
Borough of Stockton

At a meeting of the mayor aldermen and burgesses held this 2nd day of January 1823 pursuant to due notice.

The committee appointed to set out and treat for the ground required to be purchased by the Stockton and Darlington Railway Company having exhibited a plan and admeasurement thereof and reported their opinion of the value, ordered that the ground set out by such committee and described in the said plan as proposed to be purchased by the said company be sold to them at or for the price or sum of 300 guineas on the understanding or condition that the railway shall if required be continued along the wharfs and quays at Stockton so far as is authorised by the act of Parliament lately passed for making the said railway.

John Wilkinson mayor

[*col. 1*] Wm Braithwaite, Tho Jennett, Richd. Jackson, Jas: Crowe, Willm. Gent, John Grant, Jas Atkinson, John Heaviside, Jas Atkinson junior, H. Beckwith junior, Rob. Bald, Thos. Fall
[*col. 2*] W. Richmond, Robt. Jordison, Thos. Eeles [*followed by 'Jno Proctor' in pencil*].

291 In pencil. At this point the practice of pencilling in the names of signatories, who would sign in ink over them, commenced. On this page all the signatures are over such guides, except that William Sleigh signed in a different position.

[p. 408]
Borough of Stockton. At a meeting of the mayor aldermen and burgesses held this twenty ninth day of March 1823 pursuant to due notice to authorise the raising and appropriating the requisite fund for carrying into effect the resolutions lately entered into for erecting new Shambles.

Resolved that sufficient information not having been given by the committee to this meeting to enable them to judge of the propriety of authorising the said committee to lay out the sum required it would be highly impudent for this meeting to give authority for raising the same.

John Wilkinson, mayor
Richd. Walker senior, [in pencil: 'Thos Walker', W. Bursey'], H. Beckwith junior, [in pencil: 'John Jackson'], Wm. Dale, [in pencil: 'Joseph Pickering'], Thos Heaviside, Matthew Watson, C. Robinson, Willm. Gent, Jas. Atkinson junior, B. Unthank, Jas Atkinson, Watson Alcock, Jas. Crowe.

Borough of Stockton.[292] At a meeting of the mayor aldermen and burgesses held this 8th day of April 1823 pursuant to due notice.

Ordered that the case laid before counsel inspecting the Shambles and the opinion thereon be submitted to the next meeting.

[col. 1] Wm. Skinner, [in pencil: 'Thos Eeles', 'Danl Pearson']
[col. 2] Thos Heavisides, R. Jordison, [in pencil: 'M. Wadeson']
[col. 3] W. Richmond, Thos. Jennet, Thos. Fall.

[p. 409]
Borough of Stockton. At a meeting of the mayor aldermen and burgesses held this third day of June 1823 pursuant to due notice.

Ordered that the resolution of the twenty seventh day of December 1822 be confirmed and that the new Shambles[293] ordered to be erected

---

292 A double line across the page and a change of hand separate this entry from those above.
293 Two proposals were considered: repair of the old Shambles at £680 and a new Shambles at the cost above, 'after an animated discussion'. The new

be constructed according to the plan \now/ produced by Mr Jennett and that they be 114 feet long, 53 feet wide, and 14 feet high from the ground line, and that the mayor be empowered to procure the sum of twelve hundred pounds on \security of/ the funds of the corporation to carry the same into effect and to execute such documents as may be necessary to secure the same.

Ordered that the resolution of the meeting on the 8th day of April last respecting the production of the case laid before counsel relative to the Shambles, with his opinion thereon, be rescinded.

[*col. 1*] John Wilkinson mayor, Wm. Skinner, Thos Jennett, Wm Braithwaite, Richd. Jackson, Wm Skinner junior,[294] John Dixon, Mattw: Wadeson, Thos: Fall, Robt Bald, Rob: Jordison, W: Richmond [*col. 2*] Wm. Bradley, Joseph Welch, Charles Barrett, Henry Beckwith junior, Wilfred Sadler, H. W. Foxton, Anth[on]y Dobing, Richd Walker senior, Thos Coser, Willm Gent, John Filiner.

[p. 410]
Borough of Stockton. At a meeting of the mayor aldermen and burgesses held this nineteenth day of September 1823 pursuant to due notice.

The conveyance of the ground sold to the Stockton and Darlington Railway Company having been produced and read over, ordered that the same is executed and that a copy of the deed and plan referred to be lodged amongst the records of the corporation.

Shambles were commenced on 21 July but several burgesses objected to 'encroachments on their rights' and demolished the new wall. Thirteen people were summoned before a magistrate the following day, but the case was dismissed. It was said that opposition to the reconstruction was so great that 'when being erected the [new Shambles] were twice levelled to the ground'. On 18 June 1824, a sheriff's court was held in Stockton to determine whether the extension of the Shambles was 'injurious to the King or any of his subjects'. The court ruled not. The foundation stone was laid on 26 May 1825 and the new Shambles opened on 28 September, the day after the Stockton and Darlington Railway. They bore the name of John Wilkinson, mayor, at the south end of the building. John Brewster thought that 'whatever objection may be made to the situation, [the new building] is certainly ornamental to the street': Heavisides, *Annals*, p. 21; Richmond, *Local Records*, pp. 140, 142, 145–6; Brewster, *History*, p. 223.

294 It is unclear whether this reads 'Sr' or 'Jr'.

John Wilkinson mayor, Wm. Braithwaite alderman, Richd. Jackson alderman, Willm. Gent, John Grant, Henry Beckwith junior, William Watson, Daniel Pearson, Jno. Atkinson, B. Unthank, Thos. Eeles, James Atkinson junior, James Atkinson, Thomas Coser, Robt. Bald, Mattw: Wadeson, John Dixon, W: Richmond.

[p. 411]
Borough of Stockton. At a meeting of the mayor aldermen and burgesses held this 20th day of October 1823 pursuant to due notice.

Thomas Fall, William Richmond, Wilfred Sadler, Robert Bald, Thomas Coser, John Grant and William Gent were elected a committee of repairs for the current year which will expire on the first Tuesday next after the twenty ninth day of September next.

Matthew Wadeson, Henry Beckwith junior and James Atkinson junior were elected auditors of accounts for the same period.

Thomas Eeles, John Grant, Robert Jordison, Henry Beckwith junior and John Dixon were elected a committee to assist the mayor in the regulation of the market and any two or more of them declared competent to act.

The accounts of John Wilkinon Esq. late mayor of this borough for the year ending the first Tuesday after New Michaelmas Day now last past allowed by the auditors being produced and there appearing to be a balance of four hundred and eight pounds four shillings and four pence halfpenny due to the said John Wilkinson we do direct that the same shall be paid to him with five per cent interest from the day out of the first monies that shall become due to the corporation.

[p. 412]
Ordered that the subscription of twenty pounds to Mr Thomas Gray the master of the Grammar School be continued to him during the present year.

Ordered that the sum of twenty pounds be paid to James Ward as a compensation for his services as constable and police officer for this borough for the ensuing year if he should be continued in those offices.

John Wilkinson mayor, Thos. Jennett, Thos. Fall, W: Richmond, Robt. Jordison, Thomas Coser, Robt. Bald, Mattw: Wadeson, Thomas Eeles,

Wilfred Sadler, Henry Beckwith junior, Anth[on]y Dobing, Richd. Jackson, James Atkinson, Willm. Gent, John Grant, James Atkinson junior, Daniel Pearson, Jno. Atkinson, William Watson.

[p. 413]
Borough of Stockton. At a meeting of the mayor aldermen and burgesses held this 9th day of December 1823 pursuant to due notice.

Resolved that the property belonging to the corporation and now in lease to Mr Foxton except the Shambles, be relet to him for the term of six years \from Mayday next/ at the yearly rent of one hundred and seventy pounds payable half yearly at Mayday and Martinmas without any allowance or deduction whatsoever excepting two pounds for ringing the town hall bell as usual and two guineas as a compensation for acting as mayor's sergeant yearly and that when the corporation think fit to let the Shambles he have a preference and that Mr William Richmond and Mr John Fox be accepted as sureties for the due payment of the rent and the fulfilment of the covenants to be contained in the lease on the tenant's part.

Also resolved that a donation of five pounds be given to the School of Industry[295] at Stockton.

Also resolved that the sum of two shillings and six pence be paid to the proprietors for each coble load of seafish which shall hereafter be brought and retailed at the wharf or quay belonging to the corporation called the Custom House Quay as an encouragement [p. 414] to the fishermen upon the coast to resort to this place.

Also resolved that as the plan of the borough is in some degree defaced a committee be appointed to prepare a new one distinguishing each borough right and the present divisions thereof and setting forth also the names of the several proprietors and that they take the present plan for the guide as far as circumstances will admit, and that they do exhibit to the plan so prepared by them to a meeting of the mayor aldermen and burgesses to be convened to take the same into consideration accompanied with a report of such

295 The School of Industry for females was instituted by Mrs Sutton in 1803, but the work was industrious rather than industrial, being 'woman's work of every kind': Brewster, *History*, p. 253. George Sutton had donated £300 to it.

observations as may occur to them. That such committee consist of Mr James Crowe,[296] Mr Matthew Wadeson and Mr William Gent, and that they have power to procure any assistance they may think proper at the expence of the corporation.

[*col. 1*] John Wilkinson mayor, Wm. Braithwaite, Thos. Jennett, Wm. Skinner, Richd. Jackson, Willm. Gent, Anth. Dobing, John Heaviside, Richd. Wright, M. Kirtley, Thos: Fall, James Atkinson junior, Wm Farmer, Jno. Atkinson, William Watson
[*col. 2*] Robt. Jordison, Henry Beckwith junior, Matthew Watson, Wilfred Sadler, Robt. Bald, Thos. Eeles, Mattw: Wadeson, Robt. Hodgson.[297]

[p. 415]
Borough of Stockton. At a meeting of the mayor aldermen and burgesses held this 19th day of October 1824 pursuant to notice.

Robert Bald, William Richmond, William Gent, John Grant, Robert Jordison, Thomas Richmond [and] Wilfred Sadler were elected a committee of repairs for the current year which will expire on the first Tuesday next after the twenty ninth day of September next.

Matthew Wadeson, James Atkinson junior [and] Anthony Dobing were elected auditors of accounts for the same period.

The accounts of John Wilkinson Esq.[298] the late mayor of this borough for the year ending the first Tuesday after New Michaelmas Day now last examined and found correct by the auditors were produced and inspected.

Ordered that the subscription of twenty pounds to Mr Thomas Gray the master of the Grammar School be continued during the present year

296 This is the last mention of James Crowe before he died on 31 March 1825: Richmond, *Local Records*, p. 144. See also Richmond, *Nonconformity*, pp. 59–61, which also mentions the close ties between the Cooke and Crowe families, and Crowe's abolitionist activities.

297 A Robert Hodgson lived in Finkle Street in 1827: P&W, p. 315.

298 Wilkinson was elected for the third time on 5 October 1824, 'after a very severe contest': Richmond, *Local Records*, p. 142.

Ordered that the sum of twenty pounds be paid to James Ward as a compensation [p. 416] for his services as a constable and police officer for this borough for the year ensuing if he shall be continued in those offices.

John Wilkinson mayor, Wm. Braithwaite, Thos. Jennett, Wm. Skinner, Richd. Jackson, William Watson, Jno. Atkinson, James Atkinson junior, Thos. Richmond, Anth[on]y Dobing, John Heaviside, Mattw: Wadeson, Wilfred Sadler, John Grant, William Gent, W: Richmond, Robt. Bald, Robt. Jordison.

[p. 417]
Borough of Stockton. The court leet with view of frankpledge and court baron of the honorable and right reverend father in God Shute lord bishop of Durham held at the Town House in Stockton in and for the said borough on Friday the twenty second day of October one thousand eight hundred and twenty four before John Wilkinson Esq. mayor and Leonard Raisbeck[299] gentleman, steward.

The accounts of John Wilkinson Esq. late mayor of this borough for the year ending the first Tuesday after New Michaelmas Day now last past allowed by the auditors being produced and there appearing to be a balance of five hundred and seventeen pounds ten shillings and twopence halfpenny due to the said John Wilkinson we do direct that the same shall be paid to them him with five per cent interest from this day out of the first monies that shall become due to the corporation.

[col. 1] John Wilkinson mayor, Thos. Jennett, Wm. Skinner, Richd. Jackson
[col. 2] Mattw: Wadeson, Thomas Fall, W: Richmond, Robt. Bald, Jos[ep]h Wade, Anth[on]y Dobing, Thos. Eeles, Henry Beckwith junior, Richd Ableson, John Grant, Robert Welch, Willm. Gent.

---

299 Leonard Raisbeck, solicitor, having been recorder of the corporation for many years, had been presented with an epergne by the mayor, aldermen and burgesses on 9 January 1824. He was described as 'always affable and gentlemanly, and in his habits of business extremely punctual'. He was also presented with a sword by the Stockton Volunteers when they disbanded: Heavisides, *Annals*, p. 22, Brewster, *History*, pp. 447–50; Bayley, 'Genealogical Additions', pp. 98–9.

[p. 418]

Borough of Stockton. At a meeting of the mayor aldermen and burgesses held this eighth day of March 1825 pursuant to due notice.

Ordered that the sum of two thousand eight hundred pounds be borrowed[300] on the security of the revenues of the corporation to cover the sum of one thousand two hundred pounds ordered by the meeting held on the third day of June 1823 and the remaining one thousand six hundred pounds be applied in discharging the other debts and sums of money now due from the corporation and that a proper mortgage be prepared and executed for the same, Mr Walker having offered to lend the above sum at the rate of four pounds and five shillings per cent interest.

Ordered that the same be accepted.

Also Ordered that the accommodations at St John's Well be enlarged and improved under the direction of a committee to be now appointed and with the approbation of the mayor so as the expence do not exceed three hundred pounds in the whole and that such committee consist of Mr Jennett, Mr Jackson, Mr William Skinner, Mr Sadler and Mr William Richmond and that any three of them shall be competent to act.

Also Ordered that the property belonging to the corporation at or near Cottage Row be advertised in the months of July & August next to be let by proposal for one year to enter upon at Martinmas next.

Also Ordered that a committee be appointed to survey the common sewers and drains within the town and borough and report the state thereof and their opinion as to [p. 419] any improvements which can be adopted for the general benefit and accommodation of the inhabitants and that such committee consist of Mr Bald, Mr Skinner, Mr William Richmond, Mr Wadeson, Mr Jordison, Mr William Gent and the surveyors of the highways for the town and borough and that any three or more of them shall be competent to act.

---

300 Richmond records that £2,800 was borrowed. He also states that £300 was voted for the construction of hot and cold baths in connection with St. John's Well. Richmond and Wilkinson were also involved in the oversight of a new Mechanical and Scientific Institution: Richmond, *Local Records*, pp. 143–4.

Also Ordered that application be made to Mr Commerall the owner of the shop now occupied by Mr Robert Garbutt to ascertain whether he will dispose of the same and the lowest price he will accept.

[*col. 1*] John Wilkinson mayor, Wm. Braithwaite, Richd. Jackson alderman, Tho. Jennett, James Atkinson junior, W. Richmond, Wm Skinner junior, Thos. Richmond, Thos. Eeles, Wilfred Sadler, Thomas Walker, Thos. Fall, Willm. Gent, Anth[on]y Dobing, Jno. Atkinson, Robt. Bald, Robert Welch
[*col. 2*] Robt. Jordison, Martin Kirtley, Jos^h Wade.

[p. 420]
Borough of Stockton. At a meeting of the mayor aldermen and burgesses held this sixth day of September 1825 pursuant to notice.

Ordered that the offers of the Stockton and Darlington Railway Company for the cottages Nos 1, 2, 3, 4 & 5 at \the rent of/ £6 10s. each, of Mr Richard Mills for the Bond Yard at present occupied by Mr Robert Botcherby at the yearly rent of £14, of Mr William Richmond for the garden occupied by him at the rent of £3, of Messrs Wilkinson & Co. for the parcel of ground between Mr Hixon's mill and the ground belonging to the Stockton & Darlington Railway Company at the yearly rent of £6 10s., & of Mr James Atkinson for the remainder of the property at \the rent of/ £44 be respectively accepted for one year from Martinmas next.

At this meeting the mortgage to Messrs Walker & others and the lease of the Town House &c to Mr Foxton were executed.

[*col. 1*] John Wilkinson mayor, Wm. Braithwaite, Wm. Skinner, Thos. Jennett, Robt. Bald, Wilfd. Sadler, William Watson, W: Richmond
[*col. 2*] James Atkinson junior, William Gent, Thos. Richmond.

[p. 421]
Borough of Stockton. At a meeting of the mayor aldermen and burgesses held the twenty first day of October 1825 pursuant to due notice.

Robert Bald, William Richmond, William Gent, John Grant, Wilfrid Sadler, John Lodge [and] Thomas Fall were elected a committee of repairs for the current year which will expire on the first Tuesday after the twenty ninth day of September next.

Matthew Wadeson, James Atkinson junior [and] Anthony Dobing were elected auditors of accounts for the same period

Ordered that the sum of twenty pounds be paid to James Ward as a compensation for his services as a constable and police officer for this borough for the year ensuing if he shall be continued in those offices.

Ordered that the subscription of twenty pounds to Mr Thomas Gray or whoever else may be the master of the Grammar School for the present year be continued.

Resolved that an ~~donation of~~ annual subscription of five pounds be given to the School of Industry at Stockton to commence from the last year.

Ordered that each coble \coming to Stockton/ laden with fish from Hartlepool, Redcar or any other place be allowed the sum of five shillings provided they [p. 422] retail their own fish.

Ordered that the annual sum of five guineas be allowed towards the Stockton Cattle Show.

Wm Skinner junior mayor, Thos Jennett, Wm Skinner, Richd Jackson, Jno Wilkinson, Robt Bald, W: Richmond, Wilfred Sadler, F. R. Richmond, John Lodge, Willm. Gent, Henry Beckwith junior, Anth[on]y Dobing, Jno. Atkinson,[301] Thos. Richmond, William Watson.

[p. 423]
Borough of Stockton. At a meeting of the mayor aldermen and burgesses held this twenty first day of February 1826 pursuant to due notice.

A proposition having been made on the part of Mr Henry Wade Foxton and his assignees and sureties that the existing lease of the Town House and market dues shall be forthwith surrendered, and that in consideration of accepting the same the corporation shall be paid out of the effects of the said Henry Wade Foxton the half year's rent due at Martinmas last and also be entitled to receive or retain the accruing rents for the shops \&/ coffee room, let off by the said

---

301 A John Atkinson was a sailcloth manufacturer in 1827: P&W, p. 315.

Henry Wade Foxton and the several allowances for the use of the magistrates room for public and private meetings and also the sums agreed to be paid to the said Henry Wade Foxton for executing the offices of town sergeant and bell ringer up to Mayday next, and should also be entitled to all the market dues collected and to be collected between the fourteenth instant and the said thirteenth day of May next, the said sureties undertaking to collect and account for the same until a new tenant can be procured and the same assignees undertaking to have the House[302] carried on in the mean time in order to preserve the custom thereof.

Ordered that such proposition be accepted and that the premises be advertized to be relet \for the term of six years/ in the two York, two Durham and one of the Newcastle newspapers and proposals to be examined on or before the tenth day of [p. 424] March next to which day this meeting is adjourned and to be then held at eleven o'clock in the forenoon for the purpose of taking such proposals into consideration.

Wm Skinner junior mayor, Wm Braithwaite, Wm Skinner, Thos Jennett, J. Wilkinson, Willm Gent, Anth[on]y Dobing, John Heaviside, Jno: Dixon, Thomas Walker, Thos Richmond, John Grant, Robt. Bald, W: Richmond, Danl. Pearson.

Borough of Stockton. At a meeting of the mayor aldermen and burgesses held this first day of March 1826 pursuant to due notice

Ordered that an offer made by Mr Otley on behalf of the Stockton and Darlington Railway Company to take a lease of as much of the vacant ground at Cottage Row as shall be lie between a line to be drawn at the distance of 21 feet admeasured northwards from the northernmost staith at or near to Cottage Row and a line to be drawn at the distance of 50 feet admeasured southwards from the mill belonging to or in the occupation of Mr Walker at the yearly rent of £30 for 7 years to commence from this day, be accepted.

Error see entry of meeting 1st March 1827 post.[303]

---

302 Presumably referring to the Town House.
303 Entered in a different hand, between the heading and the deleted order; see below, p. 251.

[p. 425]
Borough of Stockton
At a meeting of the mayor aldermen and burgesses held this tenth
day of March 1826 pursuant to an adjournment from the twenty first
day of February last past.

Ordered that the Townshouse and market dues & other property
lately in lease to Mr Foxton be let to Mark Ryder for the term of
six years from Mayday next at the yearly rent of one hundred and
seventy pounds to be payable quarterly and that a lease be executed
to him accordingly in which it is to be stipulated that the tenant is
to pay all taxes and assessments as well parliamentary as parochial.

[*col. 1*] Wm Skinner junior mayor, Wm Braithwaite, Thos Jennett,
Wm Skinner, Richd. Jackson, John Wilkinson, Thomas Walker, Robt
Bald, W. Sadler, Jno: Dixon, William Watson, Danl. Pearson, John
Filiner, Anth[on]y Dobing
[*col. 2*] John Heaviside, John Grant, Willm. Gent, Mark Ryder.

[p. 426]
Borough of Stockton. At a meeting of the mayor aldermen and
burgesses held this eighteenth day of April 1826 pursuant to due
notice for the purpose of taking into consideration the expediency
of closing up the slip or watering place at the Custom House Quay.

The Stockton and Darlington Railway Company having been required
to continue the railway along the wharfs and quays at Stockton
pursuant to their engagement to that effect with the corporation on the
second day of January 1823 and having proposed in order to form a
foundation for the same to fill up the west end of the slip or watering
place at the Custom House Quay and to erect and place steps to lead
from the south west corner of the part filled up close to the north
side of the Custom House Quay to low water mark of the river and
to execute the work at their expence, and it appearing from frequent
complaints made that it is attended with danger to the public to keep
the slip open in its present state, ordered that leave be given to the
Stockton and Darlington Railway Company to carry their proposition
into effect so as the work be done to the satisfaction of Mr Wadeson,
Mr Francis Richardson Richmond and Mr Bald or any two of them.

[*col. 1*] Wm Braithwaite, [*in pencil: 'W Sadler'*], William Watson, [*in
pencil: 'M. Wadeson', 'G. Richmond'*]

[*col. 2*] Wm Skinner junior mayor, Wm. Skinner, John Wilkinson, John Richardson, F. R. Richmond, Thomas Coser, Robt. Bald.

[p. 427]
Borough of Stockton. At a meeting of the mayor aldermen and burgesses held this ninth day of May 1826 pursuant to due notice.

Ordered that the assignees of Mr James Atkinson be requested to give notice to the sub tenants of the property held by them under the corporation and that on their doing so and paying the rent due to the corporation up to the thirteenth instant and authorizing the mayor to receive the half year's rents which will become due from the subtenants at Martinmas next, their application to be released from their contract be acceded to.

At this meeting a notice from Mr Thomas Walker requiring five per cent interest for the £2800 lent on mortgage of the corporation property was produced.

Ordered that a meeting of the members of the corporation be held on Tuesday next at eleven o'clock in the forenoon to take into consideration as well such notice, as the letting of all the property belonging to the corporation at Cottage Row to take place from Martinmas next, and the renewal of the arrangements respecting the Grammar School on the termination of the present engagement.[304]

[*col. 1*] Anth[on]y Dobing, Danl. Pearson, Thomas Walker
[*col. 2*] Wm. Skinner junior mayor, Thos Jennett, Jno. Wilkinson, Robt. Jordison, Robt. Bald, William Watson.

[p. 428]
Borough of Stockton. At a meeting of the mayor aldermen and burgesses held this sixteenth day of May 1826 pursuant to due notice.

Resolved that the thanks of this meeting be given to Leonard Raisbeck Esq.[305] for his long and valuable services as recorder and steward of the borough & that he be requested to continue the office of recorder.

---

304 In left margin a symbol akin to '(+')'.
305 In 1827, Leonard Raisbeck lived in Cleveland Row: P&W, p. 315.

The lease of the Town House and stallage agreed to be let to Mark Ryder being produced and explained, ordered that the same be executed by affixing the corporation seal to the same.

And Messrs Walker and others the mortgagees of the corporation property having required to be paid five per cent interest for the principal sum of £2800 lent by them to commence from the end of the current half year, ordered that the same be complied with, the mortgagees having agreed to accept notice in October next in case it should be considered necessary to pay in the principal sum in May next.

Also Ordered that the requisite notices be given for the purposes of obtaining a licence for a public house in Cottage Row, at the next Brewster Sessions,[306] and that a committee be [p. 429] appointed to enquire and consider in what manner and for what purpose the property at Cottage Row can be let to the best advantage and do consist of Mr Robert Bald, Mr Robert Jordison, Mr Anthony Dobing, Mr William Watson and Mr Richard Jackson and that any three of them be competent to act – That they be requested to report their sentiments to a meeting of the corporation to be convened by them as soon as conveniently may be.

Also Ordered that the mayor be requested to give notice to Mr Thomas Gray the master of the Grammar School that his contract will expire at Christmas next and that the disposal of the school be taken into consideration at the next meeting of the corporation.

[col. 1] William Skinner junior mayor, [in pencil: 'W Braithwaite'], Thos Jennett, Richd. Jackson, Jno. Wilkinson, Robt. Bald, [in pencil: 'Mr Thos Richmond']
[col. 2] Rt. Jordison, William Watson, Daniel Pearson, Anth[on]y Dobing, Thomas Walker,[307] [in pencil: 'Mr Jno Lodge'].

[p. 430]
Borough of Stockton. At a meeting of the mayor aldermen and burgesses held this tenth day of August 1826 pursuant to due notice.

---

306 Brewster Sessions were annual meetings of licensing justices to deal with the granting, renewal and transfer of licenses to sell intoxicating liquor.
307 A Thomas Walker, flax merchant, lived on Hanover Square in 1827: P&W, p. 316.

The committee appointed at the last meeting having recommended that that part of the property in Cottage Row which is now let to John Cummins, Matthew Hunton and John Cockerton and their subtenants and described in the plan now exhibited shall be appropriated for a public house.

Ordered that that recommendation be complied with and that the whole of the property at Cottage Row be advertized to be let by proposal on Tuesday the 26th of September next. And that proposals in writing be required to be delivered in on \or/ before the 25th of that month.

Wm Skinner junior mayor, Richd. Jackson, Jno. Wilkinson, Anth[on]y Dobing, William Watson, Rob. Jordison, Robt. Bald, W: Richmond.

[p. 431]
Borough of Stockton. At a meeting of the mayor aldermen and burgesses held this 26th day of September 1826 pursuant to notice.

Ordered that the property in Cottage Row to be appropriated as an inn be let to William Blenkinsop for the term of three years \from Martinmas next/ at the yearly rent of thirty five pounds ~~each~~ either party to be at liberty to determine the tenancy on giving six months notice of his intention to the other at the end of any one year.

Also Ordered that the offer of Mr William Richmond for the garden occupied by him at the rent of three pounds per annum, of Mr Robert Jordison for the cottages Nos. 1, 2, 3 & 4 including the garden attached to No. 1 but exclusive of the stable in the possession of Thomas Huddart the late tenant of No. 1 at the rent of twenty two pounds \per annum/, & of John Cummins for the cottage No. 6 at the rent of six pounds ten shillings \per annum/ be accepted. And that the letting to them be also for the term of three years from Martinmas next determinable at the end of any one year of that term upon six months previous notice by either party.

And the rest of the property in Cottage Row is ordered to be let for the like term by Mr Robert Bald, Mr Robert Jordison, Mr Anthony Dobing, Mr William Watson and Mr Richard Jackson or any three of them at such rents as they may deem reasonable, taking into consideration the offers laid before the meeting this day for the same.

Application having been made to this meeting for part of the ground at Cottage Row to be appropriated as a scite for warm baths, ordered that the application be submitted to the consideration of the above committee [p. 432] and that they be requested to ascertain the precise quantity of ground and the terms on which the same is requested to be granted and to report the same with their sentiments to the next meeting of the corporation.

Wm. Skinner junior mayor, Wm. Skinner, Richd. Jackson, Jno. Wilkinson, John Grant, Anth[on]y Dobing, William Watson, John Heaviside, Jno: Dixon, W. Richmond, Robt. Jordison.

[p. 433]
Borough of Stockton. At a meeting of the mayor aldermen and burgesses held this ~~19th~~ nineteenth day of October 1826 pursuant to due notice.

Robert Bald, William Richmond, William Gent, John Grant, Wilfred Sadler, John Lodge [and] Thomas Fall were elected a committee of repairs for the current year which will expire on the first Tuesday after the twenty ninth day of September next.

Matthew Wadeson, Robert Jordison [and] Anthony Dobing were elected auditors of accounts for the same period.

The accounts of John Wilkinson Esq. as mayor of this borough for the year ending the first Tuesday after New Michaelmas Day 1825 not having been produced and examined at the meeting held the 21st of October 1825 in consequence of the several persons employed in building the new Shambles not being able \at that time/ to make up their bills and state the amount of their respective demands against the corporation. The same accounts examined and found correct by the auditors were this day produced and examined & there appearing to be a balance of four hundred and ninety pounds eleven shilling and four pence due to the said John Wilkinson, we do direct that the same shall be paid to him with five per cent interest from the eleventh day of April last (when such balance was disbursed) out of the first monies that shall become due to the corporation.

The accounts of William Skinner junior Esq. the late mayor of this borough for the year ending the first Tuesday after New Michaelmas Day last examined and found correct by the [p. 434] auditors were produced and inspected and there appearing to be a balance of one hundred and ninety pounds ten shillings and one penny three farthing due to the said William Skinner, we do further direct that the same shall be paid to him \with interest/ after the rate of five per cent from this day out of the first monies that shall become due to the said corporation after the said balance due to the said John Wilkinson shall have been liquidated.

Ordered that Mr Thomas Gray be continued as master of the Grammar School for one year from Christmas next and that the subscription of twenty pounds for that year be continued to him.

Ordered that the sum of twenty pounds be paid to James Ward as a compensation for his services as a constable and police officer for this borough for the next year if he shall be continued in those offices.

The Committee appointed at the last meeting having made the following report. 'The committee appointed to survey the Cottage Row property and to set out a piece of ground for the purpose of building new baths do recommend that a right of road be granted to Mr Hixon not exceeding twelve feet from the south end of his mill steps to the proposed north side of the new baths and that the said baths extend not exceeding eight yards to the south and that a lease be offered to the proposed subscribers for a term not exceeding twenty five years they binding themselves to erect a building of not less value than £300 and after that period the said erection to be continued as a bath by the corporation. Thomas Harris accepts the cottage No 3 \5/ at £6 per annum and we recommend that Nos. 10 and 11 be offered to Matthew Hunton for the yearly rent of £6 and that No 7 occupied by Thomas Jackson be continued at £6 per annum and that No 8 accepted by Thomas Lanchester be continued at £3 per annum, No. 9 occupied by Jane Spelling be continued at £3 per annum. We further recommend that the Stockton and Darlington Railway Company be requested to make a drain from the north end of Cottage Row to the common shore south of the building leading to the River Tees and that the whole of that property be inspected and made drop dry. (Signed) Robert Jordison, Richard Jackson, William Watson, Anthony Dobing.[308]

---

308 The report of the committee is entered in a different hand from the rest of the minutes.

[p. 435]
Ordered that the said report be confirmed that the same committee be ~~requested~~ named as a committee to treat with Mr Hixon for the sale of the said right of road and that any two of the said committee be competent to act.

Wm. Skinner junior mayor, Thos. Jennett, Richd. Jackson, Jno. Wilkinson, Jno. Dixon, W. Richmond, W. Sadler, Mattw: Wadeson, Wm. Smith, Wm. Gent, Robt. Bald.

[p. 436]
Borough of Stockton
At a meeting of the mayor aldermen and burgesses held this nineteenth day of January 1827 pursuant to due notice.

It having been represented that the Stockton and Darlington Railway has been laid so near to the houses in Cottage Row belonging to the corporation as to occasion inconvenience, ordered that the mayor be requested to desire the agent for the railway company to meet the committee appointed on the sixteenth of May last on an early day to determine upon the necessary alteration for the line of railway to obviate the objection stated.

Also ordered that the further sum of £1200 shall be forthwith borrowed, for the purpose of discharging the outstanding claims upon the corporation, and that the mayor be authorized to procure the same and to execute a proper security for it upon the revenues of the corporation.

Wm. Skinner junior mayor, Richd. Jackson, Jno. Wilkinson, Robt. Bald, W: Richmond, Anth[on]y Dobing, W. Sadler, Willm. Gent, Jno. Heaviside.

[p. 437]
Borough of Stockton. At a meeting of the mayor, alderman and burgesses held this first day of March 1827 pursuant to due notice.

Mr Richard Otley the agent of the Stockton and Darlington Railway Company having attended this meeting and stated the wish of the company to rent of the corporation the whole or any part of the vacant ground at Cottage Row adjoining the River Tees belonging to the corporation, ordered that an offer be made to the committee of the railway company to let them so much of such vacant ground as shall lie between a line drawn at the distance of 21 feet admeasured northwards from the northernmost staith at or near to Cottage Row belonging to the said company and a line to be drawn at the distance of 50 feet admeasured southwards from the mill belonging to or in the occupation of Mr Walker at the yearly rent of thirty pounds for seven years to commence from the period of the company's signifying their acceptance of such offer.

William Skinner junior mayor

[col. 1], Richd. Jackson, Thos. Jennett, John Wilkinson, [in pencil: 'Thos Heaviside'], Anthony Dobing, Robt. Bald
[col. 2] W: Richmond, W. Sadler, Wm. Skinner, Willm. Gent.

[p. 438]
Borough of Stockton. At a meeting of the mayor aldermen and burgesses held this twenty seventh day of March 1827 pursuant to due notice.

Mr Otley having attended on behalf of the Stockton and Darlington Railway Company to treat for a lease of ~~the Stockton and Darlington Railway~~ part of the vacant ground at Cottage Row, and having been offered a lease for seven years of the piece of ground described in the order made at the last meeting of the corporation, and of the other parcel of ground previously rented of the corporation by the railway company at the yearly rent of thirty pounds per annum to commence from the 13th day of May next and having accepted such offers on the part of the railway company, ordered that a lease of the premises to the said railway company for the term and at the rent above mentioned be forthwith executed and that the rent be reserved to be payable half yearly at Mayday and Martinmas and that the lease contain such covenants and clauses as are usual in the like cases, and also a clause authorizing the railway company at the termination of the leases to remove any erections that they may put up upon the premises, but at the same time restraining them from removing any piles or other works which they may put up for the support and defence of the ground.

An application having been made by Mr John Hixon to be allowed a right of road over the corporation grounds at the south end of his mill and it appearing desirable for [erasure] the [p. 439] corporation to have the privilege of moving vessels so as to lay partly in front of the said mill, ordered that Mr John Wilkinson, Mr Richard Jackson and

Mr Robert Jordison be and they are hereby appointed a committee to treat with Mr Hixon and be empowered to agree to the corporation granting the right \of road/ required by him under such regulations and restrictions as they may think proper, in consideration of his granting to the corporation and their tenants for vessels resorting to their property such privilege of laying and moving vessels partly in front of the said mill as they may deem expedient to stipulate for on behalf of the corporation.

William Skinner junior mayor, Thos. Jennett, Richd. Jackson, John Wilkinson, Thomas Walker, Willm. Gent, Wilfred Sadler, Robt. Bald, Rt. Jordison, Thomas Coser.

[p. 440]
Borough of Stockton. At a meeting of the mayor aldermen and burgesses held this twenty fourth day of July 1827 pursuant to due notice.

A letter from the collector and comptroller of the customs bearing date the twenty third day of July instant and addressed to the mayor requesting to be informed whether the corporation are disposed to enlarge the present Custom House the lease of which will expire in April next or whether they have any other house to offer to the Crown having been laid before the meeting, ordered that an answer be returned acquainting the collector and comptroller that no enlargement of the building will be made and that the corporation have no other house to offer.

Also ordered that the property contained in the above indenture of lease shall pursuant to the general order of the mayor aldermen and burgesses made on the 27th day of November 1817 be advertized to be let at a meeting of the corporation to be held on the 28th day of September next at seven o'clock in the evening.

Wm. Skinner junior mayor, Wm. Skinner, John Wilkinson, Robert Bald, Willm. Gent, A. Dobing, Robt. Jordison, John Heaviside, Mattw: Wadeson, Thomas Coser, Thos. Jennett, William Watson.

[p. 441]
Borough of Stockton. At a meeting of the mayor aldermen and burgesses held this 28th day of September 1827 pursuant to ~~due notice~~ adjournment.

Ordered that this meeting be adjourned to Friday the 26th day of October next at 7 o'clock in the evening.

Wm. Skinner junior, mayor

[*col. 1*] John Wilkinson, Thomas Walker, John Filiner, Robt. Bald, Robt. Cass, William Watson[309]
[*col. 2*] Thomas Coser, Willm. Gent, A. Dobing, W. Richmond.

[p. 442]
Borough of Stockton. At a meeting of the mayor aldermen and burgesses held this 26th day of October 1827 pursuant to adjournment.

Ordered that this meeting be adjourned to Tuesday next at 11 o'clock in the forenoon.

Thomas Walker mayor, Thos. Jennett, Wm. Skinner, Richd. Jackson, Wm. Skinner junior, Willm. Gent, Willm. Watson, Thomas Coser, Robt. Bald, John Filiner, W: Richmond.

[p. 443]
Borough of Stockton. At a meeting of the mayor aldermen and burgesses held this thirtieth day of October 1827 pursuant to due notice.

Messrs[310] William Richmond, William Gent, John Grant, Robert Bald, Wilfred Sadler, Henry Beckwith junior[311] [and] Thomas Eeles were elected a committee of repairs for the current year which will expire on the first Tuesday after the 29th day of September next.

Mr Matthew Wadeson, William Richmond [and] Robert Jordison were elected auditors of accounts for the same period.

The accounts of William Skinner junior Esq. the late mayor of this borough for the year ending the first Tuesday after New Michaelmas Day last (examined and certified to be correct by the auditors) were

309 William Watson was Chief Constable of Stockton Ward and adjuster of weights and measures, living in Finkle Street, and part of Globe Insurance: P&W, p. 316.

310 Here and in later lists of appointments, the first name is prefaced by 'Mr' and subsequent names by 'ditto' marks.

311 In 1827, a Henry Beckwith, gentleman, lived on the High Street: P&W, p. 315.

produced and inspected and there appearing to be a balance of ninety nine pounds nineteen shilling and four pence due to the said William Skinner we do direct that the same shall be paid to him with interest after the rate of five per cent from this day out of the first monies that shall come become due to the said corporation.

It being ascertained that the sum of £1200 ordered to be borrowed at the meeting held on the nineteenth day of January last is not adequate for the purposes \therein mentioned/ and to defray the expence of for the further improvements since made in the property of the corporation and it appearing that the outstanding bills still due after [p. 444] the application of that sum amount to the sum of six hundred pounds and upwards, ordered that the further sum of six hundred pounds shall be forthwith borrowed for the purpose of discharging such outstanding claims and that the mayor be authorized to procure the same and to execute a proper security upon the revenues of the corporation for it.

And it being stated that the sum due and ordered to be paid to Mr Raisbeck on the eighth day of March 1825 has not yet been discharged, ordered that he be allowed interest for the same from that day until payment at the rate of five per cent.

Ordered that Mr Thomas Gray be continued as master of the Grammar School for one year from Christmas next and that the subscription of twenty pounds for that year be continued to him.

Ordered that the committee appointed to superintend the building of the Shambles be deputed to adjust and settle the disputed account of William Jeckyls and that in case they and he cannot agree upon the same that they be authorized to refer the difference to arbitration and to appoint the referrees for that purpose.

Ordered that Mr William Braithwaite, Mr Richard Jackson and Mr John Wilkinson be appointed a committee for appropriating and letting the room called the Corn Exchange so as to render the same productive to the corporation in such manner as they or any two of them shall think fit.

Also ordered that the sum of four hundred pounds be annually appropriated and applied to answer the payment of [p. 445] the interest of the debt due from the corporation and to pay the salaries or allowances usually made and granted by the corporation and to defray the expence of repairs and improvements and that the whole of the income of the corporation over and above such sum of £400 shall be reserved and set apart and be impro placed out and improved at interest to form a fund to be applied from time to time under the order of the corporation towards the reduction of the debt until the whole of such debt shall be liquidated.

Also ordered that Mr Nathan Thompson[312] the collector of the anchorage and plankage dues for the corporation be allowed a salary at the rate of ten per cent upon the net sum received for his trouble to take place from the first day of October 1826.

Also ordered that the sum five guineas be subscribed towards the fund for premiums to be distributed at the cattle shows in Stockton for the year ensuing.

Also ordered that the committee of repairs do examine the state of the Custom House and take into consideration \and make a report/ whether it will more for the advantage of the corporation to appropriate it for an inn or to let it to some other and what purpose and what alterations and repairs will be proper to be made and at what expence will attend the same and that Thomas Salmon shall have the preference as a tenant.

Also ordered that James Ward be allowed the sum of two guineas for acting as mayor's sergeant for the year ensuing and that he have also the further salary of thirty pounds for such year for which he shall collect and receive under the correction direction of the mayor the rents of the stalls and \of/ the Shambles \&/ of the property at Cottage [p. 446] Row and any other revenues of the corporation which the mayor shall order and shall also regularly and duly attend to the proper regulation of the market and execute and fulfil the duties of a police officer for the borough and any other services which have been hitherto performed by him for the mayor.

---

312 Nathan Thompson, collector's clerk and warehouse keeper in customs, lived on the High Street in 1827 (P& W, p. 316). He supplied extracts from the customs house book to Robert Surtees (Surtees, *History*, pp. 177–80), who added data from Brewster (*History*, pp. 72, 75).

Also ordered that Mr William Richmond, Mr Robert Jordison and Mr Robert Bald be appointed a committee to assist the mayor in the regulation of the market.

Also ordered that the sum of five pounds be subscribed towards the fund of the School of Industry at Stockton and that so much of the sum of forty pounds advanced by Mr John Wilkinson and thirty pounds advanced by Mr William Skinner junior for the services of James Ward as shall not be repaid by means of the subscription entered into towards the salary of the said James Ward shall be paid out of the sinking fund agreed to be established after the same shall be sufficient for that purpose over and above the sum of two hundred pounds.

Thomas Walker, mayor

[*col. 1*] Thos. Jennett, Wm. Skinner, Richd. Jackson, Jno. Wilkinson, W. Skinner junior, Willm. Gent, Willm. Watson, Robt. Jordison, Robt. Bald, W. Richmond[313]
[*col. 2*] Mattw: Wadeson, Anth[on]y Dobing, Robt. Sherwood, F. R. Richmond.

[p. 447]
Borough of Stockton. At a meeting of the mayor aldermen and burgesses held this first day of March 1828 pursuant to due notice.

Ordered that petitions \be presented/ to both Houses of Parliament in favor of the bill now pending for the further improvement of the River Tees and that the corporation seal be affixed thereto.[314]

---

313 In 1827, a William Richmond was in the Phoenix Fire and Pelican Life insurance office in the High Street: P&W, p. 316.
314 The course of the River Tees had already been shortened between Stockton and Portrack by the 'Old Cut' across the neck of the river's loop at Mandale. It is said that William Sleigh, mayor 1790–1, had, in his term of office, made 'considerable exertions' in support of a cut at Portrack to shorten the river, originally proposed by Edmund Harvey, pewterer, but this was not pursued until 1802, when a committee (consisting of John Carr, Matthew Davison, Matthew Wadeson, James Crowe, Richardson Ferrand and William Mellanby) was appointed to take the project forward: the cut eventually opened on 18 September 1810, accompanied by 'great rejoicings'. At the opening, Leonard Raisbeck proposed the advantages of improved transport between Stockton and the western parts of Co. Durham, and was instrumental in setting up a large committee to investigate a railroad or canal (Brewster, *History*, pp. 211–12;

Also ordered that William Skinner Esq. junior, Mr John Wilkinson and Mr Richard Jackson be and they are hereby appointed a committee to prepare such petition.

Thomas Walker, mayor

Tho. Jennett,[315] Richd. Jackson, W. Skinner junior, Wm. Gent, [*in pencil: 'D. Pearson'*], Willm. Watson, [*in pencil: 'Robt Pearson, Jno Heaviside, – Ableson'*], Robt. Bald, W. Richmond, Robt. Jordison, Jno. Wilkinson, Wm. Skinner, Ro. Lamb.[316]

[p. 448]
Borough of Stockton. At a meeting of the mayor aldermen and burgesses held this tenth day of April 1828 pursuant to due notice.

It appearing to this meeting that the property of the corporation will be materially decreased in value by the proposed extension of the Stockton and Darlington Railroad to Middlesbrough, ordered that petitions be presented to both houses of Parliament against the bill now pending to enable the Stockton and Darlington Railway Company to make that extension and that William Skinner Esq. junior be and he is hereby authorized to take those petitions to London and to adopt such measures as he may deem best for vigorously opposing the said bill in its progress through Parliament.

Ordered that all expences attendant upon or incident to such opposition shall be defrayed out of the first monies that shall become due to the corporation.

[*In pencil: 'Present'*] Thomas Walker mayor, Thos. Jennett, Richd. Jackson, Jno. Wilkinson, W. Skinner junior, Wm. Skinner, Robt. Bald, W. Richmond, [*in pencil: 'Robt Jordison, Martin Kirtley, Wm Sleigh, Thos Fall junior, Thos Richmond'*], Willm. Watson, [*in pencil: 'Anthony Dobing, John Heaviside'*].

Surtees, *History*, p. 177; Heavisides, *Annals*, pp. 55–8; P&W p. 315; Richmond, *Local Records*, pp. 115–16). A 'New Cut', to the east of the Old Cut, arose from the petition recorded here, and opened in 1831: *VCH Durham III*, p. 348.

315 Thomas Jennet was in the Sun insurance office in the High Street: P&W, p. 316.

316 A Robert Lamb was an iron merchant of Brunswick Street in 1827: P&W, p. 315.

[p. 449]
Borough of Stockton. At a meeting of the mayor aldermen and burgesses held this seventeenth day of October 1828 pursuant to due notice.

Messrs William Richmond, William Gent, John Grant, Robert Bald, Robert Cass, Henry Beckwith junior [and] Thomas Eeles were elected a committee of repairs for the current year which will expire on the first Tuesday after the 29th day of September next.

Mr Matthew Wadeson, William Richmond [and] Robert Jordison were elected auditors of accounts for the same period.

The accounts of Thomas Walker Esq. the mayor of this borough for the year ending the first Tuesday after New Michaelmas Day last (examined and certified to be correct by the auditors) were produced and inspected and there appearing a balance of two hundred and thirty six pounds fourteen shillings and six pence farthing due to the said Thomas Walker, we do direct that the same shall be paid to him with interest after the rate of five per cent from this day out of the first monies that shall become due to the said corporation.

Ordered that Mr Thomas Gray be continued as master of the Grammar School for one year from Christmas next and that the subscription of twenty pounds for that year be continued to him.

Also ordered that the sum of five guineas be subscribed towards the fund for premiums to be distributed at the cattle shows in Stockton for the year ensuing.

Also ordered that James Ward be allowed the sum of two guineas for acting as mayor's serjeant for the year ensuing and that he have also the further salary of thirty pounds for such year for which he shall collect and receive under the direction of the mayor the rents of the stalls of the [p. 450] Shambles and of the property at Cottage Row and any other revenues of the corporation which the mayor shall order and shall also regularly and duly attend to the proper regulation of the market and execute and fulfil the duties of a police officer for the borough and any other services which have been hitherto performed by him for the mayor.

Also ordered that Mr Richard Jackson, Mr William Richmond and Mr Robert Jordison be appointed a committee to assist the mayor in the regulation of the market.

Also ordered that the sum of five pounds be subscribed towards the fund of the School of Industry at Stockton.

Also ordered that each coble coming to Stockton during the year next ensuing laden with fish from Hartlepool, Redcar or any other place for sale by retail be allowed the sum of five shillings provided the fish have been caught by the crew and not purchased.

Also ordered

That Mr Ryder the lessee of the corporation having represented that Robert Sherwood refused to pay his stallage dues and that he cannot obtain the same without proceeding at law for the purpose, ordered that he be supported by the corporation in suing for the same and be indemnified by them against any loss or expence which may be occasioned thereby.

Thomas Walker mayor, Wm Skinner, Richd. Jackson, Thos. Jennet, [*in pencil: 'J Wilkinson'*], Willm. Gent, William Watson, Robt. Jordison, Robt. Bald, W: Richmond.

[p. 451]
Borough of Stockton. At a meeting of the mayor aldermen and burgesses held this twentieth day of October 1829 pursuant to due notice.

Messrs William Gent, William Watson, Daniel Pearson, Martin Kirtley, Pickering Pick, John Coates [and] Robert Jordison were elected a committee of repairs for the current year which will expire on the first Tuesday after the 29th day of September next.

Messrs Matthew Wadeson, Francis Richardson Richmond [and] Henry Beckwith junior were elected auditors of accounts for the same period.

The accounts of Thomas Walker Esq. the mayor of this borough for the year ending the first Tuesday after New Michaelmas Day last (examined and certified to be correct by the auditors) were produced and inspected and there appearing a balance of two hundred and seven pounds three shillings due to the said Thomas Walker we do direct that the same shall be paid to him with interest after the rate of five per cent from this day out of the first monies that shall become due to the said corporation.

Ordered that Mr Thomas Gray be continued as master of the Grammar School for one year from Christmas next and that the subscription of twenty pounds for that year be continued to him.

[p. 452]
Also ordered that the sum of five pounds five shillings be subscribed towards the fund for premiums to be distributed at the cattle shew in Stockton for the year ensuing.

Also ordered that James Ward be allowed the sum of two pounds two shillings for acting as mayor's serjeant for the year ensuing and that he have also the further salary of thirty pounds for such year for which he shall collect and receive under the direction of the mayor the rents of the stalls of the Shambles and of the property at Cottage Row and any other revenues of the corporation which the mayor shall order and shall also regularly and duly attend to the proper regulation of the market and execute and fulfil the duties of a police officer for the borough and other services which hath been hitherto performed by him for the mayor.

Also ordered that Mr William Watson, William Smith and Robert Jordison be appointed a committee to assist the mayor in the regulation of the market.

Also ordered that the sum of five pounds be subscribed towards the fund of the School of Industry at Stockton.

Also ordered that each coble coming to Stockton during the year next ensuing laden with fish from Hartlepool, Redcar or any other place for sale by retail be allowed the sum of five shillings provided the fish have been caught by the crew and not purchased.

[p. 453]
Also ordered that the tenants of the butchers' stalls shall henceforth pay one quarter of a year's rent in advance.

Also ordered that the piece of ground belonging to the corporation lying between Mr Hixon's mill and the ground occupied by the Stockton and Darlington Railway Company and now in the possession of Mr John Wilkinson, shall be let to him upon lease for the term of fourteen years to be computed from the thirteenth of May last at the yearly rent of five pounds and that at the expiration of the term the lessee may remove to and for his own use and benefit any erections or buildings he may construct thereon if the corporation shall decline taking them at such price as shall be fixed upon by two persons one appointed by each party and in case of their differing in opinion then by an umpire nominated by such two persons but that the premises shall notwithstanding such erections or buildings may be taken away be left in as good a condition as they are in at present and that the mayor shall affix the corporation seal to such lease when presented to him for that purpose.

Also ordered that the lease of the corporation property be renewed upon the terms offered by the bishop of Durham.

Ro. Lamb mayor, Thos. Jennett, Wm. Skinner, J. Wilkinson, Rd. Jackson, [*in pencil 'Kirtley, Jordison'*], Thomas Walker, Robt. Bald, Rich. Jackson, [*in pencil: 'Wm Smith, Thos. Walker, Rd. Jackson'*].

[p. 454]
Borough of Stockton. At a meeting of the mayor aldermen and burgesses held this first day of July 1830 pursuant to due notice.

Resolved that the mayor be authorised to let the garden now occupied by Mr Richmond for the best rent that can be obtained for the same for the purpose of the lessee erecting a public coal staith thereon.

The person taking the same to have a lease for such time as the mayor shall deem expedient and such lease to become void if the lessee at any time during the term exercise or carry on the trade of a coal fitter and that the lessee may take away at the expiration of his term any erections he may put thereon if the lessors do not take the same at a valuation to be made by two indifferent persons one to be chosen by each party and the two parties so chosen to be at liberty to elect an umpire whose decision shall be final.

Ro. Lamb mayor, Thos. Jennett, J. Wilkinson, Robt. Bald, Rich. Jackson, M. Kirtley.

[p. 455]
Borough of Stockton. At a meeting of the mayor aldermen and burgesses held this first day of July 1830 pursuant to due notice.

A proposition from the Stockton and Darlington Railway Company to lay at their own expence a branch or siding through the gardens belonging to the corporation lying behind the houses in Cottage Row for the use of the staiths the property of the corporation at the north end of Cottage Row aforesaid having been read and taken into consideration and the corporation feeling anxious to afford every facility to the increased trade of the port, ordered that the mayor be authorised to inform the Stockton and Darlington Railway company that their proposition is acceded to upon the following terms, namely that the Stockton and Darlington Railway Company shall lay two branches or sidings through the gardens in question at their own expence for the use of the staiths before mentioned and discharge all claims that may be substantiated by the occupiers of those gardens for compensation and all other expences whatsoever incident to or attending upon the execution of the work; that the soil and freehold of the gardens shall still remain the property of the corporation and the Stockton and Darlington Railway Company shall pay the sum of one shilling yearly for the occupation thereof and hold the same for the term of fourteen years and be at the expiration of that term at full liberty to take the rails away for their own use.

A request from Messrs Harris and Taylor that the corporation would erect an additional office for them on the property in Cottage Row having read and taken into consideration, ordered that the mayor assisted by the committee of repairs be requested to ascertain the expence of the work and be at full liberty to grant or refuse the request as he may judge most conducive to the interests of the corporation.

[p. 456]
A proposal having been laid before this meeting on the part of the churchwardens of the parish to give to the corporation a pew containing six sittings at the west entrance of the church in lieu of or in exchange for the pew belonging to the corporation situate near the communion table and containing two sittings, ordered that that proposal be accepted and that the pew so given to the corporation shall be immediately fitted up in such manner as this mayor may think proper at the corporation's expense.

Also ordered that the sum of £40 mentioned in an order made on the thirtieth day of October 1827 as having been advanced by Mr John Wilkinson for fo the services of James Ward to be paid to Mr Wilkinson by the mayor prior to his going out of office in October next.

Present
[*col. 1*] Rt. Lamb mayor, Wm. Skinner, Rich. Jackson, J. Wilkinson, Robt. Bald
[*col. 2*] Mattw: Wadeson, [*in pencil: 'Wm Watson'*], Martin Kirtley.

[p. 457]
Borough of Stockton. At a meeting of the mayor aldermen and burgesses held this twenty first day of October 1830 pursuant to due notice.

Messrs William Watson, Martin Kirtley, Pickering Pick, Robert Jordison, Robert Bald, Anthony Dobing [and] Robert Cass were elected a committee of repairs for the current year which will expire on the first Tuesday after the 29th day of September next.

Messrs Henry Beckwith, Matthew Wadeson [and] Thomas Eeles were elected auditors of accounts for the same period.

The accounts of Robert Lamb Esq. the mayor of this borough for the year ending the first Tuesday after New Michaelmas Day last (examined and certified to be correct by the auditors) were produced and inspected and there appearing a balance of forty one pounds four shillings due to the said Robert Lamb we do direct that the same shall be paid to him with interest after the rate of five per cent from this day out of the first monies that shall become due to the said corporation.

Ordered that Mr Thomas Gray be continued as master of the Grammar School for one year from Christmas next and that the subscription of twenty pounds for that year be continued to him.

Also ordered that the sum of five pounds five shillings be subscribed towards the fund for premiums to be distributed at the cattle shew for the year next ensuing.

[p. 458]
Also ordered that James Ward be allowed the sum of two pounds two shillings for acting as mayor's sergeant for the year ensuing and that he have also the further salary of thirty pounds for such year in which he shall collect end receive under the direction of the mayor the rents of the stalls of the Shambles and of the property at Cottage Row and any other of the revenues of the corporation which the mayor shall order and shall also regularly and duly attend to the proper regulation of the market and execute and fulfil the duties of a police officer for the borough and other services which have been hitherto performed by him for the mayor.

Also ordered that Mr William Watson, Mr Robert Jordison and Mr Thomas Smith be appointed a committee to assist the mayor in the regulation of the market.

Also ordered that the sum of five pounds be subscribed towards the fund of the School of Industry at Stockton.

Also ordered that each coble coming to Stockton during the year next ensuing laden with fish from Hartlepool, Redcar or any other place for sale by retail be allowed the sum of five shillings provided the fish have been caught by the crew and not purchased.

Also ordered that Mr Faber be requested to ascertain from the executors of the late Mr Richard Walker on or before the first of November next if they are willing to accept four and a half per cent interest for the money secured to them by mortgage of the corporation property and that if their reply be in the negative they be informed that this principal money and all interest to be then due thereon will be paid to them at the expiration of six calendar months from that day.

[p. 459]
Also ordered that the Mariners Tavern in Cottage Row be advertized to be let by proposal from the twenty third of November next when Mr Blenkinsop's term therein will expire.

Present
[*col. 1*] Ro. Lamb mayor, Rich. Jackson, [*in pencil: 'Wm Watson'*]
[*col. 2*] Robt. Bald, Anth[on]y Dobing, [*in pencil: 'Martin Kirtley'*].

Borough of Stockton. At a meeting of the mayor aldermen and burgesses held this 11th day of November 1830 pursuant to due notice.

Ordered that the offer made by Mr Barnes for & on behalf of Mr Guest to take the Mariners Tavern at £55 per year be accepted and that the same be let to him for 3 years at that yearly rent on such security being given for the same payable quarterly as is satisfactory to the mayor.

The butchers' Shambles being found too small, ordered that the room called the Exchange be converted into butchers' Shambles and that the work be let by tender and be executed under the direction of the mayor and committee of repairs.

[*col. 1*] Robert Lamb mayor, Thos. Jennett, [*in pencil: 'Rd. Jackson, Wm Skinner'*], Martin Kirtley, [*in pencil: 'Thos Walker'*]
[*col. 2*] Anthony Dobing, [*in pencil: 'Jno Heaviside'*], Robt. Bald, [*in pencil: 'Wm Watson, Th. Sherwood'*].

[p. 460]
Borough of Stockton. At a meeting of the mayor aldermen and burgesses held this twenty first day of October 1831 pursuant to due notice.

Messrs William Watson, Martin Kirtley, Joseph Wade, Robert Jordison, Robert Bald, Anthony Dobing [and] Robert Cass were elected a committee of repairs for the current year which will expire on the first Tuesday after the 29th day of September next.

Messrs Henry Beckwith, Thomas Eeles [and] Thomas Richmond were elected auditors of accounts for the same period.

The accounts of Robert Lamb Esq. the mayor of this borough for the year ending the first Tuesday after New Michaelmas Day last (examined and certified to be correct by the auditors) were produced and inspected and there appearing a balance of three hundred and forty one pounds fourteen shillings and tenpence due to the said Robert Lamb we do direct that the same shall be paid to him with interest after the rate of five per cent from this day out of the first monies that shall become due to the said corporation.

Mr ~~Thomas~~ \George/ Hardcastle having been appointed master of the Grammar School in the place of Mr Thomas Gray deceased, ordered that the new master shall enter into an agreement similar to that signed by Mr Gray on his appointment and that the sum of twenty pounds be paid as a subscription to Mr George Hardcastle as such master in case he shall perform the duties of that office [p. 461] to the satisfaction of the mayor until the first Tuesday after the 29th day of September next.

Also ordered that the sum of five pounds five shillings be subscribed towards the fund for premiums to be distributed at the cattle show for the year next ensuing.

Also ordered that James Ward be allowed the sum of two pounds two shillings for acting as mayor's sergeant for the year ensuing and that he have also the further salary of thirty pounds for such year for which he shall collect and receive under the direction of the mayor the rents of the stalls of the Shambles and of the property at Cottage Row and any other of the revenues of the corporation which the mayor shall order and shall also shall regularly and duly attend to the proper regulation of the market and execute and fulfill the duties of a police officer for the borough and other services which have hitherto been performed by him for the mayor.

Also ordered that Mr William Watson, Mr Robert Jordison and Mr Robert Dalton be appointed a committee to assist the mayor in the regulation of the market.

Also ordered that the sum of five pounds be subscribed towards the fund of the School of Industry at Stockton.

[p. 462]
Also ordered that each coble coming to Stockton during the year next ensuing laden with fish from Hartlepool, Redcar or any other place for sale by retail be allowed the sum of five shillings provided the fish have been caught by the crew and not purchased.

Also ordered that the Town House and other property belonging to the corporation now tenanted by Mr Mark Ryder be advertized to be let by proposal and that such proposals be taken into consideration at a meeting to be holden on the 10th day of February next.

Also ordered that notice to quit be served on the tenants of the property in Cottage Row (except the tavern \there/) and that such property be also advertised to be let by proposal and such proposals to be taken into consideration at the meeting on the said 10th day of February.

Also ordered that notice be given to Mr James Walker that if he uses the road on the south side of the mill and which road belongs to the corporation he will be deemed a trespasser and proceeded against accordingly.

Also ordered that this meeting be adjourned to the 10th day of February next.

Present
[*col. 1*] Rt. Lamb mayor, Wm. Skinner junior, Martin Kirtley, Robt. Bald
[*col. 2*] Anthony Dobing, [*in pencil: 'Wm Watson'*], Joseph Wade, [*in pencil: 'Thos Richmond'*].

[p. 463]
Borough of Stockton. At a meeting of the mayor aldermen and burgesses held this 10th day of February 1832 pursuant to adjournment from the 21st day of October last.

Ordered that the Town House and market dues and other property in lease to Mark Ryder be again let to him the said Mark Ryder for the further term of six years commencing from the expiration of the present demise at the yearly rent of two hundred and twenty pounds to be payable quarterly and that a lease be executed to him accordingly in which it is to be stipulated that the tenant is to pay all taxes and assessments as well parliamentary as parochial.

Present
[*col. 1*] Rt. Lamb mayor, Thos. Jennett, J: Wilkinson, Wm. Skinner, Robt. Bald, Jno. Dixon, Robt. Jordison
[*col. 2*] M. Kirtley, C. Swenne, Joseph Wade, [*in pencil: 'Wm Watson, Rt Sherwood'*], Anthony Dobing, Thos. Richmond.

[p. 464]
Copy of a requisition addressed by the mayor aldermen & burgesses to Leonard Raisbeck Esq. their recorder.

We the undersigned the mayor aldermen and burgesses of the borough of Stockton upon Tees, having a deep regard for the prosperity of the town of Stockton and the interests connected with the trade and commerce of the port and feeling assured of the influence of your valuable aid in support of those interests from the zeal and anxiety you have on every occasion evinced to promote the welfare of the inhabitants of your native place, do hereby respect-fully request you will permit us to place your name in nomination for the office of mayor for the ensuing year.

[*col. 1*] Robert Lamb mayor, Thos. Jennett alderman, Wm Skinner alderman, John Wilkinson alderman, Wm Skinner junior alderman, Thomas Walker alderman, Robt. Jordison, Thos. Mills, Robt. Bald, Robt. Cass, Jno. Dixon, Robinson Watson, Thos. Fall, Jno. Coates, William Sleigh, Thos. Richmond, Henry Beckwith senior, John Heaviside, Saml. Braithwaite
[*col. 2*] Cutht. Swennie, John Bell, Cutht. Robinson, Martin Kirtley, Richd. Walker senior, Ralph Briggs, Wm. Bradley, Anty. Sands, Thomas Page, John Atkinson, Anthy. Dobing, Thos Eeles.

[p. 465]
Borough of Stockton. At a meeting of the mayor aldermen and burgesses held this 16th day of October 1832 pursuant to due notice.

Messrs Martin Kirtley, Robert Bald, Joseph Wade, Robert Sherwood, Anthony Dobing, Thomas\John/Heaviside, Robert Jordison [and] John Atkinson were elected a committee of repairs for the current year which will expire on the first Tuesday after the twenty ninth day of September next.

Messrs Henry Beckwith, Thomas Eales [and] Thomas Richmond were elected auditors of accounts for the same period.

The accounts of Robert Lamb Esq. the late mayor of this borough for the year ending the first Tuesday after New Michaelmas Day last (examined and certified to be correct by the auditors) were produced and inspected and there appearing a balance of one hundred and thirty nine pounds and four pence due to the said Robert Lamb, we do direct that the same shall be paid [p. 466] to him with interest after the rate of five per cent from this day out of the first monies that shall become due to the said corporation.

Ordered that Mr George Hardcastle be continued as master of the Grammar School for one year from Christmas next and that the subscription of twenty pounds for that year be continued to him.

Also ordered that the sum of five pounds five shillings be subscribed towards the fund for premiums to be distributed at the cattle show for the year next ensuing.

Also ordered that James Ward be allowed the sum of two pounds two shillings for acting as mayor's serjeant for the year ensuing and that he have also the further salary of thirty pounds for such year for which he shall collect and receive under the direction of the mayor the rents of the stalls of the Shambles and of the property at Cottage Row and any other of the revenues of the corporation which the mayor shall order and shall also regularly and duly attend to the proper regulation of the market and execute and fulfill the duties of a police officer for the borough and other services which have hitherto [p. 467] been performed by him for the mayor.

Also ordered that Mr Robert Jordison, Mr William Wadeson Watson and Mr Robert Dalton be appointed a committee to assist the mayor in the regulation of the market.

Also ordered that the sum of five pounds be subscribed towards the fund of the School of Industry at Stockton on condition that the mayor be allowed the privilege of sending five children to that school and having always that number of his nomination and appointment there.

Also ordered that each coble coming to Stockton during the year next ensuing loaden with fish from Hartlepool, Redcar or any other place for sale by retail be allowed the sum of five shillings provided the fish have been caught by the crew and not purchased.

A misunderstanding having arisen between the corporation and Mr George William Todd as to the terms of the lease agreed to be granted to him of the piece of ground mentioned in the order [p. 468] of the 1st day of July 1830, ordered that Mr Robert Lamb and Mr Robert Bald be and they are hereby appointed a committee to communicate with Mr Todd on the subject and report the result of their conference to the next meeting of the corporation.

A claim made by Mr Mark \Ryder/ of £12 12[s.] as a rent for the room in which the justices meet for the transaction of their magisterial duties for the last six years having been taken into consideration, ordered that the same be disallowed but that the sum of £6 6[s.] be paid to him by the mayor as a gratuity in consideration of a room having previously to this period been occasionally occupied for that purpose not upon market days upon the express understanding that in future the corporation are not to be considered to liable to any charge whatever of a similar nature.

A further claim made by Mr Ryder against the corporation for the use of the news room for public meetings having also been brought forward and considered, [p. 469] resolved that such claim is entirely a novel one and that the same be entirely disallowed and that where the news room is made use of by a public meeting convened by the mayor no charge whatever ever has been or is in future to be made for the use thereof and also that this resolution be communicated to Mr Ryder and his new lease which is not yet executed to be made conformable thereto.

Leo. Raisbeck mayor, Wm. Skinner, Wm. Skinner junior, Jn: Wilkinson, Ro. Lamb, Thomas Walker, Robt. Bald, Martin Kirtley, Thomas Heaviside, Joseph Wade [*to right, in pencil:'Robert Harwood'*].

[p. 470]
Borough of Stockton. At a meeting of the mayor aldermen and burgesses held this 14th \6th/ day of February \November/ 1832 pursuant to due notice.

This meeting having taken into consideration the expediency of altering or rescinding an order made at a corporate meeting holden on the 30th day of October 1827 whereby it was directed that the sum of £400 should be annually applied for the purposes therein mentioned and that the whole of the income of the corporation over & above such sum should be placed out at interest to form a sinking fund for the payment of their debt and it appearing to this meeting that the above sum of £400 is greatly inadequate to answer the purposes specified and that it is highly [*blank*][317] the appropriation

317 The missing text may perhaps have been 'desirable that'.

of the income of the corporation to further improvements should be unrestricted.

Resolved that as well the above mentioned order as all and every other orders directing an accumulation of the income of the corporation or any part thereof be and the same are hereby absolutely rescinded.

And ordered that the mayor be authorised to borrow a sum of money (not exceeding in the whole the sum of £700) as will enable him to pay off and discharge all outstanding claims now due from the corporation exclusive of the p[rincipa]l[318] money and interest secured on mortgage of their property.

Various bills claimed to be due from the corporation having been laid before and inspected by this meeting, [p. 471] ordered that the same be referred for examination and adjustment to the mayor and that Mr William Skinner junior, Mr Robert Bald and Mr Robert Lamb be and they are hereby appointed a committee to assist him in the investigation thereof and that so much of the amount as he shall find to be justly due shall be satisfied and paid by him out of the money to be borrowed as aforesaid. Also that in case any doubt or difficulty as to the legality or justice of any of the said claims or any part thereof shall arise he shall have power either to admit or to compound the amount in question or to refer the same to arbitration as he may deem expedient or proper.

The committee appointed at the last meeting to communicate with Mr Todd as to the misunderstanding that had arisen between the corporation and himself relative to the terms of his intended lease having reported that Mr Todd had consented to take the lease on the Terms mentioned in the order of the 1st day of July 1830, ordered that the lease be prepared accordingly and that the mayor be authorised to execute the same and to attach the corporation seal thereto.

[col. 1] Leo. Raisbeck mayor, Thomas Walker, Wm. Skinner, W. Skinner junior, Jno. Wilkinson, Anth[on]y Dobing
[col. 2] [in pencil: 'Mr R Jordison'], John Atkinson, M. Kirtley, Robt. Bald.

318 Reading uncertain.

[p. 472]
Borough of Stockton. At a meeting of the mayor aldermen and burgesses held this 14th February 1833 pursuant to due notice.

Ordered that the sum to be borrowed by the mayor under the authority of the order passed at the last meeting be £700 and that the seal of the corporation be affixed at this meeting to the mortgage deed now produced for securing that further amount to the present mortgagees.

Also ordered that Mr Robert Jordison, Mr Robert Lamb, Mr Anthony Dobing, Mr Martin Kirtley, Mr Thomas Walker be and they are hereby appointed a committee with full power for any three of them to act to investigate and ascertain the amount of sundry claims for ~~money~~ sums expended by former burgesses prior to the year 1825 for law expenses and stamps or still remaining due from them for the benefit of the corporation. And that such sums as shall be found by such committee to be justly due shall be paid off and discharged by the mayor as soon as the funds of the corporation will enable him to do so.

[*col. 1*] Leo. Raisbeck mayor, Wm. Skinner, Thos. Jennett, Jn. Wilkinson, Thomas Walker
[*col. 2*] Anth[on]y Dobing, Martin Kirtley, John Atkinson.

[p. 473]
Borough of Stockton. At a meeting of the mayor aldermen and burgesses held this 8th day of November 1833 pursuant to due notice.

Messrs Martin Kirtley, Robert Bald, Joseph Wade, Robert Sherwood, Anthony Dobing, Thomas Heaviside, Robert Jordison, John Atkinson [and] Robert Seymour were elected a committee of repair for the current year which will expire on the 1st Tuesday after the 29th day of September next.

Messrs Henry Beckwith, Thomas Richmond [and] John Dixon were elected auditors of accounts for the same period.

The accounts of Leonard Raisbeck Esq. the late mayor of this borough for the last year (examined and certified to be correct by the auditors) were produced and inspected and there appeared a balance of £180 19[s.] 4[d.] due from the said Leonard Raisbeck to the corporation.

He having proposed a mode of arranging and classifying the accounts with the view of simplifying the same and distinguishing as well the disbursements under the different heads of expenditure as the receipts ~~and~~ income derived from each particular property, or source of revenue, ordered that such arrangement be approved of and be adopted in future.

Also ordered that the committee of repairs for the time being, shall [p. 474] keep a book in which they shall enter a minit of such alterations or repairs as they shall think proper to recommend and shall submit the same to the mayor for his sanction and that no alterations or repairs shall be undertaken without his previous approbation and direction.

Great inconvenience having been experienced in consequence of persons having demands upon the corporation neglecting to deliver an account thereof to the mayor in due time, ordered that in future (save in cases where written contracts shall be entered into) no person shall be dealt with or employed on[319] behalf of the corporation except on condition of forfeiting his claim if he shall fail to render his account to the mayor on or before the 1st day of October in each year for the articles \which shall have been supplied or the work/ which shall have been done in the course of the next preceeding 12 calendar months.

Ordered that Mr George Hardcastle be continued master of the Grammar School for one year from Christmas next and that the sum of £20 be paid to him as a subscription but that he do previously execute an agreement similar to those entered into by former masters with the exception that a public examination of his scholars at Christmas yearly shall only be required.

Also ordered that the sum of £5–5–0 be subscribed towards the funds for premiums to be distributed at the cattle show at Stockton for the year next ensuing.

---

319 MS: 'or'.

Also ordered that James Ward's salary as the mayor's sergeant be increased to £5 yearly so long as the magistrate's Petty Sessions for Stockton Ward shall be holden in the Town House on condition that the said James Ward shall duly and regularly attend such meetings as a police officer or constable; and that the augmentation be paid to him for the last year. That the said James Ward have also a further salary of £30 [p. 475] for the year ensuing for which he shall collect and receive under the direction of the mayor the rents of the stalls in the Shambles and of the property in Cottage Row and any other revenues of the corporation which the mayor shall direct and shall also regularly and duly attend to the proper regulation of the market and execute and fulfil the duties of a police officer for the borough and all other services which have hitherto been performed by him for the mayor.

Also ordered that Mr Robert Jordison, Mr William Wadeson Watson and Mr Robert Sherwood be appointed a committee to assist the mayor in the regulation of the market.

Also ordered that the sum of £5 be subscribed towards the fund of the School of Industry at Stockton on the terms prescribed last year which have been assented to by the managers of that charity.

Also ordered that each coble with a full cargo of fresh sea fish which during the year next ensuing shall arrive and be disposed of at Stockton by retail shall be allowed a premium of 5s. provided the fish have been caught at sea by the crew of such boat.

Complaints having been made that a greater portion of the land at Cottage Row is occupied by Mr Wilkinson than is included in his lease and of \his/ having placed lead so as to impede or inconvenience the public footpath, ordered that the committee of repairs do communicate with Mr Wilkinson on these subjects and with the sanction of the mayor do enter into proper arrangements with him as well for abating the nuisance complained of as for adjusting the rent of the extra ground occupied by him.

A letter from Mr Otley on behalf of the Stockton and Darlington Railway Company inquring if the corporation are disposed to review the lease granted to that company which will expire at May Day next and on what terms having been read, [p. 476] ordered that it be referred to the committee of repairs to survey the property and to take the subject into consideration and afterwards to treat and agree with the Stockton and Darlington Railway Company for a renewal of their lease on such terms as shall appear to them reasonable and shall be approved of by the mayor.

It appearing that the lease of the Mariners Tavern granted to Mr Joseph Smith will expire on the 23rd instant, ordered that the committee of repairs be authorised to relet the property to him for such time and at such rent as they may think proper and the mayor shall approve of.

Also ordered that the sum of £100 be subscribed towards the fund for erecting a church or chapel at the south end of the town and for enclosing the ground there recently granted gratuitously by the bishop of Durham for a cemetery and that the same be paid to the committee who may ultimately be appointed to carry the measures into effect to be by them applied to both or either of those objects at their discretion.

[*col. 1*] Leo. Raisbeck mayor, Wm. Skinner, Ro. Lamb, Thos. Jennett, [*in pencil: 'Robt Jordison'*]
[*col. 2*] Robt. Bald, Anth[on]y Dobing, [*in pencil: 'Robt Sherwood'*], Joseph Wade, Thos. Heaviside.

[p. 477]
Borough of Stockton. At a meeting of the mayor aldermen and burgesses held this 8th day of March \1834/ pursuant to due notice.

Resolved unanimously that as the corporation is very deeply interested in retaining the trade now carried on at the town of Stockton it is highly expedient that they should unite in the measures now in progress for that object so far as circumstances will justify.

A steam navigation company having been established as a necessary expedient for preventing the removal of the London trade from Stockton to Middlesbro' which would most prejudicially affect the property and interests of the corporation, ordered unanimously that a sum of money not exceeding £300 be paid to Mr Thomas Walker, Mr Thomas Jennett, Mr William Skinner junior, Mr Robert Bald, Mr Anthony Dobing as a committee (any 3 of whom shall be competent to act) with power to lend the same to the above mentioned steam navigation company at such rate of interest and on such terms and conditions as to the committee may seem proper having regard to the desire of the corporation to manifest their disposition to assist and support that company.

A letter from the corporation of Norwich calling upon this body to send a deputation to join a general meeting of corporate bodies in London with a view to oppose any legislative measures prejudicially affecting their rights having been produced by the mayor and read, ordered that the consideration of that letter be postponed till the exact nature of the legislative enactments in contemplation be ascertained.

[p. 478]
It having been represented that a great number of butchers are contrary to law retailing meat in the town of Stockton on market days in private shops and not in the Shambles or public market, ordered that the butchers alluded to be requested to attend a meeting of the aldermen and Committee of Repairs to be convened on an early day that the illegality of their proceedings may be explained to them.

A board of trade having been just established for the protection of the trade of the town, ordered that a donation of £5 5s. be contributed to the fund for defraying the expenses thereof.

[*col. 1*] Leo. Raisbeck mayor, Wm. Skinner, Jno. Wilkinson, Thos. Jennett, M. Kirtley, [*in pencil: 'Mr W Smith'*]
[*col. 2*] Robt. Bald, Anth[on]y Dobing, [*in pencil: 'Mr C Martin'*], Thomas Walker, Joseph Wade, M. Skinner junior.

[p. 479]
Borough of Stockton
At a meeting of the mayor aldermen and burgesses held this ~~eig~~ twentieth day of June 1834 pursuant to due notice.

Ordered that Robert Seymour, John Atkinson, Thomas Heaviside, Anthony Dobing, Robert Bald & William Smith be and they are hereby appointed a committee (any 3 of whom shall be competent to act) to examine the state & condition of the building called the Old Customhouse and the drain adjoining thereto and report their opinion as to the most eligible means of putting the building into tenantable repair with an estimate of the expence.

It having been represented to this meeting by the mayor that certain ship owners at Middlesbro had refused to pay the corporation dues of anchorage & plankage & that in consequence he had directed a statement of the case to be laid before Sir James Scarlett the attorney general for the bishop of Durham (under whose title the dues are held by the corporation) and Dr Lushington and such statement with the opinions of those gentlemen confirmatory of the legal right of the corporation to the dues having been ~~read~~ produced and read, ordered that the measures already adopted by the mayor be and they are hereby fully sanctioned by this meeting and that he be authorized to obtain further opinions of counsel should circumstances render it adviseable to do so and also to institute proceedings either at law or in equity against such persons as have already refused or shall hereafter refuse to pay anchorage & plankage dues to recover & enforce payment of the same.

Various complaints having been made that several butchers have lately opened shops in or stalls near private [p. 480] houses in the town for the sale of butcher's meat on market days to the great prejudice of the corporation & the persons renting stall in the public Shambles under them, ordered that this infringement of the rights and privileges of the corporation as owners of the market be resisted and that notice thereof be given to all persons who shall use private stalls or open any private shop for the retail of butcher's meat on market days that they are thereby infringing the just rights of the corporation and that in the event of their persisting in so doing after such notice actions will be commenced against them to recover damages.

A letter received by the mayor from his Majesty's Commissioners on the Public Records requesting for historical purposes the particulars of any ancient documents of a specific description which may be in the possession of the corporation (if any) having been read, ordered that the mayor be at liberty to give the information desired.

Form of Notice & Protest to Butchers.

To [*blank*] of Stockton in the County of Durham, butcher

You having lately opened and used a shop or stall at or in a private house in the town of Stockton aforesaid, and therein sold or retailed flesh meat on the days on which the public markets are held in that place, I do hereby on behalf and by the direction of the mayor aldermen & burgesses of the borough of Stockton aforesaid give you notice, that by so doing you have infringed their just rights & privileges as owners of the market of Stockton aforesaid; and that if after this notice you shall continue to sell or retail flesh meat in any private house, shop, or stall in Stockton aforesaid, on the usual and accustomed market days an action will be commenced [*p. 481*][320] against you to recover damages for such an infringement of the rights and privileges of the said mayor aldermen and burgesses.

Dated the 3rd day of September 1834. (signed) T. H. Faber, solicitor.[321]

[*col. 1*] Leo. Raisbeck mayor, [*in pencil: 'Robt Jordison'*], Robt. Bald, Martin Kirtley
[*col. 2*] Thos. Heaviside, John Atkinson, Wm. Skinner junior, Wm. Skinner.

[*p. 482*]
Borough of Stockton. At a meeting of the mayor aldermen and burgesses held this 19th day of September \1834/ pursuant to due notice.

The report of the committee appointed at the last meeting to examine the condition of the old building called the Custom House having \been/ read and taken into consideration and it appearing advisable to ascertain the sufficiency of the foundation below low water mark by boring before any final determination be made on the subject, ordered that the same gentlemen be requested to continue to act as a committee & to cause the foundations to be bored to a sufficient depth & to report the result to a future meeting.

The mayor having produced at this meeting a vase manufactured by John Cartwright Esq. from the wood found on excavating the new channel of the river in 1830 & presented to him by that gentleman for the use of the corporation, ordered that the best thanks of the corporation be given to Mr Cartwright for his valuable present.

---

320 At this point, page numbering of the MS ceases; from p. 481, page numbers have been supplied editorially.
321 Thomas Henry Faber was also coroner for Stockton Ward for many years. He died in 1850, aged forty-nine: Heavisides, *Annals*, pp. 98–100.

[*col. 1*] Leo. Raisbeck mayor, Wm. Skinner, *John Atkinson, Mr William Watson*, W. Skinner junior, Jno. Wilkinson, Anth[on]y Dobing
[*col. 2*] [*in pencil: 'Thos Heaviside'*], Robt. Bald, [*in pencil: 'Martin Kirtley, Thos Fall'*], Jos. Wade, Thomas Walker.

[*p. 483*]
Borough of Stockton. At a meeting of the mayor aldermen and burgesses held this 17th day of October 1834 pursuant to due notice.

Messrs Martin Kirtley, Robert Bald, Joseph Wade, Robert Sherwood, Anthony Dobing, Thomas Heaviside, Robert Jordison, John Atkinson and Robert Seymour were elected a committee of repairs for the current year which will expire on the first Tuesday after the 29th day of September next.

Messrs Henry Beckwith, Thomas Richmond [and] John Dixon were elected auditors of accounts for the same period.

The account of Leonard Raisbeck Esq. the late mayor of this boro' for the year ending the first Tuesday after New Michaelmas Day last (examined and certified to be correct by the auditors) were produced and inspected and there appearing a balance of £239–15–4 due to the corporation from the said Leonard Raisbeck, we do direct that the same shall be paid to Robert Thompson Esq. the present mayor of this borough.

Ordered that Mr George Hardcastle be continued master of the Grammar School for one year [*p. 484*] from Christmas next and that the sum of twenty pounds be paid to him as a subscription but that he do previously execute an agreement similar to that entered into by former masters with the exception that a public examination of his scholars at Christmas yearly shall only be required.

Also ordered that the sum of £10. 10. 0 be subscribed towards the funds for premiums and premiums only to be distributed at the cattle show at Stockton for the year next ensuing.

Also ordered that the sum of £5 be subscribed towards the fund of the School of Industry at Stockton on the terms prescribed last year which have been assented to by the managers of that charity.

Also ordered that each coble with a full cargo of fresh sea fish which during the year next ensuing shall arrive and be disposed of at Stockton by retail shall be allowed a premium of 5s. provided the fish have been caught at sea by the crew of such boat.

Also ordered that James Ward's salary be increased to the sum of £45 yearly to be computed from the 13th day of May last for acting in and performing the several duties hereinafter mentioned (i.e.) as the mayor's sergeant so long as the magistrate's Petty Sessions for Stockton Ward shall be holden in the Townhall and for duly and regularly attending such meetings as a police officer or constable; as collector and receiver [*p. 485*] under the direction of the mayor of the rents of the stalls in the Shambles and of the property in Cottage Row and any other revenues of the corporation which the mayor shall direct; and regularly and duly attending to the proper regulation of the market and executing and fulfilling the duties of a police officer for the borough and performing all other services which have hitherto been performed by him for the mayor; and also paying and discharging all such allowances \to/ the fish cobles as shall from time to time become payable in pursuance of the order hereinbefore made relative to the same allowances.

Also ordered that Mr Robert Jordison, Mr William Wadeson Watson and Mr Robert Sherwood be appointed a committee to assist the mayor in the regulation of the market.

Also ordered that Leonard Raisbeck Esq. be respectfully requested to resume the office of recorder vacated by him on his being elected mayor of this boro'.

Also ordered that the mayor be recommended to provide himself with a gown of a similar kind to that of the aldermen and that the steward of the court be also recommended to provide himself with a gown of a similar kind to that of the recorder.

Also ordered that the interest charged on the banking [*p. 486*] account of Thomas Walker Esq. as mayor be paid out of the first monies that shall become due to the corporation.

Also ordered that the sum of £4. 15. 0 paid by Robert Lamb Esq. when mayor be repaid to him together with the sum of £2. 14. 0

charged to him on his banking account as mayor be paid out of the first monies that shall become due to the corporation.

Also ordered that the King's printers' copies of the act of parliament transmitted to the mayor be by him handed over to the recorder who at the close of each session be requested to get the same properly bound up.

[*col. 1*] Robt. Thompson mayor,[322] Thos. Jennett,[323] Wm. Skinner, W. Skinner junior, [*in pencil: 'T Jennett'*], Robt. Bald, Anth[on]y Dobing
[*col. 2*] [*In pencil: 'J Heaviside, W W Watson, J Atkinson'*].

[*p. 487*]
Borough of Stockton. At a meeting of ~~burgess~~ the mayor aldermen and burgesses held this 9th day of June 1835[324] pursuant to due notice.

The report of the committee appointed to examine the state of the old Custom House having been received read and taken into consideration, ordered that the mayor be authorized to ascertain from the Clarence Railway Company if they are willing to give possession of that building on paying the rent up to this date and that he be also empowered to refer to arbitration any dispute that may arise relative to such rent.

Also ordered that if such application be successful the committee of repairs be empowered to take immediate steps for taking down so much of the building as they may think proper and that in the event of its not being successful they may on the 26th July next take the like steps and in either case after the taking down of the building report their opinion as to the best mode of appropriating the property.

[*col. 1*] Robt. Thompson mayor, Thos. Jennett, Wm. Skinner, W. Skinner junior

---

322 R. W. Thompson, wine merchant, lived on the High Street in 1827: P&W, p. 316.

323 This signature is written in the space pencilled 'L Raisbeck'. Jennett's name is pencilled three lines below.

324 'June' appears to have been written over 'October' and the year changed from, perhaps, '1834'.

[*col. 2*] [*in pencil: 'T Jennett, J Atkinson'*], Robt. Bald, Anth[on]y Dobing
[*col. 3*] [*in pencil: 'J Heaviside, W W Watson'*].

[*p. 488*]
Borough of Stockton. At a meeting of the mayor aldermen and
burgesses held this 22nd day of October 1835.

Ordered that with reference to the provision of the Act for the
Regulation of Municipal Corporations the same gentlemen as consti-
tuted the committee of repairs and auditors of accounts and all other
officers of the corporation for the last year continue to discharge the
functions of their respective offices till the declaration of the first
election of councillors under that act.

The accounts of Robert Thompson Esq. the mayor of this borough for
the last year (examined and certified to be correct by the auditors)
were produced and inspected and there appearing a balance of
£233. 2. 6 due to the corporation from the said Robert Thompson, we
do direct that the same shall be retained by him and carried to the
next account

Ordered that it be left to the mayor to let the old Custom House
to such persons on such terms and for such times (not exceeding
21 years) as he may think proper.

Ordered that this meeting be adjourned to the 24th day of December
next at 11 o'clock in the forenoon and that the further accounts of
the mayor be made up to that day and be produced [*p. 489*] and
inspected at such adjourned meeting.

Mr Wilkinson being prevented by arrangements between the corporation and the Stockton and Darlington Railway Company from
enjoying the property he leases at Cottage Row in the manner
contemplated by him on his lease being granted and having agreed
to relinquish any claim for compensation from the corporation on
account of it, ordered that in consideration thereof Mr Wilkinson be
allowed to hold the additional portion of land he now occupies there
for the unexpired residue of the term in his lease for an additional
rent of £2 per annum to be computed from Martinmas next but
that he shall quit possession thereof at the expiration of 6 calendar
months notice if the corporation require the land for building sites
or in consequence of the erection of buildings on the west of it but

that a sufficient footpath between the said piece of ground and the hedge which divides it from the bishop of Durham's property shall always be left free open and unoccupied to the full and entire satisfaction of the mayor And that the mayor be requested to enter into a proper agreement with Mr [*p. 490*] Wilkinson in the spirit of this order and that a plan be affixed to such agreement accurately defining the piece of ground before mentioned. And that if the new council to be elected under the act before mentioned shall set aside such agreement that then Mr Wilkinson shall be at full liberty to raise the question of compensation agreed to be relinquished by him and fully and effectually to all intents and purposes as if this order with agreement in pursuance of it had not been made or entered into.

Also ordered that the sum of £10. 10. 0 be subscribed towards the funds for premiums and premiums only to be distributed at the cattle show at Stockton for the year next ensuing.

Also ordered that the sum of £5 be subscribed towards the fund of the School of Industry at Stockton on the terms prescribed last year which have been assented to by the managers of that charity.

Ordered that the mayor retain out of the balance in his hands the sum of £100 or so much as shall remain after paying all the other charges and allowances to be by him paid to such persons as he may select to be by them [*p. 491*] applied in the foundation of an infant school in Stockton.

[*col. 1*] Robt. Thompson mayor, Wm. Skinner, W. Skinner junior, [*in pencil: 'L Raisbeck'*], J. Wilkinson, Thos. Jennett, Robt. Bald, [*in pencil: 'James Atkinson'*]
[*col. 2*] [*in pencil: 'W Smith'*], Anth[on]y Dobing, [*in pencil: 'J Heaviside, Thos Richmond, Jos Wade'*], Richd. Walker.

[*p. 492*]
Borough of Stockton. At a meeting of the mayor aldermen and burgesses held this 24th day of December 1835 pursuant to adjournment.

Ordered that this meeting be adjourned to Monday next at 11 o'clock in the forenoon to examine and pass the accounts of the mayor and that a hand bill giving notice of such meeting be printed and circulated.

Robert Thompson mayor, [*in pencil: 'Leo R, Jos Wade'*], Anth[on]y Dobing, [*in pencil: 'John Dixon, Thos Lambert, Jno Farrow, Rd Walker, Thos Mills, C Lodge, Jas Robinson, C Swennie, J H Heavyside,*[325] *Rt Jordison'*].

[*p. 493*]
Borough of Stockton. At a meeting of the mayor, aldermen and burgesses held this 28th day of December 1835 pursuant to adjournment

The accounts of Robert Thompson Esq. mayor of this borough from the first Tuesday after New Michaelmas Day up to this day (examined and certified to be correct by the auditors) were produced ~~and~~ examined \and allowed/ upon which there appeared a balance of £101. 12. 2 due to the corporation.

Ordered that the mayor be requested to pay immediately out of that balance to Messrs Wilson and Faber the sum of £7. 12: 4 in discharge of their bill now produced and examined:

Robert Thomson mayor, Thos. Jennett, Rt. Lamb, Wm. Skinner, Wm. Skinner junior, Robert Bald, Anth[on]y Dobing.

[*The remaining 24 folios are blank, except for what seems to be a practice signature 'Ed: Bunting' in an eighteenth-century hand, repeated several times on the final page.*]

---

325 Reading of this name uncertain.

APPENDIX 1:
CORRESPONDENCE CONCERNING
THE 'BOOK OF ORDERS AND ACCOUNTS', 1923

The following correspondence was transcribed from Teesside Archives, Microfilm 371. This microfilm has been lost and the whereabouts of the original letters is unknown. The editor roughly transcribed the correspondence from this poor-quality microfilm in 2015, but was unable to revisit it more recently to resolve uncertainties.

1. Councillor Alexander Livingstone to Thomas Downey, town clerk, 28 May 1923
Dear Mr Downey
I have just had a visit from Mr Lang, who informs me that whilst a search was being made through the books in the possession of the YMCA, some interesting official records of the Stockton Corporation were found. I understand the record is continuous and marks the period covering 1616 to 1835. It appears this find has been shown to the mayor, who attached much importance to it. I am also told that arrangements have been made to show the record to the bishop of Durham in view of the special rights and privileges which is […] in the borough. Mr Lang informs me that the committee of management desire that this […] be shown to a formal handing over of the record at a full council meeting. I said I would acquaint you with this desire (probably the mayor has already done so). So they have asked me, as one of the old associates of the head branch, to make the presentation – before assenting I would like to […] from you as to whether it would be in order to place such a matter on the agenda. Perhaps you will kindly let me have your opinion on the matter. I may say this is the first I have heard of this discovery. I have not seen the record referred to, but the early date would seem to place its historic value beyond dispute. I am still somewhat in a […] but I shall do what I can as regards the task the YMCA people wish to impose upon me.
Yours truly,
A. Livingstone[1]

1   Alexander Livingstone was a town councillor who ran a ladies' and gentlemen's outfitters with branches in Yarm Lane and Bowesfield Lane.

2. Thomas Downey, town clerk, to Councillor Alexander Livingstone, 31 May 1923

Dear Councillor Livingstone

I am in receipt of yours of the 29th inst. I will place the matter on the next meeting's agenda of the General Purposes Committee when I trust you will be present and explain in person with regard to the matter. The committee will then consider about the presentation being made at an open council meeting.

Yours faithfully

Town Clerk.

3. […] to Councillor Alexander Livingstone, 11 June 1923

Referring to the decision of Friday night's meeting upon this matter, will you please arrange with the YMCA to attend the next council meeting for the purposes of formally handing over the minute book.

Yours faithfully

[…]

4. Councillor Alexander Livingstone to Thomas Downey, town clerk, 11 June 1923

Dear Mr Downey

Re YMCA minute book, Mr R Copeland of 19 Grange Road, Norton, honorary secretary of the YMCA, has been appointed to perform the handing over ceremony of above minute book.

Copeland is a very […] and respectable young fellow (he is a correspondence clerk at one of the large works and can be depended upon to do the task required with the necessary tact). By the way, shall I have to 'introduce' to the mayor before I make the presentation? I have asked Copeland to confine his remarks within narrow limits, say five or six minutes at most.

Yours faithfully

A. Livingstone.

5. Thomas Downey, town clerk, to Councillor Alexander Livingstone, 14 June 1923

I am obliged by yours of the 14th instant and will arrange accordingly for the next council meeting. I will inform the mayor that Mr Copeland will be present for the purpose indicated. I feel sure that he will discharge the work as you say in the right manner.

Yours faithfully,

Thomas Downey

Town Clerk

APPENDIX 2:
COMMISSION ON MUNICIPAL CORPORATIONS IN ENGLAND AND WALES, 1835: REPORT ON THE BOROUGH OF STOCKTON

BOROUGH OF STOCKTON[1]

1. The Limits of the Borough of Stockton, within which the burgage houses conferring freedom of the corporation are situate, form part of the township of Stockton; that the borough, township, and two others, compose the parish of Stockton. The borough forms but a small part of the township and only about one-fourth part of the town (in its popular sense). The town extends beyond it on all sides except on the river side.
2. This is a borough by prescription: there are no charters relating to it.
3. The Title of the corporation is, 'The Mayor, Aldermen, Burgesses and Commonalty of the Borough of Stockton.'
4. The officers of the corporation are,

Mayor	1
Deputy Mayor	1
Aldermen	8
Recorder	1
Town Clerk	1
Auditors	3
Collector of River Dues	1
Leather Searchers	2
Corn Meters	5
Bread Weighers	3
Searchers of Weights and Measures	3
Fish and Flesh Lookers	3
Butter Searchers	3
Ale Tasters	3
Bellman	1

---

1 Knight, C., *First Report of the Commissioners Appointed to Inquire into the Municipal Corporations in England and Wales*, Parliamentary Papers, Vol. XXIII (1835) pp. 1729–32. Contents page omitted here.

5. There are only 53 Burgesses. The burgage tenements conferring that right are 71 in number.

6. The Mayor is elected annually, on the Tuesday after Michaelmas Day, at a court leet composed of an indefinite number of burgesses. The mayor generally attends this meeting, at which he presides. The steward of the manor also attends, and generally the aldermen, but their presence is not essential. The election is by a majority of all the burgesses present, voting together. The mayor must be a burgess. All those burgesses who have served the office of mayor become, ipso facto, aldermen. In order to limit the number of aldermen to eight, it is said that when that number is complete, the mayor must be elected out of the aldermen; but in other cases, the choice is not confined to the aldermen, and any burgess is eligible. The legality of this rule limiting the number of aldermen, (as a compulsory one,) is however denied; and it is asserted, on the other hand, that the number of aldermen is indefinite, and that a burgess, who is not an alderman, is at all times eligible to the office of mayor. It has, however, rarely happened of late years, that the number of aldermen has amounted to eight. The mayor's office is annual.

7. The deputy mayor is appointed by the mayor, and holds office during his pleasure.

8. The aldermen, as already stated, are such of the burgesses as have served the office of mayor. They hold office for life, provided they continue burgesses. There are now six aldermen, all of whom are resident.

9. The steward of the manor, appointed by the bishop of Durham, who is lord of the manor, has generally been considered recorder, without any formal election. On the retirement of the late steward from that office, however, he was requested to retain his office of recorder, by the mayor, aldermen and burgesses, and he continued to hold that office after he had given up the office of steward. He is not required to be a burgess.

10. The steward of the manor acts as town clerk. No formal appointment is recollected to have been made.

11. The serjeant at mace is appointed by the mayor at the court leet, at which the mayor himself is elected.

12. The auditors are appointed annually, by a majority of the burgesses, at a meeting held 21 days after Michaelmas Day. Aldermen are never appointed to this office.

13. The other officers are appointed annually, on their nomination by the mayor to the jury, at the court leet held 21 days after Michaelmas Day.

14. A person seised in possession of a freehold estate, in any of the 71 qualifying burgage tenements within the borough, is a burgess during the continuance of his estate. The person entitled, is admitted to his estate, at a manor court, by the steward of the manor. On such occasion he pays a small fine to the lord of the manor, and a fee of 10s. 6d. to the town clerk.

15. There is no select body; the affairs of the corporation are managed by the whole body of the burgesses.

16. There are two committees appointed; one for superintending the repairs, and the other for regulating the market. They are appointed by the burgesses at the meeting held 21 days after Michaelmas.

17. The mayor is conservator of the peace in the borough. He is also a justice of the peace for the county, if he qualifies. He presides at the meetings of the corporation, and at the manor court. He has an allowance of £30 per annum; but he always returns this to the corporation. He has no perquisites.

18. The aldermen have no duties to perform distinct from the other burgesses.

19. The recorder is the legal adviser of the corporation. He has an annual salary of 5 guineas. There is now no recorder.

20. The town clerk attends the meetings of the corporation. He is also the steward of the lord of the manor, and he holds the manor courts. He is the attorney and solicitor of the corporation. As town clerk he receives an annual salary of £4; he has a guinea for every court which he attends, and 13s. 4d. for every adjourned court. As bishop's bailiff he receives a certain allowance out of the town dues for groundage and plankage; viz. 4d. for every British ship, and 8d. for every foreign ship that enters the port. The amount of this perquisite has very much increased of late. In the year 1821 it was £5 9s. 4d.; in 1830 it was £20, and in 1832 £39 2s. The profits of his business as attorney to the corporation do not exceed from £6 to £7 on an average in the year.

21. The serjeant at mace collects the rents for the corporation, attends the markets and acts as superintendent of the police. He has an annual salary of 2 guineas, a livery and hat; and for acting as police officer, he receives from the corporation £30 a year.

22. The auditors audit the accounts of the corporation previous to their being laid before a general meeting of the burgesses, who inspect and pass them.

23. The collector of river dues collects the groundage and plankage dues collected mentioned before and hereafter. He receives an allowance proportioned to the amount of the dues. The amount of his receipts last year was £30 8s.

24. The duties of the other officers are to be collected from the names of their several offices.

25. The only privilege of the burgesses is the being entitled to land goods at a particular quay, called the Custom House Quay, without paying any quay dues. But, as this quay is not used, the privilege is in fact nominal.

26. The corporation do not exercise any jurisdiction except at the courts of the manor. The mayor presides at these courts. Courts baron are held eight times in the year for the recovery of debts not exceeding 40s. The juries are composed of the owners of burgage tenements. The jurisdiction extends over the borough. About 15 cases are tried annually in this court.

27. Petty Sessions are held in the town by the county magistrates for the ward of Stockton, weekly.

28. The police of the borough and town consists of a superintendent, who is serjeant at mace, two constables and two watchmen. The expenses of this establishment are defrayed under a local act of parliament, by a rate, not to exceed 1s. in the pound, on houses, buildings and gardens, and market tolls. It is under the direction of commissioners, vacancies amongst whom are supplied by elections by the survivors. This force is quite sufficient to keep the peace. On extraordinary occasions, such as the races, the corporation provide and pay extra constables. The town is lighted and cleaned under the provisions of the above act. The lighting is remarkably good. The gas is supplied by a company established under a local act of parliament. The roads are repaired under the provisions of the General Highway Act.

29. There is no gaol in the borough; merely a lock-up house.

30. There is a school, built by the corporation; they appoint a schoolmaster, and pay him an annual salary of £20; this allowance is voluntary. The corporation send three boys to the school, who are taught gratis.

31. The revenue of the corporation is derived from dues, stallage, and the rents of lands and houses. Port dues, called groundage

and plankage, are levied on ships, and certain goods, entering
the port; the amount of these is 2s. 6d. on every British ship,
5s. on every foreign ship, 1s. on 120 deals imported, and 4d. on
every 100 bushels of corn. No persons are exempt from these
tolls. The amount of these dues, in 1830 was £175 4s. 3d.; in 1831
it was £236 2s. 2d.;[2] and in 1832, it was £347 11s. 4d.; and up to
November 1833, it was £303 19s. 4d. This is the gross amount;
out of it is to be deducted the before-mentioned allowance to the
bishop's bailiff and the collector. These dues are leased to the
corporation by the bishop of Durham, at a nominal rent, and are
renewed whenever the lease expires. The lease declares the toll
to be granted upon trust, to apply the profits for the making and
repairing the public streets and pavements within the borough,
or for or towards the payment of the debts contracted on that or
any other occasion, or for other public uses within the borough,
and for the public advantage and convenience thereof, in such
manner as the mayor, aldermen and burgesses shall direct and
approve. The corporation are also entitled to some dues at the
Custom-house Quay; but this right is unproductive. The market
dues are let, with some stables and other property, for £220 a
year. The houses and lands are let by public tender, and are
publicly advertised; they are let for six years. The custom-house
is let from year to year; the butchers' shambles partly from year
to year, and partly for shorter terms. The items of this amount
are distinguished in the following table of income.

32. The debt due from the corporation is £5,300, bearing interest
at 4½ per cent. and secured on mortgage of part of the corporation property. The greatest part of this amount was borrowed
in the years 1823, 1824, and 1825: it was applied in paying
off a debt then due, of upwards of £1,000 in building the
butchers' shambles, and in expenses, incurred in consequence
of proceedings having been taken against the corporation, for
building the shambles in a different part of the street from that
which they had before occupied: £700 of the debt was borrowed
recently.

33. The Expenditure appears from the following account of income
and expenditure, for the year 1833:

2   Sowler, *History*, p. 490 has £200 2s. 2d.

INCOME	£.	s.	d.	EXPENDITURE	£.	s.	d.
Balance of preceding year	49	13	2	Subscriptions	37	12	0
				Salaries	55	17	0
Slates Sold	1	5	6	Taxes and cesses	41	9	0
Town Hall market dues and				Interest of debt	245	8	0
West Row stables	220	0	0	Improvements to Town Hall &c			
					178	14	
Butchers' shambles:				Repairs	126	13	0
Arrear	4	0	0	Rents	1	18	10
Year's Rent	170	0	0	Sundries including Law	63	4	4
Quarter in advance	41	0	0				
Old Custom House	30	0	0	Balance	180	19	4
Cottage Row:							
Arrear	3	0	0				
Rent	81	15	0				
Ditto	83	7	6				
West Row	8	9	2				
Town dues	234	9	4				
Interest allowed by voucher	4	5	10				
	£931	5	6		£931	5	6

State and Prospects of the Town

34.   The population of the township was in

      1801   4,009
      1811   4,229
      1821   5,006
      1831   7,763

Annual value of real property in 1815 was £12,783.

The parochial assessments for years ending 25 March

      1825   £1,839   18
      1829   £2,272   19

Number of houses in 1831 was 1,370.

The trade of this port has increased considerably of late years, and there is every prospect of a further increase of its commercial prosperity. New coal mines of large extent, have recently been discovered in the neighbourhood, and a rail-road has been made from them to the port.

Port of Stockton
An account of the amount of tonnage on vessels entering inwards and clearing outwards with cargoes, at this port, in the last sixteen years; distinguishing the coasting from the foreign

YEARS	FOREIGN TRADE		COASTING TRADE	
ending 5th January	Inwards	Outwards	Inwards	Outwards
	Tons	Tons	Tons	Tons
1818	5,843	1,030	18,227	18,038
1819	8,908	570	19,348	18,297
1820	6,857	541	20,032	16,335
1821	5,599	777	20,057	19,594
1822	6,495	833	18,592	19,431
1823	7,875	1,397	18,720	18,360
1824	10,426	897	19,213	17,388
1825	11,234	1,338	20,771	18,383
1826	11,687	565	20,098	18,958
1827	6,828	1,526	15,813	26,097
1828	9,719	1,578	20,133	44,500
1829	9,642	1,466	31,443	70,548
1830	11,259	2,537	21,909	48,020
1831	10,592	960	30,162	106,310
1832	12,112	1,657	42,472	255,325
1833	13,929	1,735	48,746	446,816

35.   We add a List of the Local Acts:

48 George 3, c. xlviii.[3] 'An act for making a navigable cut from the east side of the River Tees near Stockton, into the said river near Portrack, in the county of Durham, and for making various other improvements, in the navigation of the said river, between the town of Stockton and the sea.'

1 George 4, c. lxii.[4] 'An act for lighting, cleansing and otherwise improving the town and – borough of Stockton, in the county of Durham.'

3 George 4, c. xxxiii.[5] 'An act for lighting with gas the town and borough of Stockton, in the county of Durham.'

9 George 4, c. xcvii.[6] 'An act to enable the Tees Navigation Company to make a navigable cut from the east side of the River Tees near Portrack in the county of Durham into the said river

3   Tees Navigation Company Act, 1808.
4   Stockton Improvement Act, 1820.
5   Stockton Gas Act, 1822.
6   Tees Navigation Act, 1828.

near Newport, in the township and parish of Acklam, in the North Riding of the county of York.'

36. We have sent, with this report, copies of the following documents:

1. Table of stallage.
2. Account of the income and expenditure of the corporation for the year 1832–33.
3. Accounts of the commissioners for lighting the town of Stockton for the year 1832–33.
4. The name, ages, professions, &c. of the principal corporate officers.

Fortunatus Dwarris

S. A. Rumbal

APPENDIX 3:
MAYORS OF STOCKTON-ON-TEES, 1616 TO 1835

Entries in Roman are recorded in the 'Book of Orders and Accounts'. Entries in italics are from Surtees, *History* unless otherwise stated in footnotes.[1]

Above, page	Date	Outgoing mayor	Incoming mayor	Amount Transferred		
				£	s	d
37	1616, Oct. 11	Thomas Lambart	Thomas Lambart	5	12	8
	1617	*Thomas Lambert*	*Thomas Lambert*[2]			
	1618	*Thomas Lambert*	*Thomas Lambert*			
	1619	*Thomas Lambart*	*Rowland Wetherell*			
	1620	*Rowland We(a)therill*	*Rowland We(a)therill*			
	1621	*Rowland Wetherell*	*William Burdon*			
	1622	*William Burdon*	*William Swainston*			
	1623	*William Swainston*	*Thomas Watson*			
	1624	*Thomas Watson*	*William Harte*			
37	1625, Oct. 19	William Hart	Thomas Lambart	0	19	1
	1626	*Thomas Lambert*	*Thomas Lambert*			
	1627	*Thomas Lambert*	*William Hart*			
	1628	*William Hart*	*William Hart*			
39	1629, Oct. 20	William Hart	William Hart	0	8	4
39	1630, Oct. 19	William Hart	Giles We(a)therill	0	18	10
	1631	*Giles We(a)therill*	*Giles We(a)therill*			
	1632	*Giles We(a)therill*	*John Jessop*			
40	1633, Oct. 15	John Jessepp	John Jessopp	3	17	0
41	1634, Oct. 14	John Jessop	Thomas Watson	0	10	18

---

1   The lists of Stockton mayors in Sowler, *History* and Surtees, *History* in this period tally, except for 1667 and 1668. Sowler has 1667 John Anson, 1668 John Anson. This is an abbreviation of Atkinson, who was mayor in 1664, but John Jessop was mayor in 1668 according to all other sources.

2   Surtees, Fordyce, Mackenzie and Ross, Richmond, and Sowler are not explicit on who was mayor in 1617 and 1618 but their lists may imply that Thomas Lambert was mayor from 1616 to 1619. Bayley, 'Genealogical Additions', p. 74 states that he was 'mayor 1616 and 1625'.

45	1635, Oct. 20	Thomas Watson	John Jessop	23	12	6[3]
45	1636, Oct. 12	John Jessopp	John Jessop	16	14	7[4]
46	1637, Oct. 17	John Jessop	Giles We(a)therill	11	17	7[5]
47	1638, Nov. 6[6]	Giles We(a)therill	John Jessopp	5	3	5
47	1638, Nov. 6	John Jessop	John Jessop	21	17	3
48	1639, Oct. 18	John Jessopp	Thomas Watson	15	5	4[7]
48	1640, Oct. 20	Thomas Watson	James Cooke	6	17	0
49	1641, Oct. 19	James Cook	Rowland Burdon	11	17	7
49	1642, Oct. 19	Rowland Burdon	Rowland Burdon	6	15	8
50	1643, Oct. 24	Rowland Burdon	James Cooke	5	13	0
50	1644, Oct. 3	James Cook	Rowland Burdon	3	4	5
50	1645, Oct. 7	Rowland Burdon	Rowland Burdon	3	2	6
51	1646, Oct. 20	Rowland Burdon	Thomas Watson	0	14	2
51	1647, Oct. 8	Thomas Watson	Thomas Watson	11	17	8
52	1648, Oct. 17	Thomas Watson	John Bunting?	11	5	9
53	1649, Oct. 16	John Bunting	John Bunting	11	4	2
53	1650, Oct. 15	John Bunting	Rowland Burdon	11	13	9
	1651	*Rowland Burdon*	*Rowland Burdon*			
	1652	*Rowland Burdon*	*Rowland Burdon*			
54	1653, Oct. 18	Rowland Burdon	Thomas Watson	0	4	2
54	1654, Oct. 17	Thomas Watson	Rowland Burdon	0	8	0½
	1655	*Rowland Burdon*	*Rowland Burdon*			
55	1656, Oct. 14	Rowland Burdon	Thomas Watson	0	4	7[8]
56	1657, Dec. 5	Thomas Watson	John Atkinson	13	12	0
56	1658, Oct. 22	John Atkinson	Thomas Jessopp	10	17	5
57	1659, Oct. 25	Thomas Jessopp	Thomas Jessopp	11	17	1½
57	1660, Oct. 20	Thomas Jessopp	William Peeres	12	0	5
	1661	*William Peers*	*William Peers*			
58	1662, Oct. 14	William Peers	Ralph Eden	16	4	6

3   A total handed over is not stated. Individual amounts listed for metage, causey money, corn dues and previous cash in hand total £23 12s. 6d. (sum of £11 10s.; 7s.; 4s. 6d.; £10 4s.; 15s. 10d.; 11s. 2d.).

4   Three sums are shown as 'resting' in his hand: £2 3s. 1d.; £13 14s. 0d.; 17s. 6d.; totalling £16 14s. 7d.

5   Made up of two resting items: £7 10s. 0d. and £4 7s. 7d.

6   There are two entries for 6 November 1638, on MS pp. 15 and 17. On MS p. 15 (above, p. 47) the recently deceased Giles Weatherill paid John Jessop £3 18s. 6d., then John Thompson, presumably stepping in, paid £1 4s. 2d. to John Jessop, making £5 3s. 5d. handed over to John Jessop. On MS p. 17 (above, p. 47), John Jessop summarises his position, with 18s. 4d. of borough corn money resting in his hands, £8 3s. 5d. of causey and other money resting, and £12 15s. 6d. for anchorage and metage, making £21 17s. 3d.

7   Made up of two amounts, one for causey money and one for borough corn and metage.

8   The MS entry states 4s. but shows 4s. 7d. in figures.

	1663	*Ralph Eden*	*John Atkinson*			
59	1664, Oct. 18	John Atkinson	Robert Jackson	0	9	4
60	1665, Oct. 17	Robert Jackson	Robert Jackson	1	19	0
61	1666, Oct. 16	Robert Jackson	Thomas Jessepp	2	18	11
62	1667, Oct. 1	Thomas Jessepp	John Atkinson	1	12	8
62	1668, Oct. 6	John Atkinson	Thomas Jessep	4	3	2
63	1669, Oct. 19	Thomas Jessepp	James Cooke	4	1	0
63	1670, Oct. 18	James Cooke	Thomas Jessopp	17	17	7
63	1671, Oct. 17	Thomas Jessepp	Robert Jackson	21	2	3¼
64	1672, Oct. 15	Robert Jackson	Nicholas Fleatham	14	4	6½
64	1673, Oct. 14	Nicholas Fleatham	Nicholas Fleatham	6	13	6
67	1674, Oct. 20	Nicholas Fleatham	James Cooke	18	19	2
68	1675, Oct. 19	James Cooke	James Cooke	56	12	7
68	1676, Oct. 19	James Cooke	Robert Jackson	23	1	8
69	1677, Oct. 16	Robert Jackson	Robert Jackson	8	7	1
71	1678, Oct. 15	Robert Jackson	William Lee	2	9	0
72	1679, Oct. 14	William Lee	William Lee	8	19	6
73	1680, Oct. 19	William Lee	William Atkinson	20	5	5
73	1681, Oct. 18	William Atkinson	William Atkinson	9	4	0
76	1682, Oct. 17	William Atkinson	Ralph Moone	4	10	0
78	1683, Oct. 16	Ralph Moone	James Burdon	10	12	0
79	1684, Oct. 14	James Burdon	James Burdon	8	8	3½
81	1685, Oct. 20	James Burdon	James Cooke	13	9	4½
83	1686, Oct. 19	James Cooke	James Cooke	9	19	3½
84	1687, Oct. 18	James Cooke	Ralph Moone	30	4	2½
85	1688, Oct. 16	Ralph Moone	Ralph Moone	23	10	10½
86	1689, Oct. 15	Ralph Moone	Thomas Wrangham	9	9	0½
88	1690, Oct. 14	Thomas Wrangham	Thomas Wrangham	24	4	2
89	1691, Oct. 20	Thomas Wrangham	Robert Jackson	7	12	9
89	1692, Oct. 18	Robert Jackson	Robert Jackson	25	11	6
90	1693, Oct. 17	Robert Jackson	James Cooke	2	13	4½
91	1694, Oct. 16	James Cooke	James Burdon	2	1	1½
92	1695, Oct. 15	James Burdon	James Burdon	10	13	0½
93	1696, Oct. 20	James Burdon	James Burdon	6	17	6½
94	1697, Oct. 19	James Burdon	William Atkinson	0	13	0½
96	1698, Oct. 18	William Atkinson	James Cooke	0	0	0
100	1699[9]	James Cooke	Thomas Wrangham	0	9	2
100	1700, Oct. 5	Thomas Wrangham	Thomas Wrangham	8	0	11½
	1701	*Thomas Wrangham*	*Ralph Bunting*			
105	1702, Oct. 20	Ralph Bunting	Ralph Bunting	1	19	6
106	1703, Oct. 19	Ralph Bunting	James Cooke	6	7	1¾
108	1704, Oct. 17	James Cooke	Thomas Readman	35	6	10
109	1705, Oct. 16	Thomas Readman	Thomas Readman	6	10	1½

9   Damage to page: date not legible.

109	1706, Oct. 15	Thomas Readman	William Hart Atkinson	2	10	5
110	1707, Oct. 14	William Hart Atkinson	Richard Bowlby	8	4	6
111	1708, Oct. 19	Richard Bowlby	Thomas Sutton	39	4	10¾
112	1709, Oct. 18	Thomas Sutton	Thomas Sutton	39	9	5½
114	1710, Oct. 17	Thomas Sutton	James Cooke	30	1	0¼
115	1711, Oct. 16	James Cooke	Ralph Bunting	10	2	3¾
117	1712, Oct. 14	Ralph Bunting	Thomas Readman	20	15	7¾
118	1713, Oct. 20	Thomas Readman	John Wells	20	14	4¾
119	1714, Oct. 19	John Wells	John Wells	32	12	9
120	1715, Oct. 18	John Wells	John Burdett	38	2	9
121	1716, Oct. 16	John Burdett	John Burdett	11	12	2
122	1717, Oct. 15	John Burdett	John Cooke	37	10	4
124	1718, Oct. 14	John Cooke	Thomas Ogle	28	0	6
125	1719, Oct. 20	Thomas Ogle	John Cooke	75	14	4
127	1720, Oct. 18	John Cooke	William Raisbeck	236	3	10
128	1721, Oct. 26	William Raisbeck	John Cooke	27	14	8½
129	1722, Oct. 16	John Cook	William Gibson	152	8	11¾
131	1723, Oct. 15	William Gibson	William Gibson	25	4	3
132	1724, Oct. 20	William Gibson	David Dowthwaite	0	10	10½
133	1725, Oct. 19	David Dowthwaite	David Dowthwaite	9	3	5½
135	1726, Oct. 18	David Dowthwaite	John Burdett	15	0	4½
136	1727, Oct. 17	John Burdett	John Burdett	17	1	8¾
137	1728, Oct. 15	John Burdett	John Finch	39	18	6½
138	1729, Nov. 25	John Finch's widow	William Sutton	12	11	0
	1730	William Sutton	William Sutton			
138	1731, May 4	William Sutton	William Sutton	7	3	11
139	1731, Oct. 19	William Sutton	Henry Brown	45	0	0
139	1732, Oct. 17	Henry Brown	Henry Brown?	13	17	10
140	1733, Oct. 16	Henry Brown	John Burdett	1	11	9¼
141	1734, Oct. 15[10]	John Burdett	Ralph Bunting	2	17	9
141	1735, Oct. 14	Ralph Bunting	David Dowthwaite	9	18	10
144	1736, Oct. 19	David Dowthwaite	James Raisbeck	1	18	0
145	1737, Oct. 18	James Raisbeck	Thomas Raisbeck	0	13	7
146	1738, Oct. 17	Thomas Raisbeck	Thomas Raisbeck	30	12	5¼
147	1739, Oct. 23	Thomas Raisbeck	Jonathan Troy	23	19	8
148	1740, Oct. 14	Jonathan Troy	Jonathan Troy	22	17	0
149	1741, Oct. 20	Jonathan Troy	William Sutton	16	9	9
149	1742, Oct. 19	William Sutton	James Raisbeck	15	19	7
150	1743, Oct. 18	James Raisbeck	William Sleigh	24	7	1
155	1744, Oct. 23	William Sleigh	William Sleigh	73	16	5¾
158	1745, Oct. 15	William Sleigh	Henry Brown	2	0	3¾
159	1746, Oct. 14	Henry Brown	James Raisbeck	14	6	6
159	1747, Oct. 20	James Raisbeck	Thomas Raisbeck	14	19	10

10   Meeting continued by adjournment to 5 Nov.

162	1748, Oct. 25	Thomas Raisbeck	Ralph Whitley	0	3	5¾
163	1749, Oct. 17	Ralph Whitley	Ralph Whitley	1	8	4¾
164	1750, Oct. 25	Ralph Whitley	Jonathan Troy	25	10	9
166	1751, Oct. 22	Jonathan Troy	Richardson Ferrand	23	1	10
166	1752, Oct. 31	Richardson Ferrand	Richardson Ferrand	17	1	11
167	1753, Oct. 16	Richardson Ferrand	William Sutton	1	1	9½
167	1754, Oct. 15	William Sutton	William Sleigh	75	1	5
169	1755, Oct. 28	William Sleigh	Henry Brown	21	1	8
171	1756, Oct. 22	Henry Brown	James Raisbeck	21	6	5
172	1757, Nov. 10	James Raisbeck	Thomas Raisbeck	57	9	8
173	1758, Oct. 17	Thomas Raisbeck	Ralph Whitley	42	12	6½
	1759	*Ralph Whitley*	*Ralph Whitley*			
173	1760, Apr. 29	Ralph Whitley	George Sutton	3	14	5¾
174	1760, Oct. 14	George Sutton	George Sutton	7	16	6
175	1761, Oct. 20	George Sutton	William Sutton	24	8	10
175	1762, Oct. 21	William Sutton	Richardson Ferrand	1	2	11
176	1763, Oct. 25	Richardson Ferrand	William Sleigh	26	4	4½
176	1764, Oct. 16	William Sleigh	Thomas Fall	41	8	4
177	1765, Oct. 15	Thomas Fall	Thomas Fall	5	3	5½
179	1766, Oct. 6	Thomas Fall	John Wilkinson	9	12	3
179	1767, Oct. 20	John Wilkinson	John Wilkinson	28	3	9
181	1768, Oct. 25	John Wilkinson	George Sutton	31	11	0½
182	1769, Oct. 31	George Sutton	George Sutton	7	6	5
	1770	*George Sutton*	*J. S. Raisbeck*			
182	1771, Apr. 16	J. S. Raisbeck	J. S. Raisbeck	5	1	1½
183	1771, Oct. 15	J. S. Raisbeck	Robert Preston	6	15	6½
183	1772, Oct. 20	Robert Preston	Robert Preston	16	17	0
	1773	*Robert Preston*	*William Sleigh*			
186	1774, Nov. 15	Robert Preston	Benjamin Lumley	75	0	0
186	1775, Oct. 17	Benjamin Lumley	Benjamin Lumley	16	13	1
187	1776, Oct. 29	Benjamin Lumley	George Hutchinson	0	1	10½
188	1777, Oct.	George Hutchinson	George Hutchinson	37	7	2¾
188	1778, Oct. 7	George Hutchinson	Jonathan Davison	62	8	4¼
	1779	*Jonathan Davison*	*Jonathan Davison*			
189	1780, Oct. 24	Jonathan Davison	Rowland Webster	41	12	9
	1781	*Rowland Webster*	*Rowland Webster*			
189	1782, Oct. 22	Rowland Webster	Charles Sleigh	35	13	3½
190	1783, Oct. 28	Charles Sleigh	John Sutton	42	9	11
190	1784, Oct. 26	John Sutton	George Sutton	102	5	6½
191	1785, Oct. 18	George Sutton	John Wilkinson	9	10	7½
192	1786, Oct. 17	John Wilkinson	Christopher Smith	28	9	6
	1787	*Christopher Smith*	*Christopher Smith*			
192	1788, Oct. 21	Christopher Smith	J. S. Raisbeck	45	14	
193	1789, Oct. 27	J. S. Raisbeck	Benjamin Lumley	62	6	7½
194	1790, Oct. 26	Benjamin Lumley	William Sleigh	80	3	6
194	1791, Oct. 24	William Sleigh	John Sutton	99	6	6½

195	1792, Nov. 2	John Sutton	George Sutton	19	19	0½
196	1793, Oct. 15	George Sutton	Rowland Burdon	8	9	4
196	1794, Nov. 3	Rowland Burdon	Rowland Burdon	39	5	3½
197	1795, Oct. 22	Rowland Burdon	*Thomas Simpson*[11]	100	7	1
	1796	*Thomas Simpson*	*Thomas Simpson*			
	1797	*Thomas Simpson*	*George Sutton*	34	14	4
198	1798, Apr. 24	Court ordered Thomas Simpson to pay the sum of £34 14s. 4d.				
199	1798, Oct. 18	George Sutton	Christopher Smith	15	16	10
199	1799, Oct. 29	Christopher Smith	Robert Wilkinson	44	13	3½
200	1800, Nov. 4	Robert Wilkinson	Robert Wilkinson	83	16	11
200	1801, Nov. 27	Robert Wilkinson	Richardson Ferrand	25	0	1
201	1802, Oct. 22	Richardson Ferrand	Richardson Ferrand	53	17	2½
203	1803, Oct. 11	Richardson Ferrand	John Carr	139	17	9½
203	1804, Oct. 30	John Carr	John Carr	78	15	6
204	1805, Oct. 22	John Carr	George Hutchinson	28	18	0
205	1806, Oct. 17	George Hutchinson	George Hutchinson	79	5	11½
206	1807, Oct. 20	George Hutchinson	Watson Alcock	26	2	10
206	1808, Oct. 25	Watson Alcock	Watson Alcock	93	12	10¾
207	1809, Oct. 17	Watson Alcock	James Walker	41	13	3¾
207	1810, Oct. 26	James Walker	John Hutchinson	53	3	8½
208	1811, Oct. 29	John Hutchinson	James Walker	115	12	4
208	1812, Oct. 16	James Walker	Thomas Hutchinson	49	13	1
209	1813, Oct. 26	Thomas Hutchinson	George Sutton	13	2	2½
209	1814, Oct. 25	George Sutton	Richard Dickson	3	3	4
210	1815, Oct. 17	Richard Dickson	Richard Dickson	127	6	4½
211	1816, Oct. 25	Richard Dickson	Henry Hutchinson	74	15	7½
211	1817, Oct. 24	Henry Hutchinson	Henry Hutchinson	129	4	7
214	1818, Oct. 27	Henry Hutchinson	William Braithwaite	59	13	7
220	1819, Oct. 21	William Braithwaite	Thomas Jennett	369	13	1
221	1820, Oct. 21	Thomas Jennett	William Skinner	48	8	6
226	1821, Oct. 18	William Skinner	Richard Jackson	163	6	1
230	1822, Oct. 11	Richard Jackson	John Wilkinson	335	7	2
236	1823, Oct. 20	John Wilkinson	John Wilkinson	408	4	4½
238	1824, Oct. 19	John Wilkinson	[No amount given]			
239	1825, Oct. 22	John Wilkinson	John Wilkinson	517	10	2½
248	1826, Oct. 21	Accounts not made up (Shambles). Due:		499	11	4
248	1826, Oct. 19	William Skinner	William Skinner	199	10	1¾
253	1827, Oct. 30	William Skinner	Thomas Walker	99	19	4
258	1828, Oct. 17	Thomas Walker	Thomas Walker	236	14	6¼
259	1829, Oct. 20	Thomas Walker	Robert Lamb	207	3	0
263	1830, Oct. 21	Robert Lamb	Robert Lamb	41	4	0

11　Thomas Simpson was twice elected mayor, his first election being deemed void as he was not a burgess (see above, p. 198 n. 252).

265	1831, Oct. 21	Robert Lamb	Robert Lamb	341	14	10
268	1832, Oct. 16	Robert Lamb	Leonard Raisbeck	139	0	4
272	1833, Nov. 8	Leonard Raisbeck	Leonard Raisbeck	180	19	4
279	1834, Oct. 17	Leonard Raisbeck	Robert Thompson	239	15	4
282	1835, Oct. 22	Robert Thompson	Robert Thompson	233	2	6
284	1835, Dec. 28	Robert Thompson	Robert Thompson?	101	12	2

APPENDIX 4:
STEWARDS, SERGEANTS AND CONSTABLES

Entries in Roman are from direct mentions in the MS. Entries in italics are direct mentions elsewhere: Sowler's *History*, pp. 424–5, unless otherwise noted.

			Above, page
1629	Robert Kitchin	sergeant	39
1629	Thomas Raw	sergeant	39
1633	John Thompson	sergeant	40
1649	Thomas Goldsborough	[sergeant]	53
1653	Anthony Fleatham	sergeant	54
1653	*John Turner*	*steward/recorder*	
1654	Anthony Fleatham	sergeant	55
1656	Anthony Fleathan	sergeant	55
1662	*Richard Matthew*	*steward/recorder*	
1664	Miles Stapleton		60
1666	*Miles Stapylton*	*steward/recorder*	
1669	William Cuthbert	sergeant	63
1669	*Thomas Gibson*	*steward/recorder*	
1672	William Cuthbert	sergeant	64
1672	*George Moorcroft*	*steward/recorder*	
1673–5	Ralph Bunting	sergeant	65, 68
1679	Ralph Bunting	sergeant	72
1680	John Porrett	steward	73
1680	*John Porrett*	*steward/recorder*	
1681–1727	John Porett	steward	74–137
1732	John Porrett	steward	139
1733	Edmund Bunting	steward	140
1733	*Edmund Bunting*	*steward/recorder*	
1734–64	Edmund Bunting	steward	141–77
1735	Francis Eden	sergeant	144
1736	Ralph Bradley	deputy steward	144
1740	Peter Dunning	deputy steward	148
1743	Ralph Bradley	deputy steward	150
1744	*David Hilton*	*steward/recorder*	
1744, 1748	John Gibson	deputy steward	155, 161
1745	Peter Dunning	deputy steward	156
1755–7	Tomlinson Bunting	deputy steward	169–75

1758	Tomlinson Bunting	steward	173
1760–2	Tomlinson Bunting	steward	173–5
1763–5	J. S. Raisbeck	deputy steward	176
1765	J. R. Raisbeck	steward	177
1765	*J. R. Raisbeck*	*steward/recorder*	
1766–8	J. R. Raisbeck	steward	179–81
1768	D'arcy Fowler	deputy steward	181
1769	Gascoigne Finch	steward	182
1769	*Gascoigne Finch*		
1771–2	Gascoigne Finch	steward	182–3
1773–4	John Carter	steward	184–5
1774	*John Carter*	*steward/recorder*	
1775–7	John Carter	steward	186–8
1778	*Robert Preston*	*steward/recorder*	
1778	Timothy Smallwood	deputy steward	188
1780	Robert Preston	steward	189
1781	*Robert Preston junior*		
1782–90	Robert Preston, younger	steward	189–94
1791	J. S. Raisbeck	steward	194
1791	*J. S. Raisbeck*	*steward/recorder*	
1792–4	J. S. Raisbeck	steward	195–6
1795	Robert Clark	steward	197
1795	*Robert Clark*	*steward/recorder*	
1798–1804	Robert Clark	steward	198–203
1805–19	Leonard Raisbeck	steward	204–20
1805	*Leonard Raisbeck*	*steward/recorder*	
1818–19	H. R. E. Wright	deputy steward	214
1823–6	James Ward	constable	236, 239, 242, 249
1826	Henry Wade Foxton	sergeant	243
1826	Leonard Raisbeck	recorder and steward	245
1826	*Thomas Henry Faber*	*steward/recorder*[1]	
1827	*William Watson*	*chief constable*[2]	
1827–34	James Ward	sergeant	255–6, 258, 260, 263–4, 266, 269, 274, 280
1832–4	Leonard Raisbeck	recorder	267, 280

---

1   Faber would be Town Clerk from 1835 until 1850 under the new corporation.
2   P&W, p. 316.

APPENDIX 5:
PERSONAL MARKS

Handwriting and Literacy

In the earlier part of the period documented by the 'Book of Orders and Accounts', there is evidence of illiteracy or partial literacy among the burgesses, though most burgesses were probably among the more educated citizens. The extent to which the ability to sign documents indicates literacy has been subject to considerable debate.[1] It is likely that a signature in a flourishing, unique hand has been penned by a person with solid reading and writing skills, but what of people who signed with a mark? Some of these marks are an initial/capital letter or two. If those with a little education had learnt letters first, they may be partly literate rather than totally illiterate. It is also possible that some people could read a little but not write. Some historians regard signatures as being of little use as indicators of literacy levels,[2] but Hailwood maintains that a significant percentage of people in sixteenth- and seventeenth-century England could use a pen and therefore make a mark consistently. Rather than separate into literate (signature) and non-literate (mark), we can usefully study the marks themselves, which vary from single strokes through initials to relatively complex symbols. This appendix presents images of personal marks used by signatories to the 'Book of Orders and Accounts'.

The signatures and personal marks recorded in a document such as this do not form a strong evidence base from which to estimate the literacy and writing proficiency of the wider population, but it is noticeable that, in entries with a larger number of signatures – that is, beyond the core group of burgesses seemingly managing the town's affairs at any given time, the number of personal marks is greater, at least in the seventeenth century. There are also several men, like John

---

1   Mark Hailwood, 'Rethinking literacy in rural England, 1550–1700', *Past & Present*, 260 (1) (August 2023), pp. 38–70.
2   Margaret W. Ferguson, *Dido's Daughters: Literacy, Gender, and Empire in Early Modern England and France* (Chicago, 2003), p. 77.

Carter, William Hart, Thomas Mitchell, Ralph Ware, John Osborne and members of the Coates and Fewler families, who often used marks but show consistent involvement in the town's affairs. They must have understood the significance of documents, and making a mark made them active participants in governance.

Those who used a mark in this volume were, therefore, not necessarily totally illiterate or completely 'unlettered'. Their mark might be their initials, for example, 'AC' for Anthony Coates, 'H' for Thomas Hart, 'B' for John Bainbridge and 'TF' for Thomas Fewler. Many other marks are just simple geometric shapes. In assessing the literacy of the population of Terling (Essex) in the early modern period, Wrightson and Levine suggest that a genuine signature is a reasonable indicator of literacy, because reading ability is normally ahead of writing ability.[3] However, that study considered signatures on a wide range of documents over a broader demographic base than is represented in this volume, in which the cross-section of the Stockton community reflected in the book's signatures is no doubt very narrow. The limited evidence here suggests broadly that literacy among men (almost all the people mentioned in this book are men) improved in the seventeenth century, and that in the eighteenth century there was general literacy among the burgesses and merchants. However, three signatories – John Carter (or possibly two men of that name), Thomas Mitchell and Ralph Ware – continued to make marks over an extended period, during which the use of marks otherwise disappeared.

There is a difficulty counting signatories in this volume due to the possible confusion with duplicate names within one family or across families with common surnames. Sometimes the time gap between two men of the same name is sufficient that they must be different people, and sometimes they are distinguished by calling one 'junior' or 'the younger', but there is scope for error.

The personal marks in this volume fall into the following categories (using Hailwood's classification), making reasonable assumptions about whether repeated marks are the same person:

---

3   Keith Wrightson and David Levine, *Poverty and Piety in an English Village: Terling, 1525–1700* (Oxford, 1995).

Category	No. of Individuals with marks in the category
Cross	13
Circle	2
Single initial	26
Double initial	8
Icon	0
Single stroke	4
Two strokes	12
>2 strokes	18
Indistinct	1
Total	*84*

The Marks

Where marks against a name are consistent, one exemplar is given below. Further instances may be located using the name index. Significant variations in the marks are shown, as are variants of titles, e.g. 'John Fewler', 'John Fewler the weaver', 'John Fewler, junior'. No attempt has been made to identify exact relationships between men of the same name, nor to trace lineage where identical names are too far separated in time to be the same person. Family reconstitution, or at least some research in parish records and other sources, would be required and might still not be conclusive.

Name	Mark	Above, page
John Bainbridge		38
Roger Bainbridge		38
William Bainbridge		38
Christopher Barrett		95
William Brown		165

Name	Mark	Pages
Henry Burdon		38
John Carr		171
John Carter		128, 152, 164–6
		144, 147–8, 150, 154–64, 167, 169, 171–3
Robert Catchaside		128
Anthony Coates		56, 63, 65–6, 71, 75, 95, 97
Anthony Coates, senior		80
Christopher Coates		64–5
John Coates		97
Christopher Coats		56
Roger Coats		50

Christopher Coots		56
Brian Cottes		37, 40
Robert Dale		57
Joseph Davison		75
Christopher Denneham		75
George Denam		54
John Fewler, weaver		39, 40
John Fewler junior		39
Leonard Fewler		54, 71
Roger Fewler, senior		39
Thomas Fewler		65–6, 71–2
William Fewler		38

William Fewler, senior		39
Thomas Fleathem		38
Thomas Fowler		75
Christopher Garbutt		164
Robert Guy		55
Thomas Harrison		128
Thomas Hart		38, 55–6
William Hart		39, 40, 45, 52, 54
John Hazelhurst		227
Thomas Heringson		123
Matthew Heron		39
Thomas Hope		67

Gregory Hurworth		39
John Jeckel		39
John Jeckel		40
John Jeckel		71
John Johnson		54–5
John Johnson, junior		60
William Lambart		39
Thomas Marchant		66
Thomas Murshant		71
John Maineard		73, 75, 90
John Maineard, senior		80, 82
John May		71

Thomas Mitchell		158–67, 169, 171, 173
Robert Nicholson		64
Robert Nicholson		65
Robert Nicholson		66
Robert Nicholson		71
Robert Nicholson		75
John Osburne		39
John Osburne		39
John Osburne, junior		54
John Osburn, senior		56
Augustine Perkin		145
Austin Perkin		147

Christopher Read		38
Christopher Read		40–1
George Simpson		103, 123
George Simpson		128
Hannah Smith		165
Thomas Sparrow		126
Anthony Storye		38
Anthony Storie		37
William Storye		55
Averell Swainston		165
Thomas Swinbank		123
Jacob Taylor		144

Thomas Ward		49, 66, 80
Thomas Ward		71
Ralph Ware		140
Ralf Ware		140
Ralph Ware		144
Ralph Ware		148, 152, 154–8
Ralph Welfoot		39
Richard Wilson		72
Richard Wilson		95

APPENDIX 6:
STOCKTON BURGAGE HOLDERS IN 1602

The following list is taken from Brewster, *History*, pp. 99–100. It is not known whether the interposed comments were in the original document or were added by Brewster. The list begins at the corner-house opposite the Dove-cote house, and continues along the west side of the street, running south.

1. Ralfe Lambert
2. Thomas Lambert
3. Roger Anderson
4. John Dossey
5. Nicholas Fleatham
6. William Raw
7. William Raw
8. William Burdon
9. Henry Burdon
10. Anthony Harperley
11. Anthony Bambridge
12. The Queen's Majesty
13. Bambridge/Roger Fewler
(Cross the end of the street called Ram's Wind)[1]
14, 15, 16. Roger Fewler
17. Tobias Tunstal
18. John Osburn
19. Thomas Osburn
20, 21. Thomas Fleatham
22, 23. John Fewler
(The street called the West Row, beginning at the north)
24. Christofer Wilson
25. Roger Wylson Clarke
26. Leonard Fewler

---

1   Also called Ramsgate or Ram's Lane.

27. Richard Harperley
28. John Fewler
29.
30. Wife of John Bunting
31. Thomas –
(*East side of the street, beginning at the north*)
32. The Queen's Majesty
33. Giles Weatherell
34. William Swainston
35. Richard Halliman
(*Across the end of Custom-house street*)[2]
36. Giles Weatherell
37. Thomas Burdon
38. Heirs of John Bambridge
39. Mr Saire
40. William Thompson
41. Ralph Heron
(*A water course to the Tease*)
42. Thomas Watson
43, 44. John Osborne
45. Bryan Swainston
46. Jane Swainston
47. John Swainston
(*A water course to the River Tease*)
48. The Queen's Majesty
49. Isobel Fleatham
50. The Queens' Majesty
51, 52. Persevell Bambridge
53. John Fewler
54. Thomas Lambert
(*End of the borough to the south next the street*)
–
(*From the south by the river to the Custom-house street*)
55. Christopher Fleatham
56. John Symme
57. The Queen's Majesty
58. William Swainston
59. Bryan Swainston
60. John Osburne

2   Later named Finkle Street.

61. Thomas Watson
62. The Queen's Majesty
63. William Wright
64. Christofer –

(South side of Custom-house street, beginning next the river)

65. Anthony Bambridge
66, 67, 68. Bryan Heart
69. Mr Sayer

(North side of Custom-house street)

70. Bryan Heart
71. William Fewler
72. Mr John Saire

BIBLIOGRAPHY

Manuscript Sources

Preston Hall Museum, Stockton-on-Tees

STCMG:2011.0264 Stockton-on-Tees Book of Orders and Accounts.

Stockton-on-Tees Reference Library

Microfilm No. 54 Stockton Parish Registers; originals in DCRO,
Ep/Sto/Section 1
Overseers Accounts, 1718–1732.

Teesside Archives, Middlesbrough

Microfilm No. 371 Microfilm of the 'Book of Orders and Accounts'
and related correspondence.
U/PG Pargeter Collection.

The National Archives, Kew

E190 186/1 Exchequer Port Book, Overseas, Customer,
Newcastle with Stockton, 1601–2.
E190 186/2 Exchequer Port Book, Coastal, Surveyor,
Stockton with Hartlepool, 1601–2.

Tyne-Wear Archives, Newcastle

GU.TH.201–203 Primage account summaries for Stockton.
Trinity House, Newcastle, 1623–1661.
GU.TH.213 Covenant to build lighthouse on the Tees, 1641.

Printed Sources

Place of publication is London, except where noted.

Bayley, W. D., '"Genealogical Additions" to the History of Stockton upon Tees', in J. G. Nichols (ed.), *The Topographer and Genealogist*, Vol. II (1853), pp. 73–123 and 550–9

Barrow, Tony, *The Port of Stockton-on-Tees 1702–1802*, Papers in North Eastern History, No. 14 (Middlesbrough, 2005)

Barton, Peter, 'The port of Stockton-on-Tees and its creeks: a problem in port history', *Maritime History*, 1 (2) (Sep. 1971), pp. 121–57

Betteney, Alan, *Shipbuilding in Stockton and Thornaby* (Stockton-on-Tees, 2003)

Brewster, John, *The Parochial History and Antiquities of Stockton-upon-Tees* (1796, 2nd edn 1829; reprinted Stockton-on-Tees, 1972)

Calendar of Close Rolls, Edward I, Vol. 4, 1296–1301 (1906)

Calendar of Close Rolls, Edward III, Vol. 1, 1327–1330 (1896); Vol. 3, 1333–1337 (1898)

Calendar of State Papers Domestic, Charles I, 1639–40 (1877); 1641–43 (1887)

Chase, Malcolm, 'Chartism 1838–58: responses in two Teesside towns', *Northern History*, 24 (1) (1998), pp. 146–71

Chase, Malcolm, *Chartism: A New History* (Manchester, 2007)

Clark, Peter and Hosking, Jean (eds), *Population Estimates of English Small Towns, 1550–1851* (Leicester, 1993)

Defoe, Daniel, *A Tour through the Whole Island of Great Britain* (1762)

Drury, J. Linda, 'The bishop of Durham's horse ferry, Stockton, c.1469', *Cleveland History*, No. 75 (Summer 1999)

Drury, J. Linda, 'Estate records of medieval Stockton', *Cleveland History*, No. 83 (2002)

Drury, J. Linda, 'Records of the bailiff of Stockton Manor or Castle', *Cleveland History*, No. 91 (2006)

Fordyce, William, *The History and Antiquities of the County Palatinate of Durham*, 2 vols (Newcastle upon Tyne, 1855–7)

Green, Adrian, *County Durham Hearth Tax Assessment Lady Day 1666*, British Academy Hearth Tax Project (2006)

Hailwood, Mark, 'Rethinking literacy in rural England, 1550–1700', *Past & Present*, 260 (1) (2023)

Harrison, Barry J. D., 'The borough of Stockton in the late Middle Ages', *Stockton Local History Journal*, No. 49 (Autumn 1985)

Heavisides, Henry, *Annals of Stockton-on-Tees with Biographical Notes* (Stockton-on-Tees, 1865)

Hill, Christopher, *Continuity and Change in the Seventeenth Century* (1974, revised edn 1991)

Hodgson, Robert Ian, *Demographic Trends in County Durham 1560–1801: Data Sources and preliminary findings with particular reference to north Durham*. University of Manchester School of Geography Research Paper No. 5 (March 1978)

Hodgson, Robert Ian, 'The progress of enclosure in County Durham 1550–1870', in H. S. A. Fox and R. A. Butlin, *Change in the Countryside, Essays on Rural England, 1500–1900* (1979)

Husbands, Chris, 'Hearths, wealth and occupations: an exploration of the Hearth Tax in the later seventeenth century', in Kevin Schürer and Tom Arkell (eds), *Surveying the people: The interpretation and use of document sources for the study of population in the later seventeenth century* (Oxford, 1992), pp. 65–77

Hutchinson, William, *The History and Antiquities of the County Palatine of Durham*, 3 vols (Newcastle, 1785–94; Durham, 1823)

Knight, C., *First Report of the Commissioners Appointed to Inquire into the Municipal Corporations in England and Wales*, Parliamentary Papers, Vol. XXIII (1835)

Levine, David and Wrightson, Keith, *The Making of an Industrial Society: Whickham* (Oxford, 1991)

Little, John, 'Merchants, mariners and yeomen: What does the Hearth Tax tell us about early modern Stockton?', *Cleveland History*, No. 105 (2014), pp. 3–32

Little, John, 'Joseph Ritson and the Stockton Jubilee', *Cleveland History*, No. 110 (2016)

Little, John, 'The other James Cooke: trade on the Tees in the seventeenth century', *Bulletin of DCLHS*, No. 82 (March 2018), pp. 5–25

Little, John, 'Review of *Sunderland Wills and Inventories 1651–1675*', SS Vol. 224, *The Local Historian*, 52 (10) (January 2022), pp. 83–5

Mackenzie, Eneas and Ross, Marvin, *An Historical, Topographical and Descriptive View of the County Palatine of Durham*, 2 vols (Newcastle, 1834)

Meikle, Maureen M. and Newman, Christine M., *Sunderland and its Origins: Monks to Mariners* (2007)

North, G. A., *Teesside's Economic Heritage* (Cleveland County Council, 1975)

Parsons, William and White, William, *History, Directory and Gazetteer of the Counties of Durham and Northumberland*, 2 vols (Leeds, 1827)

Pattenden, D. W., *The History of the River Tees in Maps* (Cleveland and Teesside Local History Society, 2001)

Richmond, Thomas, *History of Protestant Nonconformity and of the Society assembling in the Old Meeting-House, High-Street, Stockton* (Stockton-on-Tees, 1856)

Richmond, Thomas, *The Local Records of Stockton and the Neighbourhood* (Stockton-on-Tees and London, 1868; reprinted Stockton-on-Tees, 1972)

Ritson, Joseph, *The St*ckt*n Jubilee or Shakespeare in all his Glory: A Choice Pageant for Christmas Holidays* (Newcastle, 1781). The only known surviving copy is in the Folger Shakespeare Library, Capitol Hill, Washington D.C.

Sowler, Tom, *History of the Town and Borough of Stockton-on-Tees* (Teesside Museums and Art Galleries Department, 1972)

Sowler, Tom, *Town House, Stockton-on-Tees* (revised edn, Stockton-on-Tees, 1986)

Sowler, Tom, *The Parish Church of Stockton-on-Tees* (Stockton-on-Tees, 1990)

Surtees, Robert, *History and Antiquities of the County Palatine of Durham*, Vol. 3 (1823, reprinted East Ardsley, 1972)

Tittler, Robert (ed.), *Two Weather Diaries from Northern England, 1779–1807: The Journals of John Chipchase and Elihu Robinson*, SS Vol. 222 (Woodbridge, 2019)

Wardell, John Wilford, *A Short History of Stockton-on-Tees* (Stockton-on-Tees, 1963)

Welford, Richard (ed.), *Records of the Committee for Compounding, etc. with Delinquent Royalists in Durham and Northumberland 1643–60*, SS Vol. 111 (1905)

Wood, H. M. (ed.), *Durham Protestations or the Returns made to the House of Commons in 1641–2 for the Maintenance of the Protestant Religion for the County Palatine of Durham*, SS Vol. 135 (Durham, 1922)

Wrightson, Keith, *English Society 1580–1680* (2nd edn, 2002)

Wrightson, Keith and Levine, David, *Poverty and Piety in an English Village: Terling, 1525–1700* (Oxford, 1995)

Theses

Daniels, Robin, *An Archaeological and Historical Survey of the Township of Norton In Cleveland*. Unpublished BA Dissertation, University of Leicester, 1979. Copy in SRL

Online Sources

Sound Toll Registers: http://www.soundtoll.nl/index.php/en/over
-het-project/sonttol-registers

North East Inheritance Database, Durham University Library: http://
familyrecords.dur.ac.uk/nei/data/neisearch.php

Hearth Tax Online, Centre for Hearth Tax Research, Roehampton
University: www.roehampton.ac.uk/hearthtax/index.html

INDEX OF NAMES

Variant spellings of surnames are given in brackets; most forenames have been modernised. Places are identified by county, using the following abbreviations: Du: Co. Durham; Fi: Fife; Nb: Northumberland; No: Norfolk; Yo: Yorkshire. The location of streets and suburbs is indicated by the town name in brackets.

Robert   23, 30, 57–9, 60–9, 71–3,
    75–6, 78–82, 84, 86–93, 95–7,
    100–1, 103–4
Thomas   249
Jeckel(l) (Jeckkel, Jeckyl), John
    39–40, 43, 71, 310
William   254
Jefferson, George   71, 73, 75–6, 80,
    83, 86–7
Isaac   96, 100, 105–6, 108
John, junior   193–4
Jenkin(g)s, Humphrey   58
John   17, 43–4
Jennet, Mr   227–8, 235, 240
Alderman   232
Thomas   199, 203–8, 210–15,
    220–2, 224–8, 231–3, 235–6,
    238–9, 241–6, 250–3, 256–7,
    259, 261, 265, 267–8, 272,
    275–6, 281–4
Jessop (Jessep(p), Jessepps) family
    107 n.136
 –   61
Mr   41, 46, 48, 60
Alderman   75, 102
John   30, 40, 43, 45–8, 59, 62
Thomas   30, 51–4, 56–60, 62–6,
    68–9, 71–3, 75, 78–84, 86–8,
    90–1, 93, 95–7, 100–3, 105–7
Johnson, John   54–5, 310
John, junior   60, 310
William   61, 63–6
Jordison, –   261
Mr   271, 288
Robert   211–15, 220, 222–7, 229,
    233–6, 238–40, 245–9, 252–3,
    256–60, 263–9, 272, 274–5,
    278, 280, 284

Kaye, William   167, 169
Kemp, Johnson   223
Kingston, Thomas   195–207
Kirtley, Martin   199–203, 205, 211,
    238, 241, 257, 259, 261, 263–5,
    267–8, 270–2, 276, 278–9

Kitchin(g), James   62, 64, 71
Robert   39, 44, 302

Lamb, Robert   257, 261, 263–5,
    267–9, 270–2, 280, 284
Lambert (Lambart), Mr   61
Mrs   42
John   40, 42, 45, 49–50, 58
Ralph   39, 314–15
Ralph, elder   42
Thomas   2, 31, 37–8, 42, 284, 315
William   39, 45, 310
Lanchester, Thomas   249
Lang, Mr   1, 285
Largo (Fi)   14
Lawrence, Mr   201
Lee, William   31, 66, 69, 71–3, 75–6,
    78–82, 84, 86–7
Lees, James   61
Leighton, R.   178
Levingston, James   17
Liddell, Charles   195–7
Litster, J.   61
Livingston, Alexander   1, 285–6
Lockey, William   199, 203–6
Lodge, C.   284
John   241–2, 246, 248
Ralph   204–7
London   14, 16, 23, 58, 141, 257,
    275–6
Longhorn, John   145–9, 156, 163,
    167, 171
Lumley, Benjamin   185–96, 198
Lushington, Dr   277

Males, William   61. *See also* Mayles
Mandale (in Thornaby)   256 n.314
Mariner's Tavern (in Stockton-
    on-Tees)   264–5, 267
Marr, Richard   134
Marshal(l) (Marshell), James
    140–2, 145 n.217
Walter   103, 115, 118, 124–6, 129,
    131–2
William   113
Martin, C.   276

SUBJECT INDEX